# Instructor's Manual with Video Guide

---

# CONSUMER BEHAVIOR
## Buying, Having, and Being
### *Seventh Edition*

## Michael R. Solomon

---

## Andrew T. Norman
*Drake University*

**PEARSON**

Prentice
Hall

Upper Saddle River New Jersey 07458

**VP/Editorial Director:** Jeff Shelstad
**Senior Acquisitions Editor:** Katie Stevens
**Project Manager:** Melissa Pellerano
**Associate Director, Manufacturing:** Vincent Scelta
**Production Editor & Buyer:** Carol O'Rourke
**Printer/Binder:** Offset Paperback Manufacturing

**Pearson Prentice Hall**[TM] **is a trademark of Pearson Education, Inc.**

10  9  8  7  6  5  4  3  2  1
ISBN 0-13-218695-0

# CONTENTS

Introduction

**PROFESSORS ON THE GO!** ...............................................................................................1

**CHAPTER-BY-CHAPTER INSTRUCTIONAL MATERIAL**

SECTION 1: CONSUMERS IN THE MARKETPLACE

Chapter 1: Consumers Rule ...............................................................................39

SECTION 2: CONSUMERS AS INDIVIDUALS

Chapter 2: Perception ...............................................................................64

Chapter 3: Learning and Memory ...............................................................................86

Chapter 4: Motivation and Values ...............................................................................108

Chapter 5: The Self ...............................................................................130

Chapter 6: Personality and Lifestyles ...............................................................................152

Chapter 7: Attitudes ...............................................................................173

Chapter 8: Attitude Change and Interactive Communications ...............................................192

SECTION 3: CONSUMERS AS DECISION MAKERS

Chapter 9: Individual Decision Making ...............................................................................216

Chapter 10: Buying and Disposing ...............................................................................242

Chapter 11: Group Influence and Opinion Leadership ...............................................................266

Chapter 12: Organizational and Household Decision Making ...............................................290

# SECTION 4: CONSUMERS AND SUBCULTURES

Chapter 13: Income and Social Class ................................................................................316

Chapter 14: Ethnic, Racial, and Religious Subcultures ....................................................338

Chapter 15: Age Subcultures ...........................................................................................358

# SECTION 5: CONSUMERS AND CULTURE

Chapter 16: Cultural Influences on Consumer Behavior .....................................................378

Chapter 17: The Creation and Diffusion of Global Consumer Culture ...............................400

**VIDEO GUIDE** ..............................................................................................................425

# INTRODUCTION

## HOW TO USE:

The Seventh Edition of Michael R. Solomon's *Consumer Behavior* has a complete set of supplemental learning and teaching aids. The *Instructor's Manual* plays a central role in organizing this package. This manual has been designed so the instructor can plan lectures, demonstrations, discussions, visual presentations, Internet exercises, and written assignments in a coordinated and efficient manner.

All 17 chapters of the textbook have been carefully reviewed in order to develop the most logical and helpful manual for you, the instructor. Primary features of the *Instructor's Manual* are described below.

## PROFESSORS ON THE GO!

New to the seventh edition of the *Instructor's Manual* is a section entitled *Professors on the Go!* This section was created with the busy professor in mind. It serves to bring key material upfront in the manual, where an instructor who is short on time can take a quick look and find key concepts, activities, and exercises that he/she can incorporate into the lecture, without having to page through all the material provided for each chapter. The material in the *Professors on the Go!* section is categorized by individual objectives for each chapter to facilitate teaching by these objectives.

## CHAPTER OBJECTIVES

Objectives are listed clearly at the beginning of each chapter of the *Instructor's Manual*. These objectives should be the focus as lesson plans are created.

## CHAPTER SUMMARY

Each chapter of the textbook is summarized in the *Chapter Summary*. This section provides the instructor with a condensed version of the information included in the chapter.

This material is consistent with the *Chapter Summary* material found at the end of each chapter in the text. This overview of the chapter material is especially helpful in planning chapter sequence presentation and any desired chapter combinations. In addition, this section may help the instructor plan introductory lecture remarks.

## CHAPTER OUTLINE

This section is the core of the *Instructor's Manual*. This teaching outline is a thorough outline (specifically tied to the actual phrases and definitions used in the textbook) of the material included in the text chapters. This outline includes major and minor headings from the textbook. The instructor will notice special information sections that appear periodically in the body of the outline. This material is indicated with **bold type** and **bold asterisks (****)** in outlined text boxes. The purpose of these information blocks is to indicate to the instructor where key material appears in the textbook and when to use teaching aids. These information blocks may contain the following items of information: **chapter Figures; chapter Tables; and, Consumer Behavior Challenge questions.** It is recommended that the instructor carefully review the *Chapter Outline* prior to preparing a chapter lecture. This review will help in coordinating the learning activities that are available with the textbook. Remember that this *Chapter Outline* is a condensed summary of the text material; therefore, it is always wise to use along with the *Test Item File* when planning, developing, and constructing examinations or quizzes.

Lastly, the instructor will find it useful to use the *Discussion Opportunity* text boxes that periodically appear in the *Chapter Outline* to aid discussion of the pertinent issues. The suggestions in these boxes are designed to prompt students to discuss the concepts that are being taught, as well as to provide examples that are not found in the textbook. Since this material does not appear in the textbook, it must be given to students firsthand. In most instances, the questions can be answered with a minimum of preparation and thought. These discussion opportunities are one of many discussion/activity oriented features of this *Instructor's Manual* and textbook designed to provide instructors with flexible options for making lessons interactive.

Because it is virtually impossible to do everything that is included here in your course, a good way to use this Chapter Outline is to highlight the portions of the outline you would like to use in class, the questions you would like to pose, and the ancillary materials you will need. This helps to make a class flow more smoothly.

# End-of-Chapter Support Material

This section of the *Instructor's Manual* supports features contained in the chapters of the textbook itself, as well as material available to students at the end of each chapter.

## SUMMARY OF SPECIAL FEATURE BOXES

Throughout each chapter of the text, there are special feature boxes. These include *Marketing Opportunity, Net Profit, The Tangled Web, Marketing Pitfall,* and *The Global Looking Glass.* The material in these sections is very helpful in illustrating the main concepts of the chapter. Thus, the instructor may wish to focus on selected special features as a part of class material. This summary simply lists all special feature boxes found in the chapter and identifies which section or sub-section of the text the special feature supports.

## REVIEW QUESTIONS

These questions were designed directly around material contained in the text. There are specific, correct answers for each. In addition to the same questions that students have in their textbooks, answers are provided in the *Instructor's Manual.* These answers are, for the most part, taken directly from text material.

## CONSUMER BEHAVIOR CHALLENGE

These questions are meant to challenge the students' understanding of chapter material and to enable them to develop an ability to creatively use the chapter material to solve problems. The questions may be used purely for discussion (if so, they might be assigned in advance of the discussion), they can be given to selected students for in-class presentation, they can be used as short essay questions on in-class quizzes or on formal examinations, or they can be used by the students to enhance the chapter summary. It should be noted that because of the nature of these questions, there is no "right" answer. Thus, the responses that are provided are merely ideas for what students might come up with, as well as directions for instructors to guide discussion.

These questions are given in two sections, *Discussion* and *Application.* This should be noted as some of the *Discussion* questions are designed to be presented to students in class, and the *Application* questions are designed to be given as more involved out-of-class assignments. The questions appear in this section, as well as responses that have been formulated for each. While the questions appear in the textbook, the comments only appear in the *Instructor's Manual.* Note that proper placement of a discussion question is up to the instructor; however, placement suggestions do appear in the *Chapter Outline* section.

# CASE STUDY TEACHING NOTES

This section is designed as a supplement for the cases found at the end of each chapter. Included here is a brief summary, suggestions for presenting the case, and suggested answers for the discussion questions.

## Additional Support Material

The material found in the *Additional Support Material* section is available only in the *Instructor's Manual.*

# STUDENT PROJECTS

This section suggests several projects that may be assigned to the students for a specific class or for several class periods (a term project). These projects may be assigned to individuals (**Individual Projects**) or to groups (**Group Projects**). The instructor may require that the material be analyzed in a written format or just as discussion motivators. As an additional tool, consider coordinating this section with the *Discussion Opportunity* boxed inserts for more beneficial discussion sessions.

Instructors might consider assigning two or three students or a group of students to do one or more of the Student Projects assignments for each class period. Ask the students to be ready to give a short **oral** presentation on the assigned topic at the beginning of class. This gets students more deeply involved in the class and gives them opportunities to work on their oral skills. You might also ask them to turn in a short paper (one or two pages) so they can also practice their writing skills. Many of these projects can be done on the Internet (which also gives them practice with their research skills). If given proper credit, the students will also see that they can earn extra points to help them over the rough spots on exams. Most instructors find that by having a few students bring in fresh ideas to each class, the class becomes more enjoyable, engaging, and personalized. Remember that when assignments are made with plenty of lead time, students tend to do a better job. Because this often presents a challenge in the first several class meetings, some of the early chapter projects might be pushed back to the second week of class.

## eLAB

This section of the *Student Projects* section allows the instructor to explore Consumer Behavior issues via the Internet. These projects may also be assigned to individuals (**Individual Assignments**) or to groups (**Group Assignments**). These assignments should be given in advance and then covered in class at the discretion of the instructor. The instructor may require that the material be analyzed in a written format or just as discussion motivators. Please consider coordinating this section with the *Discussion Opportunity* boxed inserts for more beneficial discussion sessions. Because of the rapidly changing nature of the Internet, please confirm beforehand that the URLs given are still active and that the material on the Website is relevant to the project given.

## FINAL NOTE

The Solomon team wishes to thank you for adopting the Seventh Edition of *Consumer Behavior* and hopes this supplement will aid you in creating an exciting learning experience for your students.

Should you have any questions about or difficulties with the material contained in this *Instructor's Manual*, please feel free to contact the author of this manual.

Phone: 515-271-2758
Fax: 515-271-4518
email: atnorman@drake.edu

Andrew T. Norman, Ph.D.
Assistant Professor of Marketing
Drake University

# Professors on the Go!

# CHAPTER 1—CONSUMERS RULE

## CHAPTER OBJECTIVES

**When students finish this chapter they should understand why:**

- Consumer behavior is a process.
  - o List the three stages in the consumption process. Describe the issues that you consider in each of these stages when you made a recent important purchase.
  - o Name some products or services that are widely used by your social group. State whether you agree or disagree with the notion that these products help to form group bonds, supporting your argument with examples from your list of products used by the group.

- Consumers use products to help them define their identities in different settings.
  - o The chapter states that people play different roles and that their consumption behaviors may differ depending on the particular role they are playing. State whether you agree or disagree with this perspective, giving examples from your personal life. Try to construct a "stage set" for a role you play—specify the props, costumes, and script that you use to play a role (e.g., job interviewee, conscientious student, party animal).
  - o Have students explain why they chose the clothes they are wearing to class. Probe on this one. Was there any implied symbolism? Do all students seem to be dressed in a similar fashion? Why does this occur? Can marketers learn from this? Do marketers strategically contribute to this?

- Marketers need to understand the wants and needs of different consumer segments.
  - o Have students think of a product brand that is used frequently and make a list of the brand's determinant attributes. Without sharing what was on the list, have the student ask a friend, of the same gender and approximate age, to make a similar list for the same product (although the brand may be different). Then have the student ask someone of the opposite sex to perform the same task. Have the student compare and contrast the identified attributes and report their findings to the class. Why did differences or similarities occur?
  - o Have groups select a product of interest (e.g., a car, mp3 player, vacation spot, movie, sporting event, etc.). Have each person in the group make a list of what they consider to be the product's main attributes (both physical and psychological). Compare and contrast the attributes listed by the women and by the men to see how they may vary. Next, if there are any age or ethnic differences within the group, see if differences appear. Based on these differences formulate strategies for appealing to the various subgroups within your group.

- The Web is changing consumer behavior.
  - o Do marketers have the ability to control our desires or the power to create needs? Is this situation changing as the Internet creates new ways to interact with companies? If so, how?

3

- o Ask students to consider their own consumption practices over the past decade. Have them list the ways that online consumption activities have replaced or modified their real-world consumption activities.
- o Have your group go online to three Web pages of your choice. Demonstrate how the Web pages segment markets, collect information from the consumer (after the person has come to the Web page), and might be used to build a database.

- Consumer behavior is related to other issues in our lives.
  - o A company recently introduced a teddy bear for Valentine's Day called "Crazy for You." This toy aroused the ire of mental health advocates because the cuddly bear's cuddly paws are restrained by a straitjacket and accompanied by commitment papers. Supporters of the company's decision to keep selling the bear say opponents are too politically correct. What do you think?
  - o Each group should locate an example of a company that is heavily involved in social or green marketing. Make a report on the activities of the company. Compare this company to a direct competitor that is not so extensively involved in such activities. What are the advantages/disadvantages that the social/green approach has over the other approach.
  - o Have each group discuss what the members feel is the most unethical practice now being employed on the Internet by marketers. Have them reach a consensus on this matter. Each group should comment on how to remedy the situation and be prepared to share their findings with others.

- Consumer activities can be harmful to individuals and to society.
  - o The chapter discussed a computer game called JFK Reloaded that lets players reenact President Kennedy's assassination. Have the game's developers gone too far, or is any historical event "fair game" to be adapted into an entertainment vehicle?
  - o Have each student describe a situation in which he (or someone he knows) has exhibited compulsive consumption or consumer addiction. Was this consumption or addiction harmful? Discuss.
  - o Have students identify a time when they or someone they know defrauded a company. Examples could include employee theft, shoplifting, abusing return/exchange policies, or otherwise taking advantage of the company. What was the reasoning behind the activity? Was the activity justified?

- A wide range of specialists study consumer behavior.
  - o Some researchers believe that the field of consumer behavior should be a pure, rather than an applied, science. That is, research issues should be framed in terms of their scientific interest rather than their applicability to immediate marketing problems. Give your views on this issue.

- There are two major perspectives on understanding and studying consumer behavior.
  - o What aspects of consumer behavior are likely to be of interest to a financial planner? To a university administrator? To a graphic arts designer? To a social worker in a government agency? To a nursing instructor?

# CHAPTER 2—PERCEPTION

## CHAPTER OBJECTIVES

**When students finish this chapter they should understand why:**

- Perception is a three-stage process that translates raw stimuli into meaning.
    - Go to **www.tvguide.com**. On the opening Web page, how many ads (including pop-ups) do you notice? Compare and contrast the approach of each ad to the concepts of exposure, attention, and interpretation. Comment on how the consumer goes through these steps when coming in contact with each ad. Provide an illustration of your description.
    - Go to **www.crutchfield.com**. Spend some time becoming familiar with this Web site. The group should evaluate the Crutchfield's strategy. What is it? What do you think will be the long-term result of the strategy you just described? How is the organization using exposure, attention, and interpretation to its benefit? What does the group think will be the secrets of success for Crutchfield? The seeds of failure? Which symbols should be used to ensure success? Which should be avoided?

- Products and commercial messages often appeal to our senses, but many of them will not succeed.
    - Interview three to five male and three to five female friends regarding their perceptions of both men's and women's fragrances. Construct a perceptual map for each set of products. Based on your map of perfumes, do you see any areas that are not adequately served by current offerings? What (if any) gender differences did you obtain regarding both the relevant dimensions used by raters and the placement of specific brands along these dimensions?
    - Each student should visit a shopping mall and note all of the stores for which scents are an important component of their product offerings. Does it appear that each of these is appealing to the sense of smell in a strategic manner?
    - Have students visit a grocery store and pick out five products. They should identify how each scent appeals to the five senses. How are they the same? How are they different? To what extent do any of them appear to be strategically designed to appeal to the five senses?

- The design of a product today is a key driver of its success or failure.
    - Have student groups find three examples of brands or companies that have made changes to their products (i.e., retail chain redesigning their stores, a new logo, etc.). Have them discuss how the concept of "just noticeable difference" might affect consumer perceptions of these changes. Are the changes something that the marketers wanted to be noticed?

- Subliminal advertising is a controversial—but largely ineffective—way to talk to consumers.
  - Assuming that some forms of subliminal persuasion may have the desired effect of influencing consumers, do you think the use of these techniques is ethical? Explain your answer.
  - Find an example of what you perceive to be a subliminal message. Explain your rationale to the class and show the product or message.

- We interpret the stimuli to which we do pay attention according to learned patterns and expectations.
  - Ask students to collect three different pieces of direct mail. How do the advertisers attempt to attract consumer attention? What are some of the other stimuli that could have been chosen to accomplish the same thing?
  - For this project, each student should keep a log of all the advertising information that he or she is exposed to in a single hour when out in public. The students should keep track of the quantity and not try to note the names or descriptions of each. From memory, what are some of the ways that companies attempt to get their ads noticed?
  - For this project, students will need to pay attention. The students need to notice and identify a piece of marketing material to which they have adapted and generally do not pay attention. Discuss the five factors of adaptation in relation to this particular piece of marketing material.

- The science of semiotics helps us to understand how symbols are used to create meaning.
  - Assume that you are a consultant for a marketer who wants to design a package for a new premium chocolate bar targeted to an affluent market. What recommendations would you provide in terms of such package elements as color, symbolism, and graphic design? Give the reasons for your suggestions.
  - Ask students to find three ads that contain symbolism. Examine the symbols and discuss the meaning the symbols convey. Encourage the students to identify the different types of signs used in the ads and the product qualities being communicated by each.
  - Here is a field project that students always like. Have students (you might have only one or a few students do this as a special or alternative assignment) photocopy or print a collection of brand/product symbols (an alternative would be to have students create a PowerPoint presentation with images inserted to be projected in the classroom for all to see). Then have this students quiz fellow classmates to see if they can recognize the product or company. This will show students how effective symbols are and how much involuntary learning has taken place in their life. You might give a reward to the student who had the most correct responses.
  - Here is a tough assignment for undergraduates. Ask students to spend an afternoon watching a popular soap opera or an evening watching a favorite television show. Ask them to be particularly observant of the various products and services that are used as props during the show. Do these products or services have any symbolic value? How would viewer perception be different if alternative brands or even generic brands had been used? To what extent are the props shown or mentioned? Are they used to help develop the plot? How?

# CHAPTER 3—LEARNING AND MEMORY

## CHAPTER OBJECTIVES

**When students finish this chapter they should understand why:**

- It's important for marketers to understand how consumers learn about products and services.
  - In his 2005 book *Blink: The Power of Thinking Without Thinking*, author Malcolm Gladwell argues that hallowed marketing research techniques like focus groups aren't effective because we usually react to products quickly and without much conscious thought so it's better just to solicit consumers' first impressions rather than getting them to think at length about why they buy. What's your position on this issue?

- Conditioning results in learning.
  - Ask students to visit a shopping mall or other large retail environment and observe the behavior of individual shoppers and groups of shoppers for an extended period. Have them record any behaviors that they witness that could be examples of the following concepts: vicarious learning, incidental learning, observational learning, classical conditioning, and instrumental conditioning. Have students present their findings to the class or discuss them in groups.

- Learned associations can generalize to other things—why this is important to marketers.
  - Many brands attempt to capitalize on positive associations that consumers have for competing brands by copying certain characteristics. Have students identify an example of this and relate it to the halo effect.
  - Have students identify brand or corporate names that are based on semantic associations. Then have students ask five people what comes to mind when they hear each brand name. In reporting their findings, have students discuss whether company attempts to invoke certain perceptions appear to be working.

- There is a difference between classical and instrrumental conditioning.
  - Have student groups design an experiment that would demonstrate the occurrence of either classical conditioning or instrumental conditioning. Have them conduct their experiment on members of the class.

- Observation of others' behavior can result in learning.
  - Ask students to observe their friends, roommates, and co-workers for an extended period of time to identify an incidence of modeling as it relates to a celebrity. Have them note how the four conditions of modeling are met. Is the celebrity a brand endorser? How might their behavior be positive/negative for the marketers of the brands(s) that the celebrity endorses?

- Memory systems work.
  - o Ask each student to complete the following assignment based on a popular national brand: Collect as many pieces of promotional material (ads, direct mail, etc.) as possible for the brand. Based on this promotional evidence, identify any bits of information that marketers intend to be associated with the brand. Create an associative network for the brand, integrating the documented nodes of information with other nodes.

- Our knowledge of individual products is influenced by other products we associate with them.
  - o Discuss how consumers come to know the various attributes of brands such as Hershey's Kisses and M&Ms according to activation models of memory. This question is based on the case for Chapter 3, Hershey's Versus M&Ms: The War of the Bite-Size Milk Chocolates."

- Products help us to retrieve memories from our past.
  - o Some diehard fans were not pleased when the Rolling Stones sold the tune "Start Me Up" for about $4 million to Microsoft, which wanted the classic song to promote its Windows 95 launch. The Beach Boys sold "Good Vibrations" to Cadbury Schweppes for its Sunkist soft drink, Steppenwolf offered its "Born to Be Wild" to plug the Mercury Cougar, and even Bob Dylan sold "The Times They Are A-Changin' " to Coopers & Lybrand (now called PriceWaterhouseCoopers). Other rock legends have refused to play the commercial game, including Bruce Springsteen, the Grateful Dead, Led Zeppelin, Fleetwood Mac, R.E.M., and U2. According to U2's manager, "Rock 'n' roll is the last vestige of independence. It is undignified to put that creative effort and hard work to the disposal of a soft drink or beer or car." Singer Neil Young is especially adamant about not selling out; in his song "This Note's for You," he croons, "Ain't singing for Pepsi, ain't singing for Coke, I don't sing for nobody, makes me look like a joke." What's your take on this issue? How do you react when one of your favorite songs turns up in a commercial? Is this use of nostalgia an effective way to market a product? Why or why not?
  - o Have student groups create a list of things that make them nostalgic. Then, during a period of a few days, have each of them identify ways that marketers of products targeted toward them have focused on any of these elements of nostalgia. Can they identify any nostalgia brands that are focused at their feelings of nostalgia? Have them share their findings with group members.

- Marketers measure our memories about products and ads.
  - o Go to **www.ifilm.com/superbowl**. As a group, visit the Web site and review ads from the most recent Super Bowl. For the more well-known ads, create both recall and recognition tests. Give one type or the other to different students in class (this can be done after showing the ads or not showing the ads if they are well-known enough). Compare the results.

# CHAPTER 4—MOTIVATION AND VALUES

## CHAPTER OBJECTIVES

**When students finish this chapter they should understand why:**

- It's important for marketers to recognize that products can satisfy a range of consumer needs.
  - Have students think of examples of products or services that each of them has purchased that fits the three types of motivational conflicts found in Figure 4-1.
  - Find a student who is not too shy to do this one. Ask the student to search for unconscious motives by asking six people if they are wearing perfume or cologne. Make sure the student keeps asking until at least three people say, "Yes." Then have the student ask the respondents, "Why do you wear cologne?" Ask three of those who said they were not wearing cologne, "Why not?" Ask the three who said, "No" if they wore any the last time they were on a date. Share their responses with the class and evaluate them. Can the class uncover any hidden motivations?
  - Ask students to come up with a list of products or services that people primarily buy because they want to "belong." Have them explain why they listed the particular items. Then, have them explain how each of the items that they listed might also be consumed by individuals in solitude. Are there viable needs that consumers have for consuming these products both in the company of others as well as by themselves?
  - Have students find advertisements that attempt to persuade consumers to think of products as objects that satisfy one of the motives described in this chapter. Have them identify and classify that motive.

- The way we evaluate and choose a product depends upon our degree of involvement with the product, the marketing message, and/or the purchase situation.
  - Have your students think of some product or service they have purchased recently. Then have them respond to the consumer involvement scale in Table 4.1. Is their involvement with this product best described as product involvement, message-response involvement, or purchase situation involvement? Why?
  - Have the group go to a shopping center or mall and observe others' behavior. What conclusions can they make about motives, involvement, and values after having made the observation?
  - Have groups of students visit a shopping mall or a superstore. Have them evaluate the retail environment for ways that both the retailer and product manufacturers try to increase consumer involvement (refer to text if necessary for strategies to increase involvement).

- Our deeply held cultural values dictate the types of products and services we seek out or avoid.
  - Have each student list what he or she perceives to be the five most important values for themselves. For their parents? How do these values transfer to purchase decisions? How would marketers find out about their values?
  - The text specifies 9/11 as an event that changed consumer values. Have groups of students brainstorm other significant events that had an impact on the values of a given society's consumers. What were the events and what were the value changes?
  - Go to **www.wholefoods.com**. Take some time to become familiar with the Web site. Describe this company and the products that they offer. Select specific examples of products that seem to target the LOHAS values segment. Are these products that might appeal to values other than those described by LOHAS?

- Consumers vary in the importance they attach to worldly possessions, and this orientation in turn has an impact on their priorities and behaviors.
  - After reading the section "Materialism: 'He Who Dies with the Most Toys, Wins . . . ,' " have students create an argument either for or against more materialism. Does the Internet promote materialism? Explain.
  - Go to **www.burningman.com/**. Become familiar with the purpose of this festival. As a group, discuss the extent to which it is possible to achieve the purposes set forth by this organization. Discuss the irony of this.

# CHAPTER 5—THE SELF

## CHAPTER OBJECTIVES

**When students finish this chapter they should understand why:**

- The self-concept is strongly related to consumer behavior.
  - Ask a student to bring to class two brands within the same product category that project different images to the consumer. Have the student discuss the projected images by comparing and contrasting the two different brands. What techniques did the marketer use to project these images? Is the self-concept of the buyer important? Explain.
  - Ask students to interview the managers of two retail clothing stores. See if they can discover the degree to which the managers believe that consumers' personalities and self-images are important to the marketing and promotional activities of their store. Ask the students if they are in agreement with the managers' comments.

- Products often play a pivotal role in defining the self-concept.
  - Send the students out in pairs to visit a store that they feel reflects their self-concept. Ask the students to observe and describe personalities of the sales force. Now send them to visit a store they feel does not reflect their self-concept (if the two students feel their self-concepts differ, each of them may choose a store that reflects their own self-concept and that may serve as the store that does not reflect the self-concept of the other). Did they notice any difference in the personalities of the sales force? Do they think that poor or unexciting personalities will have an effect on salesmanship?
  - Assign students to collect advertisements that would tell a stranger something about their self-concept (and image). Have them put these ads on a poster board and bring them to class. Display the poster boards in class and see if the class can match the boards to the correct students.

- Sex-role identity is different than gender, and society's expectations of masculinity and femininity help to determine the products we buy to be consistent with these expectations.
  - Have students find media examples of men exhibiting agentic as well as communal goals. Have them do the same for women. How much did they find that each gender tended to adhere to the societal expectation?
  - Ask your students to compile a list of ten household chores. Then have each student interview two married couples (one newlywed and the other seasoned) to determine who usually performs that chore—the husband or the wife. If possible have the students ask the subject when their spouse is not around. Do they agree? Have students share their findings with the class.
  - Have student groups devise a list of traditional male traits with respect to personal care and hygiene. Then have them visit the cosmetics section of a major department store and interview salespeople with respect to the nature of their male customers. What are they buying, and how are they using it? Then have the groups compare their interview findings with their list of traditional characteristics.

- o Go to **www.metrosexual.com**. What is the current state of metrosexuals according to this Web site?

- A person's sex-role identity is a major component of self-definition. The media play a key role in teaching us how to behave as "proper" males and females.
  - o Have male students and female students (separately) interview three women and three men who they think are just about the right weight for their height and bone structure (instruct students to tell respondents that their responses are completely confidential). The students should ask the respondents if they think of themselves as overweight, underweight, or about right. Then see if they can determine how the subjects reached their conclusions. Next ask the subjects if they are doing anything to manage their weight. If possible, have students ask the respondents what their weight and height are. Discuss how the students seem to feel about their weight.

- The way we think about our bodies (and the way our culture tells us we should think) is a key component of self-esteem.
  - o Have each student find a good example of identity marketing in the media. Have the students share their examples during a discussion of such in class. Which ones do students see as being the greatest and most permanent modification to the consumer's life?
  - o Assign students to collect five ads that show male or female models exhibiting tattoos or body piercing (they may want to consult tattoo-related magazines or they may print ads from the Internet). Comment on the reason for the display. Did the model match the product be sold? Do people who do not have tattoos or body piercing relate well to the ad? How could you determine this?
  - o Go to **www.makeoversolutions.com**. Take the free demo. Upload a picture of yourself and perform a makeover that you feel genuinely suits you. Print a copy of the picture and bring it in to share with others who do the same. Evaluate the results in the context of the self-concept.

# CHAPTER 6—PERSONALITY AND LIFESTYLES

## CHAPTER OBJECTIVES

**When students finish this chapter they should understand why:**

- A consumer's personality influences the way he or she responds to marketing stimuli, but efforts to use this information in marketing contexts have met with mixed results.
  - o Ask students to examine advertisements and determine which appear to be Freudian or Neo-Freudian in nature. How is this determined? What were the messages in the advertisements?
  - o Have each student develop a description of his or her own pleasure principle as it relates to consumption. In other words, how is pleasure maximized and pain minimized when buying certain types of products? What are the things that marketers do to appeal to this?
  - o Have each student characterize three different people that he or she associates with (friends, co-workers, classmates, family members, etc.) based on traits (trait theory). Each of the three should be distinct. How could this information be used by an advertiser?
  - o Ask students to list three products that seem to have personalities. Describe the personalities. What types of people buy these products? Is there a match between the consumer's personality and that of the brand or product?
  - o Have students select a product category. Then have them develop a simple survey asking respondents how much they would be willing to pay for 1) a generic version of the product, 2) a minor brand in the market, and 3) the market leading brand. Have the students distribute this to ten individuals. Have the students tally the results as a demonstration of brand equity.

- Consumers' lifestyles are key to many marketing strategies.
  - o Ask students to compile a selection of recent ads that attempt to link consumption of a product with a specific lifestyle. In class, have students demonstrate what they have found. Discuss how the goal of linking product consumption to a lifestyle is usually accomplished.
  - o Ask students to think of a specific lifestyle (your own, your parents', your aspirations, etc.), and then make a list of products and services that are linked in the consumer's mind to that specific lifestyle. (Hint: You might decorate your living room, design a wardrobe, think of options for a car, etc.)
  - o Bring in some magazines targeted toward specific regional or local groups (Southern Living, Midwest Living, Progressive Farmer, Sunset, Ingrams, Arizona Highways, etc.). Have student groups look through the magazines and describe the types of articles and advertisements contained in each. How effective are the magazines in reaching their target market? How do they use lifestyles?

- Psychographics go beyond simple demographics in helping marketers understand and reach different consumer segments.
  - This chapter mentions that psychographic analyses can be used by politicians to market themselves. What are some of the marketing strategies and techniques used by politicians in recent elections? Did the candidates design special appeals to attract the attention of special target markets? What communication strategies were used? Discuss your observations with the class.
  - Tell students that the owners of a fast-food chain have asked your class to prepare a psychographic profile of families living in the communities surrounding a new location they are considering. (You—the instructor—should select any area that the students would most likely know.) Construct a ten-question psychographic inventory appropriate for segmenting families in terms of their dining-out preferences.
  - Using AIO segmentation, have groups of students design a new advertising campaign for a chain of restaurants targeting young professional college graduates. Have them explain the process they went through.
  - Have students go to **www.sric-bi.com/VALS/presurvey.shtml**. Have each of them take the survey and print out the page with the results. They should also print the list of VALS classifications and description. Then have them discuss the outcomes in groups. Specifically, they should discuss whether they feel that the results are characteristic of them.

- Identifying patterns of consumption can be superior to knowledge of individual purchases when crafting a lifestyle marketing strategy.
  - Have students use the principles of PRIZM to develop a description of their own home zip code.
  - Have students analyze their own patterns of food and beverage consumption. What values does this consumption reflect? Do your consumption patterns fit neatly within an identifiable food culture? Explain.
  - Ask students to examine their lifestyle and/or that of their family from a geodemographic perspective. Analyze your lifestyle according to the geographic levels of your neighborhood, zip code, city, and state.

# CHAPTER 7—ATTITUDES

## CHAPTER OBJECTIVES

**When students finish this chapter they should understand why:**

- It's important for consumer researchers to understand the nature and power of attitudes.
  - Have students bring in examples of promotional material that illustrate each of the four functions identified in the functional theory of attitudes.
  - Students should assemble ads for physical fitness and/or weight loss programs or products and analyze these ads in terms of how they are trying to influence or change consumers' attitudes toward their body image. What emotional and rational appeals were used (e.g., fear, health, vanity, social acceptance, peer pressure, etc.)?
  - Have students write a short paper identifying both a consumer product that they just "love" and one they just "hate." They should address how long they have felt this way, if they remember when they first developed these attitudes, why they still might feel this way, and if they have ever tried to change their attitude.

- Attitudes are more complex than they first appear.
  - Ask students to write about the sources that are influential in their attitude toward one of the following: their college or university, the Republican/Democratic Party, President Bush (or any recently elected president), Rush Limbaugh, Ralph Nader, their own religious faith, or any organized group (e.g., labor movement, Planned Parenthood, American Civil Liberties Union, Greenpeace, Moveon.org, etc.). As an alternative, interview a few friends about one of these organizations. Have students share their findings with the class. What can be learned about attitudes by having these discussions? What would be of value to a marketer?
  - Divide the class into teams and have each team come up with a set of about ten descriptive words that could be used to positively or negatively describe a specific consumer good (e.g., stereo, car, expensive clothing, etc.). Send students out to interview a friend who owns this product. Determine the length of time the respondent has owned the product, and then have the respondent evaluate the product according to some criteria determined by the class. See if the people who more recently purchased the product have a more positive attitude toward it than those who have owned it for a longer period of time. Because of time length, the instructor may wish to do this in class between groups or have only a few students participate in the project.
  - Attitudes change over time. Have groups of students brainstorm a list of products for which consumer attitudes have changed over time. Be sure to have them identify the change agent involved (either some aspect of the external environment or some aspect of the company itself).

- We form attitudes in several ways.
  - o Contrast the hierarchies of effects outlined in the chapter. How will strategic decisions related to the marketing mix be influenced by whichever hierarchy is operative among target consumers?
  - o In this project, students should identify one specific example for each of the three hierarchies of the ABC model. For each, they should give details as to the application of each component.
  - o Go to **www.dropzone.com**. Apply the ABC model of attitudes to the activity of skydiving. Which of the three hierarchies is most applicable? What modifications could be made to this?

- Consumers are motivated to maintain consistency among all the components of their attitudes, so they may alter one or more parts to realize this goal.
  - o Think of a behavior someone does that is inconsistent with his or her attitudes (e.g., attitudes toward cholesterol, drug use, or even buying things to make them stand out or attain status). Ask the person to elaborate on why he or she does the behavior and try to identify the way the person has resolved dissonant elements.
  - o It's time for true confessions. Describe three instances when your purchase behavior was inconsistent with an attitude toward the product or service you were buying. Explain why this happened. Share this with the class asking them if they agree with the explanation or whether they have other notions.
  - o Another good in-class project: Have groups of students decide on a purchase situation that they all have experience with. Then, have them discuss situations involving cognitive dissonance (buyer's remorse). What led to such?

- We can measure attitudes using sophisticated models that identify specific components and combine them to predict what a consumer's overall attitude will be.
  - o Construct a multi-attribute model for a set of local restaurants. Based on your findings, suggest how restaurant managers can improve their establishments' images via the strategies described in the chapter.
  - o Have students explain the consistency, balance, and Fishbein theories to a friend, and then ask the friend to analyze two of his or her recent experiences that seem to confirm or disconfirm one or more of these theories. Report the findings to the class.
  - o There are four strategic applications of the multi-attribute model given in the text. Have groups identify cases where companies have applied each of them.
  - o Visit **www.izod.com**. Is a multi-attribute model a good one to apply to this product to explain how attitudes are formed? Why or why not? Suggest an alternative model.

# CHAPTER 8—ATTITUDE CHANGE AND
# INTERACTIVE COMMUNICATIONS

## CHAPTER OBJECTIVES

**When students finish this chapter they should understand why:**

- The communications model identifies several important components needed to transmit messages that attempt to change consumers' attitudes toward products and services.
  - Ask one of your students to interview three people and have each respondent identify an advertisement that they have a positive attitude toward and an ad that they have a negative attitude toward. Be sure to inquire to find out how their attitudes toward the ads influence their attitudes toward the products and likelihood of purchase.
  - Have students produce an example of some type of promotion used for each of the principles of reciprocity, scarcity, authority, consistency, liking, and consensus.

- Consumers' responses to a firm's marketing messages do not necessarily have to take the form of a purchase to be important or useful to the company.
  - Pick a controversial figure. Your group's assignment is to design a public relations campaign that will change the public's image about the figure you have chosen. What principles from the chapter did your group use to accomplish your mission? Present your campaign to the class. Measure whether the image of your chosen figure was improved or not.

- Several factors influence how effective the source of a communication will be.
  - Many, many companies rely on celebrity endorsers as communications sources to persuade. Especially when targeting younger people, these spokespeople often are "cool" musicians, athletes, or movie stars. In your opinion, who would be the most effective celebrity endorser today and why? Who would be the least effective? Why?
  - People hate the ad, but still find that they purchase the product. Have students generate and discuss a list of products that have had success from annoying campaigns. Why is this the case?
  - Corporations love the buzz. Have students describe three examples of companies that have achieved positive PR benefits from the "buzz." Why did this happen? Have the students also generate a list of three companies that have flopped based on hype. What was the difference between these situations?

- The way a message is structured can exert a big impact on how persuasive it will be.
  - What are the pros and cons of using rational versus emotional appeals, that is, trying to persuade consumers by focusing on what they know as opposed to what they feel? When should marketers use one type or the other?
  - Discuss some conditions where it would be advisable to use a comparative advertising strategy.

- A marketer must decide whether to incorporate rational or emotional appeals in its communications strategy. Describe conditions that are more favorable to using one or the other.
- A government agency wants to encourage the use of designated drivers by people who have been drinking. What advice could you give the organization about constructing persuasive communications? Discuss some factors that might be important, including the structure of the communications, where they should appear, and who should deliver them. Should fear appeals be used, and if so, how?
- Have students conduct a simple content analysis by examining either print or broadcast ads. They may find such ads in real sources such as magazines, newspapers, or by watching television. They may also find such ads online at Web sites that maintain archives of advertisements. Students should view numerous ads and analyze which of the following message appeals appear to be used: emotional, rational, sex, humorous, or fear. Does the medium or specific media vehicle have an effect on which appeals are used most commonly? After conducting this analysis, have students explain which appeal(s) is most powerful? Most persuasive? Most credible?
- Why would a marketer consider saying negative things about his or her product? When is this strategy feasible? Can you find examples of it?

- Consumer variables help to determine whether the nature of the source or the message itself will be relatively more effective in communicating.
  - Describe the elaboration likelihood model and tell how it is related to the relative importance of *what* is said versus *how* it's said?

# CHAPTER 9—INDIVIDUAL DECISION MAKING

## CHAPTER OBJECTIVES

**When students finish this chapter they should understand why:**

- Consumer decision making is a central part of consumer behavior, but the ways people evaluate and choose products (and the amount of thought they put into these choices) vary widely depending upon such dimensions as the degree of novelty or risk related to the decision.
    - o As an in-class activity, discuss with the class the concept of risk. Distribute a list of several different consumer products or have a student do this. Then ask students what types of risk they would associate with each of the products. How could the risk be reduced?

- A decision is actually composed of a series of stages that results in the selection of one product over competing options.
    - o Have individual students evaluate a recent purchase of a large-scale item (e.g., expensive clothing, car, stereo system, appliance, furniture, etc.) based on the stages in the consumer decision-making process (Figure 9-1). Ask them if they think they gathered enough information before making their decision. See if they were satisfied with the quantity or quality of the information they had at their disposal.
    - o In this field project, have a student design a project to illustrate when customers use internal versus external sources of information and deliberate versus accidental sources of information during the search process.
    - o Have the students keep a diary listing their highest and lowest involvement in product purchases or service transactions for each day for a week. Have them identify the decision process they went through and how satisfied they were with their decision. Then have them write a short paper describing the lessons they learned from the purchases. What mistakes were made?
    - o This project will require student groups to conduct consumer interviews. They should contact people (acquaintances, friends, etc.) and ask them questions about a recent purchase or consideration of a purchase. Specifically, they should ask the consumer what factors led them to problem recognition. They should also ask the respondents to explain the similarities or differences that existed at decision time.

- Our access to online sources is changing the way we decide what to buy.
    - o Have students conduct research on the state of silent commerce as highlighted in the Marketing Opportunity special feature box. How prevalent are such strategies? What is the growth potential of such?
    - o Have groups of students apply the consumer decision-making model to purchasing on the Internet. Does the model work the same as does purchasing in the retail environment? Explain and illustrate.
    - o Have groups of students construct decision rules that apply only to purchasing via the Internet. Is this possible? If so, have the students demonstrate how this is so and what

value the decision might be. Have them describe how they arrived at their "new" rules. Have other students critique the "new" rules.

- Decision making is not always rational.
  - o Have student groups devise a taxonomy of categories for a product category. Then have them reposition certain brands at the subordinate level by modifying that taxonomy. How could the companies carry out such a repositioning?

- Consumers rely upon different decision rules when evaluating competing options.
  - o Based on the non-compensatory and compensatory decision rules listed at the end of the chapter, students should create examples. Then have students form their own decision rules. Have them demonstrate how their rules are different and how they might be of value in general consumer decision making.
  - o Have students choose a specific type of product. Then have them find product-rating reports from Consumer Reports or a similar organization that tests products. The student should evaluate the rating system the organization used. What other information would have been useful.
  - o Have a group of students design an experiment that would test and illustrate prospect theory. Have them conduct this experiment using the students in class. After analyzing the results, have them present them to the class.

- We often fall back on well-learned "rules-of-thumb" to make decisions.
  - o Ask a student to compile a description of three products that include both features and country-of-origin. Then have the student ask a few people to rate the quality of the products and whether they would probably buy them. See if he or she can find out why the respondents feel this way.
  - o Have a student identify countries-of-origin of popular U.S. cars. Find out how many cars that we identify as "American" are made in other countries and how many cars we identify as "foreign" are assembled in the United States. A variation on this would be to do the same with heavy equipment (such as John Deere) or with motorcycles or cars that are considered to be of Japanese origin.
  - o In groups, students should discuss popular stereotypes that discriminate against a company, a person, a country, or product. Having selected one of these, they should design a strategy that would help to reduce the stereotype's negative effects.
  - o Go to **www.peapod.com**. Online grocery is alive and well. While most grocery purchases that we make fall into the category of habitual decision making, somehow, this concept is working for some people. Spend some time on this site and assemble a grocery order. What are the pros and cons of using an online service for habitual decision-making decisions?

# CHAPTER 10—BUYING AND DISPOSING

## CHAPTER OBJECTIVES

**When students finish this chapter they should understand why:**

- The outcome of an actual transaction is influenced by many factors over and above the qualities of the product or service. Factors operating at the time of purchase can dramatically influence the consumer decision-making process.
  - o Have students employ the Day Reconstruction method to document their own behavior for a day and report on the findings. What trends do they notice? Are there things that they found that they did not expect?
  - o Have someone visit a local supermarket and question the manager regarding how shelf space is allocated. What and who determines which products are placed on the shelves, how much space they are allocated, and at what level they are displayed on the shelf?

- In addition to what a shopper already knows or believes about a product, information provided in the store on a Web site can strongly influence his purchase decisions.
  - o Have students go to a shopping mall. Have them analyze the behavior of shoppers based on observation only. Can they determine the nature of people's reasons for shopping? Have them keep track and present the results to the class.
  - o Ask a student to visit competing discount houses, supermarkets, department stores, or specialty shops in your area and describe the image they have of each store. What factors account for the image differences? For the poorest image store, design a strategy for upgrading its image.
  - o Student teams should go to an activity store to interview the manager. Given that the concept of the store is built around participating in the production of a good, ask the manager what benefits they perceive in this model, both from the consumer perspective and from the company perspective.
  - o Student groups should visit three small clothing stores and assess their layouts. What differences do they observe? What factors might account for these differences? Would the student recommend any layout changes based on observation?
  - o Go to **www.mountaindew.com**. One of the primary features of this Web site is the entertainment provided for the viewer. What features do you find? Were you entertained or was this page really for another market segment (if so, who)? What would an entertaining Web site have to do with encouraging the consumer to buy the product? Because the consumer cannot buy the product online, does this Web site make much sense? Explain.

- A salesperson can be the crucial link between interest in a product and its actual purchase.
  - o Go to **www.customerssuck.com** and **www.northworstair.org**. As a group, examine accounts given by both employees and customers as to the outrageous behavior observed in retail settings. Summarize the findings. What conclusions can be made from this?
  - o Ask a team of students to visit a nearby popular mall to observe the activities of customers and employees. What nonretailing activities do they observe (e.g., art exhibits,

performances, fitness walking, socializing, etc.)? Are these activities beneficial or harmful to retailers?

- Marketers need to be concerned about a consumer's evaluations of a product after the person buys it as well as before.
  - o Have students talk to other students at the university or college. What forms of complaint behavior do they observe? What strategies could the university or college follow to alleviate these complaints?
  - o Ask a student to relate to the class a purchase experience in which dissatisfaction resulted from the product or service purchased. Have the student tell the class how he or she reacted in terms of post-purchase dissonance. How could the seller avoid future similar incidents?
  - o Have groups or pairs of students interview a complaint handler for a local department store to describe a recent experience with a dissatisfied customer. The complaint handler should explain why the customer was unhappy. Do the complainers seem to have any common traits?

- Getting rid of products when they are no longer needed or wanted is a major concern both to marketers and to public policy makers.
  - o Many consumers have become more interested in conserving than in "throwing away." Have students think of ideas they have for creative recycling. Then see if they can figure out ways to profitably market these ideas to the public?
  - o Give students the assignment of selling something through an online auction site that they think is worthless junk. Have them share their results with the class. Were the results unexpected? Was it worth the time to do this? What was the highest selling price of a person's "junk"?
  - o Freecycle something. Then take something off of **www.freecycle.com**. Report on the experience including the feelings of giving/receiving, the benefit or value to the giver/receiver, and so on.
  - o Have each student think of a time when he or she had to get rid of something that had been significant to them. Analyze this situation in terms of divestment rituals.

# CHAPTER 11—GROUP INFLUENCE AND OPINION LEADERSHIP

## CHAPTER OBJECTIVES

### When students finish this chapter they should understand why:

- A consumer doesn't make purchase decisions in a vacuum. He often is heavily influenced by others whose opinions and product choices exert various kinds of power over the individual.
  - o Have students in class write down the various groups to which they are members. In which of these groups are conformity pressures the greatest? Why do they think this is the case?
  - o Ask a group of students to make a list of aspirational reference groups that are of interest to many college students. Then ask them to bring to class a few print ads that are targeted to college students with these particular aspirations.
  - o Have groups of students consider and identify what special language, clothes, props, and sets are characteristic of various groups present in society. You may wish to require students to make actual observations in a public place such as a shopping mall or airport.

- Consumers often seek out others who share similar interests in products or services.
  - o Each student group will have the task of forming or joining a brand community. Have them decide upon a brand that none of them really use. Then, have them research the brand extensively and begin their own pro-product dialogue among themselves. If they wish to establish an online chat room or message board, that would be all the better. After having done this for a set period of time, have group members discuss how they feel about the brand. Whether they have purchased or not, do they feel more "loyal"? Have they developed positive attitudes? Do they find themselves engaging in WOM outside the group?

- We may be motivated to buy or use products in order to be consistent with what other people do.
  - o Ask a student to interview someone who has attended a home party where products were sold (e.g., Amway, cookware, Tupperware, Sarah Coventry jewelry, Mary Kay, lingerie). What types of group power (such as referent, expert, reward, coercive) can be identified?

- The things that other consumers tell us about products (both good and bad) are often more influential than the advertising we are exposed to about those products.
  - o Students should collect ads that attempt to influence or promote word-of-mouth communications. Have them comment on the credibility of the ads. Is the promoter used in the ad an effective influencer?
  - o Have a student think about some goods and services that he or she has purchased recently. To what extent did word-of-mouth communication influence purchases?
  - o Encourage a student to think of something he or she recently purchased in which advice was actively sought from others. For what reasons was advice sought? Why was the particular person selected to provide this advice?

- Online technologies are accelerating the impact of word-of-mouth communication.
  - Have each student try to purchase all of their necessities for one week using nothing but online purchasing. Describe the process, its successes, and its failures. What was learned? Have the students evaluate the future of online purchasing.
  - Have each student identify one case of guerrilla marketing. It should be the objective to find a case where the maximum amount of promotional benefit was achieved with the least amount of resources. They should attempt to find information that will allow for estimates of these figures. Upon sharing cases with the class, keep track to determine the most effective campaign based on this ROI type of measure.
  - Describe how opinion leaders can be formed and found on the Internet. Describe the advantages and disadvantages of using opinion leaders on the Web. How would this form of opinion leadership be different from any other form of opinion leadership (if at all)?
  - Go to **www.gogorillamedia.com/gogorillamedia.html**. This is an agency that specializes in guerilla marketing tactics. Summarize five such tactics, identifying benefits and examples of using each.
  - Go to **http://forums.prospero.com/foxidol/start**. This is the main forum page on the official Web site for American Idol. Register as a user (if necessary). Then read through the message threads posted by members. Document and summarize communications that are brand-building and those that are brand-damaging.

- Certain people are particularly likely to influence others' product choices.
  - Ask each student to think about individual family members, friends, and acquaintances. On paper, have the students identify the people who act as opinion leaders, product innovators, and market mavens. Describe what each person does. Have a few students share their observations with the class.
  - Ask a student to find one magazine advertisement for a consumer product that uses "the expert" as a reference group appeal and another that features a top corporate executive. Have the student discuss the impact of each appeal on consumers.

# CHAPTER 12—ORGANIZATIONAL AND HOUSEHOLD DECISION MAKING

## CHAPTER OBJECTIVES

**When students finish this chapter they should understand why:**

- Marketers often need to understand consumers' behavior rather than consumer behavior, since in many cases more than one person is involved in deciding what to buy.
  - o Conduct this as an in-class activity with each student doing his or her own work. Distribute a list of ten products/services and have each student indicate on the list whether the decision to purchase each product is probably made by the husband alone, the wife alone, or jointly by both parties. Does there seem to be a trend developing? If so, what evidence does the class have that they are probably correct?

- Companies as well as individuals make purchase decisions. The decision-making process differs when people are choosing what to buy on behalf of a company versus a personal purchase.
  - o Interview the purchasing manager of a small- to medium-sized organization about how the organization does purchasing. Does the organization have a buying center? If so, describe it. If not, who fulfills the roles as defined by the buying center?
  - o Student groups should interview a corporate purchase agent at length about their purchasing practices. What are the factors that affect the purchase decision? Are there multiple individuals involved in the process? Who affects the purchase decision and in what way?

- Many important demographic dimensions of a population relate to family and household structure.
  - o Have each student research the pager market. What is the current status of this market? How has it evolved since the early 1990s? Why?
  - o Have students compile a list of magazines that appeal to young women. Then have them do the same for young men. How are appeals used in such magazines similar to and/or different from each other? Have students bring in example ads to illustrate their conclusions.
  - o Have students go to the library and research advertisements in a women's magazine (i.e., *Good Housekeeping, Ladies' Home Journal, Family Circle,* and *Woman's Day*) over the past twenty years. How have advertisers adapted their copy and art work to account for the changing roles of women? Are there things that have not changed?
  - o Each student should consider the market for cell phones. In segmenting the market for cell phones and cell phone service, discuss the impact of family life cycle stage, sex, age, education, or important factors? What marketing and promotional strategies would you devise to reach the segment(s) you selected? Why?
  - o Have your group interview a group of senior citizens about what was "hot" and what was not when they were teens. How has the world changed for teens since these seniors were teens? Are there value similarities, music preferences, and relationships with peers that

are worth commenting about? How can marketers use information about a senior's past to market to them today? Explain.

- Our traditional notions about families often are outdated.
  - Have a student bring to class three advertisements that show the changing roles of men and women. Also bring in three ads that show the traditional roles of men and women. Which ads does the class like best? Which do they find more credible? Try to analyze their responses.

- Members of a family unit play different roles and have different amounts of influence when making purchase decisions.
  - Ask a student to visit a store (e.g., clothing store, shoe store, furniture store, appliance store, restaurant, etc.) and interview the store manager regarding how the family life cycle concept is employed in their inventory selection, pricing, and/or advertising and sales promotion.
  - Have each student consider a purchase that they were recently a part of that involved multiple individuals (roommates, their family, a fraternity, etc.). Have them analyze this purchase by identifying specific people who played each of the roles in the buying center (initiator, gatekeeper, influencer, buyer, and user).
  - Groups should identify three local restaurants that seem to target clientele in three different family life cycle stages (e.g., young singles; young married without children; married with young children; married with youngest child older than six; empty nesters with the breadwinner still in the work force; empty nesters out of the work force; sole survivors). Each restaurant should be visited by a team member. How does each establishment attract its target market? Sometimes it is fun to run a 2-minute video of the clientele entering and leaving each different type of restaurant.
  - Ask a student or a group of students to describe different purchase situations in which they (or another family member) play the role of initiator, influencer, information gatherer, decision maker, purchaser, or user.

- Children learn over time what and how to consume.
  - Ask a student to go to a toy store, a toy department, or a cereal aisle in the grocery store and watch several interactions between a parent and child. Have the student make an oral report on how the children "made their wishes known" and how parents reacted to their children's "needs and wants."
  - Student groups should interview youth of three different age groups (early, mid, and late teens; mall intercept format may work best) as to the purchases that they typically make in a week. Find out about how much they usually spend and on what types of things they usually spend it. How do they get their spending money? About how much do they have to spending on average? Results should be reported, including the identification of developing patterns.

# CHAPTER 13—INCOME AND SOCIAL CLASS

## CHAPTER OBJECTIVES

**When students finish this chapter they should understand why:**

- Our decisions about whether to spend our money are influenced by both personal and social conditions.
  - Have a student visit a high-end specialty store for a luxury good (i.e., Louis Vuitton, Coach, Burburry, etc.). Have him or her interview a sales associate or manager in regard to the existence of the mass class segment. Can they identify the difference between upper class people and middle to lower class people who buy the products? What are the noted differences? How prevalent are the mass culture members?
  - Students should conduct an assessment of consumer confidence in their home country according to the accepted measures of such. Do this for each year in the last five years. What is the trend? What are the economic implications of this?
  - Conduct a brief secondary research project on what happens to people after they win a large lottery. Summarize the results and share them with the class.
  - Have a student interview small business owners, large business owners, or a couple of both for their opinions of the state of the economy. How do they think an increase in Social Security taxes—or Americans with Disabilities Act, Flat Tax Proposal, NAFTA, or some other currently proposed federal regulation or mandate—would affect them? Have the student find out what major signals the owners study and watch before making their business forecasts.

- We can group consumers into social classes that say a lot about an individual's standing in society.
  - Conduct this as an in-class activity. Prepare a list of fifteen occupations and distribute copies to the class. Ask each student to rank the occupations according to prestige. Compile the results (either during class or after for the next class period). Discuss the results with the class. Are there consistencies? Why do these form? What implications do these perceptions have on consumer behavior?
  - Ask students to find at least two manufacturers' ads for the same type of product (e.g., clothing, food product, personal care product, etc.) that they think are aimed at different social classes. How do these ads differ?
  - Ask a student to compile a collection of ads that depict consumers of different social classes. What medium and vehicle is each ad found in? Have students generalize about the reality of the stories told in these ads.
  - Have a student interview one or more salespeople from one of the following product categories: new or used cars, stereo equipment, clothing, insurance, or real estate. Ask the student to determine the social classes or status of their customers. Does the student recommend that the sales approach will vary depending on the customer's social class?
  - How can online marketers use social class in marketing efforts? Give examples of good and bad usage. Go online to do this if possible.

o Have student groups visit two sections of a community—one where residents are professionals and business people and one where residents are mostly working class. Ask them to note how the homes vary in terms of color, architecture, and the general appearance of the lawn and landscape. Have them check the paper or call a realtor to find the general value of homes in the area. What types of stores are in the neighborhood and how are they promoted?

o Ask students to make a list of slang terms that are used to disparage social classes. Why are these terms used? How do marketers disparage or make fun of social classes (which they do not target)? What is the best way to treat all classes with ethics and dignity?

o Have your group designate which social class would most accurately describe each member's current position. Where do the members expect to be in five years with respect to social class? What differences will occur if the anticipated movement in social class occurs? Discuss the changes in class.

- Consumer behavior often is affected by a person's desire to make a statement about her social class or the class to which she would like to belong.

o Ask a student to bring in an ad in which the brand being marketed was at one time a status symbol, but fell out of fashion for a time (e.g., Cadillac, Parker Pen, Izod-Lacoste, etc.). Have the student discuss whether the ad still attempts to create that perception. What new product, if any, has replaced the featured product as a status symbol?

o What status symbols motivate you to purchase? Pick an example product and give an illustration.

o Have a group of students compile a list of ten colleges and universities. Then have them go out and have other students rank them. Have the students comment on the results. Are there any marketing implications to the results?

o Go to **www.cadillac.com**. Once the ultimate status symbol, Cadillac's image began a slow decline around 1980. The brand is now on a major quest to reclaim its title. Although they are seeing some success, they may be hitting certain target markets with some of their products that actually detract from the image they are trying to achieve. Specifically regarding the Escalade line of SUVs, how do you perceive the conflict between Cadillac's traditional target market and that of new market segments that are embracing the brand (i.e., hip hop culture)? How should Cadillac address this issue? Design a promotional strategy outline.

o Go to **www.hammacher.com**. How does Hammacher Schlemmer use prestige and the desire to be different in its marketing effort? Give illustrations from the company's Web site to support your conclusions. Is this a good strategy for the company to follow? Explain.

# CHAPTER 14—ETHICAL, RACIAL, AND RELIGIOUS SUBCULTURES

## CHAPTER OBJECTIVES

**When students finish this chapter they should understand why:**

- Consumers' memberships in ethnic, racial, and religious subcultures often play a big role in guiding their consumption behaviors.
  - o Assign students to interview a member of a subculture other than his or her own (e.g., African American, Hispanic American, Asian American, white, Catholic, Mormon, Jewish, etc.) to discover what types of products or services are purchased because of membership in this particular group. What are some marketing implications?
  - o Have groups prepare a list of holidays that are oriented toward a particular subculture (e.g., Cinco de Mayo, Martin Luther King's Birthday, Passover, Easter, St. Patrick's Day, etc.). Now have them ask a few people if they celebrate or commemorate these holidays. What are the marketing implications? (Make sure that some of the people interviewed belong to the subcultures chosen.)

- Additional influences come from our identification with microcultures that reflect a shared interest in some organization or activity.
  - o Have students interview a member of an ethnic or religious subculture (e.g., African American, Hispanic American, Asian American, Lutheran, Jewish, Baptist, etc.) to see if the person can identify additional subcultures within the subculture. What are the subtle differences and are any of these significant to marketers?

- Many marketing efforts appeal to ethnic and racial identity.
  - o Have each student list four or five major religions, then have them list products that each religion would or would not buy because of their faith. Can they find any examples of how companies have catered to such patterns?
  - o Have a student visit a toy store to observe the various types of toys that are for sale to ethnic subcultures. Have them give a report on the range of toys available and specify the intended racial or ethnic markets.
  - o Send students to a retail store of their choice and have them comment on ethnic symbols that may or may not be used in marketing the store's products. For example, are mannequins racially diverse? Should retail stores follow a policy of appealing to ethnic groups with symbols? Explain.
  - o Have students watch television programs based on ethnicity or subcultures. Watch one and describe how the show might appeal to an ethnic or subculture group. Notice the ads. Were there any differences between the products or services advertised in the show? Were there any differences between the ways the ads appeared? Comment.
  - o Assign student groups to visit two local supermarkets to find out if either has segmented their market on the basis of the subculture or ethnic background of their customers. How many subcultures are recognized by each supermarket? Have the students talk to the store manager if possible.

- o Have individual students bring to class print ads aimed at a particular subculture and show how the ads attempt to address the group. Do the students think they are effective?

- African Americans, Hispanic Americans, and Asian Americans are the three most important ethnic/racial subcultures in the United States.
  - o Assign a student group to interview an account executive from an advertising agency and ask this person about marketing to ethnic subcultures, particularly the African American and Hispanic American markets. Among other things, have them question the person on whether they see a line between marketing responsibly to such groups and carrying out racial stereotypes.
  - o Bring some magazines to class that are primarily targeted toward either African American or Caucasian audiences. Ask the students to look through each type of magazine and select advertisements that are similar, except for the models. Are there any other differences between the ads (e.g., language, models, social situation, etc.)? Explain.

- Religion and spirituality are increasingly being used to market products.
  - o Have student groups research a church. This should be done through secondary methods as well as visiting the church and making observations. An interview with the pastor might also be appropriate. How are these churches focusing on recruiting new members as well as retaining existing members? Does it appear that there is any compromising of doctrines in engaging in such activities?
  - o Assign students to talk to a religious professional (e.g., minister or priest) about his views toward marketing to consumers based on religious preferences. What is his opinion? Does he market his religion? If so, how? Comment on whether you agree with this policy or not.

# CHAPTER 15—AGE SUBCULTURES

## CHAPTER OBJECTIVES

**When students finish this chapter they should understand why:**

- People have many things in common with others merely because they are about the same age.
  - o Choose a basic product that is used by people of all age groups (soft drinks, toothpaste, automobiles, etc.). Identify different brands of this product that target different age groups (Gen Yers, Gen Xers, Boomers, seniors). Identify key differences in the product itself as well as in how these brands are promoted, priced, and distributed.
  - o Have students bring to class print ads that are aimed at a particular age group and show how these ads attempt to address that group.
  - o Have student groups interview men from different age groups (older than 60, 40-60, and 30-39, and 18-29). Ask them about how they watch sporting events. Do they have a preferred ritual (place to watch, with someone or alone, certain food items, etc.)? What are the similarities and differences? What are the implications of these results for the sports teams, networks, and other products mentioned by the respondents?

- Teens are an important age segment for marketers, but they are undergoing many changes that influence their behavior as consumers.
  - o Ask students to use a product example (i.e., food products, automobiles) to illustrate how the marketer might promote to youths to take advantage of the influence they exert on family purchase decisions.
  - o Ask students to visit two mall stores that are not department stores (i.e., Abercrombie & Fitch, American Eagle, Aeropostale, the Buckle, etc.). How do these stores appeal to the teen market? How does the design of the store differ from that of other stores targeted at other age groups? Do salespeople differ? Does promotion seem to differ?
  - o Have students interview someone in their early to mid teens. Ask them about their values, interests, and perceptions of what is "cool." What kinds of products (clothing, electronics, etc.) do they like? After doing this, each student should compare the results to a description of him- or herself at the same age.
  - o Have students give a one-page description of themselves, their time period, and their thoughts in their teenage years. How could a marketer use this information to make appeals to them? What were their favorite expressions? Do they still use these? Do they now seem very out of place except to someone of their generation?
  - o Go to **www.mtv.com**. MTV has been around for a long time. Did you watch it when you were a teen? How has it changed? What new strategies is the organization using to reach its target market of today? Where will the organization be heading in the future? How could it keep its customers and viewers from "growing up" and leaving it as a source of entertainment and information? Plot a strategy that might help with this.

- Baby boomers continue to be the most powerful age segment economically.
  - Large shopping malls draw in people of all ages. Have students visit a large mall and note the tactics used to target Gen Yers, Gen Xers, Boomers, and seniors. Are there any other single products that seem to be able to simultaneously target multiple age segments?
  - What do you think are the best ways to reach: the teen market, the Baby Boomer market, and the senior market with advertising messages? Demonstrate and explain.
  - Find magazine ads from the 1970s targeted at Boomers. Locate ads from current publications targeted at the same people. What are the similarities and differences? To what extent are these similarities and differences due to the phase of life, and to what extent are they due to the actual characteristics of the age cohort?

- Seniors will increase in importance as a market segment.
  - Have students contact their parents or grandparents. What is nostalgic to them? How have you seen this used in advertising? What products have a nostalgic appeal for them? Do they say that nostalgic appeals work on them? Have them give examples.
  - Have student groups go to a senior citizen gathering (this can be any kind of gathering) and interview three men and three women about nostalgia. What were they most nostalgic about? How could this be used in marketing to capture their attention? What did you learn from this experience?
  - Have student groups visit a local retirement village and observe how the complex is designed to meet the needs of the market segment it is serving. Have the students review the literature provided by the complex to see what techniques are used to market the facility to "seasoned citizens." Is it "cool" to live in a seniors' complex? Why or why not?
  - Ask groups to select two product categories that appear to have good potential for sales to older people but are presently not marketed very well. Design a plan for more effective marketing to take advantage of this opportunity.
  - Go to **www.peapod.com** and **www.iping.com**. Each student should identify how the services offered by these Web sites would benefit senior citizens. How can these Web sites better target this age group?

# CHAPTER 16—CULTURAL INFLUENCES ON CONSUMER BEHAVIOR

## CHAPTER OBJECTIVES

**When students finish this chapter they should understand why:**

- A culture is a society's personality, and our membership in a culture plays a big role in shaping our identities as individuals.
    - o Invite a person from a foreign culture to come to your class to discuss products commonly used in the guest's country that are seldom used in this country. In preparation, have the students develop a list of products commonly used in the United States. Ask the guest how available these products are in his or her country, where they can be purchased, and the frequency of use.
    - o Ask students to interview a person from a different culture or a foreign culture. During the interview have the student observe any nonverbal communication that is taking place, then ask what similarities and differences he has noticed between the nonverbal language of his culture and the American culture. Have the student report on these similarities and differences.
    - o Ask groups to prepare a list of products that people tend to buy more for what the products mean than for what the products do. Are there other products that could satisfy the same need and even perhaps sell for less? What makes these products have lesser status?

- Myths are stories that express the shared ideals of a culture. In modern times marketing messages are used to hand these stories down to members.
    - o More and more, email messages are forwarded that represent incorrect or even mythical information (i.e., that Bill Gates will pay people money to forward an email). Have student groups locate an email that would qualify as a myth and research the origin of the message as well as its truthfulness.
    - o Go to **www.snopes.com**. As a group, spend some time on this Web site. Then choose an urban myth that you find most interesting (disregarding whether it is true or not). Apply the four interrelated functions of myths to the one that you chose. How can the concepts of binary opposition, mediating figure, or monomyth be applied to the myth that you chose? In your opinion, has the Internet made urban myths and legends more commonplace? Why?

- Many of our consumption activities including holiday observances, grooming, and gift-giving are based upon deeply ingrained rituals.
    - o Invite someone from the wedding industry to come talk to the class regarding marketing practices in the industry. Collect literature from various wedding-related businesses to study prior to the guest speaker. Have students formulate questions prior to the class.

o Have a student briefly summarize an episode of a weekly television series that he or she watched recently. Have the class describe how the program transmitted cultural beliefs, values, and customs.

o Ask students to describe rituals they follow when visiting a shopping mall, movie theater, or restaurant. How could marketers capitalize on these rituals?

o Have students comment on the practice of drinking while attending college. What are their opinions and perceptions of the role of drinking in the college experience? Is it ritualistic? If so, how do marketers capitalize on this ritual? If a college really wanted to discourage drinking, what would be the best way to do this culturally?

o Have group members interview a ball player, an actress or actor, a student preparing for exams, a trial lawyer, and others you might choose to see if they have a certain ritual or superstition that they tend to follow in preparing for and performing their activity. Do they remember when they first started performing this ritual?

- We can describe products as either sacred or profane, and it's not unusual for some products to move back and forth between the two categories.

o Ask students to identify what they perceive to be a sacred place on campus. How is this place honored? Marketed? How is information about this place passed on to future students? How does the university or college use this sacred place to market the university or college? Is this proper?

o Each student should identify and describe a possession that most people would consider to be ordinary, but to them is sacred. Have them describe how this sacredness developed.

o Have student groups identify what they feel is the most sacred symbol on campus and establish the reasons for this. Then have the class come together and compare their results.

# CHAPTER 17—THE CREATION AND DIFFUSION OF GLOBAL CONSUMER CULTURE

## CHAPTER OBJECTIVES

**When students finish this chapter they should understand why:**

- Styles are a mirror that reflects underlying cultural conditions.
  - In the case of Crazy Frog, how have art and media influenced popular culture? Is the reverse also true?

- We can distinguish between high and low culture?
  - Go to a contemporary magazine and find illustrations of high and low culture. Indicate what type of consumers might be attracted to these different messages.

- Many modern marketers are reality engineers.
  - Rent a movie of your choice. Find ten different consumer products that would be natural fits for product placement in the movie you have just watched (these should be products for which a branded placement does not already exist in the film). Position the products (through description of the scene) where they should most appropriately be used. Explain why companies (the ten products) should be willing to pay for the exposure your group has suggested.
  - Discuss issues of ethics as they apply to reality engineering. Support your ideas with examples.
  - Find a product placement agency. Interview someone at this agency as to the general nature of product placement and how these "deals" come about. How is the practice of product placement changing? What is different about this practice today as opposed to 10 or 20 years ago?
  - Have groups select a product category of interest to them. Have them develop a formal strategy to reality engineer the product. Include specific tactics relating to different components of the marketing mix.

- New products, services, and ideas spread through a population. Different types of people are more or less likely to adopt them.
  - Find a product and describe how it was first introduced and how it has become diffused into our economy. Does it seem to fit the stages described in the text?

- Many people and organizations play a role in the fashion system that creates and communicates symbolic meanings to consumers.
  - What role do MTV and other teen media programs have in establishing fashion? How do older adults get information on fashion? How do older adults get information on fashion in business attire?
  - It should be apparent from the chapter that art and culture are in a constant state of influencing each other. It is the dynamics of how these two elements of society influence

each other that they also influence themselves. Discuss how fashion, music, and entertainment influence each other through pop culture.

- o This is one for groups to give some thought to and even do some research on. How have styles in fashion and in our economy impacted political and social conditions? Which came first, the style or the conditions?
- o Go to **www.myreplicawatch.com** and **www.fashionknockoffs.com**. Why do you think that the knockoff industry has become so big? Discuss this in terms of the fashion concepts discussed in the chapter. Also, include a discussion of the economics of buying such brands (How much does the real thing cost?).

- Fashions follow cycles.
  - o Go through magazines to find ads that display fashion used in association with some other product. Discuss the ramifications of this and present your findings to the class.
  - o Visit an upscale-fashion department store or boutique. Interview the manager about fashion. How does the manager decide on which fashion merchandise to purchase? What does he or she do with fashion merchandise once it has run its course? How does he or she know when a fashion is becoming unfashionable? Relate your results to the class.

- Western (and particularly American) culture has a huge impact around the world, though people in other countries don't necessarily ascribe the same meanings to products as we do.
  - o Divide the class into teams. Have one group take the perspective that the "Americanization" of foreign cultures and media is a proper path to take. Have one group take the perspective that the "Americanization" of foreign cultures and media is wrong and will eventually cause conflict. Debate the issue.

# Chapter-by-Chapter Material

# CHAPTER 1

# CONSUMERS RULE

## CHAPTER OBJECTIVES

When students finish this chapter they should understand why:

- Consumer behavior is a process.

- Consumers use products to help them define their identities in different settings.

- Marketers need to understand the wants and needs of different consumer segments.

- The Web is changing consumer behavior.

- Consumer behavior is related to other issues in our lives.

- Consumer activities can be harmful to individuals and to society.

- A wide range of specialists study consumer behavior.

- There are two major perspectives on understanding and studying consumer behavior.

## CHAPTER SUMMARY

As students will soon see, the field of consumer behavior covers a lot of ground. Whether the consumer is on a shopping trip to the mall or surfing on the Internet, general principles and theories of consumer behavior apply. The formal definition of consumer behavior used in the text is "the study of the processes involved when individuals or groups select, purchase, use, or dispose of products, services, ideas, or experiences to satisfy needs and desires."

Consumers can be seen as actors on the marketplace stage. As in a play, each consumer has lines, props, and costumes that are necessary to put on a good performance. The roles that consumers perform are among the most important elements to be studied in consumer behavior. Consumer behavior is also an economic process where exchanges take place. These exchanges often involve many players. In fact, consumers may even take the form of organizations or groups. Whatever the composition, the decisions made by the consumer and these other players are critical to an exchange being carried out successfully to the benefit of all concerned parties.

Market segmentation is an important aspect of consumer behavior. Consumers can be segmented along various demographic and psychographic dimensions. One of the important reasons for segmenting markets is to be able to build lasting relationships (relationship marketing) with the customers. Marketers are currently implementing many practices that seek to aid in forming a lasting bond with the often fickle consumer. One of the most promising of these practices is database marketing wherein consumers' buying habits are tracked very closely. The result of this practice is that products and messages can be tailored to people's wants and needs.

For better or for worse, we all live in a world that is significantly influenced by the actions of marketers. Marketers filter much of what we learn. Therefore, consumer behavior is affected by the actions of marketers. Domestic and global consumption practices are examined in this chapter with an eye toward the role of the marketer and the influence of such social variables as culture.

The field of consumer behavior and its application is not, however, without its critics. Ethical practices toward the consumer are often difficult to achieve. "Do marketers manipulate consumers?" is a serious question. Perhaps the answer may be found by examining several secondary questions such as: "Do marketers create artificial needs?" "Are advertising and marketing necessary?" or "Do marketers promise miracles?" The responses to these questions are formulated in this chapter.

As there was a "Dark Force" in the *Star Wars* saga, consumer behavior may also have a dark side. Excesses, illegal activities, and even theft are not uncommon. Ethical practices do offer positive solutions, however, to most of these problems.

The chapter concludes by providing a glimpse of consumer behavior as a field of study and provides a plan for study of the field. Simple decisions (buying a carton of milk) versus complex decisions (selection of a complex networked computer system) can all be explained if consumer behavior is studied carefully and creatively. Strategic focus and sound consumer research seem to be among several tools that can provide the guiding light that is probably necessary in our complex and ever-changing world.

# CHAPTER OUTLINE

**1. Consumer Behavior: People in the Marketplace**
   a. The average consumer can be classified and characterized on the basis of:
      1) **Demographics**—age, sex, income, or occupation.
      2) **Psychographics**—refers to a person's lifestyle and personality.
   b. The average consumer's purchase decisions are heavily influenced by the opinions and behaviors of their family, peers, and acquaintances.
      1) The growth of the Web has created thousands of online **consumption communities** where members share views and product recommendations.
      2) Groups exert pressure to conform.
   c. As a member of a large society, U.S. consumers share certain cultural values or

strongly held beliefs about the way the world should be structured.

    1) Some of the values are based on subcultures (such as Hispanics or teens).

d. The use of market segmentation strategies may be used to target a brand to only specific groups of consumers rather than to everybody.

e. Brands often have clearly defined images or "personalities" created by product advertising, packaging, branding, and other marketing strategies that focus on positioning a product in a certain way.

f. When a product succeeds in satisfying a consumer's specific needs or desires, it may be rewarded with many years of **brand loyalty**.

    1) This bond is often difficult for competitors to break.

    2) A change in one's life situation or self-concept, however, can weaken the bond.

g. Consumers' evaluations of products are affected by their appearance, taste, texture, or smell.

    1) A good Web site helps people to feel, taste, and smell with their eyes.

    2) A consumer may be swayed by the shape and color of a package, symbolism used in a brand name, or even in the choice of a cover model for a magazine.

h. In a modern sense, an international image has an appeal to many consumers. Increasingly, consumers opinions and desires are shaped by input from around the world.

### What Is Consumer Behavior?

i. **Consumer behavior** is the study of the processes involved when individuals or groups select, purchase, use, or dispose of products, services, ideas, or experiences to satisfy needs and desires.

    1) Consumers are actors on the marketplace stage.

        a) The perspective of **role theory** takes the view that much of consumer behavior resembles actions in a play.

*Discussion Opportunity—Ask students to consider and even write down some of the roles they play in life. Have them also consider if they were to describe themselves as a famous actor or actress, who would they be? Ask students to share what they have written, followed by the question, "What does the actor or actress you have selected have to do with the roles you play in life?"*

        b) People act out many roles and sometimes consumption decisions are affected.

        c) Evaluation criteria may change depending on which role in the "play" a consumer is following.

    2) Consumer behavior is a process.

        a) Most marketers recognize that consumer behavior is an ongoing process, not merely what happens at the moment a consumer hands over money or a credit card and in turn receives some good or service (**buyer behavior**).

        b) The **exchange**—a transaction where two or more organizations or people give and receive something of value—is an integral part of marketing.

            1. The expanded view emphasizes the entire consumption process.

            2. This view would include issues that influence the consumer before,

during, and after a purchase.

***** *Use Figure 1.1 Here; Use Consumer Behavior Challenges #5 and #7 Here* *****

3) Consumer behavior involves many different actors.
   a) A **consumer** is generally thought of as a person who identifies a need or desire, makes a purchase, and then disposes of the product during the three stages in the consumption process.
   b) The purchaser and user of a product might not be the same person.
   c) A separate person might be an *influencer*. This person provides recommendations for or against certain products without actually buying or using them.
   d) Consumers may be organizations or groups (in which one person may make the decision for the group).

***** *Use Consumer Behavior Challenge #1 Here* *****

## 2. Consumers' Impact on Marketing Strategy
   a. Understanding consumer behavior is good business. A basic marketing concept states that firms exist to satisfy consumers' needs.
   1) Consumer response is the ultimate test of whether a marketing strategy will succeed.
   2) Data about consumers helps organizations to define the market and to identify threats and opportunities to a brand.

Segmenting Consumers
   b. The process of **market segmentation** identifies groups of consumers who are similar to one another in one or more ways and then devises strategies that appeal to one or more groups. There are many ways to segment a market.
   1) Companies can define market segments by identifying their most faithful, core customers or **heavy users.**
   2) **Demographics** are statistics that measure observable aspects of a population, such as birth rate, age distribution, and income.
      a) The U.S. Census Bureau is a major source of demographic data on families.
   3) Important demographic dimensions include:
      a) Age.
      b) Gender.
      c) Family structure.
      d) Social class and income.
      e) Race and ethnicity.
      f) Geography.
   4). Lifestyles: Beyond Demographics. Segmentation variables that involve values, activities, and the ways that people see themselves are known as lifestyle or psychographic variables.

*Discussion Opportunity—Have students describe themselves demographically. Ask: Does this have any bearing on your purchase patterns? How could a marketer find out about you in a demographic sense? Describe one purchase occasion where a demographic dimension had an impact on your purchase decision.*

### Relationship Marketing: Building Bonds with Consumers

c. **Relationship marketing** occurs when a company makes an effort to interact with customers on a regular basis, giving them reasons to maintain a bond with the company over time.

*Discussion Opportunity—Provide the class with an example of relationship marketing. Ask: What types of organizations can make best use of relationship marketing? Have students offer additional examples of relationship marketing.*

d. **Database marketing** involves tracking consumers' buying habits very closely and crafting products and messages tailored precisely to people's wants and needs based on this information. Wal-Mart is a good example of a company that effectively utilizes database marketing.

***** *Use Consumer Behavior Challenge #6 Here* *****

*Discussion Opportunity—Ask: How can database marketing help an organization improve its relationship marketing? What databases are you in? How did you get there?*

## 3. Marketing's Impact on Consumers

a. For better or worse, we all live in a world that is significantly influenced by the actions of marketers.

### Marketing and Culture

b. **Popular culture** consists of the music, movies, sports, books, celebrities, and other forms of entertainment consumed by the mass market; it is both a product of and an inspiration for marketers. ***Product icons*** often become central figures in popular culture.

1) The meaning of consumption—A fundamental premise of consumer behavior is that people often buy products not for what they do, but for what they mean.
2) People, in general, will choose the brand that has an image (or even a personality) that is consistent with his or her underlying needs.

*Discussion Opportunity—Give some examples of products that might be consumed strictly for image. Have students offer examples of products that they purchase for this reason. Ask: How does the image of the product enhance your sense of self when you use or consume the product?*

3) People may have various relationships with a product:
   a) ***Self-concept attachment***—the product helps to establish the user's identity.
   b) ***Nostalgic attachment***—the product serves as a link with a past self.

c) *Interdependence*—the product is a part of the user's daily routine.

d) *Love*—the product elicits emotional bonds of warmth, passion, or other strong emotion.

---

*Discussion Opportunity—Ask students to give an illustration of a product that they have a strong attachment for and explain the relationship. How did this relationship develop?*

---

4) The global consumer. One highly visible—and controversial—byproduct of sophisticated marketing strategies is the movement toward a **global consumer culture**, where people around the world are united by their common devotion to brand name consumer goods, movie stars, and musical celebrities.

5) Virtual consumption. The Digital Revolution is one of the most significant influences on consumer behavior right now.

   a) Online shopping.

   b) Electronic marketing has increased convenience by breaking down many of the barriers caused by time and location.

   c) New venues include **B2C e-commerce** and **C2C e-commerce**.

   d) Virtual brand communities.

      1. Chat rooms.

      2. The ability to exchange information in new and exciting venues.

   e) Security concerns.

   f) An altered shopping experience.

   g) Will the Web bring us closer together or drive us into our on little private world? Are we, for example, spending less time with friends and family in the traditional way?

---

*Discussion Opportunity—Ask: What are the pros and cons of the virtual world? How has the virtual world altered your lifestyle? What will the future bring with respect to this topic?*

---

Blurred Boundaries: Marketing and Reality

c. Marketers and consumers co-exist in a complicated, two-way relationship. There is often a "blurring" between the two.

---

*Discussion Opportunity—Ask: What other "blurring" do you see occurring in the marketing field? Give examples to illustrate your thoughts. If no suggestions are offered, consider pointing out that there is a blurring of boundaries between promotional and entertainment material, in addition to the blurring between the marketing world and consumers' real worlds.*

---

## 4. Marketing Ethics and Public Policy

Business Ethics

a. **Business ethics** are rules of conduct that guide actions in the marketplace—the standards against which most people in a culture judge what is right and what is wrong, good, or bad. There are various universal values.

> ***\*\*\*\*\* Use Consumer Behavior Challenge #2 Here \*\*\*\*\****

> *Discussion Opportunity—Ask: What other values do you think might affect consumption?*

Needs and Wants: Do Marketers Manipulate Consumers?

b. One of the most stinging criticisms of marketing is that marketing (especially advertising) is responsible for convincing consumers that they "need" many material things that they honestly do not need.

1) In the old days, companies called the shots in what was called **marketspace**.

2) Today, consumers seem to be taking more control of what might be called **consumerspace**.

3) Consumers still "need" companies—but in new ways and on their own terms.

4) Do marketers create artificial needs? Before answering, consider that a need is a basic biological motive and a want represents one way that society has taught us that the need can be satisfied.

> ***\*\*\*\*\* Use Consumer Behavior Challenge #10 Here \*\*\*\*\****

5) Are advertising and marketing really necessary? Yes, if approached from an information dissemination perspective. The view of advertising as consumer information is known as **economics of information.**

6) Do marketers promise miracles? Not it if they are honest. They do not have the power to create miracles. Many marketers do not know enough about consumers to manipulate them.

Public Policy and Consumerism

c. Consumer activism: America™ Adbusters is one of various organizations that has the objective of discouraging rampant commercialism.

1) Such organizations employ the strategy of **culture jamming** that aims to disrupt efforts by the corporate world to dominate our cultural landscape.

2) Recent scandals in corporate America have fueled the arguments presented by culture jammers.

3) Consumer activism has developed to the extent that coordinated consumer protest movements are becoming more common.

> *Discussion Opportunity—Ask: Has cultural jamming ever affected you and your consumption behavior? Any of your friends? If so, why do you think the behavior occurred?*

d. Consumerism and consumer research.

1) A famous essay on consumerism was *The Jungle* by Upton Sinclair (1906).

2) Consumer and product safety have been important issues in Congress for most of the twentieth century.

3) Other famous consumer proclamations include:

a) President John F. Kennedy's *Declaration of Consumer Rights* in 1962.

b) Rachel Carson's *Silent Spring* in 1962.

   c) Ralph Nader's *Unsafe at Any Speed* in 1965.
   4) **Social marketing** uses marketing techniques normally employed to sell beer or detergent to encourage positive behaviors such as increased literacy and to discourage negative activities such as drunk driving.
   5) As a response to consumer efforts, many firms have chosen to protect or enhance the natural environment as they go about their business activities. This practice is known as **green marketing**.

> ***** *Use Table 1.1 Here* *****

> *Discussion Opportunity—Ask: What do you think is the worst "anti-consumer" practice used by business? What do you think should be done about it?*

## 5. The Dark Side of Consumer Behavior

> ***** *Use Consumer Behavior Challenge #3 Here* *****

   a. Despite the best efforts of researchers, government regulators, and concerned industry people, sometimes consumers' worst enemies are themselves. Examples are:

Consumer Terrorism
   1) The terrorist attacks of 2001 had a tremendous impact on consumerism throughout the world. Such effects give the indication that both natural and man-made disruptions to financial, electronic, and supply networks can be devastating.
   2) Although **bioterrorism** has occurred in the past, the threat of such attacks are more prevalent than ever.

Addictive Consumption
   3) **Consumer addiction** is a physiological and/or psychological dependency on products or services. New examples of this might be Internet or SMS addictions.

> *Discussion Opportunity—Ask: What are some types of consumer addiction that you are aware of? Discuss.*

Compulsive Consumption
   4) **Compulsive consumption** refers to repetitive shopping, often excessive, as an antidote to tension, anxiety, depression, or boredom. These people are often called "shopaholics." Note that compulsive consumption is different from impulse buying.
   5) Negative or destructive consumer behavior. Three aspects are:
      a) The behavior is not done by choice.
      b) The gratification derived from the behavior is short-lived.
      c) The person experiences strong feelings of regret or guilt afterward.

6) Gambling is an example of consumption addiction that touches every segment of society.

| ***** Use Consumer Behavior Challenge #9 Here ***** |
|---|

*Discussion Opportunity—Ask: What is the difference between consumer addiction and compulsive consumption? Besides gambling, what other compulsions or addictions can you name that demonstrate excesses in consumer behavior? Who has the responsibility for taking corrective action to curb these excesses?*

Consumed Consumers

7) People who are used or exploited, whether willingly or not, for commercial gain in the marketplace can be thought of as **consumed consumers**. Examples include:
   a) Prostitutes
   b) Organ, blood, and hair donors
   c) Babies for sale

| ***** Use Consumer Behavior Challenge #11 Here ***** |
|---|

Illegal Activities

8) Consumer activities that are illegal are exemplified by:
   a) Consumer theft—**shrinkage** is an industry term for inventory and cash losses due to shoplifting and employee theft. A growing form of fraud involves "serial wardrobers" who abuse exchange and return policies.

*Discussion Opportunity—Ask: Do you think that shoplifting significantly adds to the cost of the products that you buy? How?*

   b) Some types of destructive consumer behavior can be thought of as **anticonsumption** whereby products and services are deliberately defaced or mutilated.
   c) Anticonsumption is manifested by a range of activities from relatively harmless acts such as gifting dog manure, to destructive political protests.

| ***** Use Consumer Behavior Challenge #9 Here ***** |
|---|

## 6. Consumer Behavior as a Field of Study
   a. It is a rather recent practice that consumers have become the objects of formal study. Most colleges did not even offer a course in consumer behavior prior to the 1970s.

Interdisciplinary Influences on the Study of Consumer Behavior
   b. Consumer behavior may be studied from many points of view—such as psychology, sociology, social psychology, cultural anthropology, economics, etc.

*****Use Figure 1.2 Here; Use Table 1.2 Here*****

The Issue of Strategic Focus

c. Many regard the field of consumer behavior as an applied social science.
Accordingly, the value of the knowledge generated should be evaluated in terms
of its ability to improve the effectiveness of marketing practice.

The Issue of Two Perspectives on Consumer Research

d. One general way to classify consumer research is in terms of the fundamental
assumptions the researchers make about what they are studying and how to study
it. This set of beliefs is known as a **paradigm**. A paradigm shift may now be
underway.

1) The dominant paradigm currently is called **positivism** (or sometimes called
*modernism*). It emphasizes that human reason is supreme, and that there is a
single, objective truth that can be discovered by science. Positivism
encourages us to stress the function of objects, to celebrate technology, and to
regard the world as a rational, ordered place with a clearly defined past,
present, and future.

2) The emerging paradigm of **interpretivism** (or *postmodernism*) questions the
previous assumptions.

  a) Proponents argue that there is too much emphasis on science and
technology in our society, and that this ordered, rational view of consumers
denies the complex social and cultural world in which we live.

  b) Others say positivism puts too much emphasis on material well-being,
and that this logical outlook is dominated by an ideology that stresses the
homogeneous views of a culture dominated by white males.

  c) Interpretivists instead stress the importance of symbolic, subjective
experience and the idea that meaning is in the mind of the person.

***** Use Table 1.3 Here; Use Consumer Behavior Challenge #8 Here *****

*Discussion Opportunity—Ask students to consider whether they are more of a "positivist" or an
"interpretist." Do not allow them to take the easy way out by saying "both." All are to some
extent.*

**7. Taking It From Here: The Plan of the Book**

a. The plan is simple—it goes from micro to macro.

b. Each chapter provides a "snapshot" of consumers, but the lens used to take each
picture gets successively wider.

*****Use Figure 1.3 Here *****

# End-of-Chapter Support Material

## SUMMARY OF SPECIAL FEATURE BOXES

1. **Net Profit**

   This box features the key term, *U-commerce*—the use of ubiquitous networks that are slowly becoming part of us. More specifically, it highlights the future of wireless networks for "smart products" that can communicate with individuals through a variety of electronic interfaces. This feature supports the section "Virtual Consumption."

2. **The Global Looking Glass**

   A description is given here of the changing retail landscape in Shanghai, China. With the economic growth, there are more job opportunities for young, affluent Chinese. Rather than leave to become educated and stay away, they are now coming back. With this changing demographic comes a wave of high-end Western retailers to meet the tastes of these individuals.

3. **The Tangled Web I**

   This box examines the controversial issue of the widespread availability of consumers' personal information online. Discussed are the consumer trends of paying for privacy as well as selling one's personal information. This feature supports the section "Business Ethics."

4. **The Tangled Web II**

   This box highlights Internet addiction in South Korea, the country with the largest high-speed Internet market penetration. The impact of this problem on social dynamics and cultural values is discussed. This feature supports the section "Addictive Consumption."

5. **The Tangled Web III**

   This box highlights the practice of e-mail scams by *advanced fee fraud artists*. These scams offer the consumer extreme amounts of money but require an up-front fee. This feature supports the section "Illegal Activities."

## REVIEW QUESTIONS

1. Provide a definition of consumer behavior. *It is the study of the processes involved when individuals or groups select, purchase, use, or dispose of products, services, ideas, or experiences to satisfy needs and desires.*

2. What are demographics? Give three examples of demographic characteristics. *Demographics are statistics that measure observable aspects of a population, such as*

*birthrate, age distribution, and income.*

3. What is the difference between a culture and a subculture? *People of large populations share certain cultural values or strongly held beliefs about the way the world should be structured. Members of subcultures, or smaller groups within the culture, also share values.*

4. Define market segmentation. *The use of market segmentation strategies means targeting a brand only to specific groups of consumers rather than to everybody—even if it means that other consumers who don't belong to this target market aren't attracted to that product.*

5. What is role theory, and how does it help us to understand consumer behavior? *The perspective of role theory takes the view that much of consumer behavior resembles actions in a play. As in a play, each consumer has lines, props, and costumes necessary to put on a good performance. Because people act out many different roles, they sometimes alter their consumption decisions depending on the particular "play" they are in at the time. The criteria they use to evaluate products and services in one of their roles may be quite different from those used in another role.*

6. What do we mean by an exchange? *A transaction in which two or more organizations or people give and receive something of value.*

7. Why is it important for businesses to learn about their heavy users? *Because they account for such a substantial proportion of revenues. They are the customers that are more likely to be loyal. These customers represent the best opportunity to cross-sell and up-sell.*

8. What is database marketing? Give an example of a company that uses this technique. *Database marketing involves tracking specific consumers' buying habits very closely and crafting products and messages tailored precisely to people's wants and needs based on this information. Wal-Mart is the example given in the book. Online companies such as Dell that require customer information in order to complete transactions and deliver products have an advantage in database marketing as well.*

9. What is popular culture, and how does this concept relate to marketing and consumer behavior? *Popular culture, consisting of the music, movies, sports, books, celebrities, and other forms of entertainment consumed by the mass market, is both a product of and an inspiration for marketers. Our lives are also affected in more far-reaching ways, ranging from how we acknowledge cultural events such as marriage, death, or holidays to how we view social issues such as air pollution, gambling, and addictions.*

10. The chapter states that "people often buy products not for what they do, but for what they mean." Explain the meaning of this statement and provide an example. *The core functional benefits provided by products are only the bare minimum. Because most all brand options provide these, consumers go beyond the basics. All things being equal, people will choose the brand that has an image (or even a personality!) consistent with*

*their underlying needs. Almost any product can be used as an example. Focus on the clothing brands that students wear.*

11.     Describe two types of relationships a consumer can have with a product.

- *Self-concept attachment: The product helps to establish the user's identity.*
- *Nostalgic attachment: The product serves as a link with a past self.*
- *Interdependence: The product is a part of the user's daily routine.*
- *Love: The product elicits emotional bonds of warmth, passion, or other strong emotion.*

12.     What is meant by the term "global consumer culture"? *A culture in which people around the world are united by their common devotion to brand name consumer goods, movie stars, celebrities, and leisure activities.*

13.     What is the difference between B2B and B2C e-commerce? *Simply put, B2B is business-conducting transactions with other businesses, B2C is businesses conducting transactions with consumers.*

14.     The economics of information perspective argues that advertising is important. Why? *This view emphasizes the economic cost of the time spent searching for products. Accordingly, advertising is a service for which consumers are willing to pay, because the information it provides reduces search time.*

15.     Provide two examples of important legislation that relates to American consumers. *The Pure Food and Drug Act in 1906 and the Federal Meat Inspection Act in 1907 are the examples given in the text. The list is endless now.*

16.     Define social marketing and give an example of this technique. *Social marketing uses marketing techniques normally employed to sell beer or detergent to encourage positive behaviors such as increased literacy and to discourage negative activities such as drunk driving.*

17.     Define consumer addiction and give two examples. *Consumer addiction is a physiological or psychological dependency on products or services. These problems of course include alcoholism, drug addiction, and cigarettes—and many companies profit from addictive products or by selling solutions.*

18.     What is an example of a consumed consumer? *Consumed consumers are people who are used or exploited, willingly or not, for commercial gain in the marketplace. Examples include prostitutes and organ donors.*

19.     What is shrinkage, and why is it a problem? *Shrinkage is the industry term for inventory and cash losses from shoplifting and employee theft. This is a massive problem for businesses that is passed on to consumers in the form of higher prices (about 40 percent of the losses can be attributed to employees rather than shoppers). Shopping malls spend*

*$6 million annually on security, and a family of four spends about $300 extra per year because of markups to cover shrinkage.*

20.   Define anticonsumption, and provide two examples of it. *Anticonsumption is defined by events in which products and services are deliberately defaced or mutilated. Anticonsumption can range from relatively mild acts like spray-painting graffiti on buildings and subways to serious incidences of product tampering or even the release of computer viruses that can bring large corporations to their knees.*

21.   Name two different disciplines that study consumer behavior. How would their approaches to the same issue differ? *The text lists numerous associations including the American Association of Family and Consumer Sciences, the American Statistical Association, the Association for Consumer Research, the Society for Consumer Psychology, the International Communication Association, the American Sociological Association, the Institute of Management Sciences, the American Anthropological Association, the American Marketing Association, the Society for Personality and Social Psychology, the American Association for Public Opinion Research, and the American Economic Association.*

22.   What are the major differences between the positivist and interpretivist paradigms in consumer research? *Positivism (or sometimes modernism) has significantly influenced Western art and science since the late sixteenth century. It emphasizes that human reason is supreme, and that there is a single, objective truth that can be discovered by science. Positivism encourages us to stress the function of objects, to celebrate technology, and to regard the world as a rational, ordered place with a clearly defined past, present, and future.*

*The paradigm of interpretivism (or postmodernism) questions these assumptions. Proponents of this perspective argue that there is too much emphasis on science and technology in our society, and that this ordered, rational view of behavior denies the complex social and cultural world in which we live. Others feel that positivism puts too much emphasis on material well-being, and that its logical outlook is directed by an ideology that stresses the homogenous views of a culture dominated by (dead) white males. Interpretivists instead stress the importance of symbolic, subjective experience, and the idea that meaning is in the mind of the person—that is, we each construct our own meanings based on our unique and shared cultural experiences, so there are no right or wrong answers.*

# CONSUMER BEHAVIOR CHALLENGE

## Discussion Questions

1.    The chapter states that people play different roles and that their consumption behaviors may differ depending on the particular role they are playing. State whether you agree or disagree with this perspective, giving examples from your personal life. Try to construct a "stage set" for a role you play—specify the props, costumes, and script that you use to play a role (e.g., job interviewee, conscientious student, party animal).

*Most students will be able to identify the different roles that individuals play at different times, so agreement should be almost universal. After agreeing with this notion, the student will be more likely to accept the idea that consumption behavior is intimately tied with the role itself. The goal of this exercise is to make the student aware that consumption helps to define the roles consumers play and is a central part of those roles. For example, many family social occasions are accompanied by food and drink, and the consumption of these goods act as a shared bond that the group uses to define membership in that group. Another example is the styles of clothing worn by young people to define their group membership.*

*Each student's stage set will be unique to their own "role." Each student should also relate these "roles" to consumer behavior.*

2.    A company recently introduced a teddy bear for Valentine's Day called "Crazy for You." This toy aroused the ire of mental health advocates because the cuddly bear's cuddly paws are restrained by a straitjacket and accompanied by commitment papers. Supporters of the company's decision to keep selling the bear say opponents are too politically correct. What do you think?

*Because this is an ethics-oriented question, responses illustrating both sides of this issue are likely to emerge. Instructors should focus on the definition of business ethics given in the text (rules of conduct that guide actions in the marketplace – the standards against which most people in a culture judge what is right and what is wrong, good or bad.) as a means of guiding the discussion. This will force students to take a stand on whether the product in question is morally right or morally wrong.*

3.    The chapter discussed a computer game called *JFK Reloaded* that lets players reenact President Kennedy's assassination. Have the game's developers gone too far, or is any historical event "fair game" to be adapted into an entertainment vehicle?

*In a manner similar to question 2, this is another ethics-oriented question that will prompt responses on both ends of the "morally right/morally wrong" spectrum. However, where question 2 deals only with issues of offensiveness, this question additionally deals with criminal and legal issues. Among the critics of this video game was Senator Joseph Lieberman, a leader of many U.S. Senate decency campaigns. He highlighted the fact that making threats or conspiring to commit violence against elected officials is a crime, and that the line between the fantasy version in this game and reality is too close. Legal critics suggest that this argument holds no water, as the subject in question in not a living person.*

*Additionally, an argument may arise about the link between violent media and the commission of violence. The scientific community has produced evidence that individuals who view violent media programming or play violent video games are more likely to become aggressive and even commit violent acts. However, the flip side of this argument is that there is not a one-to-one correlation between the two, and that a person cannot be prosecuted unless there is actually a commission of violence.*

*Ultimately, a discussion of this question should bring out the difference between ethical and legal issues. In other words, even if this video game company has done nothing illegal, has it done something immoral?*

4.  Some researchers believe that the field of consumer behavior should be a pure, rather than an applied science. That is, research issues should be framed in terms of their scientific interest rather than their applicability to immediate marketing problems. Give your views on this issue.

    *Instead of viewing research in an either/or framework (i.e., consumer behavior research must be either pure scientific research or applied knowledge), the student should be encouraged to view it as both. Much research is done on a "knowledge for knowledge sake" basis, but the field of consumer behavior has the potential to make a significant contribution to how the makers of goods and services can best reach the consumer. For example, business firms are able to take the knowledge developed in a pure science research setting and apply it to their marketing efforts by utilizing the results of studies that investigate how consumers process advertising messages. Areas such as space exploration have been able to use pure science research and apply their findings to immediate problems. Consumer behavior knowledge has this same quality.*

5.  Name some products or services that are widely used by your social group. State whether you agree or disagree with the notion that these products help to form group bonds, supporting your argument with examples from your list of products used by the group.

    *Discussion of this question is similar to that pertaining to the first question. In both cases, the focus is on whether consumption behavior has a wider meaning—that of group bonding or identification. The actual products used are not the most important aspect of this discussion. Instead, the focus should be on consumption behavior as more than the satisfying of primary (basic/physiological) needs. It is assumed that most students will agree that consumption has meaning beyond satisfying primary needs. Differences will be found, however, in 1) the situations in which consumption takes on this additional meaning, 2) the products that do so, and 3) the form of the broadened meaning. Encourage students to examine the products that bring forth meaning, as well as their consideration as to why this phenomenon occurs.*

6.  Although demographic information on large numbers of consumers is used in many marketing contexts, some people believe that the sale of data on customers' incomes, buying habits, and so on constitutes an invasion of privacy and should be stopped. Is Big Brother watching? Comment on the issue from both a consumer's and a marketer's point of view.

    *As with many questions of this type there are few objectively right or wrong answers. The goal is, of course, to make the student think about the issues and to be able to critically examine the arguments on both sides. Regardless of the student's specific comments on this issue, the discussion should acknowledge the legitimate interest of both parties and the possibility of a compromise suitable to both groups. This discussion could draw upon the student's personal experiences with receiving mail that obviously came as a result of information about the student being sold to a company that compiles lists. Ask the student about his or her reactions to it and encourage the student to make a special attempt to discuss the advantages and disadvantages to both the direct marketer and potential buyer.*

    *Do the students think their university or college sells demographic information about them to database firms? If so, do they think this is legal? How might casino personnel monitor gambling habits? (See chapter information on database marketing.)*

7.  List the three stages in the consumption process. Describe the issues that you consider in each of these stages when you made a recent important purchase.

    *Students can use the material presented in Figure 1.1. The three stages in the consumption process shown are:1) prepurchase, 2) purchase, and 3) post purchase. The student selected should develop fairly unique sets of issues related to each of these phases based on the different products and purchase situations. Figure 1.1 provides a list of issues for each stage from both the consumer's and marketer's perspectives.*

8.  What aspects of consumer behavior are likely to be of interest to a financial planner? To a university administrator? To a graphic arts designer? To a social worker in a government agency? To a nursing instructor?

    *The listing of the aspects of consumer behavior corresponding to these positions should reflect the particular aspects of each position. For example, a financial planner depends on consumers' willingness to postpone consumption in order to save and invest money to have more later. A social worker must be concerned about people's attitudes toward government, social work in general, and the role of government in people's lives. What each of these positions share, and what should underlie the discussion, is their connection to the consumption process and the fact that consumers themselves will have different needs and wants associated with their consumption. Each of the listed parties would attempt to influence consumers by using a different aspect of consumption, and these differences need to be discussed and analyzed.*

9.    Critics of targeted marketing strategies argue that this practice is discriminatory and unfair, especially if such a strategy encourages a group of people to buy a product that may be injurious to them or that they cannot afford. For example, community leaders in largely minority neighborhoods have staged protests against billboards promoting beer or cigarettes in these areas. On the other hand, the Association of National Advertisers argues that banning targeted marketing constitutes censorship and is thus a violation of the First Amendment. What are your views regarding both sides of this issue?

*Discussion of this question closely parallels discussion of question 4. It is important to guide discussion to the legitimate interests on both sides. In this situation, however, the discussion should also examine the legitimacy of each side's basic point. For what groups should target marketing not be allowed? Or under what specific circumstances should target marketing be allowed? Is the argument that target marketing unduly influences those who cannot resist its appeal reasonable? Is the counterargument that banishing target marketing amounts to censorship and is unconstitutional equally specious? Discussion should initially focus on the validity of each argument and then evolve toward a compromise that will protect target-marketing efforts while recognizing the needs of society.*

10.   Do marketers have the ability to control our desires or the power to create needs? Is this situation changing as the Internet creates new ways to interact with companies? If so, how?

*For better or worse, we live in a world that is significantly influenced by the actions of marketers. As indicated in the text, marketers supply vast amounts of stimuli in the form of advertisements, and much of what we learn (especially younger consumers who watch a great deal of television) about the world is filtered by marketers. Marketers are always on top of popular culture and, therefore, close to the heart of our society. The boundary between marketing and reality is often blurred. The chapter identifies several issues that might be pertinent with respect to this question (and supplies a response to each indictment): Do marketers create artificial needs? Are advertising and marketing necessary? Do marketers promise miracles?*

*With respect to the influence of the Internet, students should give illustrations of "new connections" that arise from using the Internet for marketing purposes. Consider when the consumer contacts a marketer, when a marketer contacts a consumer, and when a consumer contacts another consumer.*

*The honest answer is that only the consumer has the ability to control his or her own desires—marketers do not create needs. Addictive behavior shows that the picture is not black and white, however, but a rather dull gray. This question will test the students' depth of understanding and should provide for an interesting discussion. Save this question until the end of the chapter for discussion.*

11. An entrepreneur made international news when he set up a Web site to auction the eggcells of fashion models to the highest bidder (minimum bid: $15,000). He wrote, "Just watch television and you will see that we are only interested in looking at beautiful people. This site simply mirrors our current society, in that beauty usually goes to the highest bidder . . . Any gift such as beauty, intelligence, or social skills will help your children in their quest for happiness and success. If you could increase the chance of reproducing beautiful children, and thus giving them an advantage in society, would you?" Is the buying and selling of humans just another example of consumer behavior at work? Do you agree that this service is simply a more efficient way to maximize the chance of having happy, successful children? Should this kind of marketing activity be allowed? Would you sell your eggs or sperm on a Web site?

*This question should spark discussion revolving around various ethical issues. One issue is that of the consumed consumer. Is the selling of all or part of a human being an acceptable practice if that person has given their consent? In such a case, is the person truly being exploited for commercial gain? Both sides of this issue will emerge as some students will adamantly profess that such practices are morally wrong while others will view this as a perfectly acceptable way for consumers to become suppliers, thereby exercising their rights as participants in the free enterprise system.*

*Another issue that should emerge is that of the emphasis that society places on physical beauty. Again, some will contend that this is simply a cultural value that has come about naturally and that there is nothing wrong with it. Others will focus more on the role that marketing has played in "artificially" increasing the importance of physical characteristics as a value.*

*A third issue that students may identify is somewhat related to the previous. Does marketing foster incorrect perceptions of how to achieve happiness? Numerous examples might arise such as owning products with a high-status image, engaging in leisure activities, or even consuming various food and beverage items. Although numerous promotions may imply that purchasing such products leads to happiness, the example given in this question is much more blatant.*

## Application Questions

12. To what degree will consumers trade lower prices for less privacy? Car owners now can let insurance companies monitor their driving using a new technology in exchange for lower rates. Customers who sign up for Progressive's TripSense program get a device the size of a Tic Tac box to plug into their cars. The device will track speed and how many miles are driven at what times of day. Every few months, customers unplug the device from the car, plug it into a computer, download the data and send it to the company. Depending on results, discounts will range from 5 percent to 25 percent. In Great Britain, a major insurer is testing a program called Pay as You Drive. Volunteers will get a device the size of a Palm computer installed in their cars. The gadget will use global positioning satellite technology to track where the car goes, constantly sending information back to

the insurance company. Cars that spend more time in safer areas will qualify for bigger discounts. Of course, the potential downside to these efforts is that the insurance companies may be able to collect data on where you have driven, how long you stayed in one location, and so on. Conduct a poll of 10 drivers of various ages where you describe these programs and ask respondents if they would participate in order to receive a discount on their insurance premiums. What reasons do they give pro and con? Do you find any differences in attitudes based on demographic characteristics such as age or gender?

*This question of exchanging privacy for lower prices (or convenience, or any of a number of other benefits) can be applied in many contexts these days, particularly in e-commerce. As the student reports are discussed, the instructor can relate this issue to various topics. These include value (what benefits are people gaining and what cost are they "paying"?), ethics (what are the implications of companies having such a depth of information on consumers?), public policy (should there be attempts to regulate such business activities?), and demographic segmentation. Probe students as to what types of trade-offs they have made (providing personal, credit card, bank account, and other information in order to conduct business online).*

13. While you're talking to car owners, probe to see what (if any) relationships they have with their vehicles. Do these feelings correspond to the types of consumer/product attachments we discussed in the chapter? How do these relationships get acted upon (hint: see if any of the respondents have nicknames for their car, or if they "decorate" them with personal items).

*The types of relationships referred to in the text are the following:*

- *Self-concept attachment: The product helps to establish the user's identity.*
- *Nostalgic attachment: The product serves as a link with a past self.*
- *Interdependence: The product is a part of the user's daily routine.*
- *Love: The product elicits emotional bonds of warmth, passion, or other strong emotion.*

*Student reports should attempt to classify their findings based on these relationships. They should also attempt to show how the consumption patterns that they engage in with their cars reflects such relationships.*

14. Many college students "share" music by downloading clips from the Internet. Interview at least five people who have downloaded at least one song or movie without paying for it. Do they feel they are stealing? What explanations do they offer for this behavior? Try to identify any common themes that come out of these interviews. If you were devising an ad campaign to discourage free downloading, how might you use what you have learned to craft a convincing message?

*Obviously, ethical issues of right and wrong should emerge here. But these issues should reflect the ethical behavior of the consumer (is it wrong to download for free?) as well as that of the corporations (are they ripping customers off by charging too much?). Reports should also revolve around "dark side" issues. Specifically, is this activity stealing? Is it on the same level as shoplifting (this discussion question can be combined with individual project #11)? Certainly, the explanations given will fall into the category of justification. Thus, from the marketer's perspective, the suggested ad campaign should be designed in a way to persuade consumers that their justified behavior is wrong.*

# CASE STUDY TEACHING NOTES

## Chapter 1 Case Study: Mexoryl

### Summary of Case

A recent phenomenon involves the illegal importation and consumption of sunscreens containing Mexoryl, a chemical proven effective at blocking harmful UVA rays. Although Mexoryl has been available in sunscreen products in Canada and Europe for over 10 years, the F.D.A. has not yet approved it for consumption in the United States. This has left U.S. consumers without a choice of products that contain an effective UVA blocker. Although sunscreens here contain UVB blockers, these are much less effective at preventing premature aging and skin cancer. U.S. consumers are not waiting for F.D.A. approval. Rather, they are buying Mexoryl products on the Internet, on the black-market, or in Canada.

### Suggestions for Presentation

As an introduction to the text, Chapter 1 covers a very broad range of topics. This case could be used in conjunction with many of these, including demographics and psychographics, market segmentation, the consumer behavior process, how consumer needs and desires affect marketing strategy, and virtual consumption, just to name a few. However, this case has its most direct applications to the concepts of ethics and public policy. Use it to illustrate the purpose of policy making federal agencies such as the F.D.A. The discussion questions should provide an interesting twist on this, however. To what extent are such agencies protecting consumers and to what extent are they harming them? This case also provides a glimpse at illegal consumption. Most students will recognize the problems associated with more blatant acts of illegal consumption, but what will they think of "minor" illegal acts such as the consumption of Mexoryl? Consumer importation and consumption of this product, while illegal, is evidently not even being prosecuted. Is it therefore wrong?

### Suggested Answers for Discussion Questions

1.      Consider that a product such as Mexoryl can prevent deadly diseases. If such a product is available in other first world countries, discuss the ethical implications of the F.D.A. not allowing the same product to be available to U.S. consumers. Is the F.D.A. protecting people, or harming people?

*The F.D.A. is one of many federal agencies that has the purpose of protecting citizens in consumer-related activities. The definition of business ethics as identified in the chapter should be discussed in laying a foundation of discussion for this question. It should be obvious to students that the basic mission of the F.D.A. (that of protecting consumers against harmful food and drug products) is ethical and, therefore, morally right. However, does this agency and it's approval process get in the way of accomplishing the very mission that it stands for? It should be discussed that at the very least, this agency has created a 12 year barrier-to-entry for a product that has been proven to protect consumers against deadly skin diseases. Not only is this harming consumers currently, but also has been for the last 12 years as other countries have received the benefit of Mexoryl. The counterpoint of possible harmful effects of the product should also be discussed.*

2.  It is illegal for people to consumer Mexoryl-based products in the United States. Is it therefore immoral to buy such products on the Internet? From black-market retailers? In Canada and bring them back? Is this any different than buying marijuana in Amsterdam or cigars in Cuba, but consuming them in the United States?

    *This is a great question to bring out the differences between that which is legal and that which is moral. Although a country's legal system is technically based on moral values, the two are distinct concepts. Student responses to each part of this question will obviously differ, and that is another point of this question: to show that moral issues are not black and white. Instructors should try to bring out both sides to each part of the question.*

# Additional Support Material

# STUDENT PROJECTS

## Individual Projects

1.  Ask a student to think of a product brand that is used frequently and make a list of the brand's determinant attributes. Without sharing what was on the list, have the student ask a friend, of the same gender and approximate age, to make a similar list for the same product (although the brand may be different). Then have the student ask someone of the opposite sex to perform the same task. Have the student compare and contrast the identified attributes and report their findings to the class. Why did differences or similarities occur?

2.  This assignment can really be fun for the class and the presenter. Have a student wear or bring to class a recent clothes purchase. Have them explain how his or her purchase decision was influenced by different economic, social, cultural, and/or psychological variables.

*in-class*

3. This activity can be done as an extension to or independent of assignment number 2. Have students explain why they chose the clothes they are wearing to class. Probe on this one. Was there any implied symbolism? Do all students seem to be dressed in a similar fashion? Why does this occur? Can marketers learn from this? Do marketers strategically contribute to this?

4. ? Assign students to identify at least five instances where a specific marketing tactic employed by an organization (for profit or non-profit) has had an impact on popular culture. Examples may include such things as an actual product, product icon, promotional campaign, celebrity endorsers, corporate sponsorship, product placement, or others. This impact may be short term (the public temporarily adopting catch-phrases such as Donald Trump's "You're fired!" or Budweiser's "Whaaaaazup!") or long term (the influence of anti-smoking campaigns in reducing the number of smokers).

5. Have students identify examples of consumer-product relationships in society or in their own lives. The text identifies four specific types: self-concept attachment, nostalgic attachment, interdependence, and love. Have students come up with an example of each of these.

6. Have students attend an entertainment event (such as a movie or play, concert or other musical performance, or a sporting event). Have them observe the behavior of others present. Have them identify how such experiences provide meaning to those in attendance by analyzing people's behavior according to each of the following consumption activities: consuming as experience, consuming as integration, consuming as classification, consuming as play.

7. Ask students to consider their own consumption practices over the past decade. Have them list the ways that online consumption activities have replaced or modified their real-world consumption activities.

8. Have each student describe a situation in which he or she (or someone they know) has exhibited compulsive consumption or consumer addiction. Was this consumption or addiction harmful? Discuss.

9. Students should visit a tattoo parlor and observe the business activities that occur there. Can consumers who patronize these establishments be classified as consumed consumers? Discuss.

10. Have each student locate an example of a marketing activity (a promotion itself or a news article about the actions of a company) that they find ethically questionable. Have them either write about or come to class prepared to discuss why they find it questionable. What moral principle does it violate?

11. Have students identify a time when they or someone they know defrauded a company. Examples could include employee theft, shoplifting, abusing return/exchange policies, or

otherwise taking advantage of the company. What was the reasoning behind the activity? Was the activity justified?

## Group Projects

1. Have groups select a product of interest (e.g., a car, mp3 player, vacation spot, movie, sporting event, etc.). Have each person in the group make a list of what they consider to be the product's main attributes (both physical and psychological). Compare and contrast the attributes listed by the women and by the men to see how they may vary. Next, if there are any age or ethnic differences within the group see if differences appear. Based on these differences formulate strategies for appealing to the various subgroups within your group.

2. Have groups collect information on at least three companies that have recently expanded into countries where they have not previously marketed their products. What kind of success/failure have they met with? Has each had any kind of impact on the society or culture entered?

3. Have groups of students find an example of a recent product, service, or program that was a failure. *Business Week, U.S.A. Today,* the *Wall Street Journal, Fortune, Forbes* or some other marketing publications are excellent sources. Have students explain to the class how knowledge of consumer behavior, or the lack of it, could have contributed to the success or failure of the effort.

4. Have your group go online to three Web pages of your choice. Demonstrate how the Web pages segment markets, collect information from the consumer (after the person has come to the Web page), and might be used to build a database.

5. Have the members of each group find and present examples of the blurred boundaries between promotional activities and programming or real life. These examples should be of activities where the program or event cannot be viewed without attending to the promotional content.

6. Each group should locate an example of a company that is heavily involved in social or green marketing. Make a report on the activities of the company. Compare this company to a direct competitor that is not so extensively involved in such activities. What are the advantages/disadvantages that the social/green approach has over the other.

7. Have each group discuss what the members feel is the most unethical practice being employed on the Internet by marketers. Have them reach a consensus on this matter. Each group should comment on how to remedy the situation and be prepared to share their findings with others.

8. Have the members (individually or in pairs) of each group interview the manager or owner of multiple retail stores. They should include at least two examples of both

national chain retail stores, as well as independent retail stores. Inquire as to the return/exchange policies of the store. What methods does management employ to prevent customers from abusing these policies? Have the group compile their findings and report on them.

# eLAB

## Individual Assignments

1.      Go to **www.rockstargames.com.** Click on the link for "games." Select three different video games marketed by this company. Discuss both sides of an ethical debate for each.

2.      Go to **www.aarp.org**. The American Association of Retired Persons is one of the largest lobbying and citizen action groups going today. Projections indicate that, as our nation ages, this organization will only get larger and more influential. After visiting this Web site, list five ways the organization is trying to influence corporate attitudes toward the older consuming public. What type of networks is the organization trying to build? How would database information from this group be useful to a marketer?

3.      Go to **www.zilo.com**. This recent addition to a growing list of youth marketing Web sites takes an MTV spin to presenting issues and potential products to teens and early twentysomethings. If you were the marketing manager for a new bottled water product that was seeking a national youth audience, plan a strategy for your new product introduction using this Web site as one of your primary promotional springboards. List what you would do, why you would do it, and what results you might expect. What does a Web site such as this teach you about consumer behavior?

4.      Go to **www.moveon.org**. What is the main variable that this site uses to segment the American public? What is the resulting segment that this site is attempting to appeal to. Extensively, describe this segment in terms of demographic and psychographic variables. What issues seem to be raised on this site? If you were an advertiser, would it be a good idea to sponsor a message on this site? Explain.

## Group Assignment

Go to **www.casino.com**. Take some time as a group to become familiar with the various sections of this site. What are the ways that this site has been designed to encourage new users to sign up, and existing users to increase their level of online gambling? Is this Web site encouraging addictive consumption? Is this unethical? After having completed this portion of the assignment, visit **www.amazinggamblingsystems.com**. What is the product being sold here? In what ways could the activities of this Web site be considered unethical?

# CHAPTER 2

# *PERCEPTION*

## CHAPTER OBJECTIVES

When students finish this chapter they should understand that:

- Perception is a three-stage process that translates raw stimuli into meaning.

- Products and commercial messages often appeal to our senses, but many of them will not succeed.

- The design of a product today is a key driver of its success or failure.

- Subliminal advertising is a controversial—but largely ineffective—way to talk to consumers.

- We interpret the stimuli to which we do pay attention according to learned patterns and expectations.

- The science of semiotics helps us to understand how symbols are used to create meaning.


## CHAPTER SUMMARY

In this chapter, students will be exposed to the study of *perception*—the process by which sensations (light, color, taste, odors, and sound) are selected, organized, and interpreted. The study of perception, then, focuses on what we add to or take away from these raw sensations as we choose which to notice, and then go about assigning meaning to them.

Marketing stimuli have important sensory qualities. We rely on colors, odors, sounds, tastes, and textures (the "feel" of products) when forming evaluations of them. Each of these sensations is discussed and placed into proper context of marketing usage and attention attraction.

How do our sensory receptors pick up sensations? The answer is exposure. *Exposure* is the degree to which people notice a stimulus that is within range of their sensory receptors. A stimulus must be presented at a certain level of intensity before it can be detected by sensory receptors. A consumer's ability to detect whether two stimuli are different (the differential threshold) is an important issue in many marketing decisions (such as changing the package design, altering the size of a product, or reducing its size). An interesting study within the exposure area is that of subliminal perception. Although evidence that *subliminal persuasion* (exposure to visual and audio messages below the level of the consumers' awareness) is effective is virtually nonexistent, many consumers continue to believe that advertisers use this technique.

All marketers would like to gain the consumer's attention. *Attention* refers to the extent to which processing activity is devoted to a particular stimulus. There are barriers that prohibit effective attention (perceptual selection, perceptual vigilance, and perceptual defense). Several factors can influence attention (such as size, color, position, and novelty). New insights are gained in the study of attention in this chapter. Attention-getting devices dominate our information-oriented society (whether in ads or on the Web). The chapter provides excellent examples that demonstrate the art of gaining attention.

If a message has gained the consumer's attention, the message must be correctly interpreted to be of value. Stimulus organization, interpretational biases, and semiotics provide direction to the study of consumer interpretation. Part of the interpretation process is using symbols to help us make sense of the world around us. The degree to which the symbolism is consistent with our previous experience affects the meaning we assign to related objects.

Perceptual positioning helps to match perceived characteristics of a product or service with the product or service's market position. Based on positions, strategies can be constructed. Perceptual maps of positions are a widely used marketing tool that evaluates the relative standing of competing brands along relevant dimensions. Modification of position can occur through repositioning.

# CHAPTER OUTLINE

**1. Introduction**
  a. We live in a world overflowing with sensations.
   1) Marketers contribute to the overflow by supplying advertisements, product packages, radio and television commercials, and billboards.
   2) Each consumer copes with the bombardment of sensations by paying attention to some stimuli and tuning out others.
  b. **Sensation** refers to the immediate response of our sensory receptors (eyes, ears, nose, mouth, fingers) to such basic stimuli as light, color, sound, odors, and textures.
  c. **Perception** is the process by which these sensations are selected, organized, and interpreted. The study of perception, then, focuses on what we add to these raw sensations to give them meaning.
  d. People undergo stages of information processing in which stimuli are input and stored. Unlike computers, people only process a small amount of information (stimuli) available to them. An even smaller amount is attended to and given meaning.
  e. The perceptual process is made up of three stages:
   1) **Exposure**.

2) **Attention**.
3) **Interpretation**.

*****Use Figure 2.1 Here *****

## 2. Sensory Systems
  a. External stimuli, or sensory inputs, can be received on a number of channels.
   1) The inputs picked up by our five senses constitute the raw data that begin the
   perceptual process.
   2) External stimuli can trigger memories from the past. The resulting responses
   are an important part of **hedonic consumption** (the multisensory, fantasy, and
   emotional aspects of consumers' interactions with products).

Hedonic Consumption and the Design Economy
  b. In recent years the sensory experiences we receive from products and services have become
   an even larger priority when we choose among competing options.
   1) People prefer additional experiences to additional possessions as income rises.
   2) Target has turned to form over function for this reason.

  Vision
  c. The unique sensory quality of a product can play an important role in helping
   it to stand out from the competition, especially if the brand creates a unique
   association with the sensation.
   1) Saturated colors such as green, yellow, cyan, and orange are considered
   the best hues to capture attention.
   2) Color is a key issue in package design.
   3) Decisions on color help to "color" our expectations of what's inside the
   package.

*Discussion Opportunity—Demonstrate how the package color affects expectation of what is inside the package. You might consider putting together a brief experiment using various products and manipulating the color. How can a marketer use color?*

*****Use Figure 2.2 Here *****

   4) Some color combinations come to be so strongly associated with a corporation
   that they become known as the company's **trade dress**, and the company may
   even be granted exclusive use of these colors (for example, Eastman Kodak's
   defense of their use of yellow, black, and red in court).

*****Use Consumer Behavior Challenge #8 Here *****

*Discussion Opportunity—Ask: What colors can you think of that are uniquely associated with a particular company or a product? Give at least three illustrations. Have you noticed any confusing similarities with these companies or products?*

Smell

d. Odors can stir emotions or create a calming feeling. They can invoke memories or relieve stress.

  1) Fragrance is processed by the limbic system, the most primitive part of the brain and the place where immediate emotions are experienced.

  2) Smell is a direct line to feelings of happiness, hunger, and even memories of happy times (such as childhood years).

  3) Scented marketing is now a $90 million business. Recent developments include scented clothes, scented stores, scented cars and planes, scented household products, and scented advertisements.

*Discussion Opportunity—Ask students to consider their most favorite and least favorite scents. Prior to class, consider your own as well. Then, engage the class in a discussion about whether or not such scents affect product purchase or avoidance.*

Hearing

e. Many aspects of sound affect people's feelings and behaviors.

  1) The Muzak Corporation estimates that 80 million people hear their "background" music everyday.

  2) Research has shown that workers tend to slow down during mid-morning and mid-afternoon. Muzak uses upbeat tempo music during these times to stimulate activity. This is called "stimulus progression."

*Discussion Opportunity—Have students close their eyes and picture themselves shopping at a mall (you might give them cues to help this visualization along). As they are doing this, tell them that they should consider that the store is completely silent. After a few seconds, have them share how this affected their experience. Then ask: What are other ways marketers might use sound to stimulate your purchasing.*

Touch

f. Though much research needs to be done in this area, moods are stimulated or relaxed on the basis of sensations of the skin. Touch has been shown to be a factor in sales interactions.

  1) *Haptic* senses appear to moderate the relationship between product experience and judgment confidence; i.e., people are more sure about what they perceive when they can touch it.

  2) The Japanese practice **Kansei engineering,** a philosophy that translates customers' feelings into design elements.

  3) People associate the textures of fabrics and other surfaces with product qualities (e.g., smooth, rough, silky, etc.).

  4) Men often prefer roughness, whereas females prefer smoothness and softness.

*****Use Table 2.1 Here *****

67

Taste
g. Our taste receptors contribute to our experience of many products, and people form
strong preferences for certain flavors.
1) Specialized companies (called "flavor houses") try to develop new concoctions
to please the ever changing and demanding palates of consumers.
2) New fads with respect to taste include products that taste "hotter" and those
that avoid harmful additives.

*Discussion Opportunity—Ask students the following: What is your favorite "new" taste? Give an illustration. How did you discover this new taste? What stimulus influenced you the most to try this "new" taste? How could marketers use this information?*

**3. Exposure**
a. **Exposure** occurs when a stimulus comes within the range of someone's sensory
receptors.
b. Consumers concentrate on some stimuli, are aware of others, and even go out of
their way to ignore some messages.

***** *Use Consumer Behavior Challenge #3 Here* *****

Sensory Thresholds
c. The science that focuses on how the physical environment is integrated into our
personal, subjective world is known as **psychophysics**.
1) When we define the lowest intensity of a stimulus that can be registered on a
sensory channel, we speak of a *threshold* for that receptor.
2) The **absolute threshold** refers to the minimum amount of stimulation that can
be detected on a sensory channel (the sound emitted by a dog whistle is
beyond our absolute threshold for example).

***** *Use Consumer Behavior Challenge #1 Here* *****

*Discussion Opportunity—Ask students to consider how the absolute threshold is an important consideration is designing marketing stimulation. Then have them give illustrations.*

3) The **differential threshold** refers to the ability of a sensory system to detect
changes or differences between two stimuli. The minimum differences that
can be detected between two stimuli is known as the **j.n.d.** or just noticeable
difference (e.g., marketers might want to make sure that a consumer notices
that merchandise has been discounted).
a) A consumer's ability to detect a difference between two stimuli is
relative. A whispered conversation will not be noticed on a busy street.
b) **Weber's Law** demonstrates that the stronger the initial stimulus, the
greater the change must be for it to be noticed. A shout followed by an
almost equal shout will pose difficulties is disguising differences,
whereas, the shout followed by a whisper will not. As an example, most

retailers believe that a price discount must be at least 20 percent for consumers to notice or to react to it.

> ***** *Use Consumer Behavior Challenge #7 Here* *****

> *Discussion Opportunity—Ask the class to write down the price of the following goods on a piece of paper: (a) a Gallon of 2% milk, (b) a Big Mac, (c) a pair of top-of-the-line Nike tennis shoes, and (d) a Chevrolet Corvette. Then see if they can figure out the differential threshold they have for these goods. (See how much price would have to change before they would actually know it.) Ask them why it is different depending on the price of the product in question.*

Subliminal Perception

d. Most marketers are concerned with creating messages above consumers' thresholds so they can be sure to be noticed. **Subliminal perception**, however, is the opposite. It occurs when the stimulus is below the level of the consumer's awareness.

  1) Though the topic has received its share of notoriety, there is virtually no proof that this process has any effect on consumer behavior.

  2) Most examples of this technique are not really subliminal, in fact, they are quite visible.

> *Discussion Opportunity—Find an example of what you perceive to be a subliminal message. Explain your rationale to the class and show the product or message.*

  3) Subliminal messages supposedly can be sent on both visual and aural channels.

   a) Embeds are tiny figures that are inserted into magazine advertising. These hidden figures (usually of a sexual nature) supposedly exert strong but unconscious influences on innocent readers.

   b) Some also believe that "satanic" messages have been embedded into contemporary music (especially the various forms of rock and roll).

e. Does subliminal perception work? Within the marketing context, most agree the answer is "probably not." Effective messages must be very specifically tailored to individuals, rather than the mass messages required by advertising. Other discouraging factors are:

1) Individuals have wide differences in their threshold levels.

2) Advertisers can't control many important variables (such as viewing distance from the television screen).

3) Consumers must give their absolute attention to the screen—most do not.

4) The specific effect can't be controlled—your thirst will not make you buy "Pepsi."

> *****Use Consumer Behavior Challenge #2 Here* *****

*Discussion Opportunity—Bring in a small can of Jolly Green Giant mushrooms. At one time the mushrooms on the front of the can seemed to spell "SEX." Or photo copy some of the illustrations from Wilson Bryan Key's book (see End Notes). See if students can find their own examples of embeds. What do they think of this technique? Under what circumstances would "subliminal stimulation" be of benefit to society?*

## 4. Attention

a. **Attention** refers to the extent to which processing activity is devoted to a particular stimulus.

1) Consumers are often in a state of sensory overload or are exposed to far more information than they are capable or willing to process.

2) Today, the average adult is exposed to about 3,000 pieces of advertising information every single day.

3) Banner ads dominate the viewing space in most Web pages. These online ads can in fact increase brand awareness after only one exposure, but only if they motivate Web surfers to click through and see what information is awaiting them.

4) Many younger people have developed the ability to **multitask**, or process information from more than one medium at a time.

***** *Use Consumer Behavior Challenge #9 Here* *****

*Discussion Opportunity—Ask: What do you think are the characteristics of the best banner ads? Give an illustration.*

b. **Perceptual selection**.

1) Because the brain's capacity to process information is limited, consumers are very selective about what they pay attention to.

2) The process of **perceptual selection** means that people attend to only a small portion of stimuli to which they are exposed.

3) Personal and stimulus factors help to decide which stimuli will be received and which will be avoided.

4) One factor that determines how much exposure to a particular stimulus a person accepts is **experience**.

5) *Perceptual filters* based on our past experiences influence what we decide to process:

a) **Perceptual vigilance**—consumers are more likely to be aware of stimuli that relate to their current needs.

b) **Perceptual defense**—people see what they want to see and vice versa.

c) **Adaptation**—the degree to which consumers notice a stimulus over time. Several factors lead to adaptation:

1. Intensity.
2. Duration.
3. Discrimination.
4. Exposure.

5. Relevance.

*Discussion Opportunity—Ask students to think of examples when they have used perceptual vigilance and perceptual defense. Think of examples and circumstances when advertisers consciously are able to overcome these effects in consumers. Identify the techniques that might be used to break through these barriers.*

6) In general, stimuli that differ from others around them are more likely to be noticed (remember Weber's Law). This contrast can be created in several ways:
   a) Size.
   b) Color.
   c) Position.
   d) Novelty.

*****Use Consumer Behavior Challenges #6 and #10 Here*****

*Discussion Opportunity—Bring a magazine illustration of each of the four contrast methods demonstrated in the chapter and discuss in class.*

## 5. Interpretation

a. **Interpretation** refers to the meaning that we assign to sensory stimuli. Two people can see the same event but their interpretation can be completely different.
   1) Consumers assign meaning to stimuli based on the **schema**, or set of beliefs, to which the stimulus is assigned. *Priming* is a process where certain properties of a stimulus typically will evoke a schema that leads us to evaluate the stimulus in terms of other stimuli we have encountered that are believed to be similar.
   2) Identifying and evoking the correct schema is crucial to many marketing decisions, because this determines what criteria will be used to evaluate the product, package, or message.

*Discussion Opportunity—Ask: What might be the schema for (a) a tuxedo, (b) a hair dryer, or (c) a calculator to be used in school?*

Stimulus Organization

b. One factor that determines how a stimulus will be interpreted is its assumed relationship with other events, sensations, or images.
   1) Our brains tend to relate incoming sensations to others already in memory based on some fundamental organizational principles.
      a) These principles are based on gestalt psychology—meaning is derived from totality of a set of stimuli. In German, *gestalt* means whole, pattern, or configuration.
      b) Sometimes the "whole is greater than the sum of its parts."
   2) Principles include:

a) The **closure principle**—people tend to perceive an incomplete picture as complete. We fill in the blanks.

b) The **principle of similarity**—consumers tend to group objects that share similar physical characteristics.

c) The **figure-ground principle**— one part of a stimulus will dominate (the figure) while other parts recede into the backdrop (the ground).

---

*Discussion Opportunity—Ask: When you walk through a room when* Wheel of Fortune *is on, do you find yourself stopping to solve the puzzle? When you hear "Less filling . . .", what do you think of? Give illustrations that demonstrate how advertisers can use or must be aware of (a) the closure principle, (b) the principle of similarity, and (c) the figure-ground principle.*

---

The Eye of the Beholder: Interpretational Biases

c. The stimuli we perceive often are ambiguous—it's up to us to determine the meaning based on our experiences, expectations, and needs.

Semiotics: The Symbols Around Us

d. For assistance in understanding how consumers interpret the meanings of symbols, some marketers are turning to a field of study known as *semiotics* that examines the correspondence between signs and symbols and their role in the assignment of meaning. Semiotics is important to the understanding of consumer behavior because consumers use products to express their social identities.

1) Marketing messages have three basic components:

   a) The **object** that is the focus of the message.

   b) The **sign** is the sensory imagery that represents the intended meanings of the object.

   c) The **interpretant** is the meaning derived.

2) Signs are related to objects in one of three ways:

   a) An **icon** is a sign that resembles the product in some way.

   b) An **index** is a sign that is connected to a product because they share some property.

   c) A **symbol** is a sign that is related to a product through either conventional or agreed-upon associations.

3) One of the hallmarks of modern advertising is that it creates a condition that has been termed **hyperreality**. This occurs when advertisers create new relationships between objects and interpretants by inventing new connections between products and benefits (e.g., equating Marlboro cigarettes with the American frontier spirit).

---

***** Use Figure 2.3 Here *****

---

Perceptual Positioning

e. A product stimulus often is interpreted in light of what we already know about a product category and the characteristics of existing brands. Perceptions of a brand consist of:

1) Functional attributes (e.g., its features, its price, and so on).

2) Symbolic attributes (its image, and what we think it says about us when we use it).

f. Our evaluation of a product typically is the result of what it means rather than what it does.

1) This meaning is called market position.

2) **Positioning strategy** is a fundamental part of a company's marketing efforts as it uses elements of the marketing mix to influence the consumer's interpretation of its meaning.

3) There are many dimensions that can be used to establish a brand's position:

a) Lifestyle.

b) Price leadership.

c) Attributes.

d) Product class.

e) Competitors.

f) Occasions.

g) Users.

h) Quality.

***** *Use Figure 2.4 Here; Use Consumer Behavior Challenge #5 Here* *****

*Discussion Opportunity—Ask students to think of a case where a product has been positioned recently (i.e., new product introduction or re-positioning of an existing product). How was it positioned? What new market was pursued? How did you find out about this position or how did you discover the position?*

# End-of-Chapter Support Material

## SUMMARY OF SPECIAL FEATURE BOXES

1.    **Marketing Pitfalls**

This box focuses on the effects that perceptions of food serving size has on consumption. Various studies have shown that the larger the container that people are presented with, the more they will eat. People also tend to eat more when portions are larger. Additionally, the height of a container has a greater impact on consumer perception of size than does the width. Container sizes can even affect perceptions of the variety contained therein.

2.    **Marketing Opportunity I**

This box takes a look at the technology of micro-editing. This technology speeds up the rate of speech for recorded media, such as radio, and audio or video recordings. In this manner, more content can be compressed into a shorter time frame, without impacting the consumer's ability to process the information.

## 3. Marketing Opportunity II

This section discusses the changing perceptions of consumer freshness for chilled foods versus frozen foods. Consumers are leaning toward chilled, so this is where much of the innovation of new products is appearing.

## 4. Marketing Opportunity III

This box explores the dynamics of hyperreality—making real that which was originally simulation. Various examples are given of fictional characters and props from the worlds of advertising, television, and cinema crossing over into the real world. This feature supports the section "Hyperreality."

# REVIEW QUESTIONS

1. Define hedonic consumption and provide an example. *The Owens-Corning Fiberglass Corporation was the first company to trademark a color when it used bright pink for its insulation material and adopted the Pink Panther cartoon character as its spokes-character. Harley-Davidson actually tried to trademark the distinctive sound made by a "hog" revving up. These responses are an important part of hedonic consumption, the multisensory, fantasy, and emotional aspects of consumers' interactions with products.*

2. Does the size of a package influence how much of the contents we eat? *When pouring or eating foods from larger boxes, these boxes suggest it is appropriate or "acceptable" to eat more than smaller ones—and we do!*

3. How does the sense of touch influence consumers' reactions to products? *Moods are stimulated or relaxed on the basis of sensations reaching the skin, whether from a luxurious massage or the bite of a winter wind. Touch has even been shown to be a factor in sales interactions. We're more sure about what we perceive when we can touch it.*

4. Identify and describe the three stages of perception. *Exposure occurs when a stimulus comes within the range of someone's sensory receptors. Attention refers to the extent to which processing activity is devoted to a particular stimulus. Interpretation refers to the meaning that we assign to sensory stimuli.*

5. What is the difference between an absolute threshold and a differential threshold? *The absolute threshold refers to the minimum amount of stimulation that can be detected on a given sensory channel. The differential threshold refers to the ability of a sensory system to detect changes or differences between two stimuli.*

6.  Does subliminal perception work? Why or why not? *Some research by clinical psychologists suggests that people can be influenced by subliminal messages under very specific conditions, though it is doubtful that these techniques would be of much use in most marketing contexts. Effective messages must be very specifically tailored to individuals, rather than the mass messages required by advertising.*

7.  "Consumers practice a form of 'psychic economy.' " What does this mean? *Psychic economy is picking and choosing among stimuli to avoid being overwhelmed.* How do they choose? *Both personal and stimulus factors help to decide.*

8.  Describe two factors that can lead to stimulus adaptation. *There are five factors that can lead to stimulus adaptation:*

    - *Intensity: Less-intense stimuli (e.g., soft sounds or dim colors) habituate because they have less sensory impact.*
    - *Duration: Stimuli that require relatively lengthy exposure in order to be processed tend to habituate because they require a long attention span.*
    - *Discrimination: Simple stimuli tend to habituate because they do not require attention to detail.*
    - *Exposure: Frequently encountered stimuli tend to habituate as the rate of exposure increases.*
    - *Relevance: Stimuli that are irrelevant or unimportant will habituate because they fail to attract attention.*

9.  Define a "schema" and provide an example of how this concept is relevant to marketing. *Consumers assign meaning to stimuli based on the schema, or set of beliefs, to which the stimulus is assigned. An applied example of a schema is given in the opening vignette to the chapter when Gary is revolted at the thought of warm milk.*

10. "The whole is greater than the sum of its parts." Explain this statement. *Gestalt roughly means whole, pattern, or configuration, and this perspective is best summarized by the saying "the whole is greater than the sum of its parts."*

11. List the three semiotic components of a marketing message, giving an example of each. *The **object** is the product that is the focus of the message (e.g., Marlboro cigarettes). The **sign** is the sensory image that represents the intended meanings of the object (e.g., the Marlboro cowboy). The **interpretant** is the meaning derived (e.g., rugged, individualistic, American).*

12. What do we mean by the idea of hyperreality? *Hyperreality refers to the process of making real what is initially simulation or "hype." Advertisers create new relationships between objects and interpretants by inventing new connections between products and benefits, such as equating Marlboro cigarettes with the American frontier spirit.*

13. What is a positioning strategy? What are some ways marketers can position their products? *A positioning strategy is a fundamental part of a company's marketing efforts*

*as it uses elements of the marketing mix (i.e., product design, price, distribution, and marketing communications) to influence the consumer's interpretation of its meaning. Marketers can use many dimensions to carve out a brand's position in the marketplace. These include:*

- *Lifestyle: Grey Poupon mustard is a "higher-class" condiment.*
- *Price leadership: L'Oréal's Noisôme brand face cream is sold in upscale beauty shops, whereas its Plenitude brand is available for one-sixth the price in discount stores—even though both are based on the same chemical formula.*
- *Attributes: Bounty paper towels are "the quicker picker upper."*
- *Product class: The Mazda Miata is a sporty convertible.*
- *Competitors: Northwestern Insurance is "the quiet company."*
- *Occasions: Wrigley's gum is an alternative at times when smoking is not permitted.*
- *Users: Levi's Dockers are targeted primarily to men in their 20s to 40s.*
- *Quality: At Ford, "Quality is job 1."*

# CONSUMER BEHAVIOR CHALLENGE

## Discussion Questions

1. Many studies have shown that our sensory detection abilities decline as we grow older. Discuss the implications of the absolute threshold for marketers attempting to appeal to the elderly.

   *It would be wise to begin this exercise by identifying the particular senses and the ways in which they decline as the consumer gets older. Once this has been done, students should brainstorm to develop a list of the ways that a message may not be received or interpreted correctly. Students might be encouraged to develop a matrix, placing the senses down the left-hand side and forms of communication across the top. The matrix then should be filled in with descriptions of how communications may fail and how these failures could be avoided. For example, print advertisements aimed at an older audience could use larger type; radio and television ads could decrease the pace of information presented and slightly increase the volume to allow older recipients to more fully process the information; and retail stores and restaurants could increase lighting.*

2. Assuming that some forms of subliminal persuasion may have the desired effect of influencing consumers, do you think the use of these techniques is ethical? Explain your answer.

   *Many students will consider the use of subliminal persuasion to be unethical. Accordingly, a discussion could focus on why subliminal messages are undesirable. An interesting issue to raise may be how, or even if, subliminal persuasion differs from other advertising consumers are exposed to every day. Once these differences have been noted, the discussion could turn toward analyzing the reasons why individuals react negatively to subliminal persuasion. Students who believe the use of these techniques is ethical should be encouraged to develop their arguments so that those representing each side of the argument might see the opposing view. Regardless of the position adopted by the majority of students, be prepared to stimulate discussion by developing an argument in favor of the use of subliminal messages. This argument could center on the idea that subliminal persuasion might result in less "clutter." Arguing for its effectiveness, the amount of advertising could decrease overall.*

3. Do you believe that marketers have the right to use any or all public spaces to deliver product messages? Where would you draw the line in terms of places and products that should be restricted?

   *This question needs to be split into two parts: 1) whether marketers have the right to use any public spaces and 2) whether they have the right to use all public spaces. These are the two extremes on the issue, and the students will most likely find themselves somewhere between complete and unlimited access for marketers on one hand and complete and total ban on the other. A key concept in this discussion is the definition of "public spaces" and, therefore, a common definition should be adopted early in the discussion. To develop their position on this issue, students should be encouraged to list both appropriate and inappropriate places for product messages and offer reasons why each place should be categorized in a particular way. See if they think signs on the highway should be eliminated. If they agree, ask them how they would ever find McDonald's!*

4. The slogan for the movie Godzilla was "Size does matter." Should this be the slogan for America as well? Many marketers seem to believe so. The average serving size for a fountain drink has gone from 12 ounces to 20 ounces. An industry consultant explains that the 32-ounce Big Gulp is so popular because "people like something large in their hands. The larger the better." Hardee's Monster Burger, complete with two beef patties and five pieces of bacon, weighs in at 63 grams of fat and more than 900 calories. Clothes have ballooned as well: Kickwear makes women's jeans with 40-inch-diameter legs. The standard for TV sets used to be 19 inches; now it's 32 inches. Hulking SUVs have replaced tiny sports cars as the status vehicle of the new millennium. One consumer psychologist theorized that consuming big things is reassuring: "Large things compensate for our vulnerability," she says. "It gives us insulation, the feeling that we're less likely to die." What's up with our fascination with bigness? Is this a uniquely American preference? Do you believe that "bigger is better"? Is this a sound marketing strategy?

   *This question comprises multiple questions. The first, "What's up with our fascination with bigness?" is very general and should spark some general comments or discussion. If anything specific is to come from this particular question, students should be directed to theorize as to "why" people in the United States prefer bigger sizes. The second question, "Is this a uniquely American preference?" can only really be addressed if and when students have a concept of product size in other countries. Thus, foreign students and students who have lived or studied abroad will be a good resource here. Another option if assigning this question as an at-home project is to have students' research product sizes in other countries to make comparisons. It might be helpful if you give a few specific products for them to research, such as soft drinks, automobiles, and televisions. The third question, "Do you believe that 'bigger is better'?" should be directed toward whether or not larger sizes benefit the consumer. The final question examines whether super-sized products benefit the marketer. (Possible At-Home Project Idea)*

## Application Questions

5.  Interview three to five male and three to five female friends regarding their perceptions of both men's and women's fragrances. Construct a perceptual map for each set of products. Based on your map of perfumes, do you see any areas that are not adequately served by current offerings? What (if any) gender differences did you obtain regarding both the relevant dimensions used by raters and the placement of specific brands along these dimensions?

    *Have the students start this project by listing a number of descriptive words that are or could be used when positioning perfumes in the market place. Have them ask the respondents to position various perfumes on the map according to their impressions of the perfumes selected. (Possible Field Project Idea)*

6.  Assume that you are a consultant for a marketer who wants to design a package for a new premium chocolate bar targeted to an affluent market. What recommendations would you provide in terms of such package elements as color, symbolism, and graphic design? Give the reasons for your suggestions.

    *Most students will recognize that the label (package), the weight of the product, and the brand name of the product are all combined to communicate the image of the product. In this exercise the students are examining a premium product targeted to an affluent market. Obviously, the suggestions developed by students are likely to reflect their own experiences. What needs to be added to the discussion of product labels and names is: (1) the colors that will augment the desired premium image, (2) the smell that is associated with candy, (3) the sound of the candy wrapper in your hand, and (4) and the symbolism that may be used to position the product in the consumer's mind. The issue of symbolism may provide the best avenue for discussion, and a broader discussion of how symbols can be used in advertising and promotion would be helpful.*

7.  Using magazines archived in the library, track the packaging of a specific brand over time. Find an example of gradual changes in package design that may have been below the j.n.d.

    *You might give a few hints here. For example, Aunt Jemima, the Morton Salt Girl, and Betty Crocker are trademarks that have changed over time and can be found in ads. Package changes include Ivory Soap, Kellogg's Rice Krispies, and Campbell Soup. Students can simply examine automobile ads to see how styles of a particular car have changed over the years—the body is the car's package. (Possible Field Project Idea)*

8.  Visit a set of Web sites for one type of product (e.g., personal computers, perfumes, laundry detergents, or athletic shoes) and analyze the colors and other design principles employed. Which sites "work" and which don't? Why?

    *See if the students will notice how similar many of the products and brands are in terms of shape, weight, color, and size as depicted on the Web sites. A good way to approach this project is to pick a mainstream product such as an Apple computer (because of its bright colors). Be sure to have students state what they mean by "it will work" (a success) and how this was measured. Have one or two students go online to demonstrate how they approached this project. (Possible At-Home Project Idea)*

9.  Look through a current magazine and select one ad that captures your attention over the others. Give the reasons why.

    *After students have indicated what ad caught their attention, probe to see if there are any other reasons. Ask the class if any other aspects of the ad struck them. (Possible Field Project Idea)*

10. Find ads that utilize the techniques of contrast and novelty. Give your opinion of the effectiveness of each ad and whether the technique is likely to be appropriate for the consumers targeted by the ad.

    *Opinions will vary here. Some people like novelty in most everything, while others want people to be more serious. (Possible Field Project Idea)*

# CASE STUDY TEACHING NOTES

**Chapter 2 Case Study: The Brave New World of Subway Advertising**

## Summary of Case

Since 1999, a new segment of out-of-home advertising has been developed. Various agencies around the world have pioneered a technology that allows for static images placed in subway tunnels to appear as full-motion commercials. This represents one of many developments in recent years to break through ad clutter to capture consumers' attention with a novel type of advertising in a place that consumers do not expect it. The ad medium is rolling out in subway tunnels of major cities worldwide. The most notable part of this new development is that public reaction has been overwhelmingly positive. Transit officials, agency representatives, and corporate advertisers alike have been given kudos for turning dark and dreary tunnels into something entertaining for commuters.

## Suggestions for Presentation

This case could be assigned as an out-of-class or in-class activity. As an in-class activity, it might be more effective to have the class read it, then break them into small groups to discuss the questions. This is because a good response to the questions would require a consideration of various chapter concepts. The small group discussion could then be followed up with a large group review.

The discussion questions indicate that this case can be most appropriately tied to section in Chapter 2 that covers the concept of attention. However, the flexibility of the case would allow for some application to the sections on exposure (Which of the five senses does this ad type appeal to most? What are the implications of this for advertisers?) and interpretation (How does placement of an ad in this context affect positioning? How does the nature of different target segments of subway riders affect interpretation?). Thus, this case can be used to illustrate the entire process of perception as explained in chapter.

This case allows for the psychological processes of perception to be linked to real-world marketing implications. One item of interest not mentioned in the case that may be brought up during discussion is how this unique appeal to the perception processes of consumers has created value for multiple constituencies:

- The consumers—the positive reception indicates that the ads have entertainment value during an otherwise boring commute.
- The media agencies—these agencies are new ventures and are carving out a multi-million dollar industry. The cost of subway ads ranges from $35,000 a month to $250,000 a month depending on the route.
- The advertisers—there is no shortage of promotional choices for corporations and non-profit organizations. However, subway tunnel advertising gives marketers one of the few options that breaks through ad clutter in such a way that the consumer wants to see the ad, not to avoid it.
- The transit agencies—most metropolitan transit agencies are struggling with ever tightening budgets and with the balance of fare prices and demand. Many are therefore searching for additional revenue streams such as concessions or advertising. Although in-station and in-train advertising has been around since the early 1900s, subway tunnel agencies are forecasting that a single transit company (which would receive between 25 percent and 60 percent of the revenues) could earn as much as $200 million over 5 years.

## Suggested Answers For Discussion Questions

1. Based on the principles of attention presented in this chapter, explain why this new wave of subway ads is expected to be so effective.

    *This case is suited for illustrating various aspects of the perceptual process, including sensation, exposure, attention, and interpretation. However, the concepts that best explain why this new advertising medium should initially be successful are the stimulus selection factors of position and novelty that contribute to attention. With respect to position, subway ads come into full view, right outside the windows of subway trains where many riders are likely to be gazing. The concept of novelty exerts that stimuli that appear in unexpected places tend to grab attention. Certainly, these ads should at least initially be unexpected on the dark walls of subway tunnels. These things alone will contribute to higher than normal levels of attention which should have some effect on memory retention.*

2.   By the same principles, what should the subway tunnel agencies be considering in order to avoid the potential burnout of this medium?

*Obviously, if novelty is the biggest playing card for this advertising medium, then this should wear off. This is especially true because the image panels for these ads are placed physically in the subway tunnels and will likely remain in place for at least a month. Many subway riders are regulars. This means that they will see the same ad day after day. It won't take long before they no longer look. Additionally, after riders become accustomed to the ad medium itself, subway tunnel ads won't be any different than any other type of advertising as far as the attention grabbing benefits.*

*It is also speculated by some that the positioning of ads where riders are likely to be looking may produce negative reactions. Some riders gazing out of subway windows may enjoy the darkness as a form of relaxation or mediation.*

*Drawing upon other concepts from the chapter, in becoming familiar with these subway ads, riders are going through "adaptation" and are likely to notice them less. That is, unless the powers at be do something to change the nature of the ads.*

## Additional Support Material

# STUDENT PROJECTS

### Individual Projects

1.   Each student should visit a shopping mall and note all of the stores for which scents are an important component of their product offerings. Does it appear that each of these is appealing to the sense of smell in a strategic manner?

2.   Ask students to find three ads that contain symbolism. Examine the symbols and discuss the meaning the symbols convey. Encourage the student to identify the different types of signs used in the ads and the product qualities being communicated by each.

3.   Here is a field project that students always like. Have students (you might have only one or a few students do this as a special or alternative assignment) photocopy or print a collection of brand/product symbols (an alternative would be to have students create a PowerPoint presentation with images inserted to be projected in the classroom for all to

see). Then have this student quiz fellow classmates to see if they can recognize the product or company. This will show students how effective symbols are and how much involuntary learning has taken place in their life. You might give a reward to the student who had the **most** correct responses.

4. Here is a tough assignment for an undergraduate. Ask students to spend an afternoon watching a popular soap opera or an evening watching a favorite television show. Ask them to be particularly observant of the various products and services that are used as props during the show. Do these products or services have any symbolic value? How would viewer perception be different if alternative brands or even generic brands had been used? To what extent are the props shown or mentioned? Are they used to help develop the plot? How?

5. Have students visit a grocery store and pick out five products. They should identify how each appeals to the five senses. How are they the same? How are they different? To what extent do any of them appear to be strategically designed to appeal to the five senses?

6. Ask students to collect three different pieces of direct mail. How do the advertisers attempt to attract consumer attention? What are some of the other stimuli that could have been chosen to accomplish the same thing?

7. For this project, each student should keep a log of all the advertising information that they are exposed to in a single hour when they are out in public. They should keep track of the quantity, and not try to note the names or descriptions of each. From memory, what are some of the ways that companies attempt to get their ads noticed?

8. Send students to the library (they may need directions!) and look through several foreign magazines. How are the advertisements different from those in the United States? What sensory cues (based on the advertisements you see) seem to be cultural in nature? See if you can find an ad that is for the same product but done differently between the United States and some other country and comment on the differences (besides language).

9. While viewing one hour of television, what types of companies focus the most on factors that might affect "perceptual vigilance" in their advertisements? Have students write about examples of instances when they have used or experienced "perceptual vigilance" and "perceptual defense." Have them share their experiences with the class.

10. Assign students to find illustrations of the "closure principle," the "principle of similarity," and "figure-ground principle" in any marketing promotional or packaging material. Have them share their findings with the class.

11. Ask students to choose any two restaurants or pubs that are frequented by friends. Have them measure their image profiles by asking ten fellow students or friends to write a list of descriptive words that apply to each restaurant or pub. It will be easier for the subjects if the students provide the subjects with a list of potential descriptions. What conclusions can be drawn from this data?

12. For this project, students will need to pay attention. The student needs to notice and identify a piece of marketing material to which they have adapted and generally do not pay attention. Discuss the five factors of adaptation in relation to this particular piece of marketing material.

13. Have students find examples of an icon, an index, and a symbol. Differentiate between the three items.

14. As part of your class preparation, devise an experiment that can be done in class to demonstrate **perceptual selection**. You might even review the psychology and consumer behavior literature for ideas.

*JH to d*

15. Examples of hyperreality are becoming more and more common in our society. Have each student locate (either through their own observations or through reviewing articles in the popular and trade press) an example of hyperreality. Is the example chosen one in which the marketer strategically facilitated the "hyperreal" phenomenon, or did the transition occur independent of the marketer? How does the chosen example contribute to the relationship between the product and the consumer?

## Group Projects

1. Have three or four students identify a list of five products that are very utilitarian. Then, have them locate three examples of each product that focus on the emotional or hedonic form more than the core function.

2. Ask a group of students (seven to eight each) to list their favorite advertisements. Look at the lists. What do these ads tell you about the person that responded or the group as a whole? What do these ads do differently to increase perception or remembrance? What percentage of the ads were sexually oriented? After your respondents have given you their lists, be sure to ask whether they use the products displayed in the "favorite" ads? Comment on your results.

3. Have students (in small groups) go to various local restaurants and find menu items they would never eat. Describe these items (such as fried squid). Students should next demonstrate how perception might alter these biases. What could be done to make these "taboo" foods more acceptable? They should consider such areas as name changes, peer pressure, health benefits, and informational ads. Report the results in class.

4. Have student groups find three examples of brands or companies that have made changes to their products (i.e., retail chain re-designing their stores, a new logo, etc.). Have them discuss how the concept of "just noticeable difference" might affect consumer perceptions of these changes. Are the changes something that the marketers wanted to be noticed?

5.     Have groups of students (five to six each) think of how to demonstrate the principles of "absolute threshold" and "difference threshold" to the rest of the class. Have them develop this exercise and perform it.

# eLAB

## Individual Assignments

1.     Go to **www.tvguide.com**. On the opening Web page, how many ads (including pop-ups) do you notice? Compare and contrast the approach of each ad to exposure, attention, and interpretation. Comment on how the consumer goes through these steps when coming in contact with each ad. Provide an illustration of your description.

2.     Go to **www.scion.com**. Toyota launched its Scion brand for the 2004 model year. Already, three of the top ten hottest models (as measure by number of days spent on dealer lots) are Scion models. Not bad considering the division only has three models! Scion has focused its promotional efforts on the Internet and other non-traditional media. Is this Web site a good way to promote a car? In terms of concepts of perception, why or why not?

3.      Go to **www.leapfrog.com**. This is a Web site designed for children to facilitate learning. Analyze the Leapfrog site for sensory stimulation, attention value, and ability to promote a sale of the product. How are semiotics used on this site? Discuss briefly in class.

4.     Go to **www.bose.com**. Bose promises that once you listen to their Quiet Comfort 2 headphones you will never be satisfied with another comparable unit. Determine the competitive advantages and disadvantages of the Quiet Comfort 2. How does the company use sensory stimulation to promote the product? What key words can be used to evoke a response from consumers? Is the Bose approach effective? Explain.

## Group Assignments

1.     Go to **www.crutchfield.com**. Spend some time becoming familiar with this Web site. The group should evaluate the Crutchfield's strategy. What is it? What do you think will be the long-term result of the strategy you just described? How is the organization using exposure, attention, and interpretation to its benefit? What does the group think will be the secrets of success for Crutchfield? The seeds of failure? Which symbols should be used to ensure success? Which should be avoided?

2.     Go to **www.apple.com**. It seems like only yesterday that Steve Jobs re-joined Apple Computer and launched the company on a new product development spree that helped the ailing organization to pull itself out of its computer doldrums. Your group assignment is to analyze how Apple used color and design to differentiate the iPod line from other

mp3 players. Give illustrations of what was done. Was this a good strategy? What target markets were pursued? How did Apple use exposure, attention, and interpretation to their advantage? What are the criticisms about the iPod line? Can color and design overcome these criticisms?

# CHAPTER **3**

# *LEARNING AND MEMORY*

## CHAPTER OBJECTIVES

When students finish this chapter they should understand why:

- It's important for marketers to understand how consumers learn about products and services.

- Conditioning results in learning.

- Learned associations can generalize to other things, and why this is important to marketers.

- There is a difference between classical and instrrumental conditioning.

- Observation of others' behavior can result in learning.

- Memory systems work.

- Our knowledge of individual products is influenced by other products we associate with them.

- Products help us to retrieve memories from our past.

- Marketers measure our memories about products and ads.

## CHAPTER SUMMARY

*Learning* refers to a relatively permanent change in behavior that is caused by experience. Learning can occur through simple associations between a stimulus and a response or via a complex series of cognitive activities. Learning is an ongoing process.

It is useful in any study of consumer behavior to explore behavioral learning theories in order to gain insight into how consumers learn. Behavioral learning theories assume that learning occurs as a result of responses to external events. *Classical conditioning* occurs when a stimulus that naturally elicits a response (an unconditioned stimulus) is paired with another stimulus that does not initially elicit this response. Over time, the second stimulus (the conditioned stimulus) comes to elicit the response as well. Several experiments that demonstrate this conditioning are discussed in this chapter. Through this discussion it is found that a conditioned response can also extend to other, similar stimuli in a process known as stimulus generalization. This process is the basis for such marketing strategies as licensing and family branding, where a consumer's positive associations with a product are transferred to other contexts. The opposite effect is achieved by masked branding (where the manufacturer wishes to disguise the product's true origin).

Another view of behavioral learning is that of *instrumental* or *operant conditioning*. This form of conditioning occurs as the person learns to perform behaviors that produce positive outcomes and avoid those that result in negative outcomes. Although classical conditioning involves the pairing of two stimuli, instrumental learning conditioning occurs when reinforcement is delivered following a response to a stimulus. It is important to understand how conditioning occurs. Reinforcement is part of the process. Reinforcement is positive if reward is delivered following a response. It is negative if a negative outcome is avoided by not performing a response. Punishment occurs when a response is followed by unpleasant events. Extinction of the behavior will occur if reinforcement is no longer needed.

A third theory is called *cognitive learning*. This form occurs as the result of mental processes. For example, *observational learning* takes place when the consumer performs a behavior as a result of seeing someone else performing it and being rewarded for it.

The role of memory in the learning process is a major emphasis in this chapter. *Memory* refers to the storage of learned information. The way information is encoded when it is perceived determines how it will be stored in memory. Consumers have different forms or levels of memory. The memory systems are known as *sensory memory, short-term memory,* and *long-term memory.* Each plays a role in retaining and processing information from the outside world.

Information is not stored in isolation; it is incorporated into *knowledge structures,* where it is associated with other data. The location of product information in associative networks, and the level of abstraction at which it is coded, helps to determine when and how this information will be activated at a later time. Some factors that influence the likelihood of retrieval include the level of familiarity with an item, its salience (or prominence) in memory, and whether the information was presented in pictorial or written form. The chapter concludes with a brief discussion of how memory can be measured with respect to marketing stimuli.

# CHAPTER OUTLINE

1. **The Learning Process**
   a. **Learning** is a relatively permanent change in behavior that is caused by experience.
      1) Instead of direct experience, the learner can learn vicariously by observing events that affect others.
      2) We can learn without even really trying—just observing brand names on shelves. This casual, unintentional acquisition of knowledge is called **incidental learning**.

a) Learning is an ongoing process. Our world of knowledge is constantly being revised as we are exposed to new stimuli and receive ongoing feedback.

    i.   The concept of learning covers a lot of ground, ranging from a consumer's simple association between a stimulus such as a product logo and a response to a complex series of cognitive activities.

---

*Discussion Opportunity—Present the class with illustrations of learning vicariously and incidental learning in a consumer context. In reference to each of your illustrations, ask students what strategies marketers have used or might use to foster such learning.*

---

2. **Behavioral Learning Theories**
    a. **Behavioral learning theories** assume that learning takes place as the result of responses to external events.
        1) With respect to these theories, the mind might be perceived as being a "black box" and observable aspects of behavior are emphasized.
        2) The observable aspects consist of things that go in to the box (the stimuli—or events perceived from the outside world) and things that come out of the box (the responses—or reactions to these stimuli).
    b. The previous view is represented by two views:
        1) Classical conditioning.
        2) Instrumental conditioning.
    c. The sum of the activities is that people's experiences are shaped by the feedback they receive as they go through life. People also learn that actions they take result in rewards and punishments, and this feedback influences the way they will respond in similar situations in the future.

---

*****Use Figure 3.1 Here *****

---

Classical Conditioning
    d. **Classical conditioning** occurs when a stimulus that elicits a response is paired with another stimulus that initially does not elicit a response on its own.
        1) Over time, this second stimulus causes a similar response because it is associated with the first stimulus.
        2) This phenomenon was first demonstrated by Ivan Pavlov's "dog experiments" when doing research on digestion in animals.
            a) Pavlov induced classical conditioning learning by pairing a neutral stimulus (a bell) with a stimulus known to cause a salivation response in dogs (he squirted dried meat powder into their mouths).
            b) The powder was an **unconditioned stimulus (UCS)** because it was naturally capable of causing the response.
            c) Over time, the bell became a **conditioned response (CS)**; it did not initially cause salivation, but the dogs learned to associate the bell with the meat powder and began to salivate at the sound of the bell only.
            d) The drooling of these canine consumers over a sound, now linked to feeding time, was a **conditioned response (CR).**

3) This basic form of classical conditioning demonstrated by Pavlov primarily applies to responses controlled by the autonomic and nervous systems.

4) Classical conditioning can have similar effects for more complex reactions (such as in automatically using a credit card for purchases).

*Discussion Opportunity—Ask students to think of some examples of classical conditioning in everyday life as well as in advertising and marketing. Ask students if they think such examples represent intentional efforts to condition consumers. What are the strengths of these campaigns, if any? Be sure to point out the difference between true conditioning and mere association.*

 e. Conditioning effects are more likely to occur after the conditioned stimuli (CS) and unconditioned stimuli (UCS) have been paired a number of times (repetition). Notice how often ad campaigns are repeated. Repetition prevents decay.

 f. **Stimulus generalization** refers to the tendency of stimuli similar to a CS to evoke similar, conditioned responses. Pavlov's dogs might respond to sounds similar to a bell (such as keys jangling).

  1) People also react to other, similar stimuli in much the same way they responded to the original stimulus; a generalization known as the **halo effect.**

  2) Private brands often use "piggybacking" to build on impressions built by major brands.

  3) **Masked branding** occurs when a manufacturer deliberately hides a product's true origin.

 g. **Stimulus discrimination** occurs when a stimulus similar to a CS is *not* followed by an UCS. When this happens, reactions are weakened and will soon disappear.

  1) Manufacturers of well-established brands urge consumers not to buy "cheap imitations."

*Discussion Opportunity—Ask students the following: Can you think of some products that have similar packaging? Similar shapes? Similar names? To what extent do these examples represent stimulus generalization? In each case, which brand is the primary brand and which brand is the "me too" brand? Assuming the strategy was intentional, did it work? How can a marketer achieve stimulus discrimination?*

Marketing Applications of Behavioral Learning Principles

 h. Many marketing strategies focus on the establishment of associations between stimuli and responses. Examples would be:

  1) Distinctive brand image.

  2) Linkage between a product and an underlying need.

  3) **Brand equity** is where a brand has a strong positive association in a consumer's memory and commands a lot of loyalty as a result.

  4) Repetition can be valuable. Too much repetition, however, results in ***advertising wearout***.

 i. Advertisements often pair a product with a positive stimulus to create a desirable association.

  1) The order in which the conditioned stimulus and the unconditioned stimulus are presented can affect the likelihood that learning will occur. Normally, the

unconditioned stimulus (***backward conditioning***) should be presented prior to the conditioned stimulus.

2) Product associations can be ***extinguished***.

j. The process of stimulus generalization is often central to branding and packaging decisions that attempt to capitalize on consumers' positive associations with an existing brand or company name. Strategies include:
1) Family branding.
2) Product line extensions.
3) Licensing.
4) Look-alike packaging.

---

***\*\*\*\*\* Use Consumer Behavior Challenge #4 Here \*\*\*\*\****

---

*Discussion Opportunity—Ask students to give examples of brands that they perceive have equity over other brands. As with equity of other assets (such as real estate), can an exact monetary value be placed on brand equity?*

---

*Discussion Opportunity—Have students apply the concept of stimulus generalization to real examples of family branding or product line extensions. Have them come up with examples where the stimulus was successfully generalized and examples where it was not.*

---

k. An emphasis on communicating a product's distinctive attributes vis-à-vis its competitors is an important aspect of positioning, where consumers differentiate a brand from its competitors. Stimulus discrimination attempts to promote unique attributes of a brand.

l. Concerns for marketers relating to stimulus discrimination include the loss exclusive rights to a brand name to the public domain and brand piracy.

Instrumental Conditioning

m. **Instrumental conditioning (*operant conditioning*)** occurs as the individual learns to perform behaviors that produce positive outcomes and to avoid those that yield negative outcomes. This approach is closely associated with B.F. Skinner. (He taught pigeons and other animals to dance and play Ping-Pong using this method.)
1) Although responses in classical conditioning are involuntary and fairly simple, those in instrumental conditioning are made deliberately to obtain a goal and may be more complex.
2) Desired behavior may be rewarded in a process called **shaping**.
3) Instrumental conditioning (learning) occurs as a result of a reward received following the desired behavior.

---

*Discussion Opportunity—Have students brainstorm a list of examples of instrumental conditioning in marketing. Ask: Which do you think has more application to marketing— classical or instrumental conditioning?*

---

> *Discussion Opportunity—Relate the concept of instrumental conditioning to the Internet and eCommerce through a specific example. Have students point out why they think this example is an application of instrumental conditioning.*

    n.  Instrumental learning occurs in one of three ways:
      1)  When the environment provides **positive reinforcement** in the form of a reward, the response is strengthened and appropriate behavior is learned (a woman wearing perfume and receiving a compliment).
      2)  **Negative reinforcement** also strengthens responses so that appropriate behavior is learned.
      3)  In contrast to situations where we learn to do certain things to avoid unpleasantness, **punishment** occurs when a response is followed by unpleasant events. We learn the hard way not to repeat these behaviors.
    o.  When a positive outcome is no longer received, **extinction** is likely to occur and the learned stimulus-response connection will not be maintained.

**\*\*\*\*\*Use Figure 3.2 Here \*\*\*\*\***

> *Discussion Opportunity—What are some products that promise "good things will happen" if you buy their products? Can you think of products that tell you that you will be "punished" if you don't buy them? Can you think of products where you are told that you will be "punished" if you do buy them or use them? How would this be possible?*

    p.  An important factor in operant conditioning is the set of rules by which appropriate reinforcements are given for a behavior. Several reinforcement schedules are possible:
      1)  Fixed-interval reinforcement.
      2)  Variable-interval reinforcement.
      3)  Fixed-ratio reinforcement.
      4)  Variable-ratio reinforcement.

> *Discussion Opportunity—Provide an example of each of the previously mentioned reinforcement schedules. Ask students: Which of these examples do you think is the most effective and why? Under what conditions can each of these reinforcement schedules be effectively applied?*

Marketing Applications of Instrumental Conditioning Principles
    q.  Principles of instrumental conditioning are at work when a consumer is rewarded or punished for a purchase decision.
      1)  Most companies reinforce consumption.
      2)  A popular technique called **frequency marketing** reinforces regular purchases by giving them prizes with values that increase along with the amount purchased.

**3.  Cognitive Learning Theory**
    a.  **Cognitive learning theory** approaches stress the importance of internal mental processes. This perspective views people as problem-solvers who actively use information from the world around them to master their environment.

<u>Is Learning Conscious or Not?</u>
b. There are several schools of thought.
    1) One school believes that conditioning occurs because subjects develop conscious hypotheses and then act on them.
    2) There is also evidence for the existence of nonconscious procedural knowledge—we move toward familiar patterns (automatic responses).

<u>Observational Learning</u>
c. **Observational learning** occurs when people watch the actions of others and note the reinforcements they receive for their behaviors—learning occurs as a result of vicarious rather than direct experience.
    1) Memories are stored for later use.
    2) Imitating the behavior of others is called **modeling**.
    3) Four conditions must be met for modeling to occur (see Figure 3.3):
        a) The consumer's attention must be directed to the appropriate model, who for reasons of attractiveness, competence, status, or similarity is desirable to emulate.
        b) The consumer must remember what is said or done by the model.
        c) The consumer must convert this information into actions.
        d) The consumer must be motivated to perform these actions.

*****Use Figure 3.3 Here *****

<u>Marketing Applications of Cognitive Learning Principles</u>
d. Consumers' ability to learn in this way has helped marketers.
    1) People's willingness to make their own reinforcements has saved the marketers from having to do it for them.
    2) Consumers seem to enjoy using "models" as role models and for guidance in purchasing.

**4. The Role of Memory in Learning**

   a. **Memory** involves a process of acquiring information and storing it over time so that it will be available when needed.

      1) Contemporary approaches to the study of memory employ an *information-processing* approach.

         a) In the **encoding** stage, information is entered in a way the system will recognize.

         b) In the **storage** stage, this knowledge is integrated with what is already in memory and "warehoused" until needed.

         c) During **retrieval,** the person accesses the desired information.

---

**\*\*\*\*\*Use Figure 3.4 Here \*\*\*\*\***

---

Encoding Information for Later Retrieval

   b. The way information is encoded, or mentally programmed, helps to determine how it will be represented in memory.

      1) A consumer may process a stimulus simply in terms of its **sensory meaning** (such as its color or shape).

      2) **Semantic meaning** refers to symbolic associations, such as the idea that rich people drink champagne or that fashionable men wear earrings.

      3) **Episodic memories** are those that relate to events that are personally relevant.

      4) *Flashbulb memories* are those that are especially vivid (such as memories of September 11).

         a) One method of conveying product information is through a *narrative* or story.

         b) Much of what an individual acquires about social information is received through the narrative or story; therefore, it is a useful marketing technique for transmitting information.

---

*Discussion Opportunity—Can you give an illustration of each of the forms of meaning or memory just discussed (sensory meaning, semantic meaning, episodic memory, and flashbulb memories)? How could these forms of memory be used to motivate purchases?*

---

Memory Systems

   c. There are three distinct memory systems:

      1) **Sensory memory** permits storage of the information we receive from our senses. This storage is very temporary (it only lasts a couple of seconds).

      2) If information is retained for further processing, it passes through an **attentional gate** and is transferred to **short-term memory (STM).**

      3) **STM** also stores information for a limited period of time, and its capacity is limited. It holds information we are currently processing. This information working memory is stored by combining small pieces into larger ones in a process known as **chunking**.

         a) A chunk is a configuration that is familiar to the person and can be manipulated as a unit.

         b) An example would be a brand name.

      4) **Long-term memory** is the system that allows us to retain information for a long period of time. Catchy slogans or jingles often help in this area.

*****Use Figure 3.5 Here; Use Consumer Behavior Challenge #3 Here *****

*Discussion Opportunity—Consider the following ways to demonstrate the memory functions to the students: 1) Point out a noise that might be audible from outside the classroom (e.g., lawnmower, cars, construction) after it happens. Ask how many remember hearing it? Those that do not remember hearing it never made the jump from sensory memory to short- or long-term memory; 2) Use a phrase very clearly and audibly at the beginning of the class. Then, once you get to this point in the lecture, ask each student to write out the phrase. Because you stated it clearly, the phrase almost certainly made it in to the short-term memory. The degree of correctness of each student's statement, however, will show the difference between short-term and long-term memory. Ask students how these forms of memory (sensory, short-term, and long-term) should be taken into consideration by marketers.*

Storing Information in Memory

    d.  Relationships among the types of memory are a source of controversy.
        1)  The traditional view (**multiple-store**) is that the short-term memory and long-term memory are separate systems.
        2)  Recent work says they may be interdependent (**activation models of memory**). *Deep processing* means that the information will probably be placed in long-term memory.
    e.  Activation models propose that an incoming piece of information is stored in an association network containing many bits of related information organized according to some set of relationships. This is how the consumer can organize brands, manufacturers, and stores.
        1)  These storage units are known as **knowledge structures** (think of them as spider Webs full of knowledge).
            a)  This information is placed into **nodes** that are connected by associative links within these structures.
            b)  Pieces of information that are seen as similar in some way are chunked together under some more abstract category.
        2)  According to the **hierarchical processing model**, a message is processed in a bottom-up fashion (processing begins at a very basic level and is subject to increasingly complex processing operations that require greater cognitive capacity).
        3)  Preference categories are known as **evoked sets**. The task of the marketer is to position itself as a category member and to provide cues that facilitate its placement in the proper category.

*****Use Figure 3.6 Here; Use Consumer Behavior Challenge #5 Here *****

*Discussion Opportunity—Briefly work with students to construct an example of an associative network for a product or brand of their choosing. Illustrate the network for the class to see as it is being constructed. Refer back to this network as you teach the following concepts of spreading activation and schemas.*

f.  Consumers go through a process of **spreading activation** as they shift back and forth between levels of meaning. Memory traces are sent out. They could be:
    1) Brand-specific.
    2) Ad-specific.
    3) Brand-identification.
    4) Product category.
    5) Evaluative reactions.
g.  Knowledge is coded at different levels of abstraction and complexity.
    1)  A *proposition* links two nodes together to form a more complex meaning, which can serve as a single chunk of information.
    2) Propositions are integrated into a schema that is seen as a cognitive framework that is developed through experience.
    3) One type of schema is a *script*, where a sequence of events is expected by an individual. Scripts that guide behavior in commercial settings are known as **service scripts.** Think of all the activities one goes through when they go to the dentist.

*Discussion Opportunity—Have students give examples of scripts that they typically go through when purchasing a routine product. Why would a marketer want or not want consumers to develop such scripts?*

Retrieval Information for Purchase Decisions

h.  Retrieval is the process whereby information is accessed from long-term memory. Factors that influence retrieval are:
    1) Age.
    2) Situational variables (such as the environment).
    3) The viewing environment.
i.  In a process called *state-dependent retrieval*, people are better able to access information if their internal state is the same at the time of recall as when the information was learned.
    1) This phenomenon, called the *mood congruence effect*, underscores the desirability of matching a consumer's mood at the time of purchase when planning exposure to marketing communications.
    2) As a general rule, prior familiarity with an item enhances its recall. Familiarity can also result in inferior recall, however, because the product can be "taken for granted" and assumed to have no new information worth processing.
j.  The **salience** of a brand refers to its prominence or level of activation in memory.
    1) Almost any technique that increases the novelty of a stimulus also improves recall (called the *von Restorff Effect*).
    2) Putting a surprise element in an ad can be effective.

*****Use Consumer Behavior Challenge #3 Here (Used Previously) *****

*Discussion Opportunity—Have students share their perceptions of the salient characteristics of (a) a Subway sub, (b) a pair of Nike shoes , and (c) a Mountain Dew soda. Be sure to have students include both physical as well as psychological characteristics.*

## Factors Influencing Forgetting

k. Marketers obviously hope that consumers will not forget about their products. The forgetting process consists of:

1) **Decay**—the structural changes in the brain produced by learning simply go away.
2) Forgetting also occurs due to **interference**; as additional information is learned, it displaces the earlier information.
3) Consumers may forget stimulus-response associations if they learn new responses to the same or similar stimuli (*retroactive interference*).
4) Prior learning can interfere with new learning through a process known as *proactive interference.*
5) *Part-list cueing effect* allows marketers to strategically utilize the interference process (competitors, though known, are not easily recalled).

---

*Discussion Opportunity—Illustrate the forgetting concepts decay and interference. Have students identify types of information that a marketer might want to have consumers forget through both decay and interference. Have them do the same with information that marketers would not want consumers to forget. How can marketers combat the forgetting process?*

---

## Products as Memory Makers

l. Products and ads can themselves serve as powerful retrieval cues.

1) **Nostalgia** has been described as a bittersweet emotion, where the past is viewed with both sadness and longing. This has an appeal for many consumers.
2) Retro marketing attempts to bring back old commercials to appeal to the nostalgia market. A **retro brand** is an updated version of a brand from a prior historical period.

---

**\*\*\*\*\*Use Consumer Behavior Challenge #2 \*\*\*\*\***

---

*Discussion Opportunity—Ask students to identify what types of things are nostalgic to them. How could an advertiser appeal to this side of them and other college-age individuals? Identify recent nostalgia campaigns and present them as illustrations.*

---

## Measuring Memory for Marketing Stimuli

m. Surprisingly, consumers do a rather poor job of recalling significant pieces of information about most products. This is especially true with television ads. (Only 7 percent of television viewers can recall the product or company featured in most of the recent ads they have watched.)

1) The impression made is called *impact*.
2) Measures of impact are:
   a) *Recognition*.
   b) *Recall*.
3) Recognition tends to stay longer than recall.
4) One test for measuring recognition and recall is the *Starch Test*.

*Discussion Opportunity—How many commercials can you name from last night's television viewing experience? How many outdoor signs (billboards) can you remember from driving to class today? Have students brainstorm for one minute to see how many soft drink brands they can come up with.*

*Discussion Opportunity—As an illustration between recognition and recall, conduct this exercise to show students that they can recognize information without really recalling specifics. Show examples of various corporate symbols (brand symbols or celebrity endorsers) that students might recognize. Ask them which brands are represented by each (recognition). Then, ask them to give specific slogans, information, or other specifics related to each (recall).*

n.  Although the measurement of an ad's memorability is important, the ability of existing measures to accurately assess these dimensions has been criticized for several reasons.
1)  **Response bias**—results obtained from a measuring instrument are not necessarily due to what is being measured, but rather to something else about the instrument or the respondent. Simply, people tend to give "yes" answers.
2)  Memory lapses—people are prone to unintentionally forgetting information.
3)  Memory for facts versus feelings—it is very difficult to take "feelings" out of impressions about ads (especially if the ad raises strong emotions). Recall does not translate into preference.

*Discussion Opportunity—What is something hard for you to remember (in a personal sense and in a consumer behavior or product sense)? Why do you think this happens? What do you think would be a good strategy to attempt to overcome this problem?*

# End-of-Chapter Support Material

# SUMMARY OF SPECIAL FEATURE BOXES

## 1.  Marketing Opportunity

This box highlights the use of semantic associations in the creation of brand and company names. Such names are often created as a modification of an existing word or words in order to elicit certain concepts, feelings, or perceptions.

## 2.  Marketing Pitfalls

What happens when a sports venue is named after a sponsoring company, and the company goes bankrupt or experiences negative publicity?

## 3. Marketing Opportunity

This box examines the growing trend of nostalgia parties, specifically pajama parties. Sleepwear makers, cosmetics companies and event planners report that adult sleepovers are hot. Such companies are coming up with products to target such events.

# REVIEW QUESTIONS

1. What is the difference between an unconditioned stimulus and a conditioned stimulus? *Ivan Pavlov, a Russian physiologist doing research on digestion in animals, first demonstrated this phenomenon in dogs. Pavlov induced classically conditioned learning by pairing a neutral stimulus (a bell) with a stimulus known to cause a salivation response in dogs (he squirted dried meat powder into their mouths). The powder was an unconditioned stimulus (UCS) because it was naturally capable of causing the response. Over time, the bell became a conditioned stimulus (CS); it did not initially cause salivation, but the dogs learned to associate the bell with the meat powder and began to salivate at the sound of the bell only.*

2. Give an example of a halo effect in marketing. *People also react to other, similar stimuli in much the same way they responded to the original stimulus; this generalization is called a halo effect. A drugstore's bottle of private brand mouthwash deliberately packaged to resemble Listerine mouthwash may evoke a similar response among consumers, who assume that this "me-too" product shares other characteristics of the original.*

3. How can marketers use repetition to increase the likelihood that consumers will learn about their brand? *Many classic advertising campaigns consist of product slogans that have been repeated so many times that they are etched in consumers' minds. Conditioning will not occur or will take longer if the CS is only occasionally paired with the UCS. One result of this lack of association may be extinction that occurs when the effects of prior conditioning are reduced and finally disappear. This can occur, for example, when a product is overexposed in the marketplace so that its original allure is lost.*

4. Why is it not necessarily a good idea to advertise a product in a commercial where a really popular song is playing in the background? *A popular song might also be heard in many situations in which the product is not present.*

5. What is the difference between classical conditioning and instrumental conditioning? *Classical conditioning occurs when a stimulus that elicits a response is paired with another stimulus that initially does not elicit a response on its own. Over time, this second stimulus causes a similar response because it is associated with the first stimulus. Instrumental conditioning, also known as* operant conditioning, *occurs as the individual*

*learns to perform behaviors that produce positive outcomes and to avoid those that yield negative outcomes.*

6.  How do different types of reinforcement enhance learning? How does the strategy of frequency marketing relate to conditioning? *When the environment provides positive reinforcement in the form of a reward, the response is strengthened and appropriate behavior is learned. For example, a woman who gets compliments after wearing Obsession perfume will learn that using this product has the desired effect, and she will be more likely to keep buying the product. Negative reinforcement also strengthens responses so that appropriate behavior is learned. A perfume company might run an ad showing a woman sitting home alone on a Saturday night because she did not use its fragrance. The message to be conveyed is that she could have avoided this negative outcome if only she had used the perfume. In contrast to situations in which we learn to do certain things in order to avoid unpleasantness, punishment occurs when a response is followed by unpleasant events (such as being ridiculed by friends for wearing an offensive-smelling perfume)—we learn the hard way not to repeat these behaviors. A popular technique known as frequency marketing reinforces regular purchasers by giving them prizes with values that increase along with the amount purchased.*

7.  What is the major difference between behavioral and cognitive theories of learning? *In contrast to behavioral theories of learning, cognitive learning theory approaches stress the importance of internal mental processes. This perspective views people as problem solvers who actively use information from the world around them to master their environment. Supporters of this view also stress the role of creativity and insight during the learning process.*

8.  Name the three stages of information processing. *Encoding, storage, and retrieval.*

9.  What is external memory and why is it important to marketers? *During the consumer decision-making process, this internal memory is combined with external memory that includes all of the product details on packages and other marketing stimuli that permit brand alternatives to be identified and evaluated.*

10. Give an example of an episodic memory. *Episodic memories relate to events that are personally relevant. As a result, a person's motivation to retain these memories will likely be strong. Couples often have "their song" that reminds them of their first date or wedding.*

11. Why do phone numbers have seven digits? *Initially, researchers believed that STM was capable of processing between five and nine chunks of information at a time, and for this reason they designed phone numbers to have seven digits.*

12. List the three types of memory, and tell how they work together. *Sensory memory permits storage of the information we receive from our senses. This storage is very temporary; it lasts a couple of seconds at most. Short-term memory (STM) also stores information for a limited period of time, and it has limited capacity. Similar to a computer, this system can*

*be regarded as working memory; it holds the information we are currently processing. Long-term memory (LTM) is the system that allows us to retain information for a long period of time. Elaborative rehearsal is required in order for information to enter into long-term memory from short-term memory. This process involves thinking about the meaning of a stimulus and relating it to other information already in memory.*

13. How is associative memory like a spider Web? *Knowledge structures can be thought of as complex spider Webs filled with pieces of data. This information is placed into nodes that are connected by associative links within these structures. Pieces of information that are seen as similar in some way are chunked together under some more abstract category. New, incoming information is interpreted to be consistent with the structure already in place.*

14. How does the likelihood a person will be willing to use an ATM machine relate to a schema? *The desire to follow a script or schema helps to explain why such service innovations as automatic bank machines, self-service gas stations, or "scan-your-own" grocery checkouts have met with resistance by some consumers, who have trouble adapting to a new sequence of events*

15. Why does a pioneering brand have a memory advantage over follower brands? *Some evidence indicates that information about a pioneering brand (the first brand to enter a market) is more easily retrieved from memory than follower brands because the first product's introduction is likely to be distinctive and, for the time being, no competitors divert the consumer's attention.*

16. If a consumer is familiar with a product, advertising for it can work both ways by either enhancing or diminishing recall. Why? *As a general rule, prior familiarity with an item enhances its recall. Indeed, this is one of the basic goals of marketers who are trying to create and maintain awareness of their products. The more experience a consumer has with a product, the better use he or she is able to make of product information. However, there is a possible fly in the ointment: As noted earlier in the chapter, some evidence indicates that extreme familiarity can result in inferior learning and recall. When consumers are highly familiar with a brand or an advertisement, they may attend to fewer attributes because they do not believe that any additional effort will yield a gain in knowledge.*

17. How does learning new information make it more likely we'll forget things we've already learned? *Forgetting may occur due to interference; as additional information is learned, it displaces the earlier information.*

18. Define nostalgia, and tell why it's such a widely-used advertising strategy. *We can describe nostalgia as a bittersweet emotion; the past is viewed with both sadness and longing. References to "the good old days" are increasingly common, as advertisers call up memories of youth—and hope these feelings will translate to what they're selling today.*

19.    Name the two basic measures of memory and describe how they differ from one another. *Two basic measures of impact are recognition and recall. In the typical recognition test, subjects are shown ads one at a time and asked if they have seen them before. In contrast, free recall tests ask consumers to independently think of what they have seen without being prompted for this information first—obviously this task requires greater effort on the part of respondents.*

20.    List three problems with measures of memory for advertising. *Response biases, memory lapses, and memory for facts versus feelings.*

# CONSUMER BEHAVIOR CHALLENGE

## Discussion Questions

1.    In his 2005 book *Blink: The Power of Thinking without Thinking*, author Malcolm Gladwell argues that hallowed marketing research techniques like focus groups aren't effective because we usually react to products quickly and without much conscious thought so it's better just to solicit consumers' first impressions rather than getting them to think at length about why they buy. What's your position on this issue?

      *There are various concepts that students may apply to support both sides of this argument. Both classical conditioning and behavioral instrumental conditioning would support the idea that we make consumer decisions quickly and without much thought. However, cognitive learning theory approaches stress the importance of internal mental processes. This perspective views people as problem-solvers who actively use information from the world around them to master their environment.*

2.    Some die-hard fans were not pleased when the Rolling Stones sold the tune "Start Me Up" for about $4 million to Microsoft that wanted the classic song to promote its Windows 95 launch. The Beach Boys sold "Good Vibrations" to Cadbury Schweppes for its Sunkist soft drink, Steppenwolf offered its "Born to be Wild" to plug the Mercury Cougar, and even Bob Dylan sold "The Times They Are A-Changin'" to Coopers & Lybrand (now called PriceWaterhouseCoopers). Other rock legends have refused to play the commercial game, including Bruce Springsteen, the Grateful Dead, Led Zeppelin, Fleetwood Mac, R.E.M., and U2. According to U2's manager, "Rock 'n' roll is the last vestige of independence. It is undignified to put that creative effort and hard work to the disposal of a soft drink or beer or car." Singer Neil Young is especially adamant about not selling out; in his song "This Note's For You," he croons, "Ain't singing for Pepsi, ain't singing for Coke, I don't sing for nobody, makes me look like a joke." What's your take on this issue? How do you react when one of your favorite songs turns up in a commercial? Is this use of nostalgia an effective way to market a product? Why or why not?

*Student responses on this issue will range from support to opposition of artists selling songs for commercial application. Their reasons for either will also vary. Some will like hearing familiar songs in commercial jingles because it grabs their attention, is more relevant to them, or prompts them to recall fond memories. Some will express support simply because it is the artists' prerogative to sell what is theirs. Others will oppose this practice for reasons similar to those expressed by the artists mentioned. It is likely that among business and marketing students, however, most will find nothing wrong with the commercial application of popular songs. Responses should reflect the concept that nostalgia in marketing can be effective because it can prompt positive emotions in consumers.*

## Application Questions

3.    Devise a "product jingle memory test." Compile a list of brands that are or have been associated with memorable jingles, such as Chiquita Banana or Alka-Seltzer. Read this list to friends, and see how many jingles are remembered. You may be surprised at the level of recall.

*Students should be able to generate a large number of product jingles for this "memory test." Most of these will be highly advertised products that students have been exposed to recently. It might be surprising to note that many of the advertised products are not targeted at the student/consumer, and yet they will have high levels of recall for the jingles. As the instructor you may want to develop your own list of older jingles (many of which the students will not remember) that students will find interesting, such as those based on older, popular songs (i.e., "I'd like to buy the world a Coke").*

4.    Identify some important characteristics for a product with a well-known brand name. Based on these attributes, generate a list of possible brand extension or licensing opportunities, as well as some others that would most likely not be accepted by consumers.

*The list of characteristics will, of course, depend on the product chosen. Generally, it will include distinctive aspects of products. For example, BIC has successfully extended the brand many times over in different product categories. Also the existing brand name benefited from the characteristics consumers associate with the name BIC—namely cheap, plastic, and disposable. Their attempts in the perfume and panty hose categories, however, were disasters. Because brand extension is based on the transfer of some positive product characteristics (either physical or emotional) to the new product, the list students generate should lend itself to identification of that "something" that would enable an extension to be successful.*

5.    Collect some pictures of "classic" products that have high nostalgia value. Show these pictures to consumers and allow them to free associate. Analyze the types of memories that are evoked, and think about how these associations might be employed in a product's promotional strategy.

*Consumers' responses to "classic" product pictures should prove interesting to students. They should be encouraged to evaluate the types of meaning associated with products and asked to determine the relative effectiveness of various messages for different target consumer groups. The real emphasis, however, should be placed on students' recommendations for translating the special meaning of these products for consumers into effective promotional messages.*

# CASE STUDY TEACHING NOTES

## Chapter 3 Case Study: Hershey's Versus M&Ms: The War of the Bite-Size Milk Chocolates

### Summary of Case

Consumers have various associations for brands such as M&Ms and Hershey's, but these associations tend to be consistent. However, Hershey's is about to stir these associations up by introducing Kissables, a small bite sized piece of milk chocolate covered in a colored candy coating. Sound too familiar? It is not by accident. This is the first move by Hershey's to attempt to attack the market share of M&Ms head on. Hershey's has plans to expand the brand by introducing a variety of new products in coming years. Many of them could take on M&Ms and other candies with established concepts.

### Suggestions for Presentation

The most obvious way for using this case is as an application of associative memory networks. Having students establish a memory network for a brand is often a good way of driving that concept home. In this case, two well-known brands are given and various associations are suggested. But the interesting discussion should come about as students consider the implications of the introduction of Kissables on consumer associations for both M&Ms and Hershey's. Will it strengthen or dilute such associations? The concept of evoked set should also be woven into this discussion. When a person goes for a single serving of chocolate candy, Hershey doesn't have an entry to compete in an evoked set with M&Ms. But with this brand extension, they soon will. You may also wish to have students consider how a move such as this might affect the brand equity of both brands.

### Suggested Answers for Discussion Questions

1.  Discuss how consumers come to know the various attributes of brands such as Hershey's Kisses and M&Ms according to activation models of memory.

    *Activation models propose that an incoming piece of information is stored in an associative network containing many bits of related information organized according to some set of relationships. The consumer has organized systems of concepts relating to brands, manufacturers, and stores. We can think of these storage units, known as knowledge structures, as complex spider Webs filled with pieces of data. This information is placed into nodes that are connected by associative links within these structures. Pieces of information that are seen as similar in some way are chunked together under some more abstract category. New, incoming information is interpreted to be consistent with the structure already in place. Corporations feed information to consumers in various ways, from traditional advertising, to the product and package. If such information is integrated properly, then it becomes part of the memory store.*

2.     What are the benefits and dangers that Hershey's faces in extended a blue chip brand such as Kisses?

*The potential benefits are obvious. Hershey is attempting to broaden their market appeal by introducing products in categories where they have not previously competed. If consumers accept such extensions, then there will be more stimuli (i.e., candy-coated chocolate) that will activate the Hershey brand name in people's minds. This benefit may be enhanced by the fact that consumers will no longer think only of competing brands when presented with such stimuli. Dangers or risks include the possibility that consumers will not make the necessary link between the characteristics of the new brand extension and the core brand. In other words, that the new product concept never really catches on as a Hershey "thing." Hershey also runs the risk that introducing this extension (and other planned extensions) may dilute the concept that consumers hold currently for the brand. There is the possibility that a strongly entrenched association such as the Kiss configuration could become diluted over time.*

## <u>Additional Support Material</u>

# STUDENT PROJECTS

### <u>Individual Projects</u>

1.     Ask students to visit a shopping mall or other large retail environment and observe the behavior of individual shoppers and groups of shoppers for an extended period. Have them record any behaviors that they witness that could be examples of the following concepts: vicarious learning, incidental learning, observational learning, classical conditioning, and instrumental conditioning. Have students present their findings to the class or discuss them in groups.

2.     Many brands attempt to capitalize on positive associations that consumers have for competing brands by copying certain characteristics. Have students identify an example of this and relate it to the halo effect.

3. Have students identify brand or corporate names that are based on semantic associations. Then have students ask five people what comes to mind when they hear each brand name. In reporting their findings, have students discuss whether or not company attempts to invoke certain perceptions appear to be working.

4. Assign students to locate a print advertisement that is a clear example of a marketer employing the concepts of stimulus generalization or stimulus discrimination. Have students present the ads to the class.

5. Have students identify an example of both positive reinforcement and negative reinforcement in a marketing context. As students present their findings in class, have the class discuss how effective each example is at establishing the desired or intended behavior.

6. Ask students to observe their friends, roommates, and co-workers for an extended period of time to identify an incidence of modeling as it relates to a celebrity. Have them note how the four conditions of modeling are met. Is the celebrity a brand endorser? How might their behavior be positive/negative for the marketers of the brands(s) that the celebrity endorses?

7. Have students think of specific examples where their sensory, short-term, and long-term memory have been activated by marketing information.

8. Ask each student to complete the following assignment based on a popular national brand: Collect as many pieces of promotional material (ads, direct mail, etc.) as possible for the brand. Based on this promotional evidence, identify any bits of information that marketers intend to be associated with the brand. Create an associative network for the brand, integrating the documented nodes of information with other nodes.

9. Assign each student to ask three friends to list as many brands as they can remember for a product class of their choosing. Have them ask each friend questions about each brand on the list to get a better idea of why each might have been recalled. Then, have them identify whether familiarity, salience, or other factors influencing recall were present. Were there differences between the first brands recalled and the others?

10. Have students identify what they think are strategic efforts by marketers to cause consumer to forget about competitor information by interfering with new information of their own.

## Group Projects

1. Create a long list of brand slogans from the past 10 or more years—e.g., Ford, where quality is job one; I want my MTV; Always Coca-Cola; Pizza-pizza (Little Caesar's); BMW: the ultimate driving machine. Divide the class into teams or simply in half. Read the brand slogans one at a time, omitting the brand name. Award points to the first team to correctly identify the brand associated with each slogan. Afterward, point out how

memory was strong, even for older slogans (some may be able to identify slogans from when they were very young children). Discuss why this is the case according to the principles of memory in the chapter.

2. Have student groups design an experiment that would demonstrate the occurrence of either classical conditioning or instrumental conditioning. Have them conduct their experiment on members of the class.

3. Have student groups visit a grocery store. How are marketers taking advantage of consumer ability to "chunk" information through strategies used on packaging?

4. Ask groups of students to design an experiment to test the process of state-dependent retrieval. Have them conduct the experiment on ten individuals, five in a mood-congruent condition and five in a mood-incongruent condition. Have the groups present their experiments and findings to the class.

5. Have student groups create a list of things that make them nostalgic. Then, during a period of a few days, have each of them identify ways that marketers of products targeted toward them have focused on any of these elements of nostalgia. Can they identify any nostalgia brands that are focused at their feelings of nostalgia? Have them share their findings with group members.

# eLAB

## Individual Assignments

1. Go to the following link on the Daimler-Chrysler Web site: **http://www.daimlerchrysler.com/dccom/0,,0-5-7182-1-392150-1-0-0-348452-0-0-243-7145-0-0-0-0-0-0-0,00.html.** Video games are so popular, why haven't joysticks found their way into real automobiles? DaimlerChrysler just might have an answer to that. How does their joystick approach work? Describe the learning process of driving such a vehicle according to the principles in this chapter. Based on learning alone, what are the barriers and opportunities to the success of a joystick car for today's drivers as well as those of tomorrow? The concept of schemas should be incorporated to this discussion.

2. Go to **www.BEaREP.com.** Tens of thousands of new products are introduced every year. Due to various barriers to entry, the vast majority of new products fail. One company has an approach that will help new products gain exposure. What is the approach taken by BEaREP.com? Which learning theory in this chapter can be directly applied to this approach? Considering this learning theory, how might the BEaREP.com approach work or not work?

3. Go to **www.levis.com.** Levis Strauss is a brand that is 150 years old. But the long dominant player in the jeans and apparel industry has struggled in recent years to regain

market share that it has lost to more youthful brands. Visit their Web site and discuss what strategies the company appears to be using to attract Generation Y (30 million plus individuals born between 1979 and 1987). What forms of learning is the company attempting to use to reacquire a youthful audience? Be specific in your description and provide illustrations of your ideas from the Web site to support chapter concepts.

4. Go to **www.gogorillamedia.com.** Become familiar with the advertising product offerings from this company. What previously useless space is this company turning in to valuable advertising space? What advertisers might be most interested in the various types of ad space options? How would each affect learning and memory? What memory processes would be most critical to the success of the different ad options?

## Group Assignments

1. Go to **www.ifilm.com/superbowl.** As a group, visit the Web site and review ads from the most recent Super Bowl . For the more well-known ads, create both recall and recognition tests. Give one type of the other to different students in class (this can be done after showing the ads, or not showing the ads if they are well-known enough). Compare the results.

2. Go to **www.mitchellandness.com.** Many companies have incorporated an element of nostalgia into their strategies to help boost sales. But this company's product line relies entirely on nostalgia. Mitchell and Ness has achieved substantial success with a line of throwback sports apparel. As a group, create a profile for the market(s) you think this company is targeting. Explain how nostalgia is the cornerstone of this company's success and how this principle works by applying learning and memory processes. Based on your analysis, design a print ad that emphasizes the "nostalgia" theme for this company's products.

# CHAPTER

# *MOTIVATION AND VALUES*

## CHAPTER OBJECTIVES

When students finish this chapter they should understand why:

- It's important for marketers to recognize that products can satisfy a range of consumer needs.

- The way we evaluate and choose a product depends upon our degree of involvement with the product, the marketing message, and/or the purchase situation.

- Our deeply held cultural values dictate the types of products and services we seek out or avoid.

- Consumers vary in the importance they attach to worldly possessions, and this orientation in turn has an impact on their priorities and behaviors.

## CHAPTER SUMMARY

Marketers try to satisfy consumer needs, but the reasons any product is purchased can vary widely. The identification of consumer motives is an important step in ensuring that the appropriate needs will be met by a product. *Motivation* refers to the processes that cause people to behave as they do. Marketers are very interested in consumer *goals*, *drives*, and *wants*.

Traditional approaches to consumer behavior have focused on the abilities of products to satisfy rational needs (utilitarian motives), but hedonic motives (e.g., the need for exploration or for fun) also play a role in many purchase decisions. *Drive theory* focuses on biological needs that produce unpleasant states of arousal. This theory explains some of human behavior but not all. *Expectancy theory* suggests that behavior is largely pulled by expectations of achieving desirable outcomes—positive incentives—rather than pushed from within.

Motivational conflicts occur. Three conflicts are characterized in the chapter. First, in an approach-approach conflict, a person must choose between two desirable alternatives. Second, in approach-avoidance conflict, many products and services we desire have negative consequences attached to them. Lastly, in avoidance-avoidance conflict, consumers face a choice with two undesirable alternatives.

As demonstrated by Maslow's hierarchy of needs, the same product can satisfy different needs, depending upon the consumer's state at the time. In addition to the consumer's objective situation (i.e., whenever basic physiological needs have already been satisfied), the consumer's degree of involvement with the product must be considered.

A fact of the marketplace is that not all consumers are motivated to the same extent. *Involvement* refers to the level of perceived personal importance and/or interest evoked by a stimulus (or stimuli) within a specific situation. Involvement has many faces. Included in these are product involvement, message-response involvement, and purchase situation involvement. Degree of involvement becomes a means by which to segment a market and, therefore, devise strategies to reach different involved segments.

Consumer motivations are often driven by underlying *values*. In this context, products take on meaning because they are seen as being instrumental in helping the person to achieve some goal that is linked to a value (such as individuality or freedom). Numerous forms of values are examined in the chapter. Also examined are scales that measure the shift in values over time. This chapter concludes with an examination of the impact that the events of September 11, 2001, had on societal values.

# CHAPTER OUTLINE

**1. The Motivation Process**
  a. **Motivation** refers to the processes that cause people to behave as they do. Once a need has been activated, a state of tension exists that drives the consumer to attempt to reduce or eliminate the need.
  b. Needs can be:
    1) *Utilitarian*—a desire to achieve some functional or practical benefit.
    2) *Hedonic*—an experiential need, involving emotional responses or fantasies.
  c. The desired end state is the consumer's **goal**. Marketers try to create products and services that will provide the desired benefits and permit the consumer to reduce this tension.
  d. With the consideration of unmet needs, a discrepancy exists between the consumer's present state and some ideal state. Tension is created. The consumer seeks to reduce tension. The degree of arousal is called a **drive**.
  e. Personal and cultural factors combine to create a **want**. This is one manifestation of a need.
    1) Once a goal is attained, tension is reduced and the motivation recedes.
    2) Motivation can be described in terms of:
      a) Its *strength*.
      b) Its *direction*.

> *Discussion Opportunity*—Ask: *Pretend you are to explain motivation to a friend. What would you say? What examples would you use? (Do the same substituting goal, drive, and want.)*

> *Discussion Opportunity—Bring in examples of magazine ads that demonstrate an attempt to activate (a) a utilitarian need or (b) a hedonic need.*

## 2. Motivational Strength
  a. The degree to which a person is willing to expend energy to reach one goal as opposed to another reflects his or her underlying motivation to attain that goal.

<u>Biological Versus Learned Needs</u>
  b. Early work on motivation ascribed behavior to instinct (the innate patterns of behavior that are universal in a species). When an instinct is inferred from the behavior it is supposed to explain, this circular explanation is called ***tautology***.
  c. Drive theory focuses on biological needs that produce unpleasant states of arousal.
    1) Tension reduction has been proposed as a basic mechanism governing human behavior.
    2) **Homeostasis**—goal-oriented behavior that attempts to reduce or eliminate an unpleasant state and return to a balanced one.
    3) **Drive theory** runs into difficulty when it tries to explain why people sometimes do things that might increase a drive state (such as delaying gratification).
  d. **Expectancy theory** suggests that behavior is largely pulled by expectations of achieving desirable outcomes—positive incentives—rather than pushed from within.

> *Discussion Opportunity—Ask: Can you think of purchase situations that illustrate drive theory and expectancy theory? Which one of the theories do you think is superior?*

> *Discussion Opportunity—If a car of tourists drives into an unfamiliar town at meal time and stops at McDonald's instead of an equally attractive and price-competitive JOE'S Eats, which of the two theories (expectancy or drive) would probably be at work? How would JOE'S combat this?*

## 3. Motivational Direction
  a. Motives have direction as well as strength. Most goals can be reached by a number of paths.

<u>Needs Versus Wants</u>
  b. The specific way a need is satisfied depends on the individual's unique history, learning experiences, and his or her cultural environment.
    1) The particular form of consumption used to satisfy a need is termed a *want*.

<u>Types of Needs</u>
  c. Needs can be:
    1) ***Biogenic needs***—food, water, air, and shelter.
    2) ***Psychogenic needs***—power, status, affiliation.
    3) ***Utilitarian needs***—emphasizes objective, tangible attributes (miles per gallon).
    4) ***Hedonic needs***—subjective and experiential (excitement, self-confidence, fantasy).

Motivational Conflicts

d. A goal has **valence**, which means that it can be positive or negative. Therefore goals can be sought or avoided.

   1) Not all behavior is motivated by the desire to approach a goal.

   2) Consumers often find themselves in situations in which different motives, both positive and negative, conflict with one another.

e. Conflicts can occur. Three different types of goal conflicts are:
   1) **Approach-approach conflict**—a person must choose between two desirable alternatives.
      a) The **theory of cognitive dissonance** is based on the premise that people have a need for order and consistency in their lives and that a state of tension is created when beliefs or behaviors conflict with one another.
      b) People attempt to reduce dissonance.
      c) A state of dissonance exists when there is a psychological inconsistency between two or more beliefs or behaviors.

   2) **Approach-avoidance conflict**—many products or services we desire have negative consequences attached to them.

   3) **Avoidance-avoidance conflict**—a choice between two undesirable alternatives.

*****Use Figure 4.1 Here *****

Classifying Consumer Needs

  f. Much research has been done on classifying human needs.

    1) Various universal need classifications have been attempted.

    2) There seems to be *no universally* accepted list (though many needs are common to all lists).

      a) Murray's psychogenic needs—used as the basis for the Thematic Appreciation Test (TAT).

  g. Those needs that seem particularly relevant to buying behavior include:

    1) *Need for achievement.*

    2) *Need for affiliation.*

    3) *Need for power.*

    4) *Need for uniqueness.*

  h. Maslow's hierarchy of needs implies that the order of development is fixed. This hierarchy is most closely associated with product benefits that people might be looking for. Lower order needs must be satisfied before climbing the needs ladder. The needs are:

    1) *Physiological.*

    2) *Safety.*

    3) *Social.*

    4) *Esteem.*

    5) *Self-actualization.*

---

*****Use Figure 4.2 Here *****

---

  i. Problems with Maslow's method include:

    1) Climbing the ladder is not set in stone. Some activities cover several levels of needs.

    2) The hierarchy may be culture-bound.

    3) Consumer's have different needs priorities.

---

*****Use Consumer Behavior Challenge #6 Here *****

---

*Discussion Opportunity—(a) Tell the class about a product you could buy that could fit into all five levels of Maslow's hierarchy of needs; (b) Bring an advertisement to class that demonstrates each one of the needs (you may have to bring five ads).*

---

**4. Consumer Involvement**

  a. **Involvement** refers to "a person's perceived relevance of the object based on their inherent needs, values, and interests."

    1) Involvement can be viewed as the motivation to process information.

    2) As involvement increases, people devote more attention to ads related to the product, exert more cognitive effort to understand these ads, and focus their attention on the product-related information in them.

> **\*\*\*\*\*Use Figure 4.3 Here \*\*\*\*\***

> *Discussion Opportunity—Ask: Who can give me an example of involvement with a product category or brand? How can marketers use involvement to construct advertising campaigns?*

Levels of Involvement: From Inertia to Passion
  b. The type of information processing that will occur depends upon the consumer's level of involvement. It can range from simple to elaborate processing.
   1) **Simple processing**—only basic features of a message are considered.
   2) **Elaboration**—information is linked to one's preexisting knowledge systems.
  c. Because a person's degree of involvement can be conceived as a continuum, consumption at the low end of involvement is characterized by **inertia**.
   1) In this state, decisions are made out of habit because the consumer lacks the information to consider alternatives.
   2) To the contrary, decisions can be very passionate and carry great meaning for a person.
   3) In consumer situations of high involvement, the consumer enters a **flow state**, where the consumer is in an elated state of focus and concentration and loses track of time.
  d. **Cult products** command fierce consumer loyalty, devotion, even worship.

> **\*\*\*\*\*Use Consumer Behavior Challenge #5 Here \*\*\*\*\***

> *Discussion Opportunity—Ask the class to think of a time when they purchased something based on the concept of inertia or passion. Have students share what they thought of.*

The Many Faces of Involvement
  d. Involvement can be cognitive or emotional. There are several types of broad involvement:
   1) **Product involvement** is related to a consumer's level of interest in a particular product. Sales promotions increase this involvement. A powerful way to enhance product involvement is through **mass customization**.
   2) **Message-response involvement** (or advertising involvement), refers to the consumer's interest in processing marketing communications. **Vigilante marketing**, where freelancers and fans film their own commercials for favorite products and post them on Web sites, is a hot trend.
    a) Television is considered a low-involvement medium.
    b) Print is considered a high-involvement medium.
   3) **Purchase-situation involvement** refers to differences that may occur when buying the same object for different contexts. Social risk is considered.

> *Discussion Opportunity—Illustrate each of the "faces of involvement." How would marketers make appeals in these areas? Provide illustrations of when "gift giving" might fall under each of the involvement situations.*

## 5. Measuring Involvement

    a. Measurement of involvement is important for a variety of reasons.

      1)  An *involvement profile* can be constructed using the following components:

        a)  Personal interest in a product category.

        b)  Perceived importance of the potential negative consequences associated with a poor product choice.

        c)  The probability of making a bad purchase.

        d)  The pleasure value of the product category.

        e)  The sign value of the product category.

---

*****Use Table 4.1 and Table 4.2 Here *****

---

*Discussion Opportunity—Create a handout using the consumer involvement scale in Table 4.1 to measure involvement of two or three different products. Have the students quickly respond to the scale and total their scores. Ask for general ranges of scores for each product or have specific students share their scores. Encourage students to discuss the results and whether or not they accurately describe how they feel about each product.*

---

*Discussion Opportunity—Ask: What are some products that people buy that seem to require a great deal of involvement?*

---

      2)  It is possible to segment by involvement levels. There is diversity among involvement groups.

      3)  There are specific strategies that can be used to increase involvement.

        a)  Appeal to hedonic needs (sensory appeals).

        b)  Use novel stimuli (cinematography, sudden silences, or unexpected movements in commercials).

        c)  Use prominent stimuli (loud music, large ads, color, or fast action).

        d)  Include celebrity endorsers.

        e)  Build a bond with the consumer (relationship marketing—example, R. J. Reynolds Tobacco).

---

*****Use Consumer Behavior Challenges #8 and #5 (Used Previously) Here *****

---

*Discussion Opportunity—Construct and then discuss an example of market segmentation based on involvement.*

---

    b. A **value** is a belief that some condition is preferable to its opposite.

      1)  Two people can believe in the same behaviors but their underlying belief systems may be quite different.

      2)  Consumers often seek out those that have similar belief systems to their own.

---

*Discussion Opportunity—Ask students to share examples of how people with similar values band together. Bring in some example ads illustrating this concept.*

---

Core Values

   c. Every culture has a set of **core values** that it imparts to its members. Core values do change over time. In many cases, values are universal.

     1) What sets cultures apart is the *relative importance* or ranking of universal values. This set of rankings is a culture's **value system.**

     2) Every culture is characterized by its members' endorsement of a value system.

     3) Each set of core values that uniquely define a culture is taught to that culture by *socialization agents* (parents, friends, and teachers).

       a) The process of learning the beliefs and behaviors endorsed by one's own culture is termed **enculturation.**

       b) **Acculturation** is the process of learning the value system and behaviors of another culture.

---

*Discussion Opportunity—Ask: What are some values that are important to you? Which of these values are transferred to your purchase behavior? In what way?*

---

Applications of Values to Consumer Behavior

   d. Despite their importance, values have not been as widely applied to direct examination of consumer behavior as might be expected. The reason is that many values are very general or relative by nature (e.g., freedom, security, inner peace). Because values drive much of consumer behavior, it could be said that virtually all consumer research is ultimately related to the identification and measurement of values.

     1) Research has tended to classify values as being:

       a) *Cultural* (such as security).

       b) *Consumption-specific* (such as convenient shopping or prompt service).

       c) *Product-specific* (such as ease of use or durability).

     2) Research in values:

       a) The Rokeach Value Survey—the psychologist Milton Rokeach identified two sets of values:

         1. **Terminal values**—desired end-states that apply to many different cultures.

         2. **Instrumental values**—composed of actions needed to achieve these terminal values.

---

**\*\*\*\*\*Use Table 4.3 Here \*\*\*\*\***

---

*Discussion Opportunity—Provide an example that illustrates terminal values and instrumental values. How do these values relate to advertising attempts to influence behavior?*

---

       b) The List of Values (LOV)—identifies nine consumer segments based on the values they endorse (and then relates these to consumption).

       c) The Means-End Chain Model—specific product attributes are linked at increasing abstraction to terminal values via "laddering." **Laddering** is a technique whereby consumers' associations between specific attributes and general consequences are uncovered.

---

*****Use Figure 4.4 Here*****

---

*Discussion Opportunity—Provide an illustration of the means-end chain model. Comment on applications and usefulness of the model.*

---

   d)  Syndicated Surveys—a variety of surveys are available.
     1. The Yankelovich *Monitor* attempts to track changes in values over time.
     2. This survey identifies **voluntary simplifiers** as consumers who believe that once basic needs are met, additional income will not add to happiness.
     3. Modern syndicated surveys that track changes in values are VALS2, GlobalScan, New Wave, and the Lifestyles Study.

---

*****Use Table 4.4 Here; Use Consumer Behavior Challenge #2 Here *****

---

Materialism: "He Who Dies with the Most Toys, Wins . . ."
e. **Materialism** refers to the importance people attach to worldly possessions.
   1)  America is a highly materialistic society.
   2)  Materialists are more likely to value possessions for their status and appearance-related meanings.

---

*****Use Consumer Behavior Challenge #1 Here *****

---

*Discussion Opportunity—What is your opinion on materialism? Is it good or bad? Be careful how you answer this. How do marketers use materialism to their advantage? What is the alternative to materialism? Would this be good for our economy?*

---

Consumer Behavior in the Aftermath of September 11
a. The events of September 11, 2001, led to a marked shift in values. **Terror management theory** argues that anxiety and awareness of mortality motivates people to cling to deep-seated cultural beliefs.
b. This value shift was evident in the shift in consumer purchases from travel and hospitality to home improvement products and carryout foods.
c. One of the biggest value shifts related to consumers' willingness to sacrifice privacy for security.

# End-of-Chapter Support Material

# SUMMARY OF SPECIAL FEATURE BOXES

### 1.    Marketing Opportunity I

Those toll free numbers on product packages can be more than an outlet for customers to complain. As Nestle has learned, they can be a valuable source for conducting marketing research and gathering information on customer wants and needs.

### 2.    Net Profit

A current trend in the customer use of software is that of users designing their own **skins**. A skin is a graphical user interface that acts as both the face and the control panel of a computer program. Computer programs come with the standard or default interface. But for many, that's boring and uninviting. So for a product like Real Player, more than 15,000,000 skins have been created by users. Such skins are often made available through Web sites, allowing users to swap and customize their user experience.

### 3.    Marketing Opportunity II

**LOHAS** (lifestyles of health and sustainability) is a market segment that many marketers are recognizing. The label refers to people who worry about the environment, want products to be produced in a sustainable way, and who spend money to advance what they see as their personal development and potential. Estimates are that this group accounts for as many as a third of the U.S. adult population.

### 4.    The Global Looking Glass

This box takes a look at the global perceptions of U.S. brands and the decline in sales that many such brands have experienced. This feature supports the section "The Rokeach Value Survey."

### 5.    Marketing Opportunity III

This cultural vignette demonstrates how the values treasured by some cultures create the opportunity for products that would seem obscure to other cultures. Illustrated is Japan's fixation on time spent in the bathroom and the market that this has created for various types of toilet features. This feature supports the section "Values."

### 6.    Marketing Pitfalls I

This box focuses on the impact that cultural values can have on the marketing of products. Tampons are featured as a specific product that has met resistance in various countries. This feature supports the section "Values."

**7.** **Marketing Pitfalls II**

This box highlights the downside to shopping enthusiasm: consumers turning unruly.


# REVIEW QUESTIONS

1. What is motivation, and how is this idea relevant to marketing? ***Motivation*** *refers to the processes that lead people to behave as they do. It occurs when a need is aroused that the consumer wishes to satisfy. Once a need has been activated, a state of tension exists that drives the consumer to attempt to reduce or eliminate the need. Marketers try to create products and services that will provide the desired benefits and permit the consumer to reduce this tension.*

2. Describe three types of motivational conflicts, citing an example of each from current marketing campaigns. *In an **approach–approach conflict**, a person must choose between two desirable alternatives. A student might be torn between going home for the holidays or going on a skiing trip with friends. Many of the products and services we desire have negative consequences attached to them as well. We may feel guilty or ostentatious when buying a status-laden product such as a fur coat, or we might feel like a glutton when contemplating a tempting package of Twinkies. An **approach–avoidance conflict** exists when we desire a goal but wish to avoid it at the same time. Sometimes consumers find themselves "caught between a rock and a hard place." They may face a choice with two undesirable alternatives, for instance, the option of either throwing more money into an old car or buying a new one. Marketers frequently address an **avoidance–avoidance conflict** with messages that stress the unforeseen benefits of choosing one option (e.g., by emphasizing special credit plans to ease the pain of car payments).*

3. Explain the difference between a need and a want. *The specific way a need is satisfied depends on the individual's unique history, learning experiences, and cultural environment. A want is the particular form of consumption used to satisfy a need. For example, two classmates may feel their stomachs rumbling during a lunchtime lecture. If neither person has eaten since the night before, the strength of their respective needs (hunger) would be about the same. However, the ways each person goes about satisfying this need might be quite different.*

4. What is cognitive dissonance? *The **theory of cognitive dissonance** is based on the premise that people have a need for order and consistency in their lives and that a state of tension is created when beliefs or behaviors conflict with one another. The conflict that arises when choosing between two alternatives may be resolved through a process of cognitive dissonance reduction, where people are motivated to reduce this inconsistency (or dissonance) and thus eliminate unpleasant tension.*

5.  Name the levels in Maslow's hierarchy of needs, and give an example of a marketing appeal that is focused at each level.

    - ***Physiological***: *"I like to work in the soil."*
    - ***Safety***: *"I feel safe in the garden."*
    - ***Social***: *"I can share my produce with others."*
    - ***Esteem***: *"I can create something of beauty."*
    - ***Self-actualization***: *"My garden gives me a sense of peace."*

6.  What is consumer involvement? How does this concept relate to motivation? *We can define **involvement** as "a person's perceived relevance of the object based on their inherent needs, values, and interests." The word object is used in the generic sense and refers to a product (or a brand), an advertisement, or a purchase situation. Consumers can find involvement in all these objects.*

7.  Why would marketers want their customers to enter into a flow state when shopping for their products? *When consumers are truly involved with a product, an ad, or a Web site, they enter what a **flow state**. This state is the Holy Grail of Web designers who want to create sites that are so entrancing the surfer loses all track of time as he becomes engrossed in the site's contents (and hopefully buys stuff in the process!).*

8.  List three types of consumer involvement, giving an example of each type.

    1.  *Product involvement refers to a consumer's level of interest in a particular product. Many sales promotions are designed to increase this type of involvement. When Lifesavers announced that it was going to eliminate the pineapple flavor unless consumers went to its Web site and voted to keep it, over 400,000 consumers heard the call and saved the flavor.*
    2.  *Vigilante marketing, where freelancers and fans film their own commercials for favorite products and post them on Web sites, is hot. In one unauthorized spot produced by a teacher that got media attention in magazines like Wired and on advertising blogs like AdRants, an iPod Mini zips around to the song "Tiny Machine" by the Darling Buds. This devotion to creating a commercial is an extreme example of message–response involvement (also known as advertising involvement) that refers to the consumer's interest in processing marketing communications.*
    3.  *Purchase situation involvement refers to differences that may occur when buying the same object for different contexts. Here the person may perceive a great deal of social risk or none at all. For example, when you want to impress someone you may try to buy a brand with a certain image that you think reflects good taste. When you have to buy a gift for someone in an obligatory situation, like a wedding gift for a cousin you do not really like, you may not care what image the gift portrays.*

9.   What are some strategies marketers can use to increase consumers' involvement with their products?

   • *Appeal to the consumers' hedonic needs. For example, ads using sensory appeals generate higher levels of attention.*
   • *Use novel stimuli, such as unusual cinematography, sudden silences, or unexpected movements in commercials. When a British firm called Egg Banking introduced a credit card to the French market, its ad agency created unusual commercials to make people question their assumptions. One ad stated "Cats always land on their paws," and then two researchers in white lab coats dropped a kitten off a rooftop—never to see it again (animal rights activists were not amused).*
   • *Use prominent stimuli, such as loud music and fast action, to capture attention in commercials. In print formats, larger ads increase attention. Also, viewers look longer at colored pictures as opposed to black and white.*
   • *Include celebrity endorsers to generate higher interest in commercials. (We'll discuss this strategy in Chapter 8.)*
   • *Build a bond with consumers by maintaining an ongoing relationship with them. Learn from the actions of tobacco companies that have figured out how to keep smokers' loyalties (at least until they die). R. J. Reynolds Co. hosted nearly 3,700 Doral smokers at its factory for Western line dancing lessons, bowling, blackjack, and plenty of free cigarettes. Said one happy attendee, "I'd quit altogether before I'd change brands." Now there's a thought.*

10.  What are values, and why should marketers care? *A **value** is a belief that some condition is preferable to its opposite. For example, it's safe to assume that most people place a priority on freedom, preferring it to slavery. Others avidly pursue products and services that will make them look young, believing that this is preferable to appearing old. A person's set of values plays a very important role in consumption activities. Consumers purchase many products and services because they believe these products will help to attain a value-related goal.*

11.  What is the difference between enculturation and acculturation? *How do we figure out what a culture values? We term the process of learning the beliefs and behaviors endorsed by one's own culture **enculturation**. In contrast, we call the process of learning the value system and behaviors of another culture (often a priority for those who wish to understand consumers and markets in foreign countries) **acculturation**.*

12.  What are LOHAS, and why are they important? *Some American marketers are starting to focus on a potentially huge value segment they are calling LOHAS—an acronym for "lifestyles of health and sustainability." This label refers to people who worry about the environment, want products to be produced in a sustainable way and who spend money to advance what they see as their personal development and potential. These consumers represent a great market for products such as organic foods, energy-efficient appliances and hybrid cars as well as alternative medicine, yoga tapes, and eco-tourism.*

13.    Describe at least two alternative techniques marketing researchers have used to measure
       values.

   - ***The Rokeach Value Survey***. *The psychologist Milton Rokeach identified a set of*
     ***terminal values***, *or desired end states, that apply to many different cultures. The
     Rokeach Value Survey, a scale used to measure these values, also includes a set of
     **instrumental values**, which are composed of actions needed to achieve these
     terminal values.*
   - ***The List of Values (LOV) Scale*** *was developed to isolate values with more direct
     marketing applications. This instrument identifies nine consumer segments based on
     the values they endorse and relates each value to differences in consumption
     behaviors. These segments include consumers who place a priority on such values as
     a sense of belonging, excitement, warm relationships with others, and security.*
   - ***Means-end Chain***. *Another research approach that incorporates values is termed a
     means–end chain model. This approach assumes that very specific product attributes
     are linked at levels of increasing abstraction to terminal values. The person has
     valued end states, and he or she chooses among alternative means to attain these
     goals. Products are thus valued as the means to an end.*
   - ***Syndicated survey***. *A number of companies track changes in values through large-
     scale surveys. They sell the results of these studies to marketers, who often also pay
     a fee to receive regular updates on changes and trends.*

14.    What is the value of materialism? ***Materialism*** *refers to the importance people attach to
       worldly possessions. We sometimes take the bounty of products and services for granted,
       until we remember how recent this abundance is. For example, in 1950 two of five
       American homes did not have a telephone, and in 1940 half of all households still did not
       possess complete indoor plumbing.*

# CONSUMER BEHAVIOR CHALLENGE

## Discussion Questions

1.    "College students' concerns about the environment and vegetarianism are just a passing
      fad: a way to look 'cool.' " Do you agree?

      *Students will have mixed views about this subject. What they need to see is that a fad that
      lasts for some length of time becomes a value (or is at least tied to values). For example,
      is the trend toward not smoking a value or a fad? The value might be healthy living or
      avoidance of what is now considered to be a nasty habit. The result is not smoking. Those
      who smoke might not only do it because they like it but as a way to be peer accepted or
      make a nonconformity statement (or to shock their parents and other authority figures).
      Ask students for their feelings about these subjects. How can the marketer capitalize on
      these "value" feelings? How do consumers reinforce their deep-seated values?*

2.  Some market analysts see a shift in values among young people. They claim that this generation has not had a lot of stability in their lives. They are fed up with superficial relationships and are yearning for a return to tradition. This change is reflected in attitudes toward marriage and family. One survey of 22- to 24-year-old women found that 82 percent thought motherhood was the most important job in the world. Brides magazine reports a swing toward traditional weddings—80 percent of brides today are tossing their garters; Daddy walks 78 percent of them down the aisle. What's your take on this? Are young people indeed returning to the values of their parents (or even their grandparents)? How have these changes influenced your perspective on marriage and family?

    *Various answers are likely to arise. When asked if they are returning to the values of their parents or grandparents, many students will shudder at that thought, regardless of how they might be leaning. The way that students respond to this question will depend very much on how they have been raised. The question itself asserts that "this generation" has not had stability in their lives. Although this may be true in many instances, it is also true that many students come from very stable homes. Additionally, students may recognize that they desire more traditional values in some ways (such as a traditional wedding), but not in others (such as cohabitating or desiring a dual-income home).*

3.  How do you think consumers have changed as a result of 9/11? Are these changes long-term or will we start to revert back to our pre-2001 mindset?

    *The text mentions various ways that consumer values have changed as a result of 9/11. There were short-term effects on air travel and hospitality that seem to have recovered (although the airline industries face other problems of their own). But as for more long-term effects, people have reacted in sometimes opposing ways. Television programming saw some impact in the demand for more programming reflecting traditional values. And yet, it can also be noted that there is a higher level of crime and violence programs, many reflecting terrorism themes. Post 9/11, there was a measurable change in the number of people focusing on more utilitarian goods rather than luxury goods. But at the same time, there were many subscribing to the "can't take it with you" mentality, and have splurged even more than before. The effect that 9/11 continues to have on people and their consumer behavior likely has a great deal to do with personal views on the war on terror and how that is being handled by governments.*

4.  Core values evolve over time. What do you think are the three to five core values that best describe Americans now?

    *This question could just as easily be applied to whatever country or society that serves as the base for the student body taking the course. Regardless, responses will likely differ between those who are natives and those who are foreign. As for the core values for the United States, the basics have been the same for quite some time. U.S. citizens are more individualistic than collectivistic (more importance placed on the individual than the overall group), more monochromic than polychromic (more importance placed on punctuality and schedules), and more low context than high context (communication depending less on context and more on literal text and spoken language). However, as far as trends that tend to come and go, the core values of Americans will likely vary depending on age, ethnicity, and other demographic factors. Some factors that may arise are health, environment, and public safety, among others. However, whether or not it is determined that consumer's pay more or less attention to these issues will likely vary.*

5.    "High involvement is just a fancy term for expensive." Do you agree?

*If students have an inadequate understanding of involvement, it is likely that they will agree with this statement. What needs to be made clear is that the price of a product is only one potential determinant of product involvement. The instructor should stress the role that personal relevance of the product has for an individual and point out that it is influenced by the person, the product, and the unique purchase/consumption situation. A good exercise would be for students to develop a list of items that they would classify as high involvement. Along with the list, they should provide price estimates for each item (or simply note them as "expensive" or "not expensive"). This type of display would illustrate the lack of association between involvement and price.*

## Application Questions

6.    Devise separate promotional strategies for an article of clothing, each of which stresses one of the levels of Maslow's hierarchy of needs.

*Students should be encouraged to review Maslow's hierarchy of needs, including physiological, safety, belongingness, esteem, and self-actualization. Although their selection of clothing articles for this exercise may be diverse, there is likely to be some consistency within need categories. Examples include: 1) the promotion of name-brand/designer-label clothing stressing consumers' need to belong to a particular social group; 2) the promotion of warm and durable jackets or boots stressing consumer physiological need; 3) the promotion of protective equipment for amateur athletes (e.g., knee and elbow guards, helmets, and goggles) stressing consumers' safety needs; 4) the promotion of elegant dress or a tux for esteem; and 5) anything you want to wear (like Sam Walton did) because clothes don't matter that much to you.*

7.    Collect a sample of ads that appear to appeal to consumers' values. What value is being communicated in each ad, and how is this done? Is this an effective approach to designing a marketing communication?

*Encourage students to look at the types of values in either the Rokeach Value Survey or List of Values (LOV) to determine which consumer values they would like to share with the class. (Possible Field Project Idea)*

8. Describe how a man's level of involvement with his car would affect how he is influenced by different marketing stimuli. How might you design a strategy for a line of car batteries for a segment of low-involvement consumers, and how would this strategy differ from your attempts to reach a segment of men who are very involved in working on their cars?

   *Different levels of involvement with a product influence the amount of attention paid to marketing stimuli, affecting the amount of cognitive processing capacity directed toward stimuli (e.g., the product related information in an ad). In discussing the development of advertising targeted at low-involvement consumers, students should recognize that peripheral cues are used in place of product-related information. Behaviors resulting from such cues do not last long and are likely to change over time. (Bobby Unser uses a Die-Hard battery!) Conversely, developing advertising directed toward high-involvement consumers will rely less on peripheral cues and more on substantial product-related information (i.e., the central route to persuasion). Behaviors resulting from this emphasis will be more resistant to change. (How many amps? How many minutes of reserve capacity? What are the cold cranking amps? What are the marine cranking amps?).*

9. Interview members of a celebrity fan club. Describe their level of involvement with the "product," and devise some marketing opportunities to reach this group.

   *Student responses to this exercise might consider a variety of celebrities—movie stars, musicians, and politicians—living and dead. They might be asked to consider the Elvis Presley fan club phenomenon in terms of the tremendous marketing opportunities that have derived from tours of his home in Memphis (Graceland), his personal property displayed in "museums" (guitars, clothing, music awards, etc.), his "signature" hairstyle and sideburns, other actors' and musicians' remakes of his movies and songs, television programs, Elvis parades, books, postage stamps, etc. The quickest way to do this project is to "go online" to a "favorite site." Most of the recognized search engines (e.g., Yahoo!) will have ways for you to reach the celebrity sites.*
   *(Possible Field Project Idea)*

# CASE STUDY TEACHING NOTES

### Chapter 4 Case Study: Campbell's Soup on the Go

### Summary of Case

Campbell's Soup Company, under the direction of Chief Strategy Officer Carl Johnson, is in the midst of a major turnaround. The company that is synonymous with soup has struggled for growth for quite some time. But now, they are riding a wave of success based on a series of new product introductions. The product line highlighted in this case is the Soup at Hand line. These are soups that come in single-serving, contoured, microwaveable containers with a plastic sipping cap. They have been designed for to be sold through convenience stores for people to literally have a meal on the run.

## Suggestions for Presentation

This case is clearly applicable to the various need-based concepts as taught in the text. The discussion questions for the case have positioned the case as such. But instructors should not overlook the relationship between values and needs. In this context of this case, what are the values that have changed in the United States that are making products such as these big hits, when they likely would have failed 20 or even 10 years ago? This is a perfect product to illustrate that people in the United States are working more (including dual-income homes) and have less time for things like eating and cooking. People are also multi-tasking (eat while you drive). Although much of this has been driven by the circumstances that people find themselves in, the discussion of this case should at least touch on the possibility that today's high need for convenience has evolved and that consumers have likely been conditioned to want more and more convenience products. The case highlights the fact that opening a regular can of soup and heating it in a microwave container isn't really any more difficult than heating up a Soup at Hand soup. But, consumers perceive a big difference. That's why traditional canned soup sales are lagging, and products like these are taking off.

## Suggested Answers for Discussion Questions

1.  What consumer needs are driving the success of products like Campbell's Soup at Hand? Consider both biological and learned needs.

    *Hunger and nourishment are biological needs. But of course, those can be satisfied by any number of products. This new era of on-the-go eatables is being driven by consumer's need to save time. People are cooking at home less and less. But if one needs to eat out and eat quickly, why not go through a drive-thru? Evidently, there are plenty of people who have situations where even that takes too much time. Grabbing a soup while the car is filling up takes care of the need for quick nourishment. Putting it in the cup holder and eating while driving and talking on the cell phone ensures that eating has not taken a moment out of a person's busy schedule. As mentioned above, there are also the learned needs that consumers pick up. Companies have responded to the need for convenience with their products, but they have also taught us to want more and more convenience oriented products through offering innovations such as these.*

2.  Are some needs more powerful than others? Illustrate this by discussing the needs that customers might be sacrificing in order to satisfy other needs.

    *This could be related to Maslow's Hierarchy of Needs. Hunger is a base level need and a strong one at that. There are those that without a convenient way to eat on the go would not be able to satisfy the hunger need as often as they would like. Yet, proper nourishment is also a need, one that fits into the level of safety. Are consumers forgoing some health benefits with such products? How about taste? The case describes how the soups had to be modified in order to work in this packaging option. Evidently, some people have a stronger need for convenience than they do a need for the same soups that they are familiar with.*

# Additional Support Material

# STUDENT PROJECTS

## Individual Projects

1. Ask students to have ten people describe the personality of one of the following products or another product of the students' choosing: Mountain Dew; iPod; Buick; Prada; Wal-Mart; a specific local restaurant or pub. How are the descriptions similar? How are they different? (This question might be done as an in-class activity, assigning each student to interview five different people within the class itself. Simply direct students to mingle about the room, pairing off with another person, and interviewing each other. Allow students to continue until each has interviewed at least five other people.)

2. Have students think of examples of products or services that each of them have purchased that fit the three types of motivational conflicts found in *Figure 4.1*.

3. Find a student who is not too shy to do this one. Ask the student to search for unconscious motives by asking six people if they are wearing perfume or cologne. Make sure they keep asking until at least three people say, "Yes." Then have them ask the respondents, "Why do you wear cologne?" Ask three of those who said they were not wearing cologne, "Why not?" Ask the three who said, "No" if they wore any the last time they had a date. Share their responses with the class and evaluate them. Can the class uncover any hidden motivations?

4. Ask students to come up with a list of products or services that people primarily buy because they want to "belong." Have them explain why they listed the particular items. Then, have them explain how each of the items that they listed might also be consumed by individuals in solitude. Are there viable needs that consumers have for consuming these products both in the company of others as well as by themselves?

5. Have each student extensively describe a consumption situation that reflects each of the following: need for affiliation, need for power, and need for uniqueness.

6. Have students find advertisements that attempt to persuade consumers to think of products as objects that satisfy one of the motives described in this chapter. Have them identify and classify that motive.

7. Ask students to find a print ad that appeals to each level of Maslow's hierarchy. In class, have different students show their ads and explain why their ads appeal to each level. Ask why they think the firm selected this particular appeal. Is there overlap between levels? Is this good or bad?

8. Have individual students construct an example of the means-end chain model for a specific product or brand. Explain the thought process used.

9.  Have your students think of some product or service they have purchased recently. Then have them respond to the consumer involvement scale in Table 4.1. Is their involvement with this product best described as product involvement, message-response involvement, or purchase situation involvement? Why?

10. Have each student list what he or she perceive to be the five most important values themselves. To their parents. How do these values transfer to purchase decisions? How would marketers find out about their values?

11. After reading the section "Materialism: 'He Who Dies with the Most Toys, Wins . . .,' " have students create an argument either for or against more materialism. Does the Internet promote materialism? Explain.

12. Have each student bring in an example of vigilante marketing, where freelancers and fans film their own commercials for favorite products and post them on Web sites. Call on students to share these examples in class.

## Group Projects

1.  Assign groups of students to observe a table of people eating in either a restaurant or cafeteria setting. See if they can identify any of the major motives at work. Have them report on their conclusions. (*Hint*: Watch the respondents' behavior while they eat and during their conversation. Perhaps students might like to videotape part of the meal—five minutes maximum) .

2.  Have groups of students come up with three examples of a truly mass customized product. For each, have them give extensive reasons as to why consumers might choose the mass customized version of a product over the "off-the-rack" version.

3.  Have the class keep a diary of their consumer decisions for a two-day period. (Make sure they include both actual purchases and conscious decisions not to buy.) At the end of the period have them review their diaries and classify their apparent motives. (Maslow's scheme may be useful here.) During this process were they more aware of ads? Have students discuss their diaries in groups.

4.  Have the group go to a shopping center or mall and observe others' behavior. What conclusions can they make about motives, involvement, and values after having made the observation?

5.  In a project related to #4, have groups of students visit a shopping mall or a superstore. Have them evaluate the retail environment for ways that both the retailer and product manufacturers try to increase consumer involvement (refer to text if necessary for strategies to increase involvement).

6. Have groups evaluate a purchase made by a teenager using roles or characteristics similar to those shown in Table 4.4.

7. The text specifies 9/11 as an event that changed consumer values. Have groups of students brainstorm other significant events that had an impact on the values of a given society's consumers. What were the events and what were the value changes?

# eLAB

## Individual Assignments

1. Go to **www.benjerry.com**. Ben & Jerry's Ice Cream is famous for a well-rounded mission statement and care and concern for the environment. What is their mission? What indications are there about the organization's commitment to the environment? What values does the company try to express? How might this expression help the organization market products?

2. Go to **www.wholefoods.com**. Take some time to become familiar with the Web site. Describe this company and the products that they offer. Select specific examples of products that seem to target the LOHAS values segment. Are these products that might appeal to values other than those described by LOHAS?

3. Go to **www.burton.com**. Burton Snowboards are very popular with Gen X. How does this Web site attempt to motivate consumers to try the sport and the Burton products? Be specific with the description of strategies that Burton uses. Do you think the Burton approach is effective? Explain.

4. Go to **http://shop.vans.com**. Find the link for creating your own custom pair of Vans shoes. Go through the process and print an example of your shoes to take in to class and share. Describe the experience. Did the experience contribute to the level of involvement in shopping for such a product?

5. Go to **www.specialized.com**. Specialized Bicycles is one of the leading manufacturers and marketers of all types of bikes. Browse their Web site. Give a brief description of their different product lines. How does Specialized motivate consumers to get into biking? Are there any value statements made (either directly or indirectly)? Explain. What might Specialized do to improve the "motivation" aspect of their site (you might want to compare it to the Burton Snowboard site discussed previously)?

6. Go to **www.gallup.com** or **www.pollingreport.com**. What can we learn about consumer behavior from polls? What can we learn about motivation and values from polls? Participate in one of the polls available on the Web site. Project what might have been learned about your motivations or values by participating in the poll. Comment.

## Group Assignments

1.  Go to **www.sric-bi.com**. Your group should explore the VALS, VALS2, and iVALS methods discussed on the Web site. Describe each of the methods. Pick one of the methods for further research. Have each group member take the VALS test online. What were the results? Comment on these methods as a means to explore consumer values. Devise an experiment by which VALS studies could be used to explore consumer values.

2.  Go to **www.burningman.com**. Become familiar with the purpose of this festival. As a group, discuss the extent to which it is possible to achieve the purposes set forth by this organization. Discuss the irony of this.

# CHAPTER 5

# *THE SELF*

## CHAPTER OBJECTIVES

When students finish this chapter they should understand why:

- The self-concept is strongly related to consumer behavior.

- Products often play a pivotal role in defining the self-concept.

- Sex-role identity is different than gender, and society's expectations of masculinity and femininity help to determine the products we buy to be consistent with these expectations.

- A person's sex-role identity is a major component of self-definition. The media play a key role in teaching us how to behave as "proper" males and females.

- The way we think about our bodies (and the way our culture tells us we should think) is a key component of self-esteem.

## CHAPTER SUMMARY

The *self-concept* refers to the beliefs a person holds about his or her attributes and how he or she evaluates these qualities. In other words, consumers' self-concepts are reflections of their attitudes toward themselves. Whether these attitudes are positive or negative, they will help to guide many purchase decisions—products can be used to bolster self-esteem or to "reward" the self.

*Self-esteem* refers to the positivity of a person's self-concept. Marketing communications can influence a consumer's level of self-esteem. Self-esteem is influenced by a process where the consumer compares his or her actual standing on some attribute to some ideal. In a way, each of us really has a number of different "selves" encased in our personality. Marketers must identify these "selves" and direct their efforts toward them.

It has been said that "you are what you consume." The chapter explores the meaning of that phrase and points out links between consumption and the self-concept. In a modern sense, the self has been extended through a variety of props and settings to define a consumer's social role in society and within their own sphere.

A person's sex-role identity is a major component of self-definition or self-concept. Conceptions about masculinity and femininity, largely shaped by society, guide the acquisition of "sex-typed" products and services. Advertising and other media play an important role in socializing consumers to be male and female. Although traditional women's roles have often been perpetuated in advertising depictions, this situation is changing somewhat. Gender goals and expectations are different now than they were even 10 years ago. Segmenting by gender and sex role is examined in a new light. Alternative lifestyles have been factored into the gender equation.

A person's conception of his or her body also provides feedback to self-image. A culture communicates certain ideals of beauty, and consumers go to great lengths to attain these. Many consumer activities involve manipulating the body, whether through dieting, cosmetic surgery, tattooing, or even mutilation. Sometimes these activities are carried to an extreme, as people try too hard to live up to cultural ideals. One example is found in eating disorders, where women in particular become obsessed with thinness.

# CHAPTER OUTLINE

**1. Perspectives on the Self**
  a. Many products, from cars to cologne, are bought because the person is trying
    to highlight or hide some aspect of the self.
    1) Studies show that 72 percent of men and 85 percent of women are unhappy
      with at least one aspect of their appearance.

Does the Self Exist?
  b. The concept of the self is relatively new. It only developed in medieval times.
    Prior to that time (and in many cultures today), the collective self was emphasized.
    1) Expression of self is more popular in the Western cultures. Eastern cultures
      tend to emphasize the importance of collective self (as measured by his or her
      group).
    2) The self is seen by Western and Eastern cultures as being divided into three:
      a) Inner self
      b) Private self
      c) Outer, public self
    3) A Confucian perspective stresses the importance of "face" (others' perceptions
      of the self and maintaining one's desired status in their eyes).
      a) One dimension of face is *mien-tzu* (reputation achieved through success
        and ostentation).
    4) As opposed to the formality of Eastern cultures, Western cultures often
      emphasize casualness (as in dressing casual on Fridays).

*Discussion Opportunity—Give an example of "face" in an Eastern culture. Relate this example to products, services, or promotion.*

Self-Concept
c. The **self-concept** refers to the beliefs a person holds about his or her attributes and how he or she evaluates these qualities.
  1) Components of the self-concept include:
    a) Content—such as facial attractiveness versus mental aptitude.
    b) Positivity or negativity—such as self-esteem.
    c) Intensity, stability over time, and accuracy—the degree to which one's self-assessment corresponds to reality.

*Discussion Opportunity—Have each student evaluate themselves as to their self-concept by listing all beliefs they hold about themselves (including attributes such as personality characteristics, strengths, weaknesses, talents, roles, affiliations, etc.). Then have them select the ten most important attributes and rank order them. Have them take a good look at the ten items. Ask the students to close their eyes and picture themselves according to the ten attributes. After a few seconds, instruct them to erase the most important attribute from their self-concept and continue (eyes closed) to picture themselves without it. After a few seconds, repeat this with the second most important attribute, then the third most, then the fourth most. At the point that you feel the objective has been accomplished, have everyone open their eyes. Encourage students to share their feelings about this exercise at each phase. Was it difficult to "erase" attributes from the self-concept? Why? What happened when the first attribute was erased?*

  2) **Self-esteem** refers to the positivity of a person's self-concept.
    a) Those with low self-esteem do not think they will perform well and will try to avoid embarrassment, failure, or rejection.
    b) Those with high self-esteem expect to be successful, will take more risks, and are more willing to be the center of attention.
    c) Self-esteem is often related to acceptance by others.
  3) Marketing communications can influence a consumer's level of self-esteem.
    a) **Social comparison** is the process where a person tries to evaluate his or her self by comparing it to the people depicted in artificial images (such as ads in a magazine). This form of comparison appears to be a basic human motive.
  4) **Self-esteem advertising** attempts to change product attributes by stimulating positive feelings about the self.

*****Use Consumer Behavior Challenge #11 Here *****

*Discussion Opportunity—Find some examples of ads that promote self-esteem and show them in class.*

  5) Self-esteem is influenced by a process where the consumer compares his or her actual standing on some attribute to some ideal.

      a) The **ideal self** is a person's conception of how he or she would like to be. This self is partly molded by heroes (or advertising depictions) in one's culture.

      b) The **actual self** refers to our more realistic appraisal of the qualities we have and don't have.

---

*Discussion Opportunity—Have students make columns on a sheet of notepaper. Have them write down attributes in each column describing their ideal self, actual self, and "undesired self." Have some students share the differences and similarities that they found.*

---

6) Although most people experience a discrepancy between their real and ideal selves, for some consumers this gap is larger than for others.

      a) These people are good targets for *fantasy appeals*.

      b) A **fantasy** or daydream is a self-induced shift in consciousness that is sometimes a way of compensating for a lack of external stimulation or of escaping from problems in the real world.

      c) Marketing strategies focused on fantasies allow us to extend our vision of ourselves by placing us in unfamiliar, exciting situations or by permitting us to "try on" interesting or provocative roles.

         d) The thousands of personal Web sites people create to make a statement about themselves relate to the motivation to project a version of the self (perhaps an idealized one) into popular culture.

---

*Discussion Opportunities—Ask: How do advertisers appeal to our fantasies? Can you give some examples?*

---

*Discussion Opportunity—Describe a fantasy you have had. What role did advertisers or marketers play in expanding this fantasy (if they did)? Explain.*

---

<u>Multiple Selves</u>

  d. In a way, each of us is really a number of different people. We have as many selves as we do social roles. This causes us to prefer different products and services.

    1) The self can be thought of as having different components or *role identities*.

    2) Some of the identities are more central than others (e.g., husband, boss, mother, student).

    3) Others might be dominant in certain situations (e.g., dancer, coach, Sunday school teacher).

  e. The sociological tradition of **symbolic interactionism** stresses that relationships with other people play a large part in forming the self.

    1) Like other social objects, the meanings of consumers themselves are defined by social consensus.

    2) We tend to pattern our behavior on the perceived expectations of others in a form of *self-fulfilling prophecy* (by acting the way others expect us to act, we often wind up confirming these perceptions).

3) The **looking-glass self** is the process of imagining the reactions of others toward us (also known as "taking the role of the other").

*Discussion Opportunity—Ask: How many multiple selves do you have? When was an instance when your "looking-glass self" was operating? Explain.*

Self-Consciousness
   f. There are times when people seem to be painfully aware of themselves.
   1) Some people are more *self-conscious* than others.
   2) *Self-monitoring* is one way to measure self-consciousness. Vanity might be one aspect measured by such a scale.

*Discussion Opportunity—What was one of your most embarrassing moments? If the circumstances were different would you have been less self-conscious?*

*Discussion Opportunity—Give an illustration where you were engaged in self-monitoring.*

## 2. Consumption and Self-Concept
   a. **Identity marketing** is where consumers alter some aspect of their selves to advertise for a branded product (i.e., being paid by a company to tattoo their logo).
   b. Consumers learn that different roles are accompanied by constellations of products and activities that help to define their roles.

Products That Shape the Self: You Are What You Consume
   c. People use an individual's consumption behaviors to help them make judgments about that person's social identity.
   d. A person exhibits **attachment** to an object to the extent that it is used by that person to maintain his or her self-concept. Objects act as security blankets by reinforcing our identifies, especially in unfamiliar situations.

*Discussion Opportunity—Ask students if there has ever been a time when an object was a security blanket for them. Explain how this occurred.*

   e. **Symbolic self-completion theory** predicts that people who have an incomplete self-definition tend to complete this identity by acquiring and displaying symbols associated with it (e.g., men and their "macho" products).
   f. The contribution of possessions to self-identity is perhaps most apparent when these treasured objects are lost or stolen. The victim feels "violated."

*****Use Consumer Behavior Challenge #12 Here *****

*Discussion Opportunity—Ask: Have you ever lost (or had destroyed) an object that, because it was lost or destroyed, affected your self-concept? Explain.*

Self/Product Congruence

g. Consumers demonstrate consistency between their values.

1) **Self-image congruence models** predict that products will be chosen when their attributes match some aspect of the self. These models assume a process of cognitive matching between product attributes and the consumer self-image.

2) The ideal self seems to be more relevant for highly expressive social products such as expensive perfume. The actual self is more relevant for everyday, functional products.

3) Research tends to support the idea of congruence between product usage and self-image. This theory does not work, however, with all products (such as toasters).

*****Use Consumer Behavior Challenges #5 and #6 Here *****

*Discussion Opportunity—Give an example of self-image congruence when you have purchased something. Explain.*

The Extended Self

h. Those external objects that we consider a part of us comprise the **extended self**.

*Discussion Opportunity—Ask students to brainstorm a small list of objects that they consider to be part of their extended self? What do these objects have to do with their self-expression? How would an advertiser appeal to their extended self?*

i. Four levels of extended self have been described:

1) *Individual level*—you are what you wear.

2) *Family level*—includes your house and furniture.

3) *Community level*—includes your neighborhood and home town.

4) *Group level*—includes your religion, flag, sports team, etc.

*****Use Consumer Behavior Challenge #11 Here *****

*Discussion Opportunities—Give an illustration of the four different forms of extended self. How might these forms be used by marketers or advertisers?*

**3. Sex Roles**

a. Sexual identity is a very important component of a consumer's self-concept. We tend to conform with culture's expectations; these expectations, however, change.

*Discussion Opportunity—Ask: Have you ever made a purchase (or failed to make a purchase) because of gender issues? Explain your example.*

Gender Differences in Socialization

b. A society's assumptions about the proper roles of men and women is communicated in terms of the ideal behaviors that are stressed for each gender.

  c. Gender roles do change over time. Even in Asia, macho male stereotypes that have long dominated society in countries like Japan and South Korea are falling out of fashion as women gain power and independence.

  d. A current style for women in Japan known as the "Lolita" look illustrates the yearning of many young women there for a more idyllic feminine expression.

e. In many societies, males are controlled by **agentic goals** that stress self-assertion and mastery.

f. Females are taught to value **communal goals**, such as affiliation and the fostering of harmonious relations.

g. The field of marketing has historically been largely defined by men, so it still tends to be dominated by male values.

  1) Competition is stressed rather than cooperation.

  2) Power and control over others are pervasive themes.

---

*Discussion Opportunity—Identify goals that you think are uniquely male and female. How can marketers exploit these goals and the associated needs?*

---

*Discussion Opportunity—Find a magazine ad that demonstrates agentic goals and one that demonstrates communal goals. To which gender are these ads directed? In what publication did the ads appear? In your opinion, was there a conscious attempt to segment?*

---

Gender Versus Sexual Identity

h. Gender role identity is a state of mind as well as body.

  1) A person's biological gender does not totally determine whether he or she will exhibit **sex-typed traits** (characteristics that are stereotypically associated with one sex or the other). Subjective feelings about sexuality are also important.

  2) Masculinity and femininity are *not* biological characteristics.

  3) Characteristics of gender role change from one culture to another.

i. Many products are *sex typed*; they take on masculine or feminine attributes. This typing is often perpetuated by marketers.

  1) Masculinity and femininity are not opposite ends of the same dimension. **Androgyny** refers to the possession of both masculine and feminine traits.

  2) Differences in sex-role orientation can influence responses to marketing stimuli, at least under some circumstances. As an illustration, women who exhibit male characteristics prefer less feminine advertising messages.

  3) Sex-typed people in general are more concerned with ensuring that their behavior is consistent with their culture's definition of gender appropriateness.

---

*****Use Consumer Behavior Challenge #10 Here *****

---

*Discussion Opportunity—Ask: Why do you suppose we have boys' and girls' toys? Is society or marketing responsible for this?*

---

*Discussion Opportunity—Ask: Are there any role reversal products that you prefer (such as more feminine lotion—for a male—or a more masculine scent such as in perfume—for a female)? When might role reversal be present (single males having to cook and clean an apartment, therefore paying attention to ads about these products or a female having to wear more masculine business suits)? How do you feel about this?*

## Women's Sex Roles

j. Gender roles for women are changing rapidly. There is a move away from showing women as homemakers.

   1) The majority of women hold jobs because they have to rather than as an expression of self-fulfillment.

*Discussion Opportunity—What stereotypes of women do you feel are no longer true? How are marketers attempting to appeal to the "new" woman?*

   3) Ads many times reinforce negative stereotypes.

     a) Women are often portrayed as stupid, submissive, temperamental, or as sex objects for men.

*****Use Consumer Behavior Challenge #10 (Used Previously) Here *****

## Male Sex Roles

k. The traditional view was that the male was a tough, aggressive, muscular man who enjoyed "manly" sports and activities. Society's definition of the male role, however, is evolving.

   1) There is a field of study, **masculinism**, devoted to the study of the male image and cultural meanings of masculinity.

   2) Many males are now shown as having a "sensitive" side.

   3) "Male bonding" is a popular theme (especially in beer commercials).

   4) Male lifestyles are expressing freedom in clothing choices, raising children, and in overcoming their big, dumb jock image in advertising.

     5) Males are also rebelling against being shown as sex objects.

     6) Straight urban males who exhibit strong interest and knowledge regarding product categories such as fashion, home design, gourmet cooking, and personal care are known as **metrosexuals** (a.k.a., *prosumers* or **urban influentials**). These characteristics run counter to traditional male sex roles.

*****Use Consumer Behavior Challenge #1 Here *****

*Discussion Opportunity—Ask: Can you think of any ads where they have females performing acts that were predominately male roles in the past? Can you think of an ad in which the male is a sex object? (You might want to locate examples of each and bring them in to share with the class after they have responded.)*

Gay and Lesbian Consumers
1. In the U.S. society, in the business place, and in the market these consumers have "come out of the closet." Most marketing firms have begun to account for lifestyle segments such as these.

> *****Use Consumer Behavior Challenge #7 Here *****

> *Discussion Opportunity—Name popular movies or television shows where gay or lesbian actors or actresses are a central theme. Watch the show and note the products that are advertised during these shows. In your opinion, was this a way to reach this particular market segment? Explain.*

## 4. Body Image
a. A person's physical appearance is a large part of his or her self-concept.
  1) **Body image** refers to a consumer's subjective evaluation of his or her physical self.
  2) Consumer's often see themselves differently than they naturally are.
b. A person's feelings about his or her body can be described in terms of **body cathexis.** *Cathexis* refers to the emotional significance of some object or idea to a person, and some parts of the body are more central to self-concept than are others.
  1) Consumers who are more satisfied with their bodies use more "preening" products (such as conditioners or hair dryers).

> *Discussion Opportunity—According to the text, which parts of the body are consumers usually the most satisfied with? The least satisfied with? How might marketers use this information?*

Ideals of Beauty
c. A person's satisfaction with the physical image he or she presents to others is affected by how closely that image corresponds to the image valued by his or her culture.
  1) An **ideal of beauty** is a particular model, or *exemplar*, of appearance.
  2) Examples of ideals are physical features, clothing styles, cosmetics, hairstyles, skin tone, and body type.

> *Discussion Opportunity—Ask the Women: Write down on a piece of paper what your ideal man looks like. Ask the Men: Write down on a piece of paper what your ideal woman looks like. Discuss the results with the class. (This often leads to a wild discussion. Relate the findings to "ideals of beauty" as used by our society.)*

  3) Recent research indicates that preferences for some physical features over others are "wired in" genetically, and that these reactions tend to be the same among people around the world.
  4) Men are more likely to use a woman's body shape as a sexual cue.
  5) Marketers seem to have a lot to do with "packaging" faces (such as a fashion look).

6) History shows that women have worked hard to attain beauty. What is beautiful in one era, however, may not be considered to be so in another era.

d. Beauty is about more than aesthetics. The socialization process of any given culture establishes certain cues that people use to make inferences about people. As American media proliferates around the globe, the Western ideal of beauty is being adopted by cultures everywhere.

---

*****Use Consumer Behavior Challenge #2 Here *****

---

e. The ideal body type of Western women has changed radically over time, and these changes have resulted in a realignment of **sexual dimorphic markers**—those aspects of the body that distinguish between the sexes.

---

*Discussion Opportunity—Ask: What body "ideals" are "in" at the present time for both men and women? Why are these features deemed "beautiful"? How do advertisers use this? What happens to people who do not have these traits?*

---

Working on the Body
f. Because many consumers are motivated to match up to some ideal of appearance, they often go to great lengths to change aspects of their physical selves.
  1) As reflected in the expression "you can never be too thin or too rich," our society has an obsession with weight.

---

*****Use Figure 5.1 Here *****

---

  2) Exaggeration of appearance importance can result in disorders of great magnitude. Women especially are taught that quality of body reflects their self-worth.
    a) Eating disorders are common in women (such as **anorexia** or **bulimia**).
    b) Eating disorders in men tend to emphasize gaining, rather than losing, weight (especially in putting on more muscle).
  3) Many have elected to have cosmetic surgery to change a poor body image.
    a) Many women have the surgery done to reduce weight or increase sexual desirability.
    b) Breast size seems to be one of the main focuses. This is also emphasized either directly or indirectly by marketers.

---

*****Use Consumer Behavior Challenges #3 and #8 Here *****

---

*Discussion Opportunity—What do you think of the "thin is in" concept? (Notice the differences between the responses of males and females.) Ask students if they have ever known anyone with any of the disorders mentioned in the chapter and (if so) ask them to relate the story to the class. What would this have to do with marketing? Is there a link?*

---

g. Body decoration and mutilation is in the news on a rather regular basis. Decorating or mutilating one's self is not a new concept. It may, in fact, serve several purposes:
   1) *To separate group members from nonmembers*.
   2) *To place the individual in the social organization.*
   3) *To place the person in a gender category*.
   4) *To enhance sex-role identification*.
   5) *To indicate desired social conduct*.
   6) *To indicate high status or rank*.
   7) *To provide a sense of security*.

---

*Discussion Opportunity—Ask: How many of you have some type of body decoration? Ask individuals what form they have. Have them explain why they do this? Are there any marketing or consumption connections? Explain.*

---

h. Tattoos—both temporary and permanent—are a popular form of body adornment.
   1) A tattoo may be viewed as a fairly risk-free way of expressing an adventurous side of the self.
   2) Tattoos have also been associated with social outcasts.
i. Body piercing (decorating the body with various kinds of metallic inserts) has evolved from a practice associated with some fringe groups to become a popular fashion statement.

---

*Discussion Opportunity—Discuss tattooing and body piercing with the class. How many have done it? Why? What type of statement was being made? How might marketers and advertisers use these trends in their promotions? What do you think the long-term trend will be?*

---

# End-of-Chapter Support Material

# SUMMARY OF SPECIAL FEATURE BOXES

1.    **The Tangled Web**

Hot or Not is a Web site created by two engineers where people can submit photos that are then rated (scale of 1 to 10) by other site visitors. A brief discussion is given as to why people would submit their photo to such a site. One explanation that is offered is that of *self-handicapping* where people set themselves up for failure by submitting a bad photo. In that way, they can blame the picture rather than their own appearance if ratings are low.

## 2. Marketing Pitfalls I

This box explores the current wave of consumer sentiment against SUVs. The opinions of various groups and individuals are explored. This feature supports the section "Self/Product Congruence."

## 3. Global Looking Glass

This box discusses the impact that the purchase (by an American tycoon) of Manchester United has had on its fiercely loyal British fan base.

## 4. Marketing Opportunity I

The changing nature of gender roles is highlighted in this box. In this case, it is demonstrated how women are purchasing goods that have traditionally belonged to men.

## 5. Marketing Pitfalls II

Many promotional campaigns are stereotyping men as incompetent. *Misandry* is the act of male bashing. Also discussed is a Web site organized to boycott the worst offenders.

## 6. Marketing Opportunity II

This box illustrates how Dove has run a campaign that goes against the stereotypical images of women as thin, svelte, supermodels. The campaign features full-figured women and emphasizes that beauty comes in all forms.

## 7. Marketing Opportunity III

This box discusses how there is a reversing trend in body size for women. Whereas most ad campaigns show the women as supermodels, the reality is that women, on average, are growing bigger. The most popular sizes being purchased are larger than 20 years ago. Many companies are responding with more plus size lines.

## 8. Marketing Pitfalls III

This box highlights how the United States is not the only country with a population that is growing more obese. Many countries in Europe, as well as the Middle East, are "growing" in similar ways.

# REVIEW QUESTIONS

1.  How do Eastern and Western cultures tend to differ in terms of how people think about the self? *Furthermore, the emphasis on the unique nature of the self is much greater in Western societies. Many Eastern cultures instead stress the importance of a collective self, where a person derives his identity in large measure from his social group. Both Eastern and Western cultures see the self as divided into an inner, private self, and an outer, public self. But where they differ is in terms of which part is seen as the "real you"—the West tends to subscribe to an independent construal of the self that emphasizes the inherent separateness of each individual.*

2.  List three dimensions by which we can describe the self-concept.
    *1.   Content—facial attractiveness versus mental aptitude;*
    *2.   Positivity or negativity—self-esteem; and*
    *3.    Intensity, stability over time, and accuracy—the degree to which one's self-assessment corresponds to reality.*

3.  Compare and contrast the real versus the ideal self. List three products for which each type of self is likely to be used as a reference point when a purchase is considered. *The ideal self is a person's conception of how he or she would like to be, whereas the actual self refers to our more realistic appraisal of the qualities we have and don't have.*

4.  What does "the looking glass self" mean? *This process of imagining the reactions of others toward us is known as "taking the role of the other," or the looking-glass self. According to this view, our desire to define ourselves operates as a sort of psychological sonar: We take readings of our own identity by "bouncing" signals off others and trying to project what impression they have of us.*

5.  How do feelings about the self influence the specific brands people buy? *Because many consumption activities are related to self-definition, it is not surprising to learn that consumers demonstrate consistency between their values and the things they buy. Self-image congruence models suggest that products will be chosen when their attributes match some aspect of the self. These models assume a process of cognitive matching between product attributes and the consumer's self-image.*

6.  Define the extended self and provide three examples. *Those external objects that we consider a part of us comprise the extended self. In some cultures, people literally incorporate objects into the self—they lick new possessions, take the names of conquered enemies (or in some cases eat them), or bury the dead with their possessions. In addition to shoes, of course, many material objects ranging from personal possessions and pets to national monuments or landmarks, help to form a consumer's identity.*

7.  What is the difference between agentic and communal goals? *Many societies expect males to pursue agentic goals that stress self-assertion and mastery. On the other hand, they teach females to value communal goals, such as affiliation and the fostering of harmonious relations.*

8.      Is masculinity/femininity a biological distinction? Why or why not? *Unlike maleness and femaleness, masculinity and femininity are not biological characteristics. A behavior considered masculine in one culture might not be viewed as such in another. For example, the norm in the United States is that male friends avoid touching each other (except in "safe" situations such as on the football field).*

9.      Give two examples of sex-typed products. *Marketers often encourage the sex typing of products such as Princess telephones, boys' and girls' bicycles, or Luvs color-coded diapers.*

10.     What is body cathexis? *Body cathexis means a person's feelings about his or her body. The word cathexis refers to the emotional significance of some object or idea to a person, and some parts of the body are more central to self-concept than are others.*

11.     Have ideals of beauty in the United States changed over the last 50 years? If so, how? *A study of almost 50 years of* Playboy *centerfolds shows that the women have become less shapely and more androgynous since Marilyn Monroe graced the first edition with a voluptuous hourglass figure of 37–23–36. However, a magazine spokesman comments, "As time has gone on and women have become more athletic, more in the business world and more inclined to put themselves through fitness regimes, their bodies have changed, and we reflect that as well. But I would think that no one with eyes to see would consider playmates to be androgynous.*

12.     What is fattism? *Fattism is an obsession with weight*

13.     How did tattoos originate? *Tattoos have a long history of association with people who are social outcasts. For example, the faces and arms of criminals in sixth-century Japan were tattooed as a means of identifying them, as were Massachusetts prison inmates in the nineteenth century and concentration camp internees in the twentieth century. Marginal groups, such as bikers or Japanese yakuze (gang members) often use these emblems to express group identity and solidarity.*

# CONSUMER BEHAVIOR CHALLENGE

## Discussion Questions

1.      The "metrosexual" is a big buzzword in marketing—but is it real or just media hype? Do you see men in your age group changing their ideas about acceptable interests for males (e.g., home design, cooking, etc.)?

        *Various responses to this are possible. Given that the question asks whether students see the ideals of men they know as changing, there may not be much of response. This may be because in the past few years, men they know may not have changed. An alternative might be to ask whether they think that the characteristics of men that they know are similar or different to the descriptions given of metrosexuals in the text. Considerations should be given that in many countries (including the United States), men are buying more grooming and cosmetic products. However, whether men of the typical college age are adopting these practices may vary, given that most of these changing characteristics are occurring among urban male professionals.*

2. How prevalent is the western ideal among your peers? How do you see this ideal evolving now (if at all)? *The prevalence of the "Western Ideal" will depend on the country of the student body. Even within the United States or other western cultures, the Western ideal of beauty—big round eyes, tiny waists, large breasts, blond hair, and blue eyes—may be changing. The more enlightening discussion should come out of the "evolution" portion of the question. There is quite a bit of material in this text that indicates that the ideal is changing, based on changes that marketers have made in recent times. The question is, will individuals agree with this information?*

3. Some historians and social critics say our obsession with thinness is based less on science than on morality. They equate our society's stigmatizing obese people (treating them as "sick," disabled, or weak) with the Salem witch trials or McCarthyism (the paranoid anti-communism movement of the 1950s). These critics argue that the definition of obesity has often arbitrarily shifted throughout history. Indeed, being slightly overweight was once associated with good health (as we've seen, in some parts of the world it still is) in a time when many of the most troubling diseases were wasting diseases like tuberculosis. Plumpness used to be associated with affluence and the aristocracy (King Louis XIV of France padded his body to look more imposing), while today it is associated with the poor and their supposedly bad eating habits. What do you think? *Does the social definition of obesity change throughout time? Some of the same material that came out in question 2 might come out in the discussion of this question. However, students might also have a difficult time relating to this question, given that such changes have not occurred heavily within the realm of their memory.*

4. Should fast food restaurants be liable if customers sue them for contributing to their obesity? *This has been a hot topic since the release of the movie "Supersize Me." Various people have pursued lawsuits claiming that a fast food company caused them to be obese (none of them have won). The information from the documentary has been countered by people who have demonstrated that a fast food diet can be healthy (many have been in the press). This discussion/debate should be pretty even in terms of the number of people on each side. There will be those claiming that fast food companies have been unethical in their marketing of unhealthy products, as well as those that will claim that consumers have accountability and responsibility for what they consume.*

5. How might the creation of a self-conscious state be related to consumers who are trying on clothing in dressing rooms? Does the act of preening in front of a mirror change the dynamics by which people evaluate their product choices? Why?

*When women try on clothing in a dressing room, the presence of other women and mirrors might create a self-conscious state. In an outfit, women's self-consciousness is likely to be heightened. They may "check themselves out" in a mirror, ask other people how something looks, or listen to someone tell them that they look good. These acts and interactions will determine whether a potential customer feels confident about wearing the outfit and, therefore, is willing to buy it.*

6.  Is it ethical for marketers to encourage infatuation with the self?

    *Students will have their own opinions. Encourage them to think about self-infatuation and the related concepts of self-consciousness and self-esteem.*

7.  To date, the bulk of advertising targeted to gay consumers has been placed in exclusively gay media. If it was your decision to make, would you consider using mainstream media as well to reach gays, who constitute a significant proportion of the general population? Or, remembering that members of some targeted segments have serious objections about this practice—especially when the product (e.g., liquor, cigarettes) may be viewed as harmful in some way—do you think gays should be singled out at all by marketers?

    *Students should consider the text discussion of gay and lesbian consumers. There more likely will be a difference of opinion on this issue. The instructor might encourage different groups of students to take each side of the argument, irrespective of their personal opinions on the matter. Due to the potential sensitivity of the topic, the instructor might ask the students to think about segmentation and target marketing efforts in general and consider why this case is or is not different from targeting any other consumer group. (Possible Class Activity/Debate Idea)*

8.  Some consumer advocates have protested the use of super-thin models in advertising, claiming that these women encourage others to starve themselves in order to attain the "waif" look. Other critics respond that the media's power to shape behavior has been overestimated, and it is insulting to people to assume that they are unable to separate fantasy from reality. What do you think?

    *This is a good topic for a debate. An instructor might want to seek volunteers or to simply select two teams each consisting of one male and one female student. Give each team an opportunity to present their side of the argument and then allow time for rebuttal. (Possible In-Class Activity.)*

9.  Does sex sell? There's certainly enough of it around, whether in print ads, television commercials, or on Web sites. When Victoria's Secret broadcast a provocative fashion show of skimpy lingerie live on the Web (after advertising the show during the Super Bowl), 1.5 million visitors checked out the site before it crashed due to an excessive number of hits. Of course, the retailer was taking a risk because, by its own estimate, 90 percent of its sales are from women. Some of them did not like this display of skin. One customer said she did not feel comfortable watching the Super Bowl ad with her boyfriend: "It's not that I'm offended by it; it just makes me feel inferior." Perhaps the appropriate question is not does sex sell, but should sex sell? What are your feelings about this blatant use of sex to sell products? Do you think this tactic works better when selling to men than to women? Does exposure to unbelievably attractive men and women

models only make the rest of us "normal" folks unhappy and insecure? Under what conditions (if any) should sex be used as a marketing strategy?

*The responses to this question will depend on the background of students in each class. Ideally, responses will range from "sex should not be allowed to sell" to "more sex should be used to sell" and a healthy debate will ensue. Business and marketing students, however, often favor the rights of the company to engage in practices such as this to promote their brands. Some will likely bring up the argument that as long as promotional practices are legal, there is nothing wrong with them. Others may disagree from an ethical perspective. Still others will argue that compared to many European countries, the use of sex in advertising in the United States is mild and that people in the United States are too uptight about sex. Others may point out that there are many countries (i.e., countries with high Muslim populations) where there is far less sex and nudity allowed by law.*

## Application Questions

10. Watch a set of ads featuring men and women on television. Try to imagine the characters with reversed roles (i.e., the male parts played by women and vice versa) Can you see any differences in assumptions about sex-typed behavior?

    *Students will have fun with this challenge though it will be an eye-opener to some. An example of an ad that has women and men playing their traditional roles is a Duncan Hines cake mix commercial. The commercial shows the wife/mother making a cake. When the cake is ready, the father/husband and children are smiling and happy. The ad then says, "Nothin' says lovin' like a cake from the oven." If one switches the roles of the man and woman, the ad somehow would not correspond to our image of having a cake baked by someone who loves us. Most of the time we will want to see ads that reflect a reality as we normally perceive it. (Possible Field Project Idea)*

11. Construct a "consumption biography" of a friend or family member. Make a list and/or photograph his or her most favorite possessions and see if you or others can describe this person's personality just from the information provided by this catalogue.

    *Students might like to bring in a short videotape of the types of products the subject owns. This is usually a fun exercise, as students love to guess who the subject is. Usually, of course, they can pinpoint the person and come close to describing the person's personality. (Possible Individual Field Project.)*

12. Interview victims of burglaries or people who have lost personal property in floods, hurricanes, or other natural disasters. How do they go about reconstructing their possessions, and what effect did the loss appear to have on them?

    *This project may be somewhat difficult to do if no losses have occurred. An alternative is to have students watch news broadcasts and record their impressions of the responses and demeanor of the interviewed subjects. Given the recent El Nino effect on the lives of many U.S. citizens, there will be many stories about losses and difficulties encountered. How does a marketer deal with these situations? See if the students can find marketing responses that seem admirable and unacceptable.*

13.    Locate additional examples of self-esteem advertising. Evaluate the probable effectiveness of these appeals—is it true that "flattery gets you everywhere"?

*Most major magazines contain a variety of this type of advertisements. This is especially true of women's fashion magazines and men's sports magazines. These are the easy titles. To make the project more interesting, however, probe deeper. Go to mothers' magazines and business magazines and see how self-esteem advertising appeals are used. Are they different from the fashion magazines and sports magazines? An additional question can be raised about this form of advertising for different market segment groups. For example, how is self-esteem advertising done for teens (a group that may suffer from lack of self-esteem) or minority ethnic groups (which might also suffer from low self-esteem)? Be sure to discuss your conclusions with the class. The instructor should save the student examples for future class demonstrations.*

# CASE STUDY TEACHING NOTES

## Chapter 5 Case Study: Riding the Plus-Size Wave

### Summary of Case

This case feature the well-known plus-size company, Lane Bryant. Although the company has been around since 1900, they are riding a wave of success that is based on changing weights, body types, and perceptions of beauty. A key element in the strategy of Lane Bryant is the way that they are positioning plus-size women in society. With new product lines and promotional campaigns, they are sending the message that it's not only okay to be a plus-size, but that women in this category can be as in-style as anyone. Part of this strategy has been the signing of American Idol runner up, Kimberley Locke, as the company spokesperson.

### Suggestions for Presentation

There is quite a bit of information in the text on the ideals of beauty and how perceptions of such are changing around the world. While many countries throughout the world are adopting what has been the Western Ideal for quite some time, western countries are seeing a shift in what is considered acceptable among men and women. This case can be complemented by two of the Marketing Opportunity special feature boxes in the chapter, the one featuring Dove, and the one discussing the changing body types in western countries.

## Suggested Answers for Discussion Questions

1.  Explain the success that Lane Brant is currently experiencing in relation to self-concept, self esteem, and self consciousness.

    *The self concept: What are the beliefs that women have about their own qualities and traits and how they evaluate such?*

    *Self esteem: what is the nature of the positivity of plus-size women with respect to their self-concepts?*

    *Self consciousness: How aware are plus-sized women of how they appear to others and how they fit in relative to other women?*

2.  Discuss the real-world changes that appear to be occurring with respect to media images of women. What are the reasons for this?

    *There are two directions that this might go. The western standard is characterized by the* Playboy *study that is highlighted in the chapter showing the trend over the last fifty years has been toward women being thinner and thinner, less voluptuous. However, information contained in the two Marketing Opportunity special features (as mentioned above) provide a counterpoint to this ideal. The reality is that the average size and weight of women in the United States has been increasing. Dove's "Real Beauty" campaign has been the most famous to take on the supermodel stereotypes that the media has perpetuated for so long. But the information contained in this case also is evidence of such.*

# Additional Support Material

# STUDENT PROJECTS

## Individual Projects

1.  Ask a student to bring to class two brands within the same product category that project different images to the consumer. Have the student discuss the projected images by comparing and contrasting the two different brands. What techniques did the marketer use to project these images? Is the self-concept of the buyer important? Explain.

2.  Ask students to interview the managers of two retail clothing stores. See if they can discover the degree to which the managers believe that consumers' personalities and self-images are important to the marketing and promotional activities of their store. Ask the students if they are in agreement with the managers' comments.

3.     Have each student find a good example to identify marketing in the media. Have the students share their examples during a discussion of such in class. Which ones do students see as being the greatest and most permanent modification to the consumer's life?

4.     Have male students and female students (separately) interview three women and three men whom they think are just about the right weight for their height and bone structure (instruct students to tell respondents that their responses are completely confidential). The students should ask the respondents if they think of themselves as overweight, underweight, or about right. Then, see if they can determine how the subjects reached their conclusions. Next, ask the subjects if they are doing anything to manage their weight. If possible, have students ask the respondents what their weight and height are. Discuss how the students seem to feel about their weight.

5.     Have students find media examples of men exhibiting agentic as well as communal goals. Have them do the same for women. How much did they find that each gender tended to adhere to the societal expectation?

6.     Ask your students to compile a list of ten household chores. Then have each student interview two married couples (one newlywed and the other seasoned) to determine who usually performs that chore—the husband or the wife. If possible have the students ask the subject when their spouse is not around. Do they agree? Have students share their findings with the class.

7.     Assign students to collect advertisements that would tell a stranger something about their self-concept (and image). Have them put these ads on a poster board and bring them to class. Display the poster boards in class and see if the class can match the boards to the correct students.

8.     Have students consider the ethical consequences of the products and promotional campaigns produced by both the fashion industry and the fast-food industry. Have them develop their thoughts as a written assignment. Have them share their responses in class before turning the assignment in.

9.     Assign students to collect five ads that show male or female models exhibiting tattoos or body piercing (they may want to consult tattoo-related magazines or they may print ads from the Internet). Comment on the reason for the display. Did the model match the product be sold? Do people that do not have tattoos or body piercing relate well to the ad? How could you determine this?

10.    Students should visit a Web site for cosmetic surgeons. Have them find testimonials from actual patients that describe the reasons why they obtained the augmentations that they did.

11.    Within a 10 mile radius of the campus where the students are taking this class, have students put together a list of the tattoo parlors. Have them call each and find out how

long they have been in business. Have them visit a few of the parlors that have been around the longest and interview the owner as to how many shops there were 10 years ago. Have the students then construct a list of the tattoo shops at that point in time. Students should draw conclusions based on this comparison.

## Group Projects

1. Have each student interview four people (one each in their 20s, 30s, 40s, and 50s) to determine how important appearance is on the job. Then have students form groups in class to discuss their findings. In addition, have them discuss their own opinions on this issue as well as whether or not they feel that an employee's appearance should be considered in performance evaluations. See if their attitudes change when the employee must deal directly with customers. This activity is also interesting when you ask the subjects about the proper appearance in church or at an important social function.

2. Send the students out in pairs to visit a store that they feel reflects their self-concept. Ask the students to observe and describe personalities of the sales force. Now send them to visit a store they feel does not reflect their self-concept (if the two students feel their self-concepts differ, each of them may choose a store that reflects their own self-concept and that may serve as the store that does not reflect the self-concept of the other). Did they notice any difference in the personalities of the sales force? Do they think that poor or unexciting personalities will have an affect on salesmanship?

3. Have student groups devise a list of traditional male traits with respect to personal care and hygiene. Then, have them visit a cosmetics section of a major department store and interview salespeople with respect to the nature of their male customers. What are they buying, how are they using it? Then, have the groups compare their interview findings with their list of traditional characteristics.

4. Have each group design a role playing scenario that deals with one of the following situations: (a) A 40-year-old male suddenly announces to his wife that he plans to get a tattoo. (b) A couple, both 40 years old, discusses with their teenage son or daughter whether tattooing or body piercing would be appropriate. How can arguments be avoided? (c) A female loan officer in a bank has decided to have her nose pierced.

# eLAB

## Individual Assignments

1. Go to **www.victoriassecret.com**. How does this famous Web site use enhancement of the self to attract consumers? Would you expect males to visit the site as well as females? How could the site make it easier for males to purchase from the site (remember, males

make up a significant portion of sales in the organization's retail stores)? Is sizing easy on this site? How could it be improved?

2. Go to **www.hummer.com**. Many people might say that Hummer is a passing fad. Yet in 2005, they introduced the H3 as an all-new model for 2006. Many previous owners of Hummers say they bought the SUV because it says, "I'm Big; I'm Bad; Don't mess with me!" What does this say about the concept of the self? Which forms might be at play? How could the Web site be changed to accentuate this "don't mess with me" expression? Would this be a good move for Hummer? How does the new "baby Hummer" (H3) fit into this image?

3. Go to **www.tattoo.com**. Need a tattoo? Ever thought about getting one? Well, this Web site might just get you started in that direction. After reviewing the site, what are your impressions about tattooing? How is a self-concept involved in this process? What might cause you to get a tattoo if you don't already have one? Pretend that you are going to get a tattoo—which one of the designs would you choose? Download it (or copy it). Bring it to class; show your choice; explain why it is really "you." Have fun with this one.

4. Go to **www.metrosexual.com**. What is the current state of metrosexuals according to this Web site?

5. Go to **www.makeoversolutions.com**. Take the free demo. Upload a picture of yourself, perform a makeover that you feel genuinely suits you. Print a copy of the picture and bring it in to share with others who do the same. Evaluate the results in the context of the self-concept.

## Group Assignments

1. Go to **www.livingadspace.com**. Visit this site as a group. Become familiar with the content and history of this site. Make a summary of the different types of identity marketing tactics that individuals have taken upon themselves, or are willing to take upon themselves. Have each member of the group discuss how far they would be willing to go to advertise for a company. Would payment make a difference in this venture? How much?

2. Go to **www.bodypiercing.com**. This interesting site presents a wealth of information about body piercing. What marketing efforts are used to attract potential users? What other products were advertised? What intrigued you the most about the Web site? What can you tell about the demographics of the visitors to this Web site? How did you determine this? Did the Web site interest you in getting "pierced"? Explain. How did your group react to the information on the site?

# 6

# *PERSONALITY AND LIFESTYLES*

## CHAPTER OBJECTIVES

When students finish this chapter they should understand why:

- A consumer's personality influences the way he or she responds to marketing stimuli, but efforts to use this information in marketing contexts have met with mixed results.

- Consumers' lifestyles are key to many marketing strategies.

- Psychographics go beyond simple demographics in helping marketers understand and reach different consumer segments.

- Identifying patterns of consumption can be superior to knowledge of individual purchases when crafting a lifestyle marketing strategy.

## CHAPTER SUMMARY

The study of personality is one of the most interesting undertaken in studies of consumer behavior (it is also one of the more difficult explorations). The concept of *personality* refers to a person's unique psychological makeup and how it consistently influences the way a person responds to his or her environment. When marketers attempt to use personality in formulating marketing strategy, several difficulties may arise. Among the most common difficulties are the differences in personality traits among consumers and problems with measurement of the traits. A variety of schools of thought (such as Freudian psychology) have been applied to these studies. Only mixed results have been achieved. Several schools of thought are explored in the chapter.

In addition to the personality of the consumer being of interest to the marketer, brands are also thought to have personalities. *Brand equity* refers to the extent that a consumer holds strong, favorable, and unique associations about a brand in memory. Personality dimensions can be used to compare and contrast the perceived characteristics of brands (such as old fashioned, rugged, outdoors, sexy, etc.). The creation and communication of a distinctive *brand personality* is one of the primary ways marketers can make a product stand out from the competition and inspire years of loyalty to it.

A consumer's *lifestyle* refers to the ways he or she chooses to spend time and money and how his or her values and tastes are reflected by consumption choices. Marketers use lifestyle research as a means to track societal consumption preferences and also to position specific products and services to different segments. Marketers can segment by lifestyle differences, often by grouping consumers in terms of their *AIOs* (activities, interests, and opinions).

*Psychographic* techniques attempt to classify consumers in terms of psychological, subjective variables in addition to observable characteristics (demographics). A variety of systems, such as *VALS*, have been developed to identify consumer "types" and to differentiate them in terms of their brand or product preferences, media usage, leisure time activities, and attitudes toward such broad issues as politics and religion.

Interrelated sets of products and activities are associated with social roles to form *consumption constellations*. People often purchase a product or service because it is associated with a constellation that, in turn, is linked to a lifestyle they find desirable.

Place of residence often is a significant determinant of lifestyle. Many marketers recognize regional differences in product preferences and develop different versions of their products for different markets. A set of techniques called *geodemography* analyzes consumption patterns using geographical and demographic data and identifies clusters of consumers who exhibit similar psychographic characteristics.

The chapter concludes by discussing lifestyle trends with respect to consumer behavior for the new millennium. These major trends are characterized as being: a decline in concern for the environment, an emphasis on the value of time-saving products, decreased emphasis on dieting and nutritional foods, and a more laid-back lifestyle and casual work environment.

# CHAPTER OUTLINE

## 1. Personality
  a. **Personality** refers to a person's unique psychological makeup and how it consistently influences the way a person responds to his or her environment.
   1) There has been debate about whether personality changes with situations and circumstances.
     a) Do people appear to act consistently? Research results are mixed.
   2) Even though inconsistencies have been found in personality research, it still continues to be included in marketing strategies.
   3) Personality dimensions are usually employed in concert with a person's choices of leisure activities, political outlook, aesthetic tastes, and other individual factors to segment consumers in terms of *lifestyles*.

---

*Discussion Opportunity—Explain your own personality. Are you consistent or inconsistent with respect to this identified personality? Give examples. Ask some students to do the same.*

---

> *Discussion Opportunity—Have students collect a series of pictures from ads in magazines that would display your personality. Everyone should post these pictures on a sheet of poster board and display them around the room. Each student should explain his or her ideas of himself or herself. Does the class agree with the assessment? How well do you really know one another?*

## 2. Consumer Behavior on the Couch: Freudian Theory

   a. Sigmund Freud developed the idea that much of one's adult personality stems from a fundamental conflict between a person's desire to gratify his or her physical needs and the necessity to function as a responsible member of society. His principles (note that these terms do not refer to physiological portions of the consumer's brain) included:

     1) The **id** (which is entirely oriented toward immediate gratification). It operates on the **pleasure principle** (behavior guided by the primary desire to maximize pleasure and avoid pain).

       a) The id is selfish.

       b) The id is illogical (it acts without regard to consequences).

     2) The **superego** (which is the counterweight to the id). It is a person's conscience.

       a) It internalizes society's rules.

       b) It works to prevent the id from seeking selfish gratification.

     3) The **ego** (which is the system that mediates between the id and the superego). The ego tries to balance these two opposing forces according to the **reality principle**, whereby it finds ways to gratify the id that will be acceptable to the outside world. Much of this battle occurs in the unconscious mind.

   b. The Freudian perspective hints that the ego relies on symbolism in products to make the compromise between the demands of the id and the prohibitions of the superego.

   c. There is a connection between product symbolism and motivation (according to Freudian theory).

> *Discussion Opportunity—Ask: What are some products that are usually sold by telling you that the use of the product will make you attractive to the opposite sex?*

> *Discussion Opportunity—Ask: What are some products that make their appeals primarily to the id? What are some products that make their appeals to the superego (bring in examples if you can)? Do products make an appeal to the ego? If so, how? Describe a mediation experience where the ego functioned.*

   d. The first attempts to apply Freudian ideas to understand the deeper meanings of products and advertisements were made in the 1950s and were known as **motivational research**.

     1) This research focused on interpretations from the subconscious (unconscious motives). This form of research relies on *depth interviews* with individual consumers.

     2) Ernest Dichter pioneered this form of interview.

     3) Motivational research was attacked for two reasons:

       a) Some felt that it does work, in fact, it worked too well. It gave marketers

the power to manipulate.
  b) Others felt that the analysis technique lacked rigor and validity.
4) Positives were that:
  a) It was less expensive than traditional forms of motivational research.
  b) It was thought to aid in marketing communications.
  c) Some of the findings seem intuitively plausible after the fact.

---

**\*\*\*\*\*Use Table 6.1 Here \*\*\*\*\***

---

*Discussion Opportunity—Bring evidence of symbolism (which might be considered to be Freudian) that you have found in magazine advertisements.*

---

*Discussion Opportunity—Ask: Why is the Freudian school often associated with sex and sexuality? What ramification does this hold for marketing? Does sex sell? According to Freud, why or why not?*

---

Neo-Freudian Theories
e. Those who studied after Freud felt that an individual's personality was more influenced by how he or she handled relationships with others than by unresolved sexual conflicts. Famous advocates of this thought-path (Neo-Freudians) were:
1) Karen Horney—she proposed that people can be described as moving toward others (***compliant***), away from others (***detached***), or against others (***aggressive***).
  a) Alfred Adler—proposed that many actions are motivated by people's desire to overcome feelings of inferiority relative to others.
  b) Harry Stack Sullivan—focused on how personality evolves to reduce anxiety in social relationships.
2) Carl Jung—developed analytical psychology. He believed people were shaped by the cumulative experiences of past generations. Central to his ideas was the ***collective unconscious*** (a storehouse of memories inherited from our ancestral past).
  a) Shared memories create **archetypes**—universally shared ideas and behavior patterns.
  b) These memories would be about birth, death, and the devil (as shown in myths, stories, and dreams).
  1) Some brands have personalities. The measuring of such personalities has been problematic. Various methods have been used, including the BrandAsset Archetypes model used by Young & Rubicam.

---

**\*\*\*\*\*Use Figure 6.1 Here \*\*\*\*\***

---

*Discussion Opportunity—See if you can find illustrations of Karen Horney's and Carl Jung's theories in contemporary advertising. Indicate why you think the ads apply. Show examples if possible.*

Trait Theory

f. One approach to personality is to focus on the quantitative measurement of traits or identifiable characteristics that define a person. Common traits are:
1) *Extroversion*
2) *Innovativeness*
3) *Materialism*
4) *Self-consciousness*
5) *Need for cognition*

---

*Discussion Opportunity—Ask: What traits define you as a person? Give examples.*

---

g. The trait dimension most relevant to consumer behavior is the extent to which consumers are *inner-directed* versus *outer-directed.*
1) Inner-directed individuals consume to express a unique sense of self and tend to be classified as **idiocentrics** (having an individualistic orientation).
2) Outer-directed individuals consume to please others and fit in and tend to be classified as **allocentrics** (having a group orientation).
3) These two orientations differ in the areas of *contentment, health consciousness, food preparation, workaholism,* and *travel and entertainment.*
h. Using traits has only met with mixed success. Explanations include:
1) Many of the scales are not sufficiently valid or reliable.
2) Personality tests are often developed only for specific populations.
3) Tests may not be administered under the best conditions.
4) Researchers make changes in the research instruments to adapt them to their own situations.
5) Many trait scales are only intended to measure gross, overall tendencies.
6) Many of the scales are not well planned or thought out.

Brand Personality

i. Products, like consumers, have personalities.
1) **Brand equity** refers to the extent that a consumer holds strong, favorable, and unique associations about a brand in memory. Examples of personality dimensions include old fashioned, wholesome, traditional, and lively, among others.
2) Consumers seem to have little difficulty in assigning personality qualities to all sorts of inanimate products.
3) The creation and communication of a distinctive **brand personality** is one of the primary ways marketers can make a product stand out from the competition and inspire years of loyalty to it. This is called **animism** (whereby inanimate objects are given qualities that make them somehow alive). It is an old practice.
Types include:
a) Level 1: In the highest order of animism, the object is believed to be possessed by the soul of a being (such as spokespersons in advertising).
b) Level 2: Objects are *anthropomorphized*—given human characteristics.

---

*****Use Table 6.2 Here; Use Consumer Behavior Challenge #5 Here *****

---

> *Discussion Opportunity—Ask students if they can think of products that seem "to come alive." Have them describe how the marketer or advertiser creates this illusion. What type of impact does this have on the consumer? What are the dangers of animism?*

## 3. Lifestyles and Psychographics

> ***\*\*\*\*\*Use Figure 6.1 Here; Use Consumer Behavior Challenge #6 Here \*\*\*\*\****

<u>Lifestyle: Who We Are, What We Do</u>

a. **Lifestyle** refers to a pattern of consumption reflecting a person's choices of how he or she spends time and money. It is (in an economic sense) how one elects to allocate income.

1) A *lifestyle marketing perspective* recognizes that people sort him- or herself into groups on the basis of the things they like to do, how they like to spend their leisure time, and how they choose to spend their disposable income.

2) These choices create marketing opportunities and chances for segmentation.

3) Lifestyles can be thought of as group identities. It is more than economics and income disposal choices.

    a) Lifestyle is a statement of who one is and who one is not.

    b) Other terms used to describe *lifestyle* are:

        1. *Taste public*

        2. *Consumer group*

        3. *Symbolic community*

        4. *Status culture*

    c) Lifestyles are not set in stone unlike deep-seated values discussed in Chapter 4.

> *Discussion Opportunity—Ask: What are some different lifestyles that people about your age (those attending and not attending college) tend to follow? What are the differences between your lifestyle and someone who is a returning student (or a normal undergraduate if you are a returning student)? A graduate student?*

> *Discussion Opportunity—Ask: People who join fraternities and sororities are alike in many ways. What makes a member of a fraternity (or sorority) different from another one? If you met and talked with someone for a few minutes, could you accurately guess whether he or she was in a fraternity or sorority or to which fraternity or sorority the person belonged? What clues might the person give you?*

b. Products are the building blocks of lifestyles. Many choices are made on this basis.

c. Because a goal of lifestyle marketing is to allow consumers to pursue their chosen ways to enjoy their lives and express their social identities, a key aspect of this strategy is to focus on product usage in desirable social settings.

*Discussion Opportunity—Have students make a list of ten items you think you must have in order to attain the good life. Why do you suppose you selected these items? How might marketers use this information? Give an example.*

d. The adoption of a lifestyle-marketing perspective implies that we must look at *patterns of behavior* to understand consumers.

*****Use Table 6.3 Here; Use Consumer Behavior Challenge #12 Here *****

1) **Co-branding strategies** are used by marketers to combine products that appeal to similar patterns of behavior.
2) **Product complementarity** occurs when the symbolic meanings of different products are related to each other.
3) These products, termed **consumption constellations**, are used by consumers to define, communicate, and perform social roles.

*****Use Consumer Behavior Challenge #1 and #9 Here *****

*Discussion Opportunity—How was the "yuppie" of the 1980s defined in a product sense (e.g., Rolex watch, BMW, Gucci briefcase, white wine, etc.)? How was the Generation X grunge rocker of the 1990s defined in a product or lifestyle sense (e.g., Doc Marten combat boots, a smoker, chains, earrings, tattoos, etc.)? Bring in pictures or ads to illustrate these two lifestyles. Ask: How is your generation defined in the new millennium? Be specific.*

Psychographics
e. **Psychographics** involves the use of psychological, sociological, and anthropological factors to determine how the market is segmented by the propensity of groups within the market (and their reasons) to make a particular decision about a product, person, ideology, or otherwise hold an attitude or use a medium.

*****Use Table 6.4 Here *****

1) Psychographics can help a marketer fine-tune its offerings to meet the needs of different segments.
2) The roots of psychographics were in:
   a) *Motivational research*, which involves intensive one-to-one interviews and projective tests (yields a lot of information on a few people).
   b) *Quantitative survey research* (at the other extreme) that uses large-scale demographic research techniques.
3) Psychographics is often used interchangeably with lifestyle.
4) Psychographics focuses on *why* people buy. Demographics tells us *who* buys.
5) Psychographic analysis can take several forms:
   a) *A lifestyle profile*.
   b) *A product-specific product*.

158

c) *A study that uses personality traits as descriptors.*
d) *A general lifestyle segmentation.*
e) *A product-specific segmentation.*

---

**\*\*\*\*\*Use Consumer Behavior Challenges #7 and #11 Here \*\*\*\*\***

---

f. Most contemporary psychographic research attempts to group consumers according to some combination of three categories of variables—*activities, interests,* and *opinions* (**AIOs**).

1) To group consumers into common AIO categories, respondents are given a long list of statements and are asked to indicate how much they agree with each one. Lifestyle is "boiled down" by how consumers spend their time, what they find interesting and important, and how they view themselves and the world around them, as well as demographic information.

2) Which lifestyle segments produce the bulk of consumers? This is answered (marketers must be careful to observe) by the **80/20 rule** where only 20 percent of a product's users account for 80 percent of the volume of the product sold (in other words, the heavy users).

3) After "heavy users" are identified and understood, the brand's relationship to them is considered.

---

*Discussion Opportunity—Ask: Why would AIOs be important to marketers? How could marketers use this information to promote their products?*

---

*Discussion Opportunity—Have students conduct an AIO inventory on themselves. Then have students ask a member of their family or a roommate if he or she agrees with the inventory. What were the differences? Why did these occur?*

---

g. Uses of psychographic segmentation include:
1) *To define the target market.*
2) *To create a new view of the market.*
3) *To position the product.*
4) *To better communicate product attributes.*
5) *To develop overall strategy.*
6) *To market social and political issues.*

---

*Discussion Opportunity—Ask: Can you think of a company that uses psychographic segmentation to position its product in the marketplace? Do you think it is effective? Why or why not?*

---

h. Many research companies and advertising agencies have developed *segmentation typologies* that divide people into segments. Because these are largely proprietary, however, they are hard to get.

i. One well-known and widely used segmentation system is **VALS (Values and Lifestyles)**, developed at what is now SRI International in California. Nine lifestyle clusters have been identified. VALS2 extends this concept and uses eight groups that are determined by psychological characteristics and "resources" (such as income, education, energy levels, and eagerness to buy). The groups include:

1) *Actualizers*—successful with many resources open to change.
2) *Fulfilled*—satisfied, reflective, comfortable, practical.
3) *Achievers*—career-oriented, avoid risk, self-discovery.
4) *Experiencers*—impulsive, young, offbeat, love risk.
5) *Believers*—strong principles, favor proven brands.
6) *Strivers*—like achievers, but with fewer resources, need approval.
7) *Makers*—action-oriented, self-sufficiency, do-it-yourselfers.
8) *Strugglers*—bottom-of-the-ladder, immediate gratification.

---

*****Use Figure 6.2 Here; Use Consumer Behavior Challenge #8 Here *****

---

*Discussion Opportunity—Ask: In which of the eight VALS2 categories do you think a researcher would place you? Where do you think your parents would be placed? How might a marketer use this information to appeal to you (or in the second case, to your parents)?*

j. **Global MOSAIC** is another segmentation system that has developed fourteen common lifestyles that apply across cultures.

k. A Paris-based organization called **RISC** has developed a segmentation system that seeks to anticipate future change in social climate around the world and to identify signs of change in one country before it eventually spreads to others.
   1) RISC measures the social climate in more than forty countries.
   2) The RISC system asks a battery of questions that measure forty "trends."
   3) The system places people in a virtual space described by three axes— *exploration/stability, social/individual,* and *global/local.*
   4) Individuals fit into one of ten general category segments in this virtual space.

---

*****Use Figure 6.4 Here; Use Consumer Behavior Challenge #10 Here *****

---

l. Consumption patterns change as one moves from one region of their country to another.
   1) **Geodemography** refers to analytical techniques that combine data on consumer expenditures and other socioeconomic factors with geographic information about the areas in which people live in order to identify consumers who share common consumption patterns. "Birds of a feather flock together."
   2) *Cluster analysis* allows marketers to identify consumers who share important characteristics.
   3) **Single-source data** is where a person's actual purchasing history is combined with geodemographic data.
   4) One method that is used is **PRIZM (Potential Rating Index by Zip Market)**.

---

*****Use Consumer Behavior Challenges #2 and #3 Here;
Use Table 6.5 Here *****

---

*Discussion Opportunity—Ask: How can marketers use single-source data systems or PRIZM to identify segments? Give an illustration of how a university might use these systems to aid in its fund-raising efforts.*

# **End-of-Chapter Support Material**

# SUMMARY OF SPECIAL FEATURE BOXES

### 1.    Net Profit I

This box takes a look at research that has shown that introverts and extroverts tend to respond better to computer-generated voices that match their personality types. This feature supports the section "Trait Theory."

### 2.    The Tangled Web

This box examines how hate groups are using the Internet to expand their reach. Of particular interest is how such groups are using their core of extremists to target college-bound teens from middle- to upper-class homes. This feature supports the section "Lifestyle as Group Identities."

### 3.    The Global Looking Glass

This box highlights the fact that Vietnam is targeting American businesses by offering them one of the main American businessperson interests: golf. The Vietnamese government and national industries are focusing on developing golf courses. They have gone to great measures (including hiring Lee Trevino to design courses) to make courses that are as Western in nature as possible.

### 4.    Net Profit II

This box features the online gaming community of The Sims as a means of illustrating concept of lifestyles. This feature supports the section "Lifestyles: Who We Are and What We Do."

### 5.    Marketing Opportunity I

This box illustrates the concept of brand personalities by focusing on how Adidas has incorporated psychographic analysis to the design and marketing of their shoes and other products. Various psychographic segments are identified. This feature supports the section "Psychographics."

### 6.    Marketing Pitfalls

This box summarizes the efforts of R. J. Reynolds in targeting a new brand of cigarettes toward a specific psychographic segment of young women. This example demonstrates the irony in how applying basic marketing principles can end up being extremely controversial for companies that make certain types of products. This feature supports the section "Psychographics."

**7.     Marketing Opportunity II**

This box highlights food preferences. As a result, many marketers regionalize their offerings to appeal to different tastes. As part of this topic, the concept of a **food culture** (a pattern of food and beverage consumption that reflects the values of a social group) is discussed. A large scale analysis of 15 different countries in Europe revealed 12 different food cultures.

# REVIEW QUESTIONS

1.      Describe the id, ego, and superego and tell how they work together according to Freudian theory. *The id is entirely oriented toward immediate gratification—it is the "party animal" of the mind.The superego is the counterweight to the id. This system is essentially the person's conscience. It internalizes society's rules (especially as parents teach them to us and works to prevent the id from seeking selfish gratification. Finally, the ego is the system that mediates between the id and the superego. It is in a way a referee in the fight between temptation and virtue.*

2.      What is motivational research? Give an example of a marketing study that used this approach. *In the 1950s, a perspective called motivational research attempted to use Freudian ideas to understand the deeper meanings of products and advertisements. This approach was largely based on psychoanalytic (Freudian) interpretations, with a heavy emphasis on unconscious motives. A basic assumption is that socially unacceptable needs are channeled into acceptable outlets. Motivational research for the American Red Cross did find that men (but not women) tend to drastically overestimate the amount of blood taken from them during a donation. The Red Cross counteracted the fear of loss of virility by symbolically equating the act of giving blood with fertilization: "Give the gift of life."*

3.      Describe three personality traits relevant to marketers. *Some specific traits that are relevant to consumer behavior include: innovativeness (the degree to which a person likes to try new things); materialism (amount of emphasis placed on acquiring and owning products); self-consciousness (the degree to which a person deliberately monitors and controls the image of the self that is projected to others), and need for cognition (the degree to which a person likes to think about things and by extension expands the necessary effort to process brand information). Another trait relevant to consumer behavior is frugality. Frugal people deny short-term purchasing whims, choosing instead to resourcefully use what they already own.*

4.      Contrast idiocentrics and allocentrics. *Idiocentrics is having an individualist orientation while allocentrics is having a group orientation.*

5.      *List three problems with applying trait theory to marketing contexts. The use of standard personality trait measurements to predict product choices has met with mixed success at*

*best. In general, marketing researchers simply have not been able to predict consumers' behaviors on the basis of measured personality traits. These are some explanations for these equivocal results:*

- *Many of the scales are not sufficiently valid or reliable; they do not adequately measure what they are supposed to measure, and their results may not be stable over time.*
- *Personality tests are often developed for specific populations (e.g., mentally ill people); these tests are then "borrowed" and applied to the general population where their relevance is questionable.*
- *Often the tests are not administered under the appropriate conditions; people who are not properly trained may give them in a classroom or at a kitchen table.*
- *The researchers often make changes in the instruments to adapt them to their own situations, in the process deleting or adding items and renaming variables. These ad hoc changes dilute the validity of the measures and also reduce researchers' ability to compare results across consumer samples.*
- *Many trait scales are intended to measure gross, overall tendencies (e.g., emotional stability or introversion); these results are then used to make predictions about purchases of specific brands.*
- *In many cases, a number of scales are given with no advance thought about how these measures should be related to consumer behavior. The researchers then use a "shotgun approach," following up on anything that happens to look interesting.*

6.    Define a brand personality and give two examples. *A brand personality is the set of traits people attribute to a product as if it were a person. Many of the most recognizable figures in popular culture are spokescharacters for long-standing brands, such as the Jolly Green Giant, the Keebler Elves, or Charlie the Tuna.*

7.    How does lifestyle differ from income? *Lifestyle refers to a pattern of consumption reflecting a person's choices of how he or she spends time and money. In an economic sense, one's lifestyle represents the way one has elected to allocate income, both in terms of relative allocations to different products and services, and to specific alternatives within these categories.*

8.    What is the basic philosophy behind a lifestyle marketing strategy? *A lifestyle marketing perspective recognizes that people sort themselves into groups on the basis of the things they like to do, how they like to spend their leisure time, and how they choose to spend their disposable income.*

9.    Define psychographics, and describe three ways marketers can use it. *When marketers combine personality variables with knowledge of lifestyle preferences, they have a powerful lens with which to focus on consumer segments. We call this approach psychographics, which involves the "use of psychological, sociological, and anthropological factors . . . to determine how the market is segmented by the propensity of groups within the market—and their reasons—to make a particular decision about a product, person, ideology, or otherwise hold an attitude or use a medium."*

*Psychographic studies can take several different forms:*

- *A lifestyle profile looks for items that differentiate between users and nonusers of a product.*
- *A product-specific profile identifies a target group and then profiles these consumers on product-relevant dimensions.*
- *A general lifestyle segmentation places a large sample of respondents into homogenous groups based on similarities of their overall preferences.*
- *A product-specific segmentation tailors questions to a product category. For example, in a study done specifically for a stomach medicine, the item "I worry too much" might be rephrased as "I get stomach problems if I worry too much." This allows the researcher to more finely discriminate between users of competing brands.*

10. What are three specific kinds of AIOs? *Most contemporary psychographic research attempts to group consumers according to some combination of three categories of variables—activities, interests, and opinions—known as AIOs. Using data from large samples, marketers create profiles of customers who resemble each other in terms of their activities and patterns of product usage.*

11. What is VALS2, and how do marketers use it? *One well-known segmentation system is The Values and Lifestyles (VALS™) System, developed at SRI International in California. The original VALS™ system was based on how consumers agreed or disagreed with various social issues such as abortion rights. After about 10 years, SRI discovered that the social issues it used to categorize consumers were not as predictive of consumer behavior as they once had been. SRI searched for a more powerful way to segment consumers, and the company discovered that certain lifestyle indicators such as "I like a lot of excitement in my life" were better predictors of purchase behavior than the degree to which a person agreed or disagreed with a social value. The current VALS2™ system uses a battery of 39 items (35 psychological and four demographic) to divide U.S. adults into groups, each with distinctive characteristics.*

12. Alcohol drinkers vary sharply in terms of the number of drinks they may consume, from those who occasionally have one at a cocktail party to regular imbibers. Explain how the 80/20 rule applies to this product category. *According to a very general rule of thumb frequently used in marketing research called the 80/20 rule, only 20 percent of a product's users account for 80 percent of the volume of product sold. As far as the consumption of alcoholic beverages is concerned, a minority of the customers consumer the majority of the product. Most of the revenues for this industry are racked up by heavy users.*

# CONSUMER BEHAVIOR CHALLENGE

## Discussion Questions

1.  What consumption constellation might characterize you and your friends today?

    *Responses to this one are wide open. But students should be directed to develop a constellation of products that are complementary with respect to the symbolic meaning that they hold for the consumer. What are the social roles that a person holds? How are those social roles defined, communicated, and performed through product consumption.*

2.  Geodemographic techniques assume that people who live in the same neighborhood have other things in common as well. Why is this assumption made, and how accurate is it?

    *Although members of the U.S. culture share a common national identity, purchase and consumption patterns of different regions have been shaped by unique climates, cultural influences, and resources. For example, a student from Minnesota going to a university in the South will quickly recognize that the regional drink is iced tea or Coke rather than hot chocolate or pop. Similarly, the easterner will have a very different attitude toward space and crowding than residents of Texas or New Mexico. Just as we have come to realize that cultural differences between countries are significant, regional differences are recognized as influential (e.g., different names for the same thing—pop, soft drink, soda, soda pop, soda water, coke, tonic).*

3.  Single-source data systems give marketers access to a wide range of information about a consumer, just by knowing his or her address. Do you believe this "knowledge power" presents any ethical problems with regard to consumers' privacy? Should access to such information be regulated by the government or other bodies? Should consumers have the right to limit access to these data?

    *Students will differ in their responses to this question. Many may view single-source data as a threat of the Orwellian Big Brother nature. Others will view it as part of the public domain. The instructor should encourage students to examine both sides of the argument. How do they feel about their university or college sharing information collected about them with outside entities? Should this information be sold? Should students have the right to know to whom the information was given or sold? Should the campus (or off-campus) bookstores be allowed to share or sell information about students? What type of information must a university or college legally keep confidential and not sell or distribute (without permission)? How has information from the Internet changed our view on what information we will provide and what will not be supplied?*

4.  Should organizations or individuals be allowed to create Web sites that advocate potentially harmful practices? Should hate groups such as the White Aryan Resistance be allowed to recruit members online? Why or why not?

*This is a question for the class that is bold and wants to explore controversial issues. On the one hand is the principle of free speech as guaranteed by the Constitution. Current law extends this principle to almost all avenues of the Internet. Recent federal legislation, however, has strongly and firmly prohibited hate crimes. An interesting way to approach the dilemma posed in this question is to have a debate or invite a response from a member of a local or regional ACLU office. This always sparks controversy. Please remember that this question must be handled carefully and at all costs must not be used offensively. Set some ground rules on this one. Best used with The Tangled Web special feature box.*

Application Questions

5. Construct a brand personality inventory for three different brands within a product category. Ask a small number of consumers to rate each brand on ten different personality dimensions. What differences can you locate? Do these "personalities" relate to the advertising and packaging strategies used to differentiate these products?

   *The first thing students will have to do to answer this question is to establish the ten personality dimensions. They are free to construct these as they choose, however, some suggestions are offered by the material in the chapter. The differences will be the result of differences observed. It will be easier for them if they choose products from a brand category with which they are familiar. (Many times students will know more about the brand than what is shown in the advertisement.) Be sure the students demonstrate "how" personalities relate to the advertising and packaging used by the marketer to differentiate these products.*

6. Compile a set of recent ads that attempt to link consumption of a product with a specific lifestyle. How is this goal usually accomplished?

   *Students should be able to find a variety of advertisements to represent the link of product consumption with specific lifestyle. Examples include luxury cars, cruises, polo, and golf linked to an affluent lifestyle; used cars and furniture, small apartments, stereos, and books linked to the university student lifestyle; Miller beer linked to the young, single, sports-fanatic male lifestyle.*

7. Psychographic analyses can be used to market politicians. Conduct research on the marketing strategies used in a recent, major election. How were voters segmented in terms of values? Can you find evidence that communications strategies were guided by this information?

   *Students should recognize the power of psychographic analyses in defining target consumers and positioning political candidates for office. They should search for campaign literature that is designed for different targets and that might even contradict each other, looking for obvious and subtle differences. This type of polling data is difficult to get because it is closely guarded by the candidates and their pollsters, but often just by viewing the ads one can identify the target audience. The students might also like to comment on recent political scandals that been rampant in Washington. What do these scandals (and the ability to retain public confidence during or after the scandal) tell us about values? What data were students able to get from the most recent presidential election? Comment on the communications strategies used by the two candidates.*

8.  Construct separate advertising executions for cosmetic products targeted to the Belonger, Achiever, Experiential, and Maker VALS types. How would the basic appeal differ for each group?

    *Students should review the information in the text before trying to design advertising campaigns for the various VALS types.*

    - *Actualizers—successful with many resources open to change.*
    - *Fulfilled—satisfied, reflective, comfortable, practical.*
    - *Achievers—career-oriented, avoid risk, self-discovery.*
    - *Experiencers—impulsive, young, offbeat, love risk.*
    - *Believers—strong principles, favor proven brands.*
    - *Strivers—like achievers, but with fewer resources, need approval.*
    - *Makers—action-oriented, self-sufficiency, do-it-yourselfers.*
    - *Strugglers—bottom-of-the-ladder, immediate gratification*

9.  Using media targeted to the group, construct a consumption constellation for the social role of college students. What set of products, activities, and interests tend to appear in advertisements depicting "typical" college students? How realistic is this constellation?

    *Students should enjoy developing a consumption constellation for their role segment. The instructor might point out how the students serve as "experts" with respect to this segment and how their constellation might differ from that constructed by their professors, parents, or business executives.*

10. Extreme sports. Day trading. Chat rooms. Vegetarianism. Can you predict what will be "hot" in the near future? Identify a lifestyle trend that is just surfacing in your universe. Describe this trend in detail and justify your prediction. What specific styles and/or products are part of this trend?

    *Depending on when this exercise is assigned, the responses will vary considerably. Many trends tend to be short lived. This will be particularly true of trends that have not actually become popular yet. Many students will likely identify an underground trend simply because they identify with it. This is all okay. The objective of this exercise is to describe a trend according to lifestyle and psychographics and to identify styles and products that would be congruent with this description.*

11. In what situations is demographic information likely to be more useful than psychographic data and vice versa?

   *Demographic information is likely to be more useful than psychographic data when simple, objective criteria are sufficient in defining and distinguishing potential consumers. Demographic data are more clearly defined and directly measurable than psychographics and, therefore, make segmentation on these basis more straightforward. In contrast, psychographics are used to understand consumers' motivations for purchasing and using products. These data reflect people's tendencies to sort themselves into groups on the basis of the things they like to do, how they like to spend their leisure time, and how they choose to spend their money. Many of these characteristics are more complex and less overt than demographics but often address the underlying motivations for individuals' behaviors.*

12. Alcohol drinkers vary sharply in terms of the number of drinks they may consume, from those who occasionally have one at a cocktail party to regular imbibers. Explain how the 80/20 rule applies to this product category.

   *According to text, the 80/20 rule states that only 20 percent of a product's users account for 80 percent of the product sold. For this question, alcohol drinkers vary according to the number of drinks consumed. Consumers may be heavy, moderate, or light users. Applying the 80/20 rule, we assume that 80 percent of the alcohol is drunk by 20 percent of the drinkers (who constitute the heavy-drinker segment). What does this mean with respect to advertising? What are the legal and ethical considerations of marketing to these "heavy drinkers"?*

# CASE STUDY TEACHING NOTES

### Chapter 6 Case Study: The Magic of iPod

### Summary of Case

Before reading this case, everyone will know something about the iPod craze. Although not the pioneer of MP3 players, Apple has risen to the top rapidly. Regardless of the onslaught of competitive tactics, Apple still holds over 90 percent of the market. This case attempts to illustrate some of the reasons why. Customers are not buying iPods because they are technologically superior or because they are cheaper. They are neither. They are buying them for image reasons. IPods have personality, and users become attached to them in an emotional way. This has sparked a tremendous industry for accessory products. It has also spawned a brand community that, given the youth of the brand, is unrivaled.

## Suggestions for Presentation

This case can be used to illustrate so many of the concepts from this case. But most specifically, this case was designed to use as a teaching tool for the two concepts identified in the discussion questions: brand personality and lifestyles.

## Suggested Answers for Discussion Questions

1.  Describe the personality of the iPod. Compare this to other high-image brands.

    *What are the traits that people (students) attribute to this product? As illustrated in the case, some users may ascribe very personal characteristics to their own iPod, and only to their iPod. However, there will likely be some general personality traits that will likely emerge. Svelte, sexy, intelligent, cool, hip, stylish, artistic, flexible, efficient—just to name a few.*

2.  According to the information in this case, do iPod users seem to have a unique lifestyle? Describe it. Discuss the changes that iPod has had on music-listening lifestyle in general.

    *Actually, by the time students read this case, it should be apparent that iPod is defying market segments and lifestyles. Certainly, people that are using them are at least moderately techno-savvy. However, everyone from teens to aging professors have embraced the product and the lifestyle. Because of this, there is hardly a unique customer type or a unique lifestyle. Students may offer up that there are many identifiable lifestyles.*

    *The impact that iPod has had on the way people listen to music is another story. No longer do people listen to "albums" or CDs. No longer do people have to decide what music they should take with them. People have it all in one place and are mixing it up constantly. They are more likely to buy music on a song-by-song basis. Also, the iPod generation is more likely to be exposed to a broad variety of music, given that swapping and sharing among co-users is taking place.*

# Additional Support Material

# STUDENT PROJECTS

## Individual Projects

1.  Ask students to examine advertisements and determine which appear to be Freudian or Neo-Freudian in nature. How is this determined? What were the messages in the advertisements?

2. Have each student develop a description of their own pleasure principle as it relates to consumption. In other words, how is their pleasure maximized and pain minimized when they buy certain types of products? What are the things that marketers do to appeal to this?

3. Have students select an ad or series of ads from a well-known campaign. Based on the ad, how have archetypes been formed among consumers?

4. Have each student characterize three different people that they associate with (friends, coworkers, classmates, family members, etc.) based on traits (trait theory). Each of the three should be distinct. How could this information be used by an advertiser?

5. Ask students to list three products that seem to have personalities. Describe the personalities. What types of people buy these products? Is there a match between the consumer's personality and that of the brand or product?

6. Ask students to compile a selection of recent ads that attempt to link consumption of a product with a specific lifestyle. In class, have students demonstrate what they have found. Discuss how the goal of linking product consumption to a lifestyle is usually accomplished.

7. Ask students to think of a specific lifestyle (your own, your parent's, your aspirations, etc.) and then make a list of products and services that are linked in the consumer's mind to that specific lifestyle. (*Hint:* You might decorate your living room, design a wardrobe, think of options for a car, etc.)

8. Have students select a product category. Then, have them develop a simple survey asking respondents how much they would be willing to pay for: 1) a generic version of the product, 2) a minor brand in the market, and 3) the market leading brand. Have them distribute this to ten individuals. Have them tally the results as a demonstration of brand equity.

9. This chapter mentions that psychographic analyses can be used by politicians to market themselves. What are some of the marketing strategies and techniques used by politicians in recent elections? Did the candidates design special appeals to attract the attention of special target markets? What communication strategies were used? Discuss your observations with the class.

10. Tell students that the owners of a fast-food chain have asked your class to prepare a psychographic profile of families living in the communities surrounding a new location they are considering. (You—the instructor—should select any area that the students would most likely know.) Construct a ten-question psychographic inventory appropriate for segmenting families in terms of their dining-out preferences.

11. Have students analyze their own patterns of food and beverage consumption. What values does this consumption reflect? Do your consumption patterns fit neatly within an identifiable food culture? Explain.

12. Ask students to examine their lifestyle and/or that of their family from a geodemographic perspective. Analyze your lifestyle according to the geographic levels of your neighborhood, zip code, city, and state.

13. Have students examine their usage of the Internet. What elements from personality and lifestyle would be important to this usage? How can marketers use this information? How can marketers obtain this information?

14. Based on the ideas behind Global MOSAIC, have students research the target group of global teenagers. What are the characteristics of this group? How have similarities developed? How are marketers targeting this group?

15. Have students use the principles of PRIZM to develop a description of their own home zip code.

16. Have students identify a co-branded pair of products. Based on Figure 6.2, have the students identify the justification for these two products to be linked.


## Group Projects

1. Bring in some magazines targeted toward specific regional or local groups (*Southern Living, Midwest Living, Progressive Farmer, Sunset, Ingrams, Arizona Highways,* etc.). Have student groups look through the magazines and describe the types of articles and advertisements contained in each. How effective are the magazines in reaching their target market? How do they use lifestyles?

2. Using AIO segmentation, have groups of students design a new advertising campaign for a chain of restaurants targeting young professional college graduates. Have them explain the process they went through.

3. As an in-class activity: Ask all students to classify themselves as idiocentric or allocentric. Once everyone has done this, then have them form groups of four to six people with other that have the same classification that they do. Have students evaluate themselves in groups according to the 5 points of difference between the two groups described in the text.

4. Student groups should identify three examples of lifestyle marketing on the Internet. Have members of the group demonstrate at least one of these sites in class. Show how the site uses lifestyles to the organization's advantage.

# eLAB

## Individual Assignments

1. Go to **www.benjerry.com** and **www.bluebunny.com**. What are the primary differences between these two popular Web sites? What lifestyles are segmented? Which site better expresses values? Profile the typical consumer of both organizations. What are the differences between the two profiles? Explain how you constructed the profiles.

2. Go to **www.burtsbees.com**. How does this site use lifestyle marketing to its advantage? What lifestyle would be most associated with the products shown on this site? After reading the history of the founders, how were the founders able to project their own lifestyles into the products produced by the company? How could the company expand its sales into other lifestyle segments?

3. Go to **www.mp3.com**. Which MP3 products seem to be the greatest hit with today's youth (feel free to expand your search to other Web sites to answer the question. You might try www.kazaa.com, www.morpheus.com, or www.apple.com/itunes/). Are market segments other than Gen X adopting MP3 technology? Explain. What could MP3 add to their Web site to expand to other generations or lifestyles? Explain.

4. Go to **www.scion.com**. Explore the site and describe in detail the personality of this brand.

5. Go to **www.bebe.com**. Analyze the product offerings for this company based on the id and the superego. Do people who buy this brand do so based on one or the other? Explain how the ego may create balance.

## Group Assignments

1. Go to **www.gijoe.com** (or **www.hasbro.com**) and **www.barbie.com**. Which of these organizations has done a better job of lifestyle marketing? What can you tell about personality from visitors to these sites? How do the sites use fantasy to their advantage? How have the two sites tried to update their products to meet modern needs? How has the G. I. Joe site dealt with violence (or the aversion to it)? Evaluate the Barbie Web site's ability to allow a customer to design his or her own doll? What do you think of this customization feature? What do you project as the future for these two product groups?

2. Have students go to **www.sric-bi.com/VALS/presurvey.shtml**. Have each of them take the survey and print out the page with the results. They should also print the list of VALS classifications and description. Then, have them discuss the outcomes in groups. Specifically, they should discuss whether they feel that the results are characteristic of them.

# CHAPTER

# 7

# *ATTITUDES*

## CHAPTER OBJECTIVES

When students have finished reading this chapter they should understand why:

- It's important for consumer researchers to understand the nature and power of attitudes.

- Attitudes are more complex than they first appear.

- We form attitudes in several ways.

- Consumers are motivated to maintain consistency among all the components of their attitudes, so they may alter one or more parts to realize this goal.

- We can measure attitudes using sophisticated models that identify specific components and combine them to predict what a consumer's overall attitude will be.

## CHAPTER SUMMARY

One of the most interesting studies in consumer behavior is the study of attitudes. An *attitude* is a lasting, general evaluation of people (including oneself), objects, advertisements, or issues. These evaluations can be positive or negative.

A *functional theory of attitudes* (developed by Daniel Katz) indicates that attitudes have the following functions: utilitarian, value-expressive, ego-defensive, and knowledge. Attitudes also relate to a person's relationship to his or her social environment.

Most researchers agree that an attitude has three basic components: *affect* (how someone feels), *behavior* (what someone does—intentions), and *cognition* (what someone believes). Although all three components of attitudes are important, their relative importance will vary depending on a consumer's level of motivation with regard to the attitude object ($A_o$). Attitude researchers traditionally assumed that attitudes were learned in a fixed sequence, consisting first of the formation of beliefs (cognitions) regarding an attitude object, followed by some evaluation of that object (affect), and then some action (behavior). Depending on the consumer's level of involvement and circumstances, however, attitudes can result from other hierarchies of effects as well. These different hierarchies can be used to predict the outcome of a variety of attitude situations. Several hierarchy formats are described in the chapter.

Consumers vary in their commitment to an attitude; the degree of commitment is related to their level of involvement with the attitude object. The degrees can be described as being compliance, identification, or internalization.

One organizing principle of attitude formation is the importance of consistency among attitudinal components—that is, some parts of an attitude may be altered to be in line with others. Such theoretical approaches to attitudes as *cognitive dissonance theory*, *self-perception theory*, *social judgment theory*, and *balance theory* stress the vital role of the need for consistency.

The complexity of attitudes is underscored by *multi-attribute attitude models*, where a set of beliefs and evaluations is identified and combined to predict an overall attitude. Factors such as subjective norms and the specificity of attitude scales have been integrated into attitude measures to improve predictability. Marketers now attempt to track attitudes over time to better understand how consumers change with respect to their feelings about their environment, products, and services.

# CHAPTER OUTLINE

### 1. The Power of Attitudes
  a. The term **attitude** is widely used in popular culture. For our purposes, an attitude is a lasting, general evaluation of people (including oneself), objects, advertisements, or issues.
    1) Anything that one has an attitude toward is called an **attitude object (A$_o$)**.
    2) An attitude is lasting because it tends to endure over time.
    3) An attitude is general because it applies to more than a momentary event (such as a loud noise).
    4) Attitudes help us to make all forms of choices (some important and some minor).

*Discussion Opportunity—Ask the class to brainstorm all the ways the term* attitude *is used in our society. List them on the board.*

  The Functions of Attitudes
  b. The **functional theory of attitudes** was initially developed by psychologist Daniel Katz to explain how attitudes facilitate social behavior. According to this pragmatic approach, attitudes exist *because* they serve some function for the person. That is, they are determined by a person's motives.
  c. The following attitude functions were identified by Katz:
    1) *Utilitarian function*—based on reward and punishment.
    2) *Value-expressive function*—goes to the consumer's central values or self-concept.
    3) *Ego-defensive function*—protects the person from threats or internal feelings.
    4) *Knowledge function*—the need for order, meaning, and structure.

*Discussion Opportunity—Bring in advertisements that display each of the attitude functions.*

The ABC Model of Attitudes
d. Most researchers agree that an attitude has three components that can be remembered as the **ABC model of attitudes**:
   1) **Affect** refers to the way a consumer *feels* about an attitude object.
   2) **Behavior** involves the person's intentions to *do* something with regard to an attitude object (this intention always results in behavior).
   3) **Cognition** refers to the *beliefs* a consumer has about an attitude object.

*Discussion Opportunity—Construct an example to illustrate each of the components of the ABC model of attitudes.*

*Discussion Opportunity—Ask: Which of the three components of the ABC model of attitudes do you believe is the most common explanation of attitudes? Why?*

*Discussion Opportunity—Ask: As far as you are concerned, which of the ABCs (in the hierarchy of effects model) do you believe has the strongest influence over you when you want to buy a CD player? When you take a special friend out to lunch? When you take this same friend out to dinner? When you buy a soft drink? When you turn on the radio and the Rush Limbaugh or Howard Stern program is on? Explain your reasoning in each case.*

e. The relative importance of the components of an attitude vary depending on the level of motivation.
   1) Attitude researchers have developed the concept of a hierarchy of effects to explain the relative impact of the three components (see ABC model discussed earlier).
   2) The three hierarchies are:
      a) *The standard of living hierarchy*—this is a problem-solving process.
      b) *The low-involvement hierarchy*—based on good or bad experiences.
      c) *The experiential hierarchy*—an emotional response.
         1. The subdivision of this model could include the *cognitive-affective model* where affective judgment is the last step in a series of cognitive processes.
         2. The *independence hypothesis* says that affect and cognition are separate, partially independent systems.

*****Use Figure 7.1 Here; Use Consumer Behavior Challenge #3 Here *****

*Discussion Opportunity—Give an illustration of the three different hierarchy of effects models. Ask students how each of them apply to consumer behavior?*

*Discussion Opportunity—Ask: How can the three different hierarchy of effects models be applied to e-commerce and shopping on the Internet? Give illustrations of how marketers might use this information to make better decisions.*

<u>Product Attitudes Don't Tell the Whole Story</u>

f. Marketers must understand that in decision-making situations people form attitudes toward objects other than the product itself that can influence their ultimate selections.

   1)  People's attitudes can be influenced by advertising.

   2)  One special type of attitude object is the marketing message itself.

   3)  The **attitude toward the advertisement (A$_{ad}$)** is defined as a predisposition to respond in a favorable or unfavorable manner to a particular advertising stimulus during a particular exposure occasion. Determinates include:

      a)  Attitude toward the advertiser.

      b)  Evaluations of the ad execution itself.

      c)  The mood evoked by the ad.

      d)  The degree to which the ad affects viewers' arousal levels.

   4)  The ad also has an entertainment value.

   5)  Feelings are generated by an ad. Emotional responses can be varied.

g. At least three emotional dimensions have been identified in commercials.

   1)  Pleasure.

   2)  Arousal.

   3)  Intimidation.

h. Special feelings that can be generated are:

   1)  *Upbeat feelings*—amused, delighted, or playful.

   2)  *Warm feelings*—affectionate, contemplative, or hopeful.

   3)  *Negative feelings*—critical, defiant, or offended.

---

*Discussion Opportunity—Ask: Think of ways your attitude is affected by advertising. As an example, what is your attitude toward the "Energizer Bunny" commercial? Do you buy Energizer batteries? Relate your purchase or non-purchase to attitudes (other current ads can be used to get a response).*

---

*Discussion Opportunity—Can you think of any ads that give you an upbeat feeling? Warm feeling? Negative feeling? How do the ads do this? What affect does it have on your attitudes? Do you buy any products that project a negative attitude (what about toward competition)?*

---

## 2. Forming Attitudes

a. Attitudes can form through:

   1)  Classical conditioning—using a jingle.

   2)  Instrumental conditioning—the attitude object is reinforced.

   3)  Leaning through complex cognitive processes—one learning what to do in social situations.

---

*Discussion Opportunity—Pick one area and demonstrate how you think you learned an attitude. Give examples to illustrate. How could a marketer have influenced you?*

---

<u>Not All Attitudes Are Created Equal</u>

b. All attitudes are not formed in the same way or of equal strength.

c. Consumers vary in their ***commitment*** to an attitude; the degree of commitment is related to their level of involvement with the attitude object.

1) *Compliance*—formed to gain reward or avoid punishment.
2) *Identification*—formed to be similar to others.
3) *Internalization*—has to become part of a person's value system (hard to change once formed).

---

*Discussion Opportunity—Give an illustration of how attitudes were formed by you in each of the three ways (levels of commitment). Which were the stronger attitudes? Which were eventually replaced?*

---

The Consistency Principle

d. According to the **principle of cognitive consistency**, consumers value harmony among their thoughts, feelings, and behaviors, and they are motivated to maintain uniformity among these elements. People will change to remain consistent with prior experiences.

1) The **theory of cognitive dissonance** states that when a person is confronted with inconsistencies among attitudes or behaviors, he or she will take some action to resolve this "dissonance," perhaps by changing an attitude or modifying a behavior.
2) People seek to reduce dissonant behavior or feelings. This can be done by eliminating, adding, or changing elements.

---

*****Use Consumer Behavior Challenges #4 and #5 Here *****

---

*Discussion Opportunity—Ask students to demonstrate when the principle of cognitive consistency has occurred in their purchase decisions. Repeat the question for the theory of cognitive dissonance. Ask them if they ever catch themselves reading ads (e.g., for a car) for products that they have already purchased?*

---

*Discussion Opportunity—Find an advertisement that illustrates the theory of cognitive dissonance and the principle of cognitive consistency. Show them to the class and ask how the advertisers use these theories in their ads? How effective is each ad?*

---

e. Do attitudes necessarily change following behavior because people are motivated to feel good about their decisions?

1) **Self-perception theory** provides an alternative explanation of dissonance effects. It assumes that people use observations of their own behavior to determine what their attitudes are.
   a) Self-perception theory is relevant to the *low-involvement hierarchy*.
   b) Can use the **foot-in-the-door technique** that is based on the observation that the consumer is more likely to comply with a request if he or she has first agreed to comply with a smaller request.

---

*Discussion Opportunity—Ask: Think of an illustration when someone has used the foot-in-the-door approach on you. Did you buy the product? Why or why not?*

---

2) **Social judgment theory** stipulates that (like self-perception theory) people assimilate information. The initial attitude acts as a frame of reference, and new information is categorized in terms of this existing standard.
   a) People find information to be acceptable or unacceptable.
   b) They form **latitudes of acceptance and rejection** around an attitude standard.
   c) Messages that fall within the latitude of acceptance tend to be seen as more consistent with one's position than they actually are (*the assimilation effect*), and messages within the latitude of rejection tend to be seen even farther from one's own position than they actually are (*the contrast effect*).

---

*Discussion Opportunity—Create a demonstration that illustrates the latitudes of acceptance and rejection for some product category as evidenced by your attitudes toward the object. Ask students if they can think of marketing activities that illustrate the topic?*

---

*Discussion Opportunity—Have students apply the concept of latitudes of acceptance and rejection to shopping on the Internet. Have them explain what they did and why the concept might apply.*

---

3) **Balance theory** considers relations among elements a person might perceive as belonging together. This perspective includes *triads*. Each contains:
   a) A person and his or her perceptions.
   b) An attitude object.
   c) Some other person or object.
4) Perceptions (under balance theory) are either positive or negative. Perceptions are *altered* to make them consistent.
5) Balance theory accounts for the widespread use of celebrities in advertising.

---

*****Use Figure 7.2 Here; Use Consumer Behavior Challenges #5 (Used Previously) and #6 Here*****

---

*Discussion Opportunity—Ask students to think of a consumer behavior situation where balance theory would seem to be operating.*

---

*Discussion Opportunity—Ask: Who are some celebrity endorsers who have fallen in disfavor with the public? How do you suppose this has affected the sales of the product they endorsed? Did any of the companies stop using these endorsers? Do you believe celebrity endorsement works? If so, under which circumstances?*

**3. Attitude Models**
   a. Attitude models have been developed to specify and explore the different elements that affect attitudes.

Multiple-Attribute Attitude Models
   b. A consumer's attitude is affected by an object's attributes. **Multi-attribute attitude models** have attempted to explore the many attributes that might impact a

consumer's decision-making process.
1)  This type of model assumes that a consumer's attitude (evaluation) of an attitude object ($A_o$) will depend on the beliefs he or she has about several or many attributes of the object.
2)  Basic multi-attribute models specify three elements:
    a) *Attributes*—characteristics of the attitude object.
    b) *Beliefs*—cognitions about the specific attitude object.
    c) *Importance weights*—reflects the priority consumers place on the object.

---

*Discussion Opportunity—Create a brief illustration of a basic multi-attribute model. Explain your reasoning.*

---

c.  The most influential of the multi-attribute models is the *Fishbein model*. This model measures:
1)  **Salient beliefs**—those beliefs about the object that are considered during evaluation.
2)  **Object-attitude linkages**—the probability that a particular object has an important attribute.
3)  **Evaluation of each of the important attributes**.

---

**\*\*\*\*\*Use Table 7.1 Here \*\*\*\*\***

---

d.  Strategic applications of the multi-attribute model would include:
1)  **Capitalize on relative advantage.**
2)  **Strengthen perceived product/attribute linkages.**
3)  **Add a new attribute.**
4)  **Influence competitors' ratings.**

---

**\*\*\*\*\*Use Consumer Behavior Challenges #6 (Used Previously) and #7 Here \*\*\*\*\***

---

*Discussion Opportunity—Create an illustration to apply to the Fishbein model. Then, using the material and formula from the chapter, have the students work through this application.*

---

**4. Using Attitudes to Predict Behavior**
a.  You can't always predict from knowledge of attitudes. A consumer can love a commercial but not buy the product. A person's attitude is *not* a very good predictor of behavior.

The Extended Fishbein Model
b.  This newer model is called the **theory of reasoned action**. Additions include:
1)  *Intentions versus behavior*—past behavior is a better predictor than intentions.
2)  *Social pressure*—others have a strong influence on behavior.
3)  *Attitude toward buying*—**attitude toward the act of buying** ($A_{act}$) focuses on perceived consequences of purchase.

*Discussion Opportunity—Ask: Who are some people who tend to have a strong influence on your behavior? Can you think of anyone whose behavior you have influenced? What was the result?*

*Discussion Opportunity—Ask: Can you think of something you bought that you really didn't want to buy? Do you know why you bought it anyway?*

    c. There are certain **obstacles to predicting behavior** (the improved Fishbein model):
      1) It was designed to deal with actual behavior—not **outcomes** of behavior.
      2) Some outcomes are beyond the consumer's control.
      3) Behavior is not always intentional (impulsive actions).
      4) Direct personal experience is stronger than indirect exposure (through an advertisement).
      5) Measures of attitudes do not always correspond with the behavior they are supposed to predict.
      6) A problem can exist with respect to the time frame.
      7) The problem of personal experiences versus receiving information such as advertising (**attitude accessibility perspective**).
    d. There is another way of looking at consumers' goals and trying to attain them. The **theory of trying** states that the criterion of **behavior** is the reasoned action model that should be replaced with **trying** to reach a goal. It recognizes barriers that might arise. The theory introduces several new components:
      1) **Past frequency**.
      2) **Recency**.
      3) **Beliefs**.
      4) **Evaluations of consequences**.
      5) **The process**.
      6) **Expectations of success and failure**.
      7) **Subjective norms toward trying**.

**\*\*\*\*\*Use Figure 7.3 Here \*\*\*\*\***

Tracking Attitudes over Time
    e. When researchers attempt to track attitudes over time they must remember to take many snapshots, not just a few. Develop an **attitude-tracking program**.
      1) Attitude tracking involves the administration of an attitude survey at regular intervals.
    f. Changes to look for when tracking attitudes include:
      1) **Changes in different age groups** (the life-cycle effect).
        a) The cohort effect.
        b) Historical effects.
      2) **Scenarios about the future**.
      3) **Identification of change agents**.

**\*\*\*\*\*Use Figure 7.4 Here; Use Consumer Behavior Challenges #6 and #7 (Both Used Previously) Here \*\*\*\*\***

*Discussion Opportunity—Ask students to chart an attitude that you have had for some time. How did it develop? How has it affected your decision making? How has it changed? What changed it?*

# End-of-Chapter Support Material

## SUMMARY OF SPECIAL FEATURE BOXES

### 1. Global Looking Glass

A Canadian magazine called *Briarpatch* has the mission of informing readers about important issues. One of the issues that it is promoting is that of breaking the global "American Addiction" through boycott. The magazine provides a 10-step program for accomplishing this and is gaining support worldwide.

### 2. Marketing Opportunity I

Given that more and more television viewers are zipping, zapping, or TiVoing right over commercials, advertisers are seeking ways of getting viewers to tune in to the ads. Various examples are highlighted in this box. **Contextual marketing** is a new online advertising approach that sends pop-up ads to Web shoppers for products that compete with the ones they are examining.

### 3. Marketing Opportunity II

This box examines some of the advances that are being made in the area of emotional response measurement. Included is technology that aims to enable computers to determine the user's emotional state and make adjustments to cater to that state. This feature supports the section "The Experiential Hierarchy."

### 4. Marketing Pitfalls

This box reviews research that determines the most irritating commercials on television. Characteristics of irritating commercials are also given. This feature supports the section "Attitude Toward the Advertisement."

### 5. Marketing Opportunity III

This box illustrates balance theory by giving an example of how people publicize their connections with successful people or groups. Specifically, research is cited showing that students are more likely to wear clothing items with their school's insignia when their football team had won their weekly game. This feature supports the section "Marketing Applications of Balance Theory."

# REVIEW QUESTIONS

1.  How can an attitude play an ego-defensive function? *Attitudes we form to protect ourselves either from external threats or internal feelings perform an ego-defensive function. An early marketing study indicated that housewives in the 1950s resisted the use of instant coffee because it threatened their conception of themselves as capable homemakers.*

2.  Describe the ABC model of attitudes. *Most researchers agree that an attitude has three components: affect, behavior, and cognition. Affect refers to the way a consumer feels about an attitude object. Behavior involves the person's intentions to do something with regard to an attitude object (but, as we will discuss a later point, an intention does not always result in an actual behavior). Cognition refers to the beliefs a consumer has about an attitude object. We can remember these three components of an attitude as the ABC model of attitudes.*

3.  List the three hierarchies of attitudes, and describe the major differences among them. *The three hierarchies are 1) the Standard Learning Hierarchy (beliefs/affect/behavior), 2) the Low-Involvement Hierarchy (beliefs/behavior/affect), 3) and the Experiential Hierarchy (affect/behavior/beliefs).*

4.  How are emotions (affect) and cognitions (beliefs) related to how attitudes are formed? *That all depends on which of the three hierarchies is in process. But the basis of the ABC model of attitudes is that both affect and beliefs, along with behavior, are the main components that comprise an attitude.*

5.  Other than the direct attitude we might have about a product, what is another type of attitude that might influence the likelihood we will buy it? *Attitude toward the advertisement and attitude toward the act of buying.*

6.  How do levels of commitment to an attitude influence the likelihood it will become part of the way we think about a product in the long term? *Consumers vary in their commitment to an attitude; the degree of commitment is related to their level of involvement with the attitude object. Consumers are more likely to consider brands that engender strong positive attitudes.*

7.  What do we mean by contextual marketing? *Contextual marketing refers to providing online consumers with information about competitors at the exact time when they are searching for details or shopping for a particular product category.*

8.  We sometimes increase our attitude toward a product after we buy it. How does the theory of cognitive dissonance explain this change? *The theory of cognitive dissonance states that when a person is confronted with inconsistencies among attitudes or behaviors, he or she will take some action to resolve this "dissonance," perhaps by changing an attitude or modifying a behavior. The theory has important ramifications for attitudes, because people are often confronted with situations in which there is some*

*conflict between their attitudes and behaviors. Thus, if a person encounters negative information about a product after purchasing it, they may discount that information and focus on positive information that would reaffirm their reasons for having purchased.*

9.  What is the foot-in-the-door technique? How does self-perception theory relate to this effect? *Self-perception theory helps to explain the effectiveness of a sales strategy called the foot-in-the-door technique that is based on the observation that a consumer is more likely to comply with a request if he or she has first agreed to comply with a smaller request.*

10. What are latitudes of acceptance and rejection? How does a consumer's level of involvement with a product affect his latitude of acceptance? *People form latitudes of acceptance and rejection around an attitude standard. Ideas that fall within a latitude will be favorably received, but those falling outside of this zone will not.*

11. According to balance theory, how can we tell if a triad is balanced or unbalanced? How can consumers restore balance to an unbalanced triad? *Components of a triad can be either positive or negative. More importantly, people alter these components in order to make relations among them consistent. The theory specifies that people desire relations among elements in a triad to be harmonious, or balanced. If they are not, a state of tension will result until somehow the person changes his perceptions and restores balance.*

12. What is basking in reflected glory, and how does it create marketing opportunities? *Consumers often like to publicize their connections with successful people or organizations (no matter how tenuous the connection) to enhance their own standing. In balance theory terms, they are attempting to create a unit relation with a positively valued attitude object. Researchers call this tactic "basking in reflected glory."*

13. Describe a multiattribute attitude model, listing its key components. *A multiattribute model assumes that a consumer's attitude (evaluation) toward an attitude object ($A_o$) depends upon on the beliefs he or she has about several or many attributes of the object. The use of a multiattribute model implies that identifying these specific beliefs and combining them to derive a measure of the consumer's overall attitude can predict an attitude toward a product or brand.*

14. "Do as I say, not as I do." How does this statement relate to attitude models? *Many studies have obtained a very low correlation between a person's reported attitude toward something and his or her actual behavior toward it. Some researchers have been so discouraged that they have questioned whether attitudes are of any use at all in understanding behavior.*

15. What is a subjective norm, and how does it influence our attitudes? *The value of SN is arrived at by including two factors: (1) the intensity of a normative belief (NB) that others believe an action should be taken or not taken, and (2) the motivation to comply*

*(MC) with that belief (i.e., the degree to which the consumer takes others' anticipated reactions into account when evaluating a course of action or a purchase).*

16. What are three obstacles to predicting behavior even if we know a person's attitudes? *There are too many obstacles to list here. See the section entitled, "Obstacles to Predicting Behavior in the Theory of Reasoned Action."*

17. Describe the theory of reasoned action. Why might it not be equally valuable when it is applied to non-Western cultures? *The theory of reasoned action has primarily been applied in Western settings. Certain assumptions inherent in the model may not necessarily apply to consumers from other cultures. Several cultural roadblocks diminish the universality of the theory of reasoned action.*

18. What is the value of attitude tracking? What issues do researchers need to consider when doing this? *An attitude survey is like a snapshot taken at a single point in time. It may tell us a lot about a brand's position at that moment, but it does not permit many inferences about progress the brand has made over time or any predictions about possible future changes in consumer attitudes.*

# CONSUMER BEHAVIOR CHALLENGE

## <u>Discussion Questions</u>

1. Students often bask in reflected glory by taking credit for victories their teams earn over other colleges. Should students who just watch the games rather than play them take credit for their team's performance?

   *"Taking credit" may not be the appropriate term here. Most students are not likely to give any kind of implication that they had something to do with the fact that their team won. The greater issue here is that the student feels a connection to the university that they attend. Sports teams are very often among the main features or attributes for a university. They are often touted for recruitment of new students. Therefore, the "basking in reflected glory" phenomenon should not come as any type of surprise. If we view this connection as such, when the attribute is very positive, then attitudes of those involved will be positive. When a team wins, students want to "share the joy."*

2. One person's "contextual marketing" is another person's "spyware." Is it ethical for marketers to track which Web sites you visit, even if by doing so they can provide you with information that might help you save money by buying a competing brand?

   *Both sides to this issue are certain to arise. Most students will probably lean toward, "it's just a business practice, there is nothing wrong with it." In bringing out the different sides of this debate, instructors should distinguish between contextual marketing practices that involve software that a person has downloaded versus those that do not. If a person has downloaded software, then in essence, they have consented to being exposed to this type of promotion.*

3.  Contrast the hierarchies of effects outlined in the chapter. How will strategic decisions related to the marketing mix be influenced by which hierarchy is operative among target consumers?

    *The "standard learning" hierarchy assumes a purposeful and involved process in attitude formation leading to a decision that may lead to brand loyalty. On the other hand, the "low-involvement" hierarchy assumes a minimal amount of knowledge and sees the attitude formed "after-the-fact." The chapter specifically notes that the use of marketing stimuli would be more effective in the low-involvement situation because the consumer uses these inputs as a basis for selection and attitude formation, instead of product-related characteristics. Students should note, however, that the product is the key ingredient in the marketing mix, and consequently, long-term success is less likely to result from simple, low-involvement attitude formation.*

4.  More than 500 universities have signed up commercial companies to run campus Web sites and e-mail services. These agreements provide Web services to colleges at little or no cost. But, these actions have aroused controversy, because major companies pay to place advertising on the sites. That gives marketers entrée to influence the attitudes of thousands of students who are involuntarily exposed to product messages. One professor complained, "we're throwing our freshmen to the wolves. The University has become a shill for the corporate community." But university administrators argue that they could not provide the services by themselves—students expect to be able to fill out financial aid forms and register for classes online. Colleges that do no offer such services may lose their ability to attract students. How do you feel about this situation? Do you agree that you are being "thrown to the wolves"? Should companies be able to buy access to your eyeballs from the school you pay to attend?

    *Hopefully, the responses to this question will take in the full range of possibilities and a healthy debate will ensue. Business and marketing students, however, often favor the rights of the company to engage in practices such as this to promote their brands. Some will likely bring up the argument that as long as promotional practices are legal, there is nothing wrong with them. Others may disagree from an ethical perspective.*

## Application Questions

5.  Think of a behavior someone does that is inconsistent with his or her attitudes (e.g., attitudes toward cholesterol, drug use, or even buying things to make them stand out or attain status). Ask the person to elaborate on why he or she does the behavior, and try to identify the way the person has resolved dissonant elements.

    *Students should be able to generate many diverse examples of this type of consumer behavior. Assume you are a high school student who is health conscious but who may*

185

*smoke occasionally because your friends smoke. The reason you smoke may be to "fit in" with a group, or the behavior may serve as some type of initiation into the group. You may resolve dissonant elements by telling yourself that an occasional cigarette won't hurt you as long as you keep exercising and eating right.*

6. Devise an attitude survey for a set of competing automobiles. Identify areas of competitive advantage or disadvantage for each model you incorporate.

   *The semantic-differential scale often is used to describe a consumer's beliefs about product, brands, and/or companies. Students are likely to develop scale items reflecting a variety of beliefs about individual products, where a set of product attributes are rated on a series of scales. For example:*

   *My travel agent is:*

   | | | |
   |---|---|---|
   | *Very efficient* | *1—2—3—4—5—6—7* | *Very inefficient* |
   | *Very accessible* | *1—2—3—4—5—6—7* | *Very inaccessible* |
   | *Very friendly* | *1—2—3—4—5—6—7* | *Very unfriendly* |

   *Semantic-differential scales also may be used to compare the images of competing brands, as in the next example:*

   *Honda Accords have good interior features.*
   *Agree          1—2—3—4—5—6—7          Disagree*

   *Toyota Camry's have good interior features.*
   *Agree          1—2—3—4—5—6—7          Disagree*

   *Chevrolet Malibu's have good interior features.*
   *Agree          1—2—3—4—5—6—7          Disagree*
   *(Possible Individual or Group Field Project Idea)*

7. Construct a multi-attribute model for a set of local restaurants. Based on your findings, suggest how restaurant managers can improve their establishments' images via the strategies described in the chapter.

   *The multi-attribute models that students develop for a set of local restaurants should include:*

   - *A number of product attributes—characteristics of the restaurants, such as price, type of foods, number of menu items, location, etc.*

   - *Beliefs regarding specific restaurants (in terms of attributes).*

   - *Important weights reflecting the relative priority of specific attributes for them individually.*

*Although there likely will be some common elements in the models developed, students should be encouraged to think about how each model is reflective of the individual responsible for the product evaluation. The instructor should point out to students the complexity of consumer attitudes, as demonstrated by the diversity of attitudinal statements, product attributes, beliefs, and importance weights that might be chosen. (Possible Individual or Group Field Project Idea)*

# CASE STUDY TEACHING NOTES

### Chapter 7 Case Study: Wal-Mart

### Summary of Case

Wal-Mart is the largest retailer, not to mention the largest company, in the world. Over 80 percent of Americans make at least one purchase at Wal-Mart in a given year. Wal-Mart provides lower prices than competitors, a larger variety of goods and services, and the convenience of 24-hour operations. Studies have shown that Wal-Mart's strategies for cost-cutting have not only affected the prices of the goods that they sell, but have also had rippling effects throughout the economy as pressure has been put on manufacturers as well as other retailers to do the same. Wal-Mart is one of the most admired corporations. But it is also one of the most reviled. Reasons are given in this case for this assertion.

### Suggestions for Presentation

This case can be used to illustrate just about any concept or model in the chapter. The case is set up in a way that specific features and attributes of the brand are highlighted. Thus, it is perfect for demonstrating multi-attribute models. The information contained in the case can be used as the basis for discussing beliefs, feelings, and behaviors that are the components of the ABC model of attitudes. Principles of cognitive consistency and cognitive dissonance can be demonstrated based on the very attractive features of Wal-Mart and how these relate to either Social judgment theory can be demonstrated by showing how someone with a positive attitude might react upon learning the more negative accusations.

### Suggested Answers for Discussion Questions

1. Use a multi-attribute model to show how individuals may develop either a positive or a negative attitude toward Wal-Mart.

   *The attributes of low prices, huge variety, and convenient hours are very clearly identified in the case. Use these as three basic attributes. Then show how different people (and you might even actually call upon certain people) evaluate each of these things differently in terms of both their beliefs about each attribute as well as the importance or weight that each factor gets. One of the outcomes of Zeithaml's means-end chain value model is that for some, value IS low price. For such individuals, this feature will play a huge role in the development of a positive attitude toward Wal-Mart.*

*As far as beliefs are concerned, most people will not refute that Wal-Mart excels at these features. But different people will attach a different value to them. In the same manner, some will place a huge weight of importance while those with negative opinions will place a small weight relative to social responsibility issues like providing livable wages, and not importing goods made in sweatshops.*

2.  Explain why one's behavior might be inconsistent with their attitude toward Wal-Mart.

    *This is a great question for discussion. There are many people who harbor negative attitudes toward retailer such as Wal-Mart for very valid reasons (some listed in the case, others based on bad customer service experiences). But many will "cave" when they feel that they do not have other options (at 2 a.m. when one must have some Nyquil in order to get to sleep and nothing else is open) or when the allure of certain features (the price on a wanted item is much lower than at competing stores) is overpowering.*

# Additional Support Material

# STUDENT PROJECTS

## Individual Projects

1.  Ask students to write about the sources that are influential in his or her attitude toward one of the following: your college or university, the Republican/Democratic party, President Bush (or any recently elected President), Rush Limbaugh, Ralph Nader, his or her own religious faith, or any organized group (e.g., labor movement, Planned Parenthood, American Civil Liberties Union, Greenpeace, Moveon.org, etc.). As an alternative, interview a few friends about one of these organizations. Have students share their findings with the class. What can be learned about attitudes by having these discussions? What would be of value to a marketer?

2.  Have students bring in examples of promotional material that illustrates each of the four functions identified in the functional theory of attitudes.

3.  Students should assemble ads for physical fitness and/or weight loss programs or products and analyze these ads in terms of how they are trying to influence or change consumers' attitudes toward their body image. What emotional and rational appeals were used (e.g., fear, health, vanity, social acceptance, peer pressure, etc.)?

4. Have students explain the consistency, balance, and Fishbein theories to a friend, and then ask the friend to analyze two of his or her recent experiences that seem to confirm or disconfirm one or more of these theories. Report the findings to the class.

5. In this project, students should identify one specific example for each of the three hierarchies of the ABC model. For each, they should give details as to the application of each component.

6. Have students describe a specific example of when they have experienced an unbalanced triad in a consumer context. How did they balance the triad?

7. It's time for true confessions. Describe three instances when your purchase behavior was inconsistent with an attitude toward the product or service you were buying. Explain why this happened. Share this with the class asking them if they agree with the explanation or whether they have other notions.

8. Have students write a short paper identifying both a consumer product that they just "love" and one they just "hate." They should address how long they have felt this way, if they remember when they first developed these attitudes, why they still might feel this way, and if they have ever tried to change their attitude.

9. Ask students to take a position on one of the two following points of view and defend their position:

   • Position One—Using knowledge of attitudes is manipulative and is wrong. Advertisers and marketers should be prevented from following this practice.

   • Position Two—Using knowledge of attitudes is just a natural extension of wanting to understand the consumer. By using attitude information, a marketer (or advertiser) can more easily meet the wants and needs of the consumer.

10. Have students prepare an example of the Fishbein model and present the findings to the class.

## Group Projects

1. This is a good in-class project in which you or a group of students can lead a class discussion. Give the class a list of eight or ten common generic products (e.g., cars, peanut butter, detergent, toothpaste, gasoline, toilet paper, microwave dinners, a professional football team, an airline, and a soft drink) and ask them to list their favorite brand(s) of the product. See if those who are participating know how they developed their brand preference and how the products' attributes are related to their attitudes toward the product(s).

2.  Another good in-class project: Have groups of students decide on a purchase situation that they all have experience with. Then, have them discuss situations involving cognitive dissonance (buyer's remorse). What led to such?

3.  Divide the class into teams and have each team come up with a set of about ten descriptive words that could be used to positively or negatively describe a specific consumer good (e.g., a stereo, car, expensive clothing, etc.). Send students out to interview a friend who owns this product. Determine the length of time the respondent has owned the product and then have the respondent evaluate the product according to some criteria determined by the class. See if the people who more recently purchased the product have a more positive attitude toward it than those who have owned it for a longer period of time. Because of time length, the instructor may wish to do this in class between groups or only have a few students participate in the project.

4.  Ask a group of students to have three people write down the names of the best and worst provider of an identical service (e.g., a bank, dentist, dry cleaner, hair dresser, airline, fast food restaurant, etc.). Have the respondents give five descriptive words for each provider—ask them to use negative words that can be used in polite society. How could both service providers use this information? What would you do to change image for these firms?

5.  Ask a group of students to think about restaurants they like and don't like to patronize. Have them design a multi-attribute model for three of these restaurants, making sure both spectrums are included. Have students make suggestions of how the managers could improve the restaurants' images by following the strategies and tactics found in this chapter.

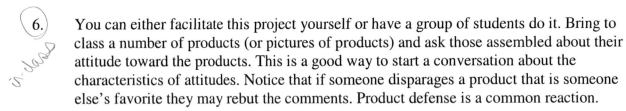

6.  You can either facilitate this project yourself or have a group of students do it. Bring to class a number of products (or pictures of products) and ask those assembled about their attitude toward the products. This is a good way to start a conversation about the characteristics of attitudes. Notice that if someone disparages a product that is someone else's favorite they may rebut the comments. Product defense is a common reaction.

7.  There are four strategic applications of the multiattribute model given in the text. Have groups identify cases where companies have applied each of them.

8.  Attitudes change over time. Have groups of students brainstorm a list of products for which consumer attitudes have changed over time. Be sure to have them identify the change agent involved (either some aspect of the external environment or some aspect of the company itself.

9.  Have groups of students go to a large retail store to participate in an observation-oriented exercise. Have them stake out different parts of the store and observe what people say about a given product. Have them keep notes on such, and identify the attitudes demonstrated and how they were likely developed.

# eLAB

## Individual Assignments

1. Go to **www.levistrauss.com**. Levi Strauss used to dominate the jeans market. It was a mainstay product for youth in the '50s, '60s, and '70s. Something happened in the '80s and '90s, however, that caused the youth to begin shifting their attention to other brands and different ways of dressing. What did attitudes have to do with this shift? How should the company best deal with these changes? Using yourself as an example, tell Levi's what they must do to once again secure your business. If you are already a customer, explain what the company must do to keep your business.

2. Go to **www.hottopic.com**. This clothing Web site provides clothing alternatives for the new millennium. Evaluate the Web site as to its use of lifestyle marketing. What attitudes seem to be most important to Hot Topic's customers? How did you determine this? Any suggestions for the company on how they might expand their business?

3. Go to **www.dropzone.com.** Apply the ABC model of attitudes to the activity of skydiving. Which of the three hierarchies is most applicable? What modifications could be made to this?

4. Visit **www.izod.com**. Is a multiattribute model a good one to apply to this product to explain how attitudes are formed? Why or why not? Suggest an alternative model.

5. Go to **http://earth.google.com**. Download the software. Explore. After having spent some time with this product, what is your attitude toward it? Why? Use concepts from the chapter to illustrate this.

## Group Assignments

1. Go to **www.lego.com**. Once your group visits this site they will recognize how far Danish toymaker Lego has come from the days when they only made plastic blocks. Today, the company is into robotics in a big way. That's right—robotics. Assume that Lego has made a functioning personal assistant robot. What attitudes must be identified, formed, or changed for this product to be successful? Be complete in your appraisal. Lastly, what features should the robot have? What would be its name?

2. Have groups of students go to **www.moveon.org.** As a group, they should spend some time reviewing the material on this Web page. Each student will likely have different attitudes. But the task here is to apply either the principle of cognitive consistency or cognitive dissonance. How is either applicable to the *experience* of having gone to this site?

# CHAPTER 8

# ATTITUDE CHANGE AND INTERACTIVE COMMUNICATIONS

## CHAPTER OBJECTIVES

When students have finished reading this chapter, they should understand why:

- The communications model identifies several important components needed to transmit messages that attempt to change consumers' attitudes toward products and services.

- The consumer who processes such a message is not necessarily the passive receiver of information marketers once believed him or her to be.

- Consumers' responses to a firm's marketing messages do not necessarily have to take the form of a purchase to be important or useful to the company.

- Several factors influence how effective the source of a communication will be.

- The way a message is structured can exert a big impact on how persuasive it will be.

- Consumer variables help to determine whether the nature of the source or the message itself will be relatively more effective in communicating.

## CHAPTER SUMMARY

This chapter focuses on how the marketer can attempt to change attitudes through persuasive and interactive communications. In fact, *persuasion* refers to an attempt to change attitudes. To begin this process of change, a good place to start is in understanding *communication models*. A standard model is presented along with ramifications for changing attitudes. Parts of this model include a source, message, medium, receiver, and feedback.

Although the traditional communications model is acceptable, it does not tell the whole story as far as consumer behavior is concerned. Consumers have more choices than ever and much more control over which messages they will choose to process. New ideas about communication (the *uses and gratifications theory*) are presented. The end conclusion is that marketers must keep pace with the rapidly changing communication environment if they wish to reach consumers with their messages and ideas.

Regardless of how or to what extent the consumer receives the message, *source effects* are an important variable to be considered by the marketer and advertiser. Under most conditions, the source of a message will have a big impact on the likelihood the message will be accepted. Two particularly important source characteristics are discussed—source *credibility* and *attractiveness*. The study of attractiveness is particularly interesting given the dramatic increase in the usage of celebrities to endorse products. Pros and cons of this approach are reviewed.

Characteristics of the message itself help to determine its impact on attitudes. Some elements of a message that help to determine its effectiveness are whether it is conveyed in words or pictures, how often the message is repeated, whether an emotional or rational appeal is employed, the frequency with which it is repeated, whether a conclusion is drawn, whether both sides of the argument are presented, and whether the message includes fear, humor, or sexual references. Each of the these elements is reviewed in this chapter.

The relative influence of the source versus the message depends on the receiver's level of involvement with the communication. The *elaboration likelihood model (ELM)* specifies that a less-involved consumer will more likely be swayed by source effects, while a more-involved consumer will more likely attend to and process components of the actual message. Marketers must learn to account for these differences if they wish to be effective communicators.

# CHAPTER OUTLINE

## 1. Changing Attitudes Through Communication
   a. Consumers are constantly bombarded by messages inducing them to change their
      attitudes. The focus of this chapter is on aspects of communication that specifically
   help to determine how and if attitudes will be created or modified.
   1) **Persuasion** refers to an active attempt to change attitudes.
   2) Persuasion is a central goal of many marketing communications.
   3) Some psychological principles that function in the persuasion process are:
      a) *Reciprocity*.
      b) *Scarcity*.
      c) *Authority*.
      d) *Consistency*.
      e) *Liking*.
      f) *Consensus*.

---

*Discussion Opportunity—Have the class think of an attitude that one or both of their parents have. Ask them to think of a way that they could persuade them to change the attitude?*

---

Decisions, Decisions: Tactical Communications Options
b. To craft persuasive messages that might change attitudes, a number of questions
   must be answered:
   1) Who is featured in the ad that seeks to change an attitude? Given the
         circumstances, who would be best? (The source of a message helps to determine
      consumers' acceptance of it as well as their desire to try the product.)
   2) How should the message be constructed?
   3) What media should be used to transmit the message?
   4) What characteristics of the target market might influence the ad's acceptance?

The Elements of Communication
c. Marketers and advertisers have traditionally tried to understand how marketing
   messages can change consumers' attitudes by thinking in terms of the
   **communications model** that specifies that a number of elements are necessary
   for communications to be achieved. The basic model can be perceived as
   having five parts:
   1) The source—where the communication originates.
   2) This meaning must be put in the form of a *message*. There are many ways to
      say something.
   3) The message must be transmitted via a *medium* (such as television or
      magazines).
   4) The message is then decoded by one or more *receivers*. The receiver interprets
      the message in light of their own experiences.
   5) Finally, *feedback* must be received by the source (who uses the reactions of
      the receivers to modify aspects of the message).

---

*****Use Figure 8.1 Here *****

---

*Discussion Opportunity—Provide an illustration of the communications model described in the
chapter. What are the strengths and weaknesses of this model? How can the source be a better
communicator?*

---

An Updated View: Interactive Communications
d. Traditional models of communications do not tell the whole story about the
   communication process.
   1) Consumers have many choices in today's dynamic world of interactivity.
   2) **Permission marketing** is a relatively new term used to describe consumers who have
      agreed to allow marketers to send them promotional information.
   3) The traditional model was developed by what was known as the
      *Frankfurt School* (it dominated communication theory for most of the last
      century).
   4) One of the flaws was that the receiver was largely seen as being passive or
      just "fed" by the media.
e. Proponents of the **uses and gratification theory** argue that consumers are
   an active, goal-directed audience that draws on mass media as a resource to
   satisfy needs. (This is contrary to the traditional model mentioned previously.)

1) This view emphasizes that media competes with other sources to satisfy needs, and that these needs include diversion and entertainment as well as information.
2) There is a blur between information and entertainment (such as with Web sites).
3) Consumers are becoming more like partners than ever before. They may seek out messages.
4) The remote control device is an example of this "seeking" behavior. Consumers are seeking to control their media environment.

---

*****Use Figure 8.2 Here; Use Consumer Behavior Challenge #9 Here *****

---

*Discussion Opportunity—Ask students to think of examples of how they are passive and active in information acquisition. Ask how they interact with the media to receive information.*

---

*Discussion Opportunity—Ask: How you are attempting to control your own Web or Internet environment.*

---

f. There has been an influx in new ways to transmit information in both text and picture form.
1) **M-commerce** (mobile commerce) involves wireless devices including cell phones, PDAs, iPods. These channels are growing and are quickly being used by marketers as alternatives channels for promotional information.
2) **Blogging** is where people post messages to the Web in diary form. There are various types of blogs, including flogs (confederate blogs created by companies to generate buzz).

---

*****Use Consumer Behavior Challenge #2 Here *****

---

g. A key to understanding the dynamics of interactive marketing communications is to consider exactly what is meant by a response. A variety of responses are possible:
1) Buying the product.
2) Building brand awareness.
3) Acquiring information about product features.
4) Reminders.
5) Building a long-term relationship (probably the most important response).
h. There are two basic types of feedback:
1) *First-order response*—a product offer that yields a transaction (an order).
2) *Second-order response*—customer feedback in response to a marketing message that is not in the form of a transaction.

---

*Discussion Opportunity—Ask students to give a personal example of a second-order response. Did this response eventually result in a transaction?*

---

*Discussion Opportunity—Ask students to think of techniques that help a second-order response end in an order. Have them list them, and then call on individuals to share.*

---

## 2. The Source

a. Regardless of how a message is received, common sense tells us that the same words uttered or written by different people can have very different effects.

1) Under most conditions, the source of a message can have a big impact on the likelihood the message will be accepted.
2) Two very important source characteristics are *credibility* and *attractiveness*.

Source Credibility

b. **Source credibility** refers to a source's perceived expertise, objectivity, or trustworthiness. The belief that a communicator is competent is important to most consumers. A credible source can be particularly persuasive when the consumer has not yet learned much about a product or formed an opinion of it.

1) Credibility can be enhanced if the source's qualifications are perceived as somehow relevant to the product being endorsed. This linkage can overcome many objections the consumer may have toward the endorser or product.
2) Even negatively perceived sources can affect attitude change in a positive manner through what is known as the **sleeper effect**. This effect demonstrates that in some instances, the differences in attitude change between positive sources and less positive sources that seem to get erased over time. Explanations of the sleeper effect include:
   a) The *dissociative cue hypothesis*—over time the message and the source become disassociated in the consumer's mind.
   b) The *availability-valence hypothesis*—emphasizes the selectivity of memory owing to the limited capacity.

*****Use Consumer Behavior Challenge #3 Here *****

*Discussion Opportunity—Ask students to think of a specific illustration of the sleeper effect.*

3) A consumer's beliefs about a product's attributes can be weakened if the source is perceived to be the victim of bias in presenting information.
   a) *Knowledge bias* implies that a source's knowledge about a topic is not accurate.
   b) *Reporting bias* occurs where a source has the required knowledge, but his or her willingness to convey it accurately is compromised.

*Discussion Opportunity—Ask: What celebrity sources do you perceive as being most credible? Is this in specific product or service categories or across the board?*

4) Often, the more involved a company appears to be in promoting its products, the less credible it becomes. This phenomenon, known as the **Corporate Paradox**, results in **hype** that is easily dismissed by consumers.
5) In contrast, **buzz** generated by word of mouth is viewed as authentic and credible.

*****Use Table 8.1 Here *****

> *Discussion Opportunity—Ask students to think of an example of word of mouth surrounding a product that could be considered buzz.*

### Source Attractiveness
c. **Source attractiveness** refers to the source's perceived social value. This quality can emanate from the person's physical appearance, personality, social status, or similarity to the receiver (we like to listen to people who are like us).
1) When used correctly, famous or expert spokespersons can be of great value. They can also be very expensive.
2) A halo effect often occurs when persons of high rank on one dimension are assumed to excel on others as well. Be careful of the stereotype "what is beautiful is good."

> *Discussion Opportunity—Ask students to give an example of the "halo effect."*

3) A physically attractive source, however, tends to facilitate attitude change.
    a) Beauty serves as a source of information.
    b) The *social adaptation perspective* assumes that information seen to be instrumental in forming an attitude will be more heavily weighted by the perceiver.
4) Celebrities embody *cultural meanings* to the general society.
5) The **match-up hypothesis** says that celebrities that match the product are the most successful endorsers.

> *****Use Consumer Behavior Challenges #5 and #15 *****

> *Discussion Opportunity—Ask students to give an example of a celebrity that they perceive to be an illustration of the match-up hypothesis.*

> *Discussion Opportunity—As a means of contrasting credibility with attractiveness, ask students to give examples of products where they would want to make sure their source is credible; examples where their source is attractive.*

6) At times, the image of celebrity endorsers can damage the image of a company or brand. For this reason, companies may seek animated characters or fictitious mascots as endorsers.
7) A more current trend sees companies utilizing endorsers in the form of an **avatar**, or cyber-character.

> *Discussion Opportunity—Ask: Can you think of company spokespersons who fit the company or the product image? Who do not fit? What should the company do about this? Give an example of a celebrity whose image has really hurt a company's marketing effort.*

### 3. The Message
  a. Are commercials effective? Research indicates that those that have a brand-differentiating message are consistently the most effective.
  b. Characteristics of the message itself have an impact on attitudes. Issues facing marketers include:
  1) Should the message be conveyed in words or pictures?
  2) How often should the message be repeated?
  3) Should a conclusion be drawn, or should this be left up to the listener?
  4) Should both sides of an argument be presented?
  5) Is it effective to explicitly compare one's product to competitors?
  6) Should blatant sexual appeals be used?
  7) Should negative emotions, such as fear, ever be aroused?
  8) How concrete or vivid should the arguments and imagery be?
  9) Should the ad be funny?

*****Use Table 8.2 Here *****

Sending the Message
c. Great emphasis is placed on sending visual messages. Words may be necessary, however, to communicate factual information. Both elements used together are especially strong.
  1) Verbal messages are stronger in high-involvement situations.
  2) Visual messages result in a stronger memory trace that aids retrieval over time. (See the idea of a "chunk" found in Chapter 3.)
d. Visual elements may affect brand attitudes.
  1) The consumer may form inferences about the brand and change his or her beliefs because of an illustration's imagery.
  2) Brand attitudes may be affected more directly through strong negative and positive reactions. (See the dual component model of brand attitudes found in Figure 8.3.)

*****Use Figure 8.3 Here *****

e. Elements:
  1) **Vividness**—powerful descriptions and graphics help us remember.
  2) **Repetition**—repetition helps us remember, but ads "wear out." Too much repetition creates **habituation**.
   a) The **two-factor theory** proposes that two separate psychological processes are operating when a person is repeatedly exposed to an ad. The positive

side increases familiarity. The negative side breeds boredom over time.
- b) Advertisers have to watch too much repetition. Provide variety in the basic message.

---

*****Use Figure 8.4 Here *****

---

*Discussion Opportunity—Ask students to think of ads that illustrate vividness and repetition. What do you remember about them? Why do you think you remember what you do?*

---

Constructing the Argument
- f. Arguments can be presented in a variety of ways. Examples include:
  - 1) The one- versus two-sided argument.
    - a) The **supportive argument** is one sided and most often used.
    - b) **Two-sided messages** give positive and negative information. This seems most effective when the audience is well educated.
    - c) **Refutational arguments** raise a negative issue and then dismiss it.

---

*Discussion Opportunity—Ask students to give an illustration of a supportive argument, a two-sided argument, and a refutational argument. Find an example of each in a print media form.*

---

  - 2) Drawing Conclusions. The question becomes should the advertiser draw conclusions or leave it to the consumer to decide? The response to this depends on the consumer's motivation to process the ad and the complexity of the arguments.
  - 3) **Comparative Advertising**. This technique compares two specifically named products and seems to be effective for new products.

---

*****Use Consumer Behavior Challenges #4, #10, and #12 Here *****

---

*Discussion Opportunity—Ask: What do you think of comparative advertising? Are the arguments more believable? Do you ever find yourself defending the "against product"?*

---

Types of Message Appeals
- g. Emotional appeals try to bond the consumer with the product. Ads that make you think through the use of rational appeals, however, are easier to recall. Effects of emotional ads are very hard to gauge.

---

*****Use Consumer Behavior Challenges #1 and #6 Here *****

---

Discussion Opportunity—*Ask students to think of situations when a rational appeal works best and when an emotional appeal works best. What is the effectiveness dependent on?*

---

- h. Sex appeals range from subtle hints to blatant displays of skin. Most assume, however, that "sex sells."

1) Does sex work?
   a) It draws attention.
   b) It is ineffective if the consumer sees it as a trick or gratuitous.
   c) It is most effective if the product is sex-related (such as perfume).

---

*****Use Consumer Behavior Challenge #11 Here *****

---

*Discussion Opportunity—Ask: Do you find more nudity in ads in men's or women's magazines? Is the nudity in either type of magazine mostly of men or of women?*

---

*Discussion Opportunity—Ask: What are your feelings about using sex in advertising? What are the dependent factors? Even if you are against it, are there circumstances when it would be Okay?*

---

i. Humorous appeals are somewhat challenging to use because what is funny to one is offensive to another.
   1) Humor can be a distraction.
   2) Subtle humor is usually the best.
   3) Humor should be appropriate to the product's image.

---

*Discussion Opportunity—What are some of your favorite ads that use humor? Do you buy those products or products from their competition?*

---

j. **Fear appeals** emphasize the negative consequences that can occur unless the consumer changes a behavior or an attitude.
   1) This appeal can be directed toward social fear.
   2) It can also be directed toward fears about careers and love life.
   3) Fear is effective if used in moderate amounts.

---

*****Use Consumer Behavior Challenge #13 Here *****

---

*Discussion Opportunity—Who can think of an ad in which the actors fear losing their jobs? Think of ways that career fear can be used.*

---

*Discussion Opportunity—Ask: What are some products that seem to use fear to attract customers?*

---

The Message as Art Form: Metaphors Be with You
   k. An **allegory** is a story told about an abstract trait or concept that has been personified as a person, animal, or vegetable.
   l. A **metaphor** involves placing two dissimilar objects into a close relationship such that "A is B," whereas a **simile** compares two objects, "A is like B." Metaphors allow the marketer to activate meaningful images and apply them to everyday events.

m. **Resonance** is another literary device that is frequently used in advertising to form a presentation that combines a play on words with a relevant picture.

> ***\*\*\*\*\*Use Table 8.3 Here; Use Consumer Behavior Challenge #14 Here \*\*\*\*\****

> *Discussion Opportunity—Give an illustration or bring an ad that displays a metaphor or resonance in advertising.*

n. The way an audience is addressed can be just as different as the story being told.
   1) Counterarguments can appear.
   2) In *transformational advertising*, the customer associates the experience of product usage with some subjective sensation.

> *Discussion Opportunity—Find an ad where a story is being told. Show or read it to the class. Ask: Do you ever catch yourself reading an ad just to see how the story ends?*

> *Discussion Opportunity—Give an illustration of transformational advertising. Ask the class to evaluate how well the ad applies the technique.*

**4. The Source Versus the Message: Sell the Steak or the Sizzle?**
   a. Variations in a consumer's level of involvement result in the activation of very different cognitive processes when a message is received.

The Elaboration Likelihood Model
   b. The **elaboration likelihood model (ELM)** assumes that once a consumer receives a message he or she begins to process it. Depending on the personal relevance of this information, one of two routes to persuasion will be followed. The routes are:
   1) Under conditions of *high involvement*, a consumer takes the *central route to persuasion*.
   2) Under conditions of *low involvement*, a *peripheral route* is taken.

> ***\*\*\*\*\*Use Figure 8.5 Here \*\*\*\*\****

c. In the central route to processing, the consumer will determine if the message is relevant. The person will actively think about the arguments presented and generate either positive (cognitive responses) or negative (counterarguments) responses. This route usually involves the traditional hierarchy of effects.

> *Discussion Opportunity—Illustrate the elaboration likelihood model by bringing in a series of print ads that illustrate either the central route or the peripheral route. Show them to the class and ask the class to identify which route is more dominant. Also ask students to point out cognitive cues and peripheral cues in either type of ad.*

d. In the peripheral route to persuasion, the consumer is not motivated to think about the argument and use other cues in deciding on the suitability of the message.

> *Discussion Opportunity—Ask: If you were the producer of a product that was being examined by the consumer in a peripheral way, what strategies could you suggest for dealing with this? In what instances would this not be bad for the producer?*

    e. The ELM model has received a lot of research support. Crucial variables to this model are:
       1) *Message-processing involvement*—high or low.
       2) *Argument strength*—use strong or weak arguments in ads.
       3) *Source characteristics*—viewed as positive or negative by receivers.

> *****Use Consumer Behavior Challenge #9 (Used Previously) Here *****

# End-of-Chapter Support Material

# SUMMARY OF SPECIAL FEATURE BOXES

**1.    Marketing Opportunity**

Companies have been turning to their "highly involved" customers as sources of valuable market information. Examples are given of companies that conducted formal market research with this group.

**2.    Global Looking Glass**

Different countries and different cultures often display differences in consumer behavior. However, when it comes to Web shopping, the customers in the United States and New Zealand are surprisingly similar. Although there are some minor differences, customers in both countries rely on the same strategies for awareness, information-gathering, and purchase decision.

**3.    Net Profit**

A popular strategy for online advertising is to disguise the source or even make one up. Specific examples are given of companies that have followed this strategy, including Burger King with their Web site, www.subservientchicken.com.

**4.    Marketing Pitfalls**

Celebrities endorsing products is hardly a new strategy. But consumers in the United States may think that they are exposed to all the products that a given celebrity endorses. However, it is very common for a star to endorse products in other countries that are not endorsed in the United States.

**5.    The Tangled Web**

Some men will do almost anything to get a girlfriend. This includes the men that have hooked up with Vivienne, the avatar that is for sale to anyone who wants to court her.


# REVIEW QUESTIONS

1.    List three psychological principles related to persuasion. *The psychological principles include reciprocity, scarcity, authority, consistency, liking, and consensus.*

2.    What is the difference between a first-order response and a second-order response? Give one example of each. *First-order response: Direct-marketing vehicles such as catalogs and television infomercials are interactive—if successful, they result in an order that is most definitely a response! Second-order response:  A marketing communication, however, does not have to immediately result in a purchase to be an important component of interactive marketing. Messages can prompt useful responses from customers, even though these recipients do not necessarily place an order immediately after being exposed to the communication.*

3.    Describe the elements of the traditional communications model, and tell how the updated model is different. *The traditional model of communication includes the components of source, channel, message, receiver, and feedback. The updated model (interactive model), recognizes that there are multiple senders and multiple receivers, all sending and receiving information simultaneously through a central medium.*

4.    Compare the perspective on media and attitude change proposed by the Frankfurt School theorists versus those who advocate a uses and gratifications perspective. *A group of theorists known as the Frankfurt School that dominated mass communications research for most of the last century, strongly influenced this model. In this view, the media exert direct and powerful effects on individuals, and often those in power use it to brainwash and exploit the population. The receiver is basically a passive being—a "couch potato" who simply is the receptacle for many messages—and who is often duped or persuaded to act based on the information he is "fed" by the media.*

5.    What are blogs and how can marketers use them? *A blog involves people posting messages to the Web in diary form. Blogging started as a grassroots movement where individuals shared their thoughts on a range of topics, from the mundane to the profound. This phenomenon hasn't slowed down yet; people post about 40,000 new blogs every day.*

6.    What is source credibility, and what are two factors that influence whether we will perceive a source to be credible? *Source credibility refers to a source's perceived expertise, objectivity, or trustworthiness. Factors affecting source credibility are: 1)*

*whether the sources qualifications are viewed as relevant, and 2) whether or not there is a bias associated with the source.*

7.  What is the difference between buzz and hype? How does this difference relate to the corporate paradox? *Buzz is word of mouth that is viewed as authentic and generated by customers. In contrast, hype is dismissed as inauthentic—corporate propaganda planted by a company with an axe to grind.*

8.  What is a halo effect, and why does it happen? *The halo effect occurs when persons who rank high on one dimension are assumed to excel on others as well.*

9.  What is an avatar, and why might an advertiser choose to use one instead of hiring a celebrity endorser? *An avatar is the manifestation of a Hindu deity in superhuman or animal form. In the computing world it means a cyberspace presence represented by a character that you can move around inside a visual, graphical world. The advantages of virtual avatars compared to flesh-and-blood models include the ability to change the avatar in real time to suit the needs of the target audience. From an advertising perspective they are likely to be more cost-effective than hiring a real person. From a personal selling and customer service perspective they have the ability to handle multiple customers at any one time, they are not geographically limited, and they are operational 24/7, thus freeing up company employees and sales personnel to perform other activities.*

10. When should a marketer present a message visually versus verbally? *Because it requires more effort to process, a verbal message is most appropriate for high-involvement situations, such as in print contexts in which the reader is motivated to really pay attention to the advertising. Because verbal material decays more rapidly in memory, these messages require more frequent exposures to obtain the desired effect. Visual images, in contrast, allow the receiver to chunk information at the time of encoding. Chunking results in a stronger memory trace that aids retrieval over time.*

    *Visual elements may affect brand attitudes in one of two ways. First, the consumer may form inferences about the brand and change his beliefs because of an illustration's imagery. For example, people in a study who saw an ad for a facial tissue accompanied by a photo of a sunset were more likely to believe that the brand came in attractive colors. Second, brand attitudes may be affected more directly; for example, a strong positive or negative reaction the visual elements cause will influence the consumer's attitude toward the ad ($A_{ad}$) that will then affect brand attitudes ($A_b$).*

11. How does the two-factor theory explain the effects of message repetition on attitude change? *The two-factor theory explains the fine line between familiarity and boredom by proposing that two separate psychological processes are operating when a person is repeatedly exposed to an ad. The positive side of repetition is that it increases familiarity and thus reduces uncertainty about the product. The negative side is that over time boredom increases with each exposure. At some point the amount of boredom incurred begins to exceed the amount of uncertainty reduced, resulting in wear-out.*

12.  When is it best to present a two-sided message versus a one-sided message? *Under the right circumstances, the use of refutational arguments, in which a negative issue is raised and then dismissed, can be quite effective. This approach can increase source credibility by reducing reporting bias. Also, people who are skeptical about the product may be more receptive to a balanced argument instead of a "whitewash."*

13.  Do humorous ads work and if so under what conditions? *Humor is more likely to be effective when the brand is clearly identified and the funny material does not "swamp" the message. This danger is similar to one we've already discussed about beautiful models diverting attention from copy points. Subtle humor is usually better, as is humor that does not make fun of the potential consumer. Finally, humor should be appropriate to the product's image. An undertaker or a bank might want to avoid humor, whereas other products may adapt to it quite well.*

14.  Should marketers ever try to arouse fear in order to persuade consumers? *Negative fear appeals are usually most effective when only a moderate threat is used, and when the ad presents a solution to the problem. Otherwise, consumers will tune out the ad because they can do nothing to solve the problem. This approach also works better when source credibility is high.*

15.  Why do marketers use metaphors to craft persuasive messages? Give two examples of this technique. *Metaphors allow the marketer to activate meaningful images and apply them to everyday events. In the stock market, "white knights" battle "hostile raiders" using "poison pills"; Tony the Tiger equates cereal with strength, and the Merrill Lynch bull sends the message that the brokerage is "a breed apart."*

16.  What is the difference between a metaphor and resonance? *A metaphor involves placing two dissimilar objects into a close relationship such that "A is B." Resonance is another type of literary device that advertisers use frequently. It is a form of presentation that combines a play on words with a relevant picture.*

17.  What is the difference between a lecture and a drama? *A lecture is like a speech in which the source speaks directly to the audience in an attempt to inform them about a product or persuade them to buy it. A drama is similar to a play or movie.*

18.  Describe the elaboration likelihood model, and tell how it is related to the relative importance of **what** is said versus **how** it's said. *The elaboration likelihood model (ELM) assumes that once a consumer receives a message she begins to process it. Depending on the personal relevance of this information, the receiver will follow one of two routes to persuasion. Under conditions of high involvement, the consumer takes the central route to persuasion. Under conditions of low involvement, she takes a peripheral route instead.*

# CONSUMER BEHAVIOR CHALLENGE

**Discussion Questions**

1.  What are the pros and cons of using rational versus emotional appeals, i.e. trying to persuade consumers by focusing on what they know as opposed to what they feel? When should marketers use one type or the other?

    *Rational appeals are better when objectives are oriented around the cognitive, as in the case of recall. However, for building relationships between the consumer and the brand, emotional appeals have the advantage. Emotional strategies are also effective when consumers do not detect significant differences between brands.*

2.  A flog is a fake blog a company posts to build buzz around its brand. Is this ethical?

    *This is another one of those "gray area" tactics that most students will see as just another way of doing business. However, if one focuses on the basic tenet of the AMA's code of ethics dealing with deceptive practices, then flogging is unethical. It is, by nature, deceptive. In fact, such will only work if the consumer is deceived.*

3.  The sleeper effect implies that perhaps we shouldn't worry too much about how positively people evaluate a source. Similarly, there's a saying in public relations that "any publicity is good publicity." Do you agree?

    *There will certainly be exceptions to this. The good thing about publicity is, it's free. Thus, when a company of any kind is getting publicity, they are getting free promotion. The extent to which negative publicity will have positive effects on consumer perceptions simply depends. One of the best-case scenarios is when the negative publicity is controversial and offends people who are not part of the target group, while being perceived in a positive manner by those who are part of the target group.*

4.  Discuss some conditions where it would be advisable to use a comparative advertising strategy.

    *Comparative advertising may be effective for low-involvement products, like convenience goods, new brands that have advantages over existing brands, and brands that are experiencing decreased sales using noncomparative advertising. For new product introductions, comparative ads benefit from the association they form between established products and new, unknown products. Students should recognize that repositioning an older established brand would also be a viable situation for comparative advertising. The discussion also might include an analysis of conditions when it would not be advisable to use comparative ads. Students should be encouraged to list ads they have seen or heard and to describe the aspects of each ad that would make the use of comparative advertising advisable or inadvisable.*

5.   The American Medical Association encountered a firestorm of controversy when it
     agreed to sponsor a line of health care products manufactured by Sunbeam (a decision it
     later reversed). Should trade or professional organizations, journalists, professors, and
     others endorse specific products at the expense of other offerings?

     *This question addresses the issue that all people who endorse products are not
     necessarily celebrities or models. The effect of the endorsement can be very strong,
     however, because of the element of trust and respect (or even the power of
     recommendation) that might be involved. Students should think of situations beyond those
     mentioned in the question that address this issue. A lively discussion should follow. How
     do the students feel about the ethics involved? In what circumstances (if any) should a
     sitting President endorse a product?*

6.   A marketer must decide whether to incorporate rational or emotional appeals in its
     communications strategy. Describe conditions that are more favorable to using one or the
     other.

     *Students' responses should include the issues of product involvement and complexity.
     Emotional appeals can be used with low involvement products to increase the level of
     consumers' involvement with the products. Emotional appeals also are appropriate for
     homogeneous or commodity-type products. Alternatively, rational appeals are
     recommended when there are significant differences between product alternatives.*

7.   Many, many companies rely on celebrity endorsers as communications sources to
     persuade. Especially when targeting younger people, these spokespeople often are "cool"
     musicians, athletes, or movie stars. In your opinion, who would be the most effective
     celebrity endorser today and why? Who would be the least effective? Why?

     *As with the previous question, students should use more than just their opinions. Direct
     them to the principles discussed in the sections on source attractiveness and source
     credibility. Some responses here will likely mirror the reality of which celebrities are
     used the most. Others will likely recognize that there are many celebrities who are not
     endorsing products that would be very effective.*

8.   The Web site for Swiss Legend, a watch brand, includes a section called "Celebrity Red
     Room," where there are photographs of famous people sporting the timepieces with their
     colorful and graphically striking designs. Swiss Legend has found its way to these
     people, despite the fact that it hasn't been around very long, in part because it has been
     "associated with" events like the SAG Awards and the Teen Choice Awards. This means
     that it has arranged to have its products given away at those events. This practice is called
     "gifting the talent." The point is not just to get celebrities to wear Swiss Legend watches,
     which sell in the $150 to $450 price range, but also to leverage the press coverage that
     focuses on what celebrities wear. The stars have been getting their Swiss Legends by way
     of Backstage Creations, one of several companies that oversee what has long since
     become a standard practice at awards shows and other galas. One method of gifting the
     talent is through "goody bags," a practice now so widely known that goody-bag contents

are listed in the celebrity press. Backstage Creations does gift bags but also offers a more elaborate approach, creating an entire backstage environment—or "retreat"—laid out and decorated by a name interior designer and filled with complimentary products. What do you think about the practice of "gifting the talent" in order to accumulate endorsements? Is this a sound strategy? Is it ethical for celebrities to accept these gifts?

*Although this may be considered by some to be a gray area promotional technique, it does not carry with it the level of deception that flogging does. Many fans and viewers are aware that when stars are wearing things at events, they have been given those items or are even paid to wear such. For those that are not aware of this, there is no information given that implies that the star bought the apparel or accessory item of their own volition. As far as whether it is a sound strategy, at the most basic level, it is a minimal investment and could potentially provide very effective coverage.*

## Application Questions

9. A government agency wants to encourage the use of designated drivers by people who have been drinking. What advice could you give the organization about constructing persuasive communications? Discuss some factors that might be important, including the structure of the communications, where they should appear, and who should deliver them. Should fear appeals be used, and if so, how?

   *Steps the government agency should take:*

   - *The target market(s) should be established (teenage drivers).*
   - *Both the source and the message must be considered.*
   - *The source must be both credible and attractive to the target audience.*
   - *Make a list of possible sources for the message.*

   *One of the largest target markets would be teenage drivers, thus making it necessary for the source to be aligned with that group. Such a person, or organization, would also have to be perceived as having social value, or having source attractiveness, to have the greatest persuasive impact. Likewise, the structure of the communication would need to be tailored to meet the processing needs and likes of the target market. Recall that uninvolved consumers will respond to peripheral cues best, and therefore the use of celebrity endorsers and other non-product-related aspects will have a greater effect. Fear appeals should be used judiciously and only with moderate emphasis on the negative aspects.*

   *(The instructor may elect to provide samples of public issue advertisements, or encourage students to collect some advertisements that can be used to stimulate discussion of issues relevant to the design of this form of advertising.) (Possible Field Project Idea)*

10.     Why would a marketer consider saying negative things about his or her product? When is this strategy feasible? Can you find examples of it?

*The use of two-sided arguments is effective when the audience is well educated and not loyal to the product. These conditions exist for many new product introductions and brand extensions. When the advertised product is complex, something negative can be said about the minor attribute without producing an overall negative affect, as long as positive descriptions of major attributes of the product also are included. For example, Curtis Mathis has advertised that its televisions are very expensive (a negative attribute) while countering with information about the superb quality, workmanship, and service provided.*

11.     Collect ads that rely on sex appeal to sell products. How often are benefits of the actual product communicated to the reader?

*Students will be able to find examples of products that use sex appeal in almost any magazine, but magazines targeted toward either men or women are the best sources. NOTE: Be sure to examine ads before they are presented to the class. Some students get carried away (especially the males) and might present material that is offensive to other class members (especially the females). The instructor should not rely solely on the students' judgment in this matter. (Possible Field Project Idea)*

12.     Observe the process of counterargumentation; ask a friend to talk out loud while watching a commercial. Ask him or her to respond to each point in the ad or to write down reactions to the claims made. How much skepticism regarding the claims can you detect?

*Students will enjoy this project. You might encourage a student to videotape a few ads and show the tape to a friend. This will give the student an opportunity to choose a few ads that make a number of claims that can be analyzed. (Possible Field Project Idea)*

13.     Make a log of all the commercials shown on one network television channel during a two-hour period. Categorize each according to product category and whether they are presented as drama or argument. Describe the types of messages used (e.g., two-sided arguments) and keep track of the types of spokespeople (e.g., TV actors, famous people, animated characters). What can you conclude about the dominant forms of persuasive tactics currently employed by marketers?

*The instructor might want to encourage students to work in pairs to better manage the recording of 10- and 15-second commercials. One person could write about one commercial while the other person is listening to the next commercial. (Possible Field Project Idea)*

14. Collect examples of ads that rely on the use of metaphors or resonance. Do you feel these ads are effective? If you were working with the products, would you feel more comfortable with ads that use a more straightforward, "hard-sell" approach? Why or why not?

*Make sure students review the section of the text that describes how metaphors and resonance are used in advertising before they go in search of ads. Encourage the students to discuss both the positive and the negative aspects of metaphors or resonance. (Possible Field Project Idea)*

15. Create a list of current celebrities whom you feel typify cultural categories (e.g., clown, mother figure, etc.). What specific brands do you feel each could effectively endorse?

*Students should be encouraged to think carefully about a variety of product categories to do this project. Listing celebrities, their characteristics, brand characteristics, and matchups is a good way to begin. Many of the matchups will be product specific. Ask students how many of the celebrities they have chosen could be used outside of specific product ranges? Encourage discussion with this question.*

16. Conduct an "avatar hunt" by going to e-commerce Web sites, online video game sites, and online communities like the Sims or Cybertown that let people select what they want to look like in cyberspace. What seem to be the dominant figures people are choosing? Are they realistic or fantasy characters? Male or female? What types of avatars do you believe would be most effective for these different kinds of Web sites as well as for associating with various brands? Explain your reasoning?

*This should be a fun exercise that students will enjoy. Hopefully, students will draw from concepts discussed in the chapter regarding celebrity and nonhuman endorsers. Specifically, encourage students to incorporate principles of source attractiveness as they consider what types of avatars would be most effective for various Web sites and products. You might also consider asking students to include an explanation of why they feel the more dominant avatars are more effective than human celebrity endorsers.*

# CASE STUDY TEACHING NOTES

**Chapter 8 Case Study: David Beckham: Professional Endorser**

<u>Summary of Case</u>

This case features the one of the top celebrity endorsers ever, soccer (football) player David Beckham. Beckham has had a long and successful career as a soccer player in Europe. However, from the earliest days as a pro, he did what Michael and Tiger did: he secured some very lucrative endorsements. Since then, he has added to his portfolio to become one of the biggest product endorsers ever.

The question is asked: "Does the brand make the player, or does the player make the brand?" Nothing is ever a sure thing, but in a case such as Beckham's, the answer is "both." This is discussed in the text. Specifically, his most recent contract with Adidas is highlighted.

## Suggestions for Presentation

This case is most directly applicable to the concepts of celebrity endorsement in the text. Within this concept, the concepts of cultural meanings and the match-up hypothesis should be discussed. But the bigger picture behind celebrity endorsement is that of source effects. This case is very appropriate for illustrating source attractiveness and source credibility. As a more indirect application, the Elaboration Likelihood Model could be discussed with respect to the types of messages that might effectively utilize a big celebrity endorser.

## Suggested Answers for Discussion Questions

1.   In the context of source effects, discuss why companies such as Adidas would be interested in being endorsed by David Beckham.

     *Source credibility: Beckham derives most of his credibility as a source from his expertise. Is he a trustworthy person? That much is debatable, especially given the information on his extramarital affair. However, he is an expert at his game, so any product associated with soccer or sports in general would benefit from that expertise. He is also an expert at being a celebrity. Good looking, fashionable, jet-setter lifestyle—fashion, apparel, and prestige products would also be good choices.*

     *Source attractiveness: This much should be obvious. Beckham is a good looking man with a beautiful and famous wife. Not every celebrity scores well on attractiveness.*

2.   Considering how attitudes are formed, what are the potential positive and negative consequences of endorsements for both the company and the celebrity?

     *One thing was mentioned in this case; that of the allegations of Beckham having an extramarital affair. Although that has not seemed to have a negative effect on his fame and popularity, this is certainly the type of thing that falls into the category of risk. If Beckham engages in any kind of behavior that is viewed as unseemly and unforgivable, public opinion on him could turn in an instant. In the same manner, what would happen if he were to suffer a career-ending injury? The risks for Beckham are similar. Any company can become the brunt of negative publicity overnight. But barring some unforeseen occurrence such as this, the risks that the endorser takes are assessable up front to some extent. Is the image of the brand one that will enhance the image of the endorser? That should be determinable without signing any contracts.*

# Additional Support Material

# STUDENT PROJECTS

## Individual Projects

1.      Ask one of your students to interview three people and have each respondent identify an advertisement that they have a positive attitude toward and an ad that they have a negative attitude toward. Be sure to inquire to find out how their attitudes toward the ads influence their attitudes toward the products and likelihood of purchase.

2.      Have students produce an example of some type of promotion used for each of the principles of reciprocity, scarcity, authority, consistency, liking, and consensus.

3.      People hate the ad, but still find that they purchase the product. Have students generate and discuss a list of products that have had success from annoying campaigns. Why is this the case?

4.      Corporations love the buzz. Have students describe three examples of companies that have achieved positive PR benefits from the "buzz." Why did this happen. Have them also generate a list of three companies that have flopped based on hype. What was the difference between these situations?

5.      Have students design a print ad for a product or service of their choosing (the product or service may be real or fictitious, but the ad should be original work). Instruct them that they may get as elaborate as they wish (employing graphic software) or they may use the old-fashioned method of designing one by hand. Also instruct them that they should apply the principles discussed in the chapter to make the ad an effective tool of persuasion. This assignment will particularly appeal to the more creative students.

6.      Have students conduct a simple content analysis by examining either print or broadcast ads. They may find such ads in real sources such as magazines, newspapers, or by watching television. They may also find such ads online at Web sites that maintain archives of advertisements. Students should view numerous ads and analyze which of the following message appeals appear to be used: (a) emotional, (b) rational, (c) sex, (d) humorous, and (e) fear. Does the medium or specific media vehicle have an effect on which appeals are used most commonly? After conducting this analysis, have students explain which appeal(s) is most powerful? Most persuasive? Most credible?

7.      Have a student bring in three television ads that employ humor. Then ask the student to analyze the ads and explain what makes the ads funny and what causes them to wear out. What types of products can change your attitude by using humor in the message?

8.      Negative attitudes are often difficult to change. Ask students to think of a company that has had some bad press. How has the company handled the news? Have they been

successful in turning the situation around? What techniques did they employ (or are they employing)? What suggestions do you have for the company?

9.  As an out-of-class assignment, ask students to reveal a social issue that they oppose (e.g., smoking, alternative lifestyles, drug use, or using alcohol). Next, have students examine their attitudes toward the subject. What could be done to change their attitudes? Bring in evidence of marketers' attempts to do so. Comment on the effectiveness of these attempts.

10. Bring in a number of print or television ads that rely on the use of metaphors or resonance (or have your students do it). Have the students discuss the ads in groups. What are their initial reactions to the ads? How effective do they think they are? Do they think some other approach would be more convincing? Why?

11. Have students identify an ad that is very evidently being repeated. Have the student estimate the frequency that the ad is being shown (they might want to do a little research [Google, Lexis-Nexis] to get some help). Is the ad experiencing positive or negative effects of the frequency of exposure?

## Group Projects

12. Bring in a number of print or television ads that use celebrity endorsers (or have students do it). Have students get into groups to discuss how effective they think the ads are. By evaluating the spokesperson as either "good" or "poor", determine whether the class likes the celebrity. Do they find the ads believable or contrived? Probe to find out why they feel this way.

13. Have student groups select a product brand and look up advertisements for it during the past 20 years or so. (Good library sources include *National Geographic, Ladies Home Journal, Reader's Digest*, and *Time*. Coke, Pepsi, Miller beer, Hallmark, and others have excellent videos of their old ads and the students tend to enjoy watching these.) Demonstrate how these ads reflect changes in consumer attitudes.

14. There is probably a pub or a restaurant near campus that is known for its lack of cleanliness. Ask student teams to take charge of this establishment and develop a promotional campaign that would change consumers' attitude toward this pub or restaurant. What is the difference between atmosphere and cleanliness? Could a manager clean the place up "too much"? Explain.

15. Have student groups collect ads that demonstrate the literary devices of allegory, metaphor, simile, and resonance. Have them discuss the effectiveness of such with the class.

16. Using the most recent national or state election as a backdrop, evaluate which candidate did the best job of changing attitudes among voters. Explain your reasoning. Give

examples if possible. How did this "attitude change attempt" figure into the outcome of the election?

17. Pick a controversial figure. Your group's assignment is to design a public relations campaign that will change the public's image about the figure you have chosen. What principles from the chapter did your group use to accomplish your mission? Present your campaign to the class. Measure whether the image of your chosen figure was improved or not.

18. Each group of students should generate a list of at least 20 current celebrity endorsers (this should not be too difficult and they can use outside source for help). Which of these companies are getting the most bang for their buck and why? Which of the celebrities are benefiting the most from the boost of the company image and why?

19. Have groups of students to take a common consumable product and apply a fear appeal to promoting the product. Have the students critique the effort with respect to the material presented in the chapter on using fear appeals. Have them do the same for applying a humor appeal to a commonly serious product.

# eLAB

## Individual Assignments

1. Go to **www.ge.com**. Pick a product from the huge portfolio of General Electric. This product should be one that you do not use and have a negative attitude against. Design a brief advertising campaign that would persuade you to use the product. Explain the process that you went through and the principles from the chapter you used in your campaign.

2. Go to **www.floss.com**. We all know that we should floss our teeth more often. Why don't we? With the help of this Web site, create a series of arguments that could get consumers to floss more often. Which products would seem to be best positioned to get consumers the most results from their increased flossing? Explain your choice.

3. Go to **http://adbusters.org/spoofads/index.php.** This is a Web site of spoof advertisements. Just how outrageous are these ads given the reality of what consumers are faced with? Discuss a few of the ads in relation to concepts from the text.

4. Go to **www.jeliowa.org**. How does this organization use fear appeals to change behavior and attitudes. Evaluate the effectiveness of the approach.

5. Go to **www.georgeforeman.com**. George Foreman has made a comeback, more than once. But long after his boxing career is over, he has been making a fortune as a brand spokespersons. What contributes to his popularity? For what products is he most

successful (how many endorsed products can you name)? Should any of these companies be worried that George is endorsing too many products? Explain.

## Group Assignments

1.    Go to **http://www.theaxeeffect.com/flash.html**. Go to the various links for the Web site of Axe body spray. Analyze the content in terms of message appeals.

2.    Go to **www.philipmorris.com** and **www.rjrt.com**. Your group's assignment is to critically evaluate both of these Web sites with respect to public relations efforts toward changing the public's view regarding the company and its products. Notice that beer, alcohol, and cigarettes are controversial products. What techniques are used? How do the companies overcome fear appeals used by their detractors? How do the companies attempt to reach consumers beyond their normal target markets? Evaluate the success of both companies. Explain your reasoning. Do legislative restrictions and lawsuits seem to have affected the companies normal business operations? If so, how?

# CHAPTER 9

## *INDIVIDUAL DECISION MAKING*

## CHAPTER OBJECTIVES

When students have finished reading this chapter, they should understand why:

- Consumer decision-making is a central part of consumer behavior, but the ways people evaluate and choose products (and the amount of thought they put into these choices) vary widely depending upon such dimensions as the degree of novelty or risk related to the decision.

- A decision is actually composed of a series of stages that results in the selection of one product over competing options.

- Our access to online sources is changing the way we decide what to buy.

- Decision making is not always rational.

- Consumers rely upon different decision rules when evaluating competing options.

- We often fall back on well-learned "rules-of-thumb" to make decisions.

## CHAPTER SUMMARY

Consumers are faced with the needs to make decisions about products and services on a constant basis. Some of the decisions are very important to the consumer and entail great effort, while others are made on virtually an automatic or impulse basis. Perspectives on decision making range from a focus on habits that people develop over time to a focus on novel situations involving a great deal of risk where consumers must carefully collect and analyze information prior to making choices.

A typical decision process involves several steps. The first step is how consumers recognize the problem (*problem recognition*). Realization that a problem exists may be prompted in a variety of ways, ranging from actual malfunction of a current purchase to a desire for new things based on exposure to different circumstances or advertising that provides a glimpse into what is needed to "live the good life." Shifts in the actual or ideal state are at the heart of problem recognition.

The second step is *information search*. This may range from simply scanning memory to determining what has been done to resolve the problem in the past to undertaking extensive fieldwork where the consumer consults a variety of sources to amass as much information as possible from a variety of sources. In many cases, people engage in surprisingly little search. Instead, they rely upon various mental shortcuts, such as brand names or price, or they simply imitate others.

In the third stage the consumer performs an *evaluation of alternatives* that were developed in the search stage. The product alternatives that are considered comprise the individual's *evoked set*. Members of the evoked set usually share some characteristics (i.e., they are categorized similarly). The way products are mentally grouped influences which alternatives will be considered, and some brands are more strongly associated with these categories than are others (i.e., they are more prototypical).

Very often, *evaluative criteria* (dimensions used to judge the merits of competing options) and *heuristics* (mental rules of thumb) are used to simplify decision making. In particular, people may develop many *market beliefs* over time. One of the most common beliefs is that price is positively related to quality. Other heuristics rely on well-known brand names or a product's country of origin as signals of product quality. When a brand is consistently purchased over time, this pattern may be due to true *brand loyalty* or simply to *inertia* because it's the easiest thing to do.

When the consumer eventually must make a product choice from among alternatives, a number of *decision rules* may be used. *Noncompensatory decision rules* eliminate alternatives that are deficient on any of the criteria the consumer has chosen to use. *Compensatory decision rules*, which are more likely to be applied in high-involvement situations, allow the decision maker to consider each alternative's good and bad points more carefully to arrive at the overall best choice.

## CHAPTER OUTLINE

**1. Consumers as Problem Solvers**
  a. Most consumers go through a series of steps when they make a purchase. They are:
  1) Problem recognition.
  2) Information search.
  3) Evaluation of alternatives.
  4) Product choice.
    a) Learning occurs on how well the choice worked out.
    b) This learning affects future choices and purchases.

---

*****Use Figure 9.1 Here *****

---

> *Discussion Opportunity—Illustrate a situation where you have gone through all of the problem-solving steps. Ask students if they think that they always go through all of these steps when making a purchase decision.*

    b. Because some purchase decisions are more important than others, the amount of
    effort we put into each differs.
      1)  Sometimes the decision is almost automatic.
      2)  Sometimes the decision is one where a great deal of thinking and analysis is
         required.
      3)  **Consumer hyperchoice** is a condition where the large number of available options
         forces us to make repeated choices that may drain psychological energy while
         decreasing our abilities to make smart decisions.

---

*****Use Consumer Behavior Challenge #1 Here *****

---

> *Discussion Opportunity—Illustrate a situation in which your decision to buy was automatic. Illustrate a situation where your decision to buy required a great deal of thought.*

<u>Perspectives on Decision Making</u>
    c. Traditionally, consumer researchers have approached decision makers from a
    **rational perspective.** In this view, people calmly integrate as much information as
    possible with what they already know about a product, painstakingly weigh the
    pluses and minuses of each alternative, and arrive at a satisfactory decision.
      1)  Though this approach is correct in many instances, it does not describe all
         forms of decision making. Sometimes actions may be contrary to those predicted by
         rational models.
      2)  **Purchase momentum** occurs when initial impulses increase the likelihood that we
         will buy even more than we need.
      3)  Consumers probably have many strategies for making decisions. This is called
         constructive processing.
      4)  Environmental cues may be used (such as buying on impulse). This form of
         decision making is called the **behavioral influence perspective**.
      5)  In other cases, consumers are highly involved in a decision, but still the
         decisions cannot wholly be explained rationally. This is called the **experiential**
         **perspective**. This approach stresses *gestalt* (or totality) of the product or
         service. Marketers in these areas focus on measuring consumers' affective
         responses to products or services and develop offerings that elicit appropriate
         subjective reactions.

---

*****Use Consumer Behavior Challenges #4, #7, and #17 Here *****

---

<u>Types of Consumer Decisions</u>
    d. Decision processes can be considered by the amount of effort that goes into the
    decision each time it must be made. Three forms exist:
      1)  **Extended Problem Solving**—There is a fair degree of risk and we use internal

search and external sources. The consumer tries to collect as much information as possible. Corresponds most closely to the traditional decision-making perspective.

2) **Limited Problem Solving**—This is a simple, straightforward decision process. Buyers use simple *decision rules* to choose among alternatives. Cognitive shortcuts are used.

3) **Habitual Decision Making**—These are characterized as simple automatic decisions. This form is characterized by *automaticity* where there is a minimal effort and an absence of conscious control.

---

*****Use Figure 9.2 Here; Use Table 9.1 Here;
Use Consumer Behavior Challenge #22 Here *****

---

*Discussion Opportunity—Provide illustrations of each of the three forms of decision processing. Ask: What do you see as the basic differences between the forms? How should marketers deal with these differences? How could marketers convert one form into another? Why might the marketer want to do this?*

---

*Discussion Opportunity—Find an advertisement that illustrates each of the forms of decision processing. Explain your choices.*

---

## 2. Problem Recognition

a. **Problem recognition** occurs whenever the consumer sees a significant difference between his or her current state of affairs and some desired or ideal state.

1) The consumer perceives there is a problem to be solved that may be large or small, simple or complex.

2) A problem can occur in two ways.

   a) The quality of the consumer's *actual state* (running out of gas, for example) can move downward (*need recognition*).

   b) The consumer's *ideal state* (e.g., desiring a newer flashy car) can move upward (*opportunity recognition*).

   c) Either way, a gulf occurs between the actual state and the ideal state.

---

*****Use Figure 9.3 Here *****

---

*Discussion Opportunity—Provide an illustration that demonstrates the actual and ideal states. Demonstrate how a gap between the two can occur.*

---

b. Need recognition can occur in several ways:

1) The quality of the person's actual state can be diminished by:

   a) Running out of a product.

   b) Buying a product that turns out to not adequately satisfy needs.

   c) Creating new needs.

c. Opportunity recognition often occurs when a consumer is exposed to different or better-quality products.

> *Discussion Opportunity—Give an illustration of the three forms of need recognition.*

> *Discussion Opportunity—Ask: How do sellers convince you that you have a problem that they can solve?*

    d. Although problem recognition can and does occur naturally, this process is often spurred by marketing efforts.
      1) Marketers attempt to create **primary demand**, where consumers are encouraged to use a product or service regardless of the brand they choose.
      2) **Secondary demand**, where consumers are prompted to prefer a specific brand over others, can only occur if primary demand already exists.

> *Discussion Opportunity—Give an illustration of primary demand and secondary demand in purchasing something via the Internet. Show how the marketer can influence each form of demand in your example.*

### 3. Information Search
    a. Once a problem has been recognized, consumers need adequate information to resolve it. Information search is the process in which the consumer surveys his or her environment for appropriate data to make a reasonable decision.

Types of Information Search
    b. Types of search that the consumer may undertake once a need has been recognized include:
      1) **Prepurchase search**—an explicit search for information.
      2) **Ongoing search**—used by veteran shoppers to keep abreast of changes in the product categories of interest to them.

> *****Use Table 9.2 Here *****

> *Discussion Opportunity—Provide an illustration of prepurchase search and ongoing search in buying or reviewing a DVD player.*

    c. Information sources can roughly be broken into:
      1) **Internal search**—a memory scan to assemble information about different product alternatives.
      2) **External search**—information is obtained from advertisements, friends, or just plain people-watching.

> *Discussion Opportunity—Ask: Where would you go to find information about a product you purchase regularly (such as a soft drink), a computer, how to have a root canal, or a new car?*

> *Discussion Opportunity—Ask students to describe a recent situation where they used internal search and external search. Be specific in your description.*

d. Search can be deliberate or accidental.
   1) Deliberate search is the result of ***directed learning***—this is an active search.
   2) Accidental search is the result of ***incidental learning***—exposure to learning over time (this is a passive search).

## 4. The Economics of Information

  a. The traditional decision-making perspective incorporates the ***economics-of-information*** approach to the search process; it assumes that consumers will gather as much data as is needed to make an informed decision.
   1) Consumers form expectations of the value of information.
   2) The utilitarian assumption implies that the most valuable units of information will be collected first.
   3) Most people, however, do not want to spend a long time collecting information.

---

*Discussion Opportunity—Ask students to relate an experience when you spent only a brief time collecting information for a decision and when you spent a long time collecting information. How did your decisions turn out?*

---

  b. Consumers do not always search rationally. Low income consumers search the least.
   1) Rational search does not always occur.
     a) The amount of external search is surprisingly small.
   2) Consumers often visit only a few stores before making a decision to purchase.
   3) Avoiding external search is less prevalent when consumers consider the purchase of symbolic items.
     a) Most external search involves the opinions of peers.
   4) Consumers are often observed to be in a state of ***brand switching***.
   5) This is often caused by a desire to switch (**variety seeking**) and usually occurs when the consumer is in a good mood.
   6) We often switch brands even if we like the old brand.

---

### *\*\*\*\*\*Use Figure 9.4 Here; Use Consumer Behavior Challenge #3 Here \*\*\*\*\**

---

*Discussion Opportunity—Ask: Have you switched brands recently? What triggered your desire to change? How do you think an advertiser could trigger this "desire to change" response?*

---

*Discussion Opportunity—Ask: If variety seeking is linked to a consumer's good mood, how could a marketer use this information to get a consumer to switch brands? Illustrate.*

---

  c. There are biases in the decision-making process.
   1) A **mental accounting** can take place.
   2) *Framing* occurs because of the way a problem is posed.
   3) The ***sunk-cost fallacy*** says that having paid for something makes us reluctant to waste it.
   4) *Loss aversion* says that people put more emphasis on loss than on gain in a

situation. An example of this would be **prospect theory**.

    5) There can always be outside influences on our selections.

---

***\*\*\*\*\*Use Consumer Behavior Challenge #21 Here \*\*\*\*\****

---

*Discussion Opportunity—Ask: What biases do you have when you search for (a) a car,( b) a computer, and (c) a university or college?*

---

How Much Search Occurs?

d. As a general rule, search activity is greater when:

    1) The purchase is important.

    2) There is a need to learn more about the purchase.

    3) The relevant information is easily obtained and utilized.

e. Consumers differ in the amount of search they tend to undertake:

    1) Females shop more than men.

    2) Younger, better-educated people shop more than others.

    3) Those who enjoy shopping shop more.

f. The consumer's prior expertise can also affect the search and shopping process.

    1) Search tends to be greatest among those consumers who are *moderately knowledgeable* about the product.

    2) The *type* of search varies with varying levels of expertise.

        a) Experts use *selective search*.

        b) Novices rely on opinions of others and "nonfunctional" attributes.

    3) As a rule, purchase decisions that involve extensive search also entail some kind of **perceived risk** or belief that the product has potentially negative consequences. Types of risk include:

        a) Objective risk forms (such as physical danger).

        b) Subjective factor risk forms (such as social embarrassment).

---

***\*\*\*\*\*Use Figures 9.5 and 9.6 Here;***
***Use Consumer Behavior Challenges #10 and #18 Here \*\*\*\*\****

---

*Discussion Opportunity—Ask students to think of products that they use that pose a risk. Ask: How does this risk affect your decision making? Try to think of products that have a social risk. What are they? What products have you not used because of the risk? How could marketers of these products overcome this risk function and get you to use their products?*

---

*Discussion Opportunity—Ask: What would be the risk in using a shopping 'bot? Explain how using a shopping 'bot could be advantageous.*

---

## 5. Evaluation of Alternatives

Identifying Alternatives

a. The alternatives actively considered during a consumer's choice process are his or her **evoked set**. In reality, this can be a very small set.

    1) The evoked set is composed of those products already in memory (the

retrieval set), plus those prominent in the retail environment.

***
**\*\*\*\*\*Use Consumer Behavior Challenge #8 Here \*\*\*\*\***
***

*Discussion Opportunity—Ask students to write down as many brands of soft drinks (or potato chips, or cars, or cologne, etc.) as they can think of in 60 seconds. Of this group (in each case), ask students to consider which they would consider purchasing? How could marketers that represent that group you did not select move into your preferred evoked set?*

Product Categorization

b. Product ***categorization*** is how consumers organize their beliefs about products or services. This is a crucial determinant of how a product is evaluated.

   1) Products in a consumer's evoked set are likely to be those that share some similar features.

   2) This knowledge is represented in a consumer's ***cognitive structure*** (the factual knowledge about products—beliefs—and the way these beliefs are organized in people's minds).

   3) There are several levels of categorization:

      a) ***Basic level***—items have much in common but a number of alternatives exist.

      b) ***Superordinate level***—abstract concepts.

      c) ***Subordinate level***—individual brands.

***
**\*\*\*\*\*Use Figure 9.7 Here; Use Consumer Behavior Challenge #15 Here \*\*\*\*\***
***

*Discussion Opportunity—Demonstrate cognitive structure using a product of your choice. How does this relate to evoked set? How could an advertiser use this information that you have provided to alter strategy?*

c. Product categorization has many strategic implications. Some of these are:

   1) ***Product positioning***—The conception of the product relative to other products in the consumer's mind. To some extent this is how a product is categorized by the consumer.

   2) ***Identifying competitors***—Are different products substitutes?

   3) ***Exemplar products***—The most known, accepted product or brand.

   4) ***Locating products***—Consumers often expect to find certain products within certain places within the store environment.

## 6. Product Choice: Selecting Among Alternatives

  a. Once the relevant options from a category have been assembled and evaluated, a choice must be made among them.

Evaluative Criteria

b. **Evaluative criteria** are the dimensions used to judge the merits of competing options. Forms can be:

   1) Differences—Significant differences among brands on an attribute (anti-lock

brakes). The attributes actually used to differentiate among choices are **determinant attributes**.
2) Supplying the consumer with decision-making rules.

> *Discussion Opportunity—Ask students to name common evaluative criteria used to evaluate (a) a computer, (b) a business suit, (c) perfume or cologne, or (d) a bicycle.*

c. When consumers make decisions, marketers often want to impact their decision making. The decision about which attributes to use is the result of *procedural learning*. To do this (effectively recommend a new decision criteria), the marketer must convey three pieces of information:
  1) It should point out that there are significant differences among the brands on the attribute.
  2) It should supply the consumer with a decision-making rule.
  3) It should convey a rule that can be easily integrated with how the person has made this decision in the past.

> ***\*\*\*\*\*Use Consumer Behavior Challenge #14 Here \*\*\*\*\****

Cybermediaries
d. In cyberspace, simplification is the key.
  1) How can people organize the vast amount of information on the Web?
  2) One type of business that is growing to meet the demand for information and service on the Web is the **cybermediary**. This intermediary helps to filter and organize online market information so that customers can identify and evaluate alternatives more efficiently. Collaborative filtering may be used.
  3) Forms include:
    a) *Directories* and *portals*.
    b) *Web site evaluators*.
    c) *Forums, fan clubs,* and *user groups*.
    d) *Financial intermediaries*.
  4) Intelligent agents are sophisticated software programs that use collaborative filtering technologies to learn from past user behavior in order to recommend new purchases.
    a) Many sites including Amazon.com and Mysimon.com use these.
    b) **Electronic recommendation agents** are software tools that try to understand a human decision maker's multiattribute preferences for a product category by asking the user to communicate his preferences.

> ***\*\*\*\*\*Use Consumer Behavior Challenges #10 (Used Previously), #12, and #22 Here \*\*\*\*****

Heuristics: Mental Shortcuts
e. Consumers often rely on **heuristics** (mental rules-of-thumb that leads to speedy decisions). These rules can be general or specific. Sometimes these shortcuts are not in the consumer's best interest.

> *Discussion Opportunity—Have students give some common general and specific heuristics that you use to make decisions with respect to purchasing products. Have these rules ever led you down a wrong path to a bad decision? Explain.*

    f. One frequently used shortcut is the tendency to infer hidden dimensions of products from observable attributes. This can result from:

      1) **Product Signals**—a visible act that signifies underlying quality.

      2) *Covariation*—perceived associations among events that may or may not actually influence one another.

    g. Other assumptions include:

      1) **Market beliefs**—knowledge of the market that is used to guide decisions.

> ***\*\*\*\*\*Use Table 9.3 Here; Use Consumer Behavior Challenge #13 Here \*\*\*\*\****

> *Discussion Opportunity—Ask: Can you think of market beliefs that you use to make decisions. Are these usually sound? Tell about some of your experiences.*

> *Discussion Opportunity—Give an example of covariation. Ask: What kind of decision might this lead to? Would the decision end in a good or bad decision? Explain.*

      2) One of the most pervasive market beliefs is the ***price-quality relationship***.

      3) **Country of origin** as a product signal.

        a) This is often a signal of quality.

        b) The consumer must avoid **stereotypes**.

        c) The tendency to prefer products or people of one's own culture over those from another country is called **ethnocentrism**.

> ***\*\*\*\*\*Use Consumer Behavior Challenge #19 Here \*\*\*\*\****

> *Discussion Opportunity—Ask students to list products where they think ethnocentrism applies. Why do you think this occurs? Does it bother you?*

    h. Branding is a marketing strategy that often functions as a heuristic.

      1) Many people tend to buy the same brand just about every time they go to the store. This consistent pattern is due to **inertia**, where a brand is bought out of habit merely because less effort is required.

      2) Brand loyalty is a form of repeat purchasing behavior reflecting a conscious decision to continue buying the same brand. There is more ***brand parity*** today and therefore brand loyalty is harder to achieve (and keep).

> ***\*\*\*\*\*Use Consumer Behavior Challenges #5 and #16 Here \*\*\*\*\****

> *Discussion Opportunity—Have students write down three brands they are most loyal to. Ask: Why are you loyal to these brands? What would it take for you to break your loyalty to them?*

Decision Rules

i. Consumers consider sets of product attributes by using different rules, depending on the complexity of the decision and the importance of the decision to them.

> *****Use Table 9.4 Here *****

j. Simple decision rules are **noncompensatory decision rules**, meaning a product with a low standing on one attribute cannot make up for this position by being better on another attribute. Rules within this structure can be:
   1) The *lexicographic rule*—the brand with the best attribute is selected.
   2) The *elimination-by-aspects rule*—must have a specific feature to be chosen.
   3) The *conjunctive rule*—the consumer processes products by brand. Cutoffs are established for each brand. Failure to meet one cutoff means the brand will be rejected.

> *****Use Consumer Behavior Challenge #9 Here *****

> *Discussion Opportunity—Provide an example of how you could use a noncompensatory decision rule. How could a marketer deal with this if you were not selecting their brand?*

k. Unlike noncompensatory decision rules, **compensatory decision rules** give a product a chance to make up for its shortcomings. You weigh the good points against the bad.
   1) There are two basic types of compensatory decision rules:
      a) *Simple additive rules*—the consumer merely chooses the alternative having the largest number of positive attributes.
      b) *Weighted additive rules*—the consumer considers the relative importance of positive attributes.

> *****Use Consumer Behavior Challenge #20 Here *****

> *Discussion Opportunity—Provide an example of when you have used a compensatory decision rule. What was the rule? Did you have regrets afterward? How do you learn to adjust these rules? How can marketers deal with these rules?*

# End-of-Chapter Support Material

## SUMMARY OF SPECIAL FEATURE BOXES

1.    **Marketing Opportunity I**

This box highlights an evolving trend known as **silent commerce**. This concept describes product transactions and information gathering to occur without human intervention. This feature supports the section "Information Search."

2.    **Net Profit**

The nature of what Internet users are doing online is shifting. This shift includes spending less time online per session and using the Internet more for information search and less for entertainment.

3.    **Marketing Pitfall I**

This box addresses the issue of misleading labels. Various examples are provided. This feature supports the section "Do Consumers Always Search Rationally."

4.    **Marketing Opportunity II**

This box reveals a line of current research called **neuromarketing**. This technique uses a brain scanning device to track blood flow in the brain and identify mental tasks. This technology is then used to identify consumer responses to marketing stimuli.

5.    **Marketing Pitfall II**

This box highlights the recent product launch by Kimberly-Clark of Cottonelle Fresh Rollwipes. Discussed are reasons why this moist toilette paper failed. This feature supports the section "Product Categorization."

6.    **Marketing Pitfall III**

This box examines the effect of U.S. foreign policy on the perceptions that global consumers have on U.S. brands. The percentage of consumers in various countries stating that they are less likely to buy American is on the rise. Coca-Cola, Starbucks, McDonald's, Mattel, and others are the object of such consumer anti-American sentiment.

7.    **The Global Looking Glass**

This special feature discusses the theory called CETSCALE that suggests that consumers with ethnocentric tendencies will typically value domestic products more favorably than imported goods. If ethnocentrism is high enough, it will be difficult for foreign producers of goods to compete in that market. This theory is applied specifically to the marketing of U.S. products in India and Pakistan. The two are compared and contrasted.

# REVIEW QUESTIONS

1.   Why do we say that "mindless" decision making can actually be more efficient? *Sometimes the decision-making process is almost automatic; we seem to make snap judgments based on very little information. At other times, coming to a purchase decision begins to resemble a full-time job. A person may literally spend days or weeks thinking about an important purchase such as a new home, even to the point of obsession.*

2.   List the steps in the model of rational decision making. *Problem recognition, information search, evaluation of alternatives, product choice, and outcomes.*

3.   What is purchase momentum, and how does it relate (or not) to the model of rational decision making? *Purchase momentum occurs when these initial impulses actually increase the likelihood that we will buy even more (instead of less as our needs are satisfied), almost as if we get "revved up" and plunge into a spending spree.*

4.   What is the difference between the behavioral influence and experiential perspectives on decision making? Give an example of the type of purchase that most likely would be explained by each perspective. *Under the circumstances of the behavioral influence perspective, managers must concentrate on assessing the characteristics of the environment, such as the design of a retail outlet or whether a package is enticing, that will influence members of a target market. In other cases, no single quality is the determining factor. Instead, the experiential perspective stresses the Gestalt, or totality, of the product or service.*

5.   Name two ways a consumer problem can arise. *1) A person's standard of comparison may be altered, 2) the quality of the consumer's actual state can move downward, and 3) the consumer's ideal state can move upward.*

6.   What is the economics of information perspective, and how does it relate to information search? *The traditional decision-making perspective incorporates the economics-of-information approach to the search process; it assumes that consumers will gather as much data as needed to make an informed decision.*

7.   Give an example of the sunk-cost fallacy. *Simply put, the sunk-cost fallacy occurs when someone has paid for something and is therefore reluctant to waste it. An example would be when someone attends a sporting event even though weather may put them at personal risk.*

8.  What is prospect theory? Does it support the argument that people are rational decision makers? *Prospect theory, a descriptive model of how people make choices, finds that utility is a function of gains and losses, and risk differs when the consumer faces options involving gains versus those involving losses. This basically says that the factors of decision making are relative. That would imply that we are not rational.*

9.  Describe the relationship between a consumer's level of expertise and how much he's likely to search for information about a product? *The relationship between prior knowledge/expertise of a product and information search is an inverted-U. When prior knowledge is very little or very great, then little information is sought. However, when prior knowledge is moderate, that's when the most information is sought.*

10. List three types of perceived risk, giving an example of each. *There are five types of perceived risk listed in the text: monetary (high dollar items), functional (product use requires exclusive commitment), physical (things that are perishable or potentially hazardous), social (socially visible or symbolic goods), and psychological (goods that may engender guilt).*

11. "Marketers need to be extra sure their product works as promised when they first introduce it." How does this statement relate to what we know about consumers' evoked sets? *People are more likely to add a new brand to the evoked set than one that we previously considered but passed over, even after additional positive information has been provided for that brand. For marketers, consumers' unwillingness to give a rejected product a second chance underscores the importance of ensuring that it performs well from the time it is introduced.*

12. Describe the difference between a superordinate category, a basic level category, and a subordinate category. *Categories exist in a taxonomy from most concrete to most abstract. The middle level, known as a basic level category, is typically the most useful in classifying products, because items grouped together tend to have a lot in common with each other but still permit a range of alternatives to be considered. The broader superordinate category is more abstract, whereas the more specific subordinate category often includes individual brands.*

13. What is an example of an exemplar product? *If a product is a really good example of a category it is more familiar to consumers and they more easily recognize and recall it. Judgments about category attributes tend to be disproportionately influenced by the characteristics of category exemplars.*

14. List three product attributes that consumers can use as product quality signals and provide an example of each. *1) Price; consumers commonly associate a higher price as an indicator of a higher level of quality. 2) Country-of-origin; a common U.S. perception is that watches that are made in Switzerland are of a higher quality than watches made in any other country. 3) Brand name; some brands have developed an image of quality (i.e., Mercedes Benz, Toyota, etc.) moreso than others (i.e., Kia).*

15. How does a brand function as a heuristic? *Branding is a marketing strategy that often functions as a heuristic. People form preferences for a favorite brand, and then they literally may never change their minds in the course of a lifetime. A study by the Boston Consulting Group of the market leaders in 30 product categories found that 27 of the brands that were number one in 1930 (such as Ivory Soap and Campbell's Soup) remained at the top over 50 years later.*

16. Describe the difference between inertia and brand loyalty. *Inertia exists when we buy a brand out of habit merely because it requires less effort. For brand loyalty to exist, a pattern of repeat purchase must be accompanied by an underlying positive attitude toward the brand.*

17. What is the difference between a noncompensatory and a compensatory decision rule? Give one example of each. *Noncompensatory decision rules are choice shortcuts where a product with a low standing on one attribute cannot make up for this position by being better on another attribute. Unlike noncompensatory decision rules, compensatory decision rules give a product a chance to make up for its shortcomings. Consumers who employ these rules tend to be more involved in the purchase and thus are willing to exert the effort to consider the entire picture in a more exacting way. The willingness to let good and bad product qualities balance out can result in quite different choices.*

# CONSUMER BEHAVIOR CHALLENGE

## Discussion Questions

1. The chapter argues that in our society having too many choices is a bigger problem than not having enough choices. Do you agree? Is it possible to have too much of a good thing?

   *This relationship will depend on the type of product. For many people looking for various product types, one choice would be enough. Anything greater than that just takes mental effort. But even in situations where we want to research the issue at hand and get the "best product," there is an optimum number of choices. And anything beyond that detracts from the decision making process.*

2. Silent commerce has the potential to automate many of our decisions. Do you see any downsides to this trend?

   *The one that rises to the top of the stack is invasion of privacy. Of course, consumers will give permission for silent commerce to occur—for the most part. But in most situations the consumer will not be aware of the implications. The more automated things become, the more our consumption patterns can be tracked on an individual basis.*

3.     The Sprite Remix strategy involves changing the composition of a product periodically but retaining the same brand name. What is your prognosis for this novel strategy—do you think it will work? Why or why not?

*More and more, people are looking for novel stimuli. However, this is fraught with risks as people get attached to a brand and like, in this case, the way it tastes. This is a very great risk with a food/beverage product. Just note the New Coke debacle.*

4.     Major American companies are affected globally by the actions of the U.S. Government in Iraq and elsewhere. Should these organizations have a say in our foreign policy?

*This is a great discussion question. Of course, there really is not much more to substantiate either side of the argument, other than opinion.*

5.     How can retailers compete if people believe they can get the same items everywhere?

*The obvious answer is through higher levels of service. However, as that becomes less and less important for every day consumables (even to the wealthy), it is no longer an important point of differentiation. Another option is to stress the exclusive nature of items that one's company carries.*

6.     Commercial Alert, a consumer group, is highly critical of neuromarketing and has called it Orwellian. The group's executive director wrote, "What would happen in this country if corporate marketers and political consultants could literally peer inside our brains and chart the neural activity that leads to our selections in the supermarket and voting booth?" "What if they then could trigger this neural activity by various means, so as to modify our behavior to serve their own ends?" What do you think—is neuromarketing dangerous?

*The idea that neuromarketing is any more dangerous than more traditional methods of market research rests on two assumptions. 1) These methods allow marketers to read minds. While the technologies employed are advanced, reading minds is far down the path. Of course, one never knows what the future will bring. 2) If marketers could read minds, that they would have the capability to trigger certain responses through any means. The bottom line is, consumers still have freedom to choose.*

7.     If people are not always rational decision makers, is it worth the effort to study how these decisions are made? What techniques might be employed to understand experiential consumption and to translate this knowledge into marketing strategy?

*In discussing the utility of studying rational decision making (or extended problem solving), the instructor should stress the importance of using different methods in investigating the complex nature of consumer decision making. What also needs to be made clear is that other less purposeful methods also play a role. To understand and apply experiential consumption to marketing strategy will require more knowledge of how consumers develop their overall impression of a product and how they integrate it into their decision-making process. Contributions from other disciplines, such as psychology and sociology, also will be important. The real challenge will be applying this disparate information to marketing strategy.*

8. Why is it difficult to place a product in a consumer's evoked set after it has already been rejected? What strategies might a marketer use in an attempt to accomplish this goal?

*It is difficult to place a product into an evoked set after it has been rejected because consumers are "cognitive misers." This means that people conserve their mental resources and expend only a minimum effort required to solve a problem. Once a product has been eliminated from consideration on the basis of some evaluation process, consumers are not likely to expend additional cognitive resources to re-evaluate that product.*

*Promotional strategies can be used to get the consumer to reconsider the product. Price discounts, coupons, special offers, rebates, or free samples will increase the possibility that a product will re-enter the evoked set. Any other means to get the consumer to try the product will increase the possibility of consideration of the product, and successful trial will increase the chances of a product being included in the consumer's evoked set.*

9. Discuss two different noncompensatory decision rules and highlight the difference(s) between them. How might the use of one rule versus another result in a different product choice?

*The use of a particular noncompensatory rule will influence the product chosen—1) The lexicographic rule will result in a choice based on a particularly important attribute; 2) the elimination-by-aspects rule will result in a choice based on the particular cut-off points established; and 3) the conjunctive rule will result in a choice based on the particular brands being considered and the cut-off points.*

*The choice of particular noncompensatory decision rules is not the crucial aspect of this exercise. It is important, however, that students appreciate the differences between the rules they choose to discuss. In addition, students should understand the more basic difference between noncompensatory and compensatory rules and how each uses different information to arrive at a decision. The instructor should encourage students to think about why particular choice rules are used and ways that marketers could appeal to consumers using each of these rules.*

10. Technology has the potential to make our lives easier by reducing the amount of clutter we need to work through in order to access the information on the Internet that really interests us. On the other hand, perhaps intelligent agents that make recommendations based only on what we and others like us have chosen in the past limit us—reducing the chance that we will stumble onto something (e.g., a book on a topic we've never heard of, or a music group that's different from the style we usually listen to). Will the proliferation of "shopping bots" make our lives too predictable by only giving us more of the same? If so, is this a problem?

*This question poses an interesting dilemma for the students—how can you get information and still have your new and interesting experiences? The instructor should begin by pointing out the benefits of being able to search for information via the Internet. Then examine the cost associated with this information search. Be sure to indicate that companies are provided data for consumers at considerable cost to themselves and are perhaps justified in their desire to be able to direct consumer purchases. The consumer is free to use information obtained to make product decisions (from the ease and convenience of their homes). How can the system be useful but still be changed to allow for originality? This should provide for a good discussion. How would students like the system to be? How could this be accomplished? What might be the cost? Would they pay for it?*

## Application Questions

11. The chapter discusses the expensive failure of the Cottonelle Fresh Rollwipe. If the company hired you as a consultant to revamp this effort, what recommendations would you make to persuade consumers to try such a sensitive product?

    *Overcome the weaknesses: 1) have small travel/sample sizes, 2) create a dispenser for the bathroom that would be incognito, and 3) come up with a tactful way to communicate the benefits of the product.*

12. Find examples of electronic recommendation agents on the Web. Evaluate these—are they helpful? What characteristics of the sites you locate are likely to make you buy products you wouldn't have bought on your own?

    *Amazon.com, Mysimon.com, and AskJeeves.com are all intelligent agents. The students may have to spend a fair amount of time to come up with actual recommendation agents.*

13. Conduct a poll based on the list of market beliefs you'll find in Table 9.3. Do people agree with these beliefs, and how much do they influence their decisions?

    *This is a very application oriented exercise. The results will vary from respondent to respondent.*

14. Pepsi invented freshness dating and managed to persuade consumers that this was an important product attribute. Devise a similar strategy for another product category by coming up with a brand new product attribute. Using the steps in procedural learning the chapter describes, how would you communicate this attribute to your customers?

    *In order for a marketer to effectively recommend a new decision criterion, its communication should convey three pieces of information:*

    *1. It should point out that there are significant differences among brands on the attribute.*

2.   *It should supply the consumer with a decision-making rule, such as if (deciding among competing brands), then . . . (use the attribute as a criterion). It should convey a rule that can be easily integrated with how the person has made this decision in the past. Otherwise, the recommendation is likely to be ignored because it requires too much mental work.*

3.   *These things should be applied to coming up with a new attribute and communicating it to the target market.*

15.   Define the three levels of product categorization described in the chapter. Diagram these levels for a health club.

   *The text discussed the following levels of product categorization:*

   1.   *Superordinate—the broadest and most abstract level (e.g., health clubs).*
   2.   *Basic Level—the most useful category to classify products because these items have much in common with each other (e.g., weight/powerlifting clubs).*
   3.   *Subordinate Level—the most specific category (e.g., Nautilus Fitness Clubs).*

16.   Choose a friend or parent who grocery shops on a regular basis, and keep a log of their purchases of common consumer products during the term. Can you detect any evidence of brand loyalty in any categories based on consistency of purchases? If so, talk to the person about these purchases. Try to determine if his or her choices are based on true brand loyalty or on inertia. What techniques might you use to differentiate between the two?

   *To begin with, the instructor should ask the students to differentiate between brand loyalty and inertia. Brand loyalty is represented by a pattern of repeat product purchases, accompanied by an underlying positive attitude toward the brand. Inertia describes consumption at the low end of involvement, where decisions are made out of habit because the consumer lacks the motivation to consider alternatives.*

   *For example a student said that her mother buys the same cereal every week. In discussing the reason for buying the cereal, her mother said she bought it because it was what the student's father liked. She considered him to be brand loyal. Techniques the student could use to find out if the father is truly brand loyal would be to ask him to try other cereals. After trying these alternatives, if he insisted that his was the best, he could be considered to be brand loyal. (Possible Field Project Idea)*

17.   Form a group of three. Pick a product and develop a marketing plan based on each of the three approaches to consumer decision making—rational, experiential, and behavioral influence. What are the major differences in emphasis among the three perspectives? Which is the most likely type of problem-solving activity for the product you have selected? What characteristics of the product make this so?

*The three approaches to consumer decision making discussed in the book are:*

1. *Rational—the consumer is a careful, analytical decision maker who tries to maximize utility in purchase decisions*
2. *Experiential—stresses the gestalt or totality of the product or service.*
3. *Behavioral—stresses that consumer decision are learned responses to cues.*

*To provide an example for individual group exercises, the instructor could first ask the class as a whole to pick one product and make suggestions for a marketing plan. The class should then be encouraged to form their own groups and devise a marketing plan for their products. It would be interesting to have groups use different approaches to market the same product and other groups use the same approach to market different products. (Possible Field Project Idea)*

18.   Locate a person who is about to make a major purchase. Ask that person to make a chronological list of all the information sources consulted prior to making a decision. How would you characterize the types of sources used (e.g., internal versus external, media versus personal, etc.)? Which sources appeared to have the most impact on the person's decision?

*The instructor could begin by reviewing the stages in the consumer decision-making process—problem recognition, information search, evaluation of alternatives, product choice, and outcomes. The following scenario might be developed in the context of this exercise:*

*Jane Smith is in the market for a new computer. She looked at store ads first to compare features and prices of many computers. The next step was to ask friends and colleagues what they thought about the brands she was considering. After much research, she finally decided on a brand and made a purchase. (The sources used were external, media, and personal. Sources that had the most impact were external and personal.) (Possible Field Project Idea)*

19.   Perform a survey of country-of-origin stereotypes. Compile a list of five countries and ask people what products they associate with each. What are their evaluations of the products and likely attributes of these different products? The power of a country stereotype can also be demonstrated in another way. Prepare a brief description of a product, including a list of features, and ask people to rate it in terms of quality, likelihood of purchase, and so on. Make several versions of the description, varying only the country from which it comes. Do ratings change as a function of the country of origin?

*Students may have strong associations for many countries tied to specific products or product categories. Examples might include European import/luxury cars, French wines, Italian leather goods, Swedish crystal, and Japanese electronics. It may be interesting to expand the notion of country of origin and ask students to talk about areas in the United States that are particularly well known for specific products. Alternatively, for both country and region of origin, students should be challenged to think of examples that represent weak or poor association that marketers would want to avoid. (Possible Field Project Idea)*

20.     Ask a friend to "talk through" the process he or she used to choose one brand over others during a recent purchase. Based on this description, can you identify the decision rule that was most likely employed?

*The instructor might begin by reviewing the two types of decision rules, namely, compensatory and noncompensatory. Compensatory decision rules involve averaging information about attributes of competing products where a poor rating on one attribute can be offset by a good rating on another. Noncomnpensatory decision rules, alternately, would find a brand with a low rating on one relevant/important attribute eliminated from the consumer's choices, despite higher ratings on less relevant/important attributes. The specific types of compensatory and noncompensatory rules also should be reviewed.*

21.     Give one of the scenarios described in the section on biases in decision making to ten to twenty people. How do the results you obtain compare with those reported in the chapter?

*This project will take some time and require a controlled structure. It is probably best done as a group project. One interesting way to accomplish this project quickly, however, is to use another class at the university or college (that would be willing to share in the learning process). In this way the other class will not have read the material in the chapter and can honestly react to the material. Be sure to draw comparisons and critique the effort (not only in results but also in methodology).*

22.     Think of a product you recently shopped for online. Describe your search process. How did you become aware that you wanted/needed the product? How did you evaluate alternatives? Did you wind up buying online? Why or why not? What factors would make it more or less likely that you would buy something online versus in a traditional store?

*This question will serve as a good application of the basic decision-making process or as a more specific illustration of the online buying process.*

# CASE STUDY TEACHING NOTES

**Chapter 9 Case Study: The Tablet PC: Revolutionizing the PC Landscape?**

<u>**Summary of Case**</u>

This case summarizes the state of the tablet PC in the overall computer market. While numerous advances have occurred with this product since its introduction in the late 1990s, overall sales still hover at around 1 percent of total mobile PC sales. This qualifies tablets as a niche product at best. What do consumers want in a tablet (a.k.a., convertible)? They want a tablet to do everything that a notebook will do, AND have the features of a tablet. In other words, they do not want to sacrifice anything. Consumers also do not want to have to pay the price premium for tablets. The features, the industry is dealing with pretty well. The price is another obstacle. On top of these issues, there is a scarcity of software.

## Suggestions for Presentation

This is clearly a "problem" case. Thus, there is a direct application for this material to the consumer decision making process, and specifically the concepts of problem identification. Use this case to illustrate different perspectives on problem solving, extended versus limited problem solving versus habitual decision making, and the different concepts that lead to problem recognition.

## Suggested Answers for Discussion Questions

1.  Generate a list of potential "problem" situations that would motivate computer customers to consider buying a tablet PC.

    *Given the stated information in the case, those that would consider buying a tablet must have a valid reason to do so. The glitz of the added features is not enough unless people really need those features. A good way to address this problem would be to consider the situations that lead to problem recognition. 1) A person's standard of comparison may be altered: a person may be accustomed to comparing the choices within the standard laptop category. Thus, manufacturers must address this in promotional material. 2) The quality of the consumer's actual state can move downward: this would be a case where a person's needs change, as in change of job responsibilities that would put a person in a position requiring the features of a tablet. 3) The consumer's ideal state can move upward: This would be a situation where the needs already exist, but the person has been unaware of the benefits of tablets. Thus, it would be necessary to identify and communicate with such.*

2.  Based on the problem situations considered in question 1, trace the path through the stages of the consumer decision making process for the identified problems.

    *   ***Problem recognition:*** *My job responsibilities have changed and I am going to be doing more one-on-one sales where I will need to demonstrate my company's software.*
    *   ***Information search:*** *I gather information on what options are available. I quickly find that traditional laptops will not meet my needs and discover the benefits of tablets.*
    *   ***Evaluation of alternatives:*** *I identify the few brands and models that best meet the criteria that I have established.*
    *   ***Product choice:*** *From my evoked set, I make the final decision.*

- **Outcomes:** *I use the product and form my own opinions as to how well it meets my needs.*

# Additional Support Material

# STUDENT PROJECTS

## Individual Projects

1.  As an in-class activity, discuss with the class the concept of risk. Distribute a list of several different consumer products or have a student do this. Then ask students what types of risk they would associate with each of the products. How could the risk be reduced?

2.  Have individual students evaluate a recent purchase of a large-scale item (e.g., expensive clothing, car, stereo system, appliance, furniture, etc.) base on the Stages in the Consumer Decision Making Process (*Figure 9.1*). Ask them if they think they gathered enough information before making their decision. See if they were satisfied with the quantity or quality of the information they had at their disposal.

3.  Based on the noncompensatory and compensatory decision rules listed at the end of the chapter, students should create examples. Then, have students form their own decision rules. Have them demonstrate how their rules are different and how they might be of value in general consumer decision making.

4.  Have students choose a specific type of product. Then, have them find product-rating reports from *Consumer Reports* or a similar organization that tests products. The student should evaluate the rating system the organization used. What other information would have been useful.

5.  Ask a student to compile a description of three products that include both features and country-of-origin. Then have the student ask a few people to rate the quality of the products and whether they would probably buy them. See if he or she can find out why the respondents feel this way.

6.  It is often revealing when a student interviews a manager of a local retail store to determine how the store is attempting to meet the consumer's need for information. After the interview, suggest that the student use powers of observation to determine how effective the approach seems to be.

7.  In this field project, have a student design a project to illustrate when customers use internal versus external sources of information and deliberate versus accidental sources of information during the search process.

8.  Have a student identify countries-of-origin of popular U.S. cars. Find out how many cars that we identify as "American" are made in other countries and how many cars we identify as "foreign" are assembled in the United States. A variation on this would be to do the same with heavy equipment (such as John Deere) or with motorcycles or cars that are considered to be of Japanese origin.

9.  What sources of information are most valuable to you when making a decision on purchasing (a) a computer, (b) an expensive piece of jewelry, (c) selecting a place to worship, and (d) something online? Explain.

10. Have the students keep a diary listing their highest and lowest involvement product purchases or service transactions for each day for a week. Have them identify the decision process they went through and how satisfied they were with their decision. Then have them write a short paper describing the lessons they learned from the purchases. What mistakes were made?

11. Ask a student to bring to class an advertisement that is designed to activate the problem-recognition process. Does the student think that the ad works on the consumer's actual state or ideal state? See if the student can improve the problem recognition features of the advertisement.

12. Given the relationship between amount of information search and product knowledge, have students devise a promotional strategy for a product targeted at consumers who have little, moderate, and extensive prior knowledge.

13. Have students conduct research on the state of silent commerce as highlighted in the Marketing Opportunity special feature box. How prevalent are such strategies? What is the growth potential of such?


## Group Projects

1.  This project will require student groups to conduct consumer interviews. They should contact people (acquaintances, friends, etc.) and ask them questions about a recent purchase or consideration of a purchase. Specifically, they should ask the consumer what factors led them to problem recognition. They should also ask the respondents to explain the similarities or differences that existed at decision time.

2.  Student groups should consider the product category of gas/electric hybrid vehicles. Based on the consumer decision making process, they should design a strategy for a company selling this product. They should cover each stage of the decision-making model used in the chapter.

3.  In groups, students should discuss popular stereotypes that discriminates against a company, a person, a country, or product. Having selected one of these, they should design a strategy that would help to reduce the stereotype's negative effects.

4.  Have student groups devise a taxonomy of categories for a product category. Then, have them reposition certain brands at the subordinate level by modifying that taxonomy. How could the companies carry out such a repositioning?

5.  Compile a list of four or five foreign countries or have a student do it. Ask the class to identify products or classes of products that they usually associate with that country. After they have selected their product categories, have the class evaluate the quality of the products that typically come from each country. What stereotypes were involved?

6.  Ask a team of students to bring to class three advertisements that attempt to change the reader's ideal states. See if the students can identify the techniques the advertisers employed to accomplish their goal. Evaluate the success of the endeavor.

7.  Have groups of students apply the Consumer Decision Making Model to purchasing on the Internet. Does the model work the same as in purchasing in the retail environment? Explain and illustrate.

8.  Have groups of students construct decision rules that only apply to purchasing via the Internet. Is this possible? If so, have the students demonstrate how this is so and what value the decision might be. Have them describe how they arrived at their "new" rules. Have other students critique the "new" rules.

9.  Have a group of students design an experiment that would test and illustrate prospect theory. Have them conduct this experiment using the students in class. After analyzing the results, have them present them to the class.

# eLAB

## Individual Assignments

1.  Go to **www.bose.com**. What makes the SoundDock iPod docking station worth $299 when similar products by competitors cost much less? Demonstrate how a consumer might evaluate such a purchase. What decision rules might be used? What strategies might Bose use to educate the consumer as to the value of their product?

2.  Go to **www.buy.com.** Pick a specific product that you might be interested in and see what alternative choices this shopping 'bot provides for you. Then, take some time to evaluate the different alternatives. Based on the information in the chapter addressing the selection of a product from alternatives, comment on your experience. Be sure to comment on consumer hyperchoice.

3.  Go to **www.kraftfoods.com/om/**. Do you eat hot dogs? Are they healthy for you? After you visit the Oscar Mayer Web site, has your opinion changed? What strategies does the Web site use to supply information and influence consumer decision making? Do the strategies seem to be successful? Did they have any effect on you? Explain.

4.     Go to **www.overstock.com**. This is a unique new retailer that stocks its online store with overstocked items from major manufacturers. As an alternative to more traditional shopping channels, how is this Web site attempting to influence the decision-making process of shoppers? What do you predict for this Web site? How long will it be around?

5.     Go to **www.peapod.com**. Online grocery is alive and well. Although most grocery purchases that we make fall into the category of habitual decision making, somehow, this concept is working for some people. Spend some time on this sight and assemble a grocery order. What are the pros and cons of using an online service for habitual decision making decisions?

## Group Assignments

1.     Go to **www.casino.com**. Become familiar with the concept of prospect theory. Spend some time as a group on this or other online gambling Web sites. What examples do you find of applying prospect theory?

2.     Go to **www.conagrafoods.com**. One of the mega-conglomerates of the modern age, ConAgra Foods boasts dozens of brands in numerous different product categories. As a group, create a categorization chart with at least three levels of abstraction to show how the brands of ConAgra fit under one umbrella category.

# 10

## *BUYING AND DISPOSING*

## CHAPTER OBJECTIVES

When students have finished reading this chapter, they should understand why:

- The outcome of an actual transaction is influenced by many factors over and above the qualities of the product or service. Factors operating at the time of purchase can dramatically influence the consumer decision-making process.

- In addition to what a shopper already knows or believes about a product, information provided in the store on a Web site can strongly influence his purchase decisions.

- A salesperson can be the crucial link between interest in a product and its actual purchase.

- Marketers need to be concerned about a consumer's evaluations of a product after the person buys it as well as before.

- Getting rid of products when they are no longer needed or wanted is a major concern both to marketers and to public policy makers.

## CHAPTER SUMMARY

A consumer's choices are affected by many personal factors, such as his or her mood, whether there is time pressure to make a purchase, and the particular situation or context for which a product is needed. Even the salesperson, such as in the purchase of a new car, can have a significant impact on the consumer's decision-making process.

Situational effects on consumer behavior can be varied. A consumption situation is defined by factors over and above characteristics of the person and of the product that influence the buying and/or using of products and services. Situation effects can be behavioral or perceptual. Smart marketers understand these influences and adapt their programs accordingly.

Retailers are especially aware of the social and physical surroundings that the consumer encounters on their shopping trips. Decor, smells, and visual stimulation are all important to the overall atmosphere of the store. Store owners are painfully aware that we are a time-oriented society and time is a resource that must be factored into marketing plans. Retailers must account for a shortage of time on the part of the consumer and arrange an environment that will speed the consumer through the store while selling effectively.

Shoppers shop for many reasons. Chief among these are for: social experiences, sharing of common interests, interpersonal attraction, instant status, and "the thrill of the hunt." Each consumer can also expect different satisfactions from the shopping experience. For example, the economic consumer will judge the shopping experience differently (primarily from economic cues) from the personalized consumer (who seeks strong attachments to store personnel).

As more and more Web sites crop up, this new format will affect how consumers and marketers conduct their business. Marketers can now reach consumers that were inaccessible only a few years ago. Because of the new e-commerce economy, however, old alliances between sellers and intermediaries are being changed. Advantages and disadvantages of doing business via the Internet are discussed.

The shopping experience is a pivotal part of the purchase decision. In many cases, retailing is like theater—that is, the consumer's evaluation of stores and products may depend on the type of "performance" he or she witnesses. This evaluation can be influenced by the actors (e.g., the salespeople), the setting (e.g., the store environment), and props (e.g., store displays). A store image, like a brand personality, is determined by a number of factors, such as perceived convenience, sophistication, knowledge of salespeople, and so on. With increasing competition from non-store alternatives, the creation of a positive shopping experience has never been more important.

Because many purchase decisions are not made until the time the consumer is actually in the store, point-of-purchase (POP) stimuli are very important sales tools. POP stimuli are particularly useful in stimulating impulse buying, where a consumer yields a sudden urge for a product.

The consumer's encounter with a salesperson is a complex and important process. The outcome can be affected by such factors as the salesperson's similarity to the customer and his or her perceived credibility. Each person must participate in the salesperson-customer relationship if a successful sale is to take place.

Consumer satisfaction is determined by the person's overall feeling toward the product after purchase. Many factors influence perceptions of product quality (such as price, brand name, and product performance). Satisfaction (or dissatisfaction) is often determined by the degree to which a product's performance is consistent with the consumer's prior expectations of how well the product will function.

Lastly, the chapter explores the area of product disposal. This is an increasingly important problem and one that the consumer often considers prior to making a purchase. Recycling options will increase in their attractiveness as the "throwaway society" fades from popularity. One of the interesting subjects discussed in this section is lateral cycling (e.g., flea markets and garage sales).

# CHAPTER OUTLINE

## 1. Introduction

a. A consumer's choices are affected by many personal factors, such as his or her mood, whether there is time pressure to make the purchase, and the particular situation or context for which the product is needed. Influences include:

1) The salesperson.
2) The store environment.
3) The World Wide Web (www).

---

**\*\*\*\*\*Use Figure 10.1 Here \*\*\*\*\***

---

Situational Effects on Consumer Behavior

b. A ***consumption situation*** is defined by factors over and above the characteristics of the person and of the product that influence the buying and/or using of products and services.

1) Situational effects can be behavioral (e.g., entertaining friends).
2) Situational effects can be perceptual (e.g., being depressed or feeling pressed for time).
3) Smart marketers understand consumer emotions change from situation to situation and tailor their efforts to coincide with situations where people are most prone to buy.
4) A research technique called the **Day Reconstruction Method** is based on consumer diaries of their emotions to track these changes.

c. In addition to functional relationships between products and usage situations, another reason to take environmental circumstances seriously is that the role a person plays at any time is partly determined by his or her ***situational self-image***, where the consumer asks "Who am I right now?"

1) Marketers often consider the major contexts where a product is used and the major users of the product.

---

**\*\*\*\*\*Use Table 10.1 Here; Use Consumer Behavior Challenge #15 Here \*\*\*\*\***

---

*Discussion Opportunity—Ask the class to think of situations where situational self-image would be very important to consider in formulating strategy.*

---

*Discussion Opportunity—Ask: What are some products that are tied to your self-image? Explain.*

---

## 2. Social and Physical Surroundings

a. A consumer's physical and social environment can make a big difference in motives for product usage and also affect how the product is evaluated.

1) Examples of the physical environment would include the decor, smells, and even temperature within the selling environment (such as a store).
2) If other consumers are present when sales are made they are called **co-consumers**.
   a) The presence or absence of other customers can be positive or negative.

    b) Crowds can make the experience more intense.
    c) Store customers can serve as a store attribute (e.g., people tend to shop
       where other shoppers are like them).
    d) Crowds can make a dull situation exciting.
    e) We can infer something about a store by examining its customers.

---

*Discussion Opportunity—Ask: What goes through your mind when you go to a new restaurant and there are empty tables everywhere? On a normal evening, what is your reaction when you go to your favorite restaurant and you are told there will be a 30- to 40-minute wait?*

---

*Discussion Opportunity—Ask students to think of a local "hot spot." Describe its characteristics. If you were going to design a similar "hot spot," what additional features would you add? Why?*

---

Temporal Factors
b. Time is one of the consumers' most precious resources. Think about how we
  talk about time:
  1) "Making time."
  2) "Spending time."
  3) "Time is money."

---

*Discussion Opportunity—Ask: What is your view toward time when shopping? How could time impact your shopping behavior?*

---

*Discussion Opportunity—Ask students to compare "time" when considering shopping on the Internet versus traditional shopping in a store. Consider the advantages and disadvantages.*

---

  c. Time is an economic variable; it is a resource that must be divided among
    activities.
    1) An individual's priorities determine his or her *timestyle*.
    2) Many consumers are affected by what they would call **time poverty**.
      a) With an increase in time poverty, researchers are noting a rise in
        *polychronic activity* (where consumers do more than one thing at a time
        or multitasking).

---

*****Use Consumer Behavior Challenge #6 Here *****

---

*Discussion Opportunity—Ask students to think of ways marketers attempt to appeal to consumers that have a sense of time poverty. Give a product illustration.*

---

*Discussion Opportunity—Give an illustration of a polychronic activity that you perform. What can a marketer learn from this activity to better present products or services to you?*

---

  d. The experience of time is subjective and is influenced by priorities and needs. Time as it
    relates to consumers is important for marketers to understand. Time has been classified

into different categories including flow time, occasion time, deadline time, leisure time, and time to kill.

e. Researchers have identified four dimensions of time: 1) *social dimension,* 2) *temporal situation*, 3) *planning orientation*, and 4) *polychronic orientation dimension* that have resulted in the identification of five metaphors that capture perspectives on time:

a) *Time is a Pressure Cooker*—Analytic in planning, other oriented, monochronic.

b) *Time is a Map*—Analytic planners, temporal orientation, polychromic.

c) *Time is a Mirror*—Analytic planners, polychromic orientation, past temporal orientation.

d) *Time is a River*—Spontaneous with a present focus.

e) *Time is a Feast*—Analytic planners with a present temporal orientation.

f. Different societies have different perspectives on time. These include:

a) *Linear separable time*—Events proceed in an orderly sequence and different times are well defined.

b) *Procedural time*—People simply decide to do something when they want to. Clocks may be ignored.

c) *Circular or cyclic time*—People are governed by natural cycles.

g. There is a psychological dimension of time or how it is experienced. This is important in **queuing theory** (a mathematical study of waiting lines). It has been found that a consumer's experience of waiting can radically influence his or her perceptions of service quality.

h. Many marketers have adopted a variety of tricks to minimize the consumer's perception of waiting time as being something that is bad (primarily by diverting their attention away from waiting).

---

*****Use Figure 10.2 Here; Use Consumer Behavior Challenges #7 and #16 Here *****

---

*Discussion Opportunity—Ask students to think of a positive and negative experience that you have had with a waiting line. Relate how the marketers handled these situations.*

---

*Discussion Opportunity—Ask: Do "waiting lines" exist on the Internet. When do you have to wait? Is it irritating? How can it be overcome?*

---

Antecedent States: If It Feels Good, Buy It . . .

i. Your mood or physiological condition can affect purchases and how products are evaluated.

1) Two dimensions, *pleasure* and *arousal*, determine if a shopper will react positively or negatively to a consumption environment.

2) A specific mood is some combination of pleasure and arousal.

3) In general, a mood state (either positive or negative) biases judgments of products and service in that direction.

4) Moods can be affected by store design, the weather, or other factors specific to the consumer (such as music or even television programming).

---

*****Use Figure 10.3 Here *****

---

*Discussion Opportunity—Have students give an illustration of how mood has affected your purchase decisions. If you were a salesperson, when would be the best time to sell to you?*

*Discussion Opportunity—Ask: If mood is an important variable in a consumer's decision to purchase, how can an Internet marketer determine your mood? If they cannot, how can they work around this inability?*

### 3. Shopping: A Job or An Adventure?

Reasons for Shopping

a. How people feel about shopping depends largely on their **shopping orientation**—or their attitudes about shopping in general.

b. Shopping is an activity that can be performed for either utilitarian (functional or tangible) or hedonic (pleasurable or intangible) reasons.

1) Hedonic shopping motives include:
   a) *Social experiences.*
   b) *Sharing of common interests.*
   c) *Interpersonal attraction.*
   d) *Instant status.*
   e) *"The thrill of the hunt."*

*****Use Consumer Behavior Challenge #3 Here *****

*Discussion Opportunity—Ask: Can you think of other reasons for shopping? How could the marketer use these (and the ones listed in the chapter) to design strategies to attract you into the store?*

*Discussion Opportunity—Ask: Are the reasons for shopping on the Internet the same as those for shopping in a store or mall? Compare and contrast the differences. How do Internet marketers appeal to your shopping motives on the Internet? Do they consciously try to lure you away from the traditional shopping format? If so, how?*

*****Use Consumer Behavior Challenge #12 Here *****

E-Commerce: Clicks Versus Bricks

c. Marketers are hotly debating how the new format of buying on the Web will affect how they conduct business.

d. For marketers, the growth of online commerce is a sword that cuts both ways.

1) On the one hand, they can reach customers that were inaccessible (even around the world).

2) On the other hand, competition just got much bigger and is no longer located just around the corner.

e. The number one thing that makes an e-commerce site successful (according to research) is good customer service.

f. From the customer's point of view, electronic marketing has increased convenience by breaking down many of the barriers caused by time and location.

g. Limitations of the virtual shopping world include:
   1) Security.
   2) The actual shopping experience—the inability to taste, touch, feel, or try on products.
   3) Potential of large shipping and return charges.

---

**\*\*\*\*\*Use Table 10.2 Here; Use Consumer Behavior Challenge #17 Here \*\*\*\*\***

---

*Discussion Opportunity—Compare the pros and cons mentioned in Table 10.2. Ask: Which do you think are the most important? Which of the cons are the easiest to overcome? What could you add to the list? If you have not shopped online, why not? How could a marketer get you to shop online? If you have shopped, what do you like the best? What could be improved in your shopping experience?*

Retailing as Theater

h. Malls are becoming giant entertainment centers. Many stores are designed around an image environment. This is a strategy known as **retail theming** and can be described based on four basic kinds of themes:
   1) *Landscape themes*—rely on associations with images of nature.
   2) *Marketscape themes*—built on associations with man-made places.
   3) *Cyberspace themes*—incorporate images of information and communications technology.
   4) *Mindscape themes*—draw on abstract ideas and concepts, introspection, and fantasy.

---

**\*\*\*\*\*Use Consumer Behavior Challenges #12 (Used Previously) and #13 Here \*\*\*\*\***

---

*Discussion Opportunity—Ask: Is there a mall or store that you like to go even if you don't want to buy something? What is the attraction?*

i. Stores today have distinct personalities or **store image**. This image includes:
   1) Location.
   2) Merchandise suitability.
   3) Knowledge and congeniality of the sales staff.

---

**\*\*\*\*\*Use Consumer Behavior Challenge #9 Here \*\*\*\*\***

---

*Discussion Opportunity—Describe a store that you think has a unique personality or image. How do you think the store maintains that image? Do you think this image was part of their original strategy?*

j. Because a store's image now is recognized as a very important aspect of retailing mix, attention is increasingly paid to **atmospherics**, or the "conscious designing of space and its various dimensions to evoke certain effects in buyers." This could include colors, scents, and sounds.

k. **Activity stores** are a fairly new trend. They allow the consumer to participate in the production of a good or service.

***** *Use Figure 10.4; Here Use Consumer Behavior Challenges #10 and #14 Here* *****

*Discussion Opportunity—Ask students to describe the atmospherics of (a) McDonald's, (b) Wal-Mart, (c) a prestige department store in your area, and (d) a bar or nightclub in your area. Do you think the atmosphere in these places accomplishes what the management intended it to?*

In-Store Decision Making

l. Despite all their efforts to "pre-sell" consumers through advertising, marketers increasingly are recognizing the significant degree to which many purchases are influenced by the store environment. For example, two of three supermarket product decisions are made in the aisles.

1) **Unplanned buying** may occur when a person is unfamiliar with a store's layout or perhaps when under some time pressure.

2) **Impulse buying**, in contrast, occurs when the person experiences a sudden urge that he or she cannot resist. Many *impulse items* are placed next to checkout stands (such as gum or candy).

3) General types of consumers include:

a) **Planner**—know specific products and brands.

b) **Partial planners**—know the products but choose brand in the store.

c) **Impulse purchasers**—do no advance planning whatsoever.

***** *Use Figure 10.5 Here* *****

*Discussion Opportunity—Ask: When it comes to shopping, would you describe yourself as a planner, partial planner, or an impulse purchaser? Give an illustration.*

m. Retailers are starting to pay more attention to the amount of information supplied within their store environment. **Point-of-purchase (POP) stimuli** is being increasingly used. This can range from displays to free samples.

***** *Use Consumer Behavior Challenge #11 Here* *****

*Discussion Opportunity—Have students list some interesting or unique POP materials that you have seen. Do you think that it is ethical to put marketing materials in public places such as restrooms or waiting rooms?*

The Salesperson

n. One of the most important in-store factors is the salesperson, who attempts to influence the buying behavior of the customer.

1) This influence can be understood in terms of **exchange theory** that stresses

that every interaction involves an exchange of value.

2) A resource exchange is "what do I get from the salesperson?" (such as expertise).

3) A buyer/seller situation is like many other dyadic encounters (two-person groups); it is a relationship where some agreement must be reached about the roles of each participant. An *identity negotiation* occurs.

4) Salespeople differ in their *interaction styles*.

---

**\*\*\*\*\*Use Consumer Behavior Challenge #5 Here \*\*\*\*\***

---

*Discussion Opportunity—Ask: What stores do you like to go to because you like the salespeople? What do you like about them? What are some of the stores you hate to shop at because of the salespeople? How do they make you feel? What specifically do you not like about them? What would you do to correct the situation if you were the management of the store?*

## 4. Postpurchase Satisfaction

a. **Consumer satisfaction/dissatisfaction (CS/D)** is determined by the overall feelings and attitude a person has about a product after it has been purchased.

---

**\*\*\*\*\*Use Consumer Behavior Challenges #4 and #5 (Used Previously) Here \*\*\*\*\***

---

Perceptions of Product Quality

b. Perceptions of product quality are primarily determined by:

1) Price.
2) Brand name.
3) Advertising.

c. Satisfaction or dissatisfaction is more than just a reaction to the actual performance quality of a product or service.

1) According to the *expectancy disconfirmation model*, consumers form beliefs about a product's performance based on prior experience with the product and/or communications about the product that imply a certain level of quality.

2) *Managing expectations*—To avoid customer dissatisfaction, marketers should avoid promising something they cannot deliver. The power of quality claims is most evident when a company's product fails.

---

**\*\*\*\*\*Use Figure 10.6 Here \*\*\*\*\***

---

3) If a person is not happy in a purchase equation, three responses can occur:

a) *Voice response*—the consumer can appeal directly to the retailer for redress.

b) *Private response*—express dissatisfaction about the store or product to friends and/or boycott the store.

c) *Third-party response*—the consumer can take legal action against the merchant or complain in a public forum.

4) The Japanese approach to TQM subscribes to the philosophy that marketers and

designers should go to the *gemba*, or the precise place where the product or service will be used.

***** *Use Figure 10.7 Here Use; Consumer Behavior Challenge #19 Here* *****

*Discussion Opportunity—Ask: What do you usually do when you are dissatisfied with a product or service? Have you ever made a legal or public complaint? If so, describe the event and the outcome.*

## 5. Product Disposal

a. Because people often do form strong attachments to products, the decision to dispose of something may be a painful one.

*Discussion Opportunity—Ask students to describe a painful disposal situation that you have encountered. What was the result? Would you do it differently if you had it to do over again? (An example might be the selling of an old car that was a favorite or throwing away something that would now be valuable, such as old baseball cards.)*

*Discussion Opportunity—Ask: How can marketers use the consumer's reluctance to part with favorite products in their marketing strategy? Apply this to a situation where you would like the consumer to part with an old product and buy a new one.*

Disposal Options

b. When a consumer decides that a product is no longer of use, three options are available:
1) Keep the item.
2) Temporarily dispose of the item.
3) Permanently dispose of the item.

*****  *Use Figure 10.8 Here; Use Consumer Behavior Challenge #8 Here* *****

Lateral Cycling: Junk Versus "Junque"

c. Interesting consumer processes occur during **lateral cycling**, where already-purchased objects are sold to others or exchanged for still other things.
1) eBay and other online auction sites have revolutionized the process of lateral cycling.
2) **Divestment rituals** involve steps that consumers take to gradually separate themselves from the things that they treasure.

*****  *Use Consumer Behavior Challenge #18 Here* *****

3) Goods and services bought through lateral cycling constitute what is known as the **underground economy**.

*Discussion Opportunity—Ask students to think of an example where you have lateral cycled something. Describe the experience. Think of something where you have purchased something that has been lateral cycled. What did you feel about the experience? How did you deal with doubts? How should the marketer try to persuade you to buy new rather than used? Where do you think new industries in lateral cycling will occur in the future?*

*Discussion Opportunity—Have students share and discuss experiences they have had buying/selling items on eBay or other online auction sites. How do they think such sites have had an impact on the underground economy?*

# End-of-Chapter Support Material

# SUMMARY OF SPECIAL FEATURE BOXES

### 1. Net Profit I

This box briefly examines emerging technology that allows signage found everywhere from restaurants to highways to change with environmental conditions. Factors that affect signs include the time of day and the weather. This feature supports the section "Situational Effects on Consumer Behavior."

### 2. Net Profit II

This box takes a look at how multi-tasking applies to eating. Prepared foods companies are responding to consumer needs with a variety of foods that can be eaten easily on the go. This feature supports the section "Temporal Factors."

### 3. The Global Looking Glass

The Western style hypermarkets have invaded Eastern Europe. But the Eastern Europeans aren't buying it. They prefer to shop the way that they always have in smaller neighborhood stores with few choices. This box highlights the hypermarket chains as well as chains that have been finding success pursuing a model based on the corner market.

### 4. Marketing Opportunity I

The concept of a **pop-up store** is featured in this box. A pop-up store is a temporary store that is opened in order to showcase new brands, concepts, or ideas. These stores by definition are shut down after a limited period of time, even if profitable.

**5.      Net Profit III**

Sony has inserted links to Pizza Hut into its online game, Everquest II. People can order Pizza while playing the game.

**6.      Marketing Pitfalls I**

This box highlights various cases of consumer abuse by retail employees. This feature supports the section "Post-Purchase Satisfaction."

**7.      Marketing Pitfalls II**

This box takes a look at the flipside of the previous feature—that of employee frustration with customers. This feature supports the section "Post-Purchase Satisfaction."

**8.      Marketing Opportunity II**

This box highlights various techniques that are being used for product disposal. These include the practice of **freecycling**, giving away unwanted goods to keep them out of landfills or simply to help someone with something that they need (see case study for this chapter).

**9.      Marketing Pitfalls III**

This box explores the positive and negative aspects of recycling consumer electronics products by sending them to third world countries. This feature supports the section "Lateral Cycling: Junk Versus 'Junque'."

# REVIEW QUESTIONS

1.      What is meant by the situational self-image? Give an example of this phenomenon. *A reason to take environmental circumstances seriously is that the role a person plays at any one time is partly determined by his situational self-image—he basically asks: "Who am I right now?"*

2.      Describe the difference between density and crowding. Why is this difference relevant in purchase environments? *Density term refers to the actual number of people occupying a space although the psychological state of crowding exists only if a negative affective state occurs as a result of this density.*

3.      What is time poverty, and how can it influence our purchase decisions? *Many consumers believe they are more pressed for time than ever before.*

4.  What are the two dimensions that determine whether we will react positively or negatively to a purchase environment? *Pleasure——a person can enjoy or not enjoy a situation, and arousal—he can feel stimulated or not.*

5.  List three separate motivations for shopping, giving an example of each. **Social experiences**: *The shopping center or department store has replaced the traditional town square or county fair as a community gathering place.* **Sharing of common interests**: *Stores frequently offer specialized goods that allow people with shared interests to communicate.* **Interpersonal attraction**: *Shopping centers are a natural place to congregate. The shopping mall has become a central "hangout" for teenagers.* **Instant status**: *As every salesperson knows, some people savor the experience of being waited on, even though they may not necessarily buy anything.* **The thrill of the hunt**: *Some people pride themselves in being able to find the best bargains.*

6.  What are some important pros and cons of e-commerce? *Numerous benefits and limitations of e-commerce are listed in Table 10.2 for both the consumer and the marketer.*

7.  List three factors that help to determine store image. *Color, scents, and sounds.*

8.  What is the difference between unplanned buying and impulse buying? *Unplanned buying may occur when a person is unfamiliar with a store's layout or perhaps when under some time pressure; or, a person may be reminded to buy something by seeing it on a store shelf. In contrast, impulse buying occurs when the person experiences a sudden urge he cannot resist.*

9.  Describe what is meant by a commercial friendship, and provide an example. *A warm personal relationship between a company employee and a client. This may be something as simple as a sales representative giving a gift to a client for a special occasion.*

10. How do a consumer's prior expectations about product quality influence his satisfaction with the product after he buys it? *Consumers form beliefs about product performance based on prior experience with the product and/or communications about the product that imply a certain level of quality. When something performs the way we thought it would, we may not think much about it. If it fails to live up to expectations, negative feelings may result. On the other hand if performance happens to exceed our expectations, we are satisfied and pleased.*

11. List three actions a consumer can take if he is dissatisfied with a purchase. *Voice response: The consumer can appeal directly to the retailer for redress (e.g., a refund). Private response: Express dissatisfaction about the store or product to friends and/or boycott the store. As we'll discuss in Chapter 11, negative word-of-mouth (WOM) can be very damaging to a store's reputation. Third-party response: The consumer can take legal action against the merchant, register a complaint with the Better Business Bureau, or perhaps write a letter to the newspaper.*

12.     What is the underground economy? *Although traditional marketers have not paid much attention to used-product sellers, factors such as concern about the environment, demands for quality, and cost and fashion consciousness are conspiring to make these "secondary" markets more important.*

# CONSUMER BEHAVIOR CHALLENGE

## Discussion Questions

1.      Is the customer always right? Why or why not? *Use this question in conjunction with the section on Post-Purchase Satisfaction to direct students to concepts that would govern whether or not the customer should always be treated as though they are right.*

2.      Are pop-up stores just a fad or a retailing concept that's here to stay? *Given that there are so many strategies that have circulated through retailing, it is likely that nothing is "here to stay." Students should be engaged in a discussion as to how long they thing that this trend will last and possible reasons that it might end (no longer providing the benefits of promoting the new idea; stores so profitable that they remain open, etc.).*

3.      Discuss some of the motivations for shopping as described in the chapter. How might a retailer adjust his or her strategy to accommodate these motivations?

        *Shopping motives listed in the chapter are:*

        - *Functional and tangible needs.*
        - *Pleasurable and intangible reasons.*
        - *Social experiences.*
        - *Sharing of common interests.*
        - *Interpersonal attraction.*
        - *Instant status.*
        - *"The thrill of the chase."*

        *Shopping is a way of acquiring needed products as well as satisfying some important social need. Retailers might adjust their strategies to accommodate these motives by creating a theme environment, like that of the Banana Republic. They might offer additional complementary services—for example, a tanning salon might include manicures, massages, and makeovers. Encourage your students to think of specific examples appropriate for their favorite stores.*

4.      What are some positive and negative aspects of requiring employees who interact with customers to wear some kind of uniform or to mandate a dress code in the office?

        *Employee uniforms will impact the overall image and atmospherics of some retail outlets. The positive aspects of requiring employees who interact with customers to wear some kind of uniform or to mandate a dress code in the office include: 1) portraying a professional image; 2) helping employees to feel "equal" in terms of dress; and 3) making it easier for customers to identify employees of the business. The negative aspects include: 1) some employees might feel uncomfortable in some uniforms; 2) others may feel their "freedom" of apparel (to look good) is being limited; and 3) employees may also feel their individuality is being restricted. Students should quite easily identify examples of some jobs or professions that require uniforms (e.g., police, firefighters, nurses, priests, or McDonald's staff.)*

5.      Think about exceptionally good and bad salespeople you have encountered in the past. What qualities seem to differentiate them?

*The instructor might ask students to recall the last time they went shopping. In the context of that shopping trip, students should describe the characteristics of the salespeople who assisted them. The instructor, or a member of the class, should generate a list of the most common traits mentioned and use the class discussion to profile both good and bad salespeople. The students also should be encouraged to consider the text discussion of source credibility, including such characteristics as similarity, attractiveness, expertise, trustworthiness, and likeability.*

6.      Discuss the concept of "timestyle." Based on your own experiences, how might consumers be segmented in terms of their timestyles?

*The concept of "timestyle" reflects how individuals allocate their time to various activities. You might want to discuss your own timestyle with the class and encourage students to do the same. A discussion of how consumers might be segmented on the basis of their timestyles should be included. Products that benefit from different timestyles also could be discussed. For example: How much time do you spend teaching, grading papers, researching, and doing college and community service? How much time do you spend with your family, doing household chores, eating, sleeping, exercising, and having fun?*

7.      Compare and contrast different cultures' conceptions of time. What are some implications for marketing strategy within each of these frameworks?

*Conceptions of time are not universal; cultural differences with regard to time exist. Examples of such that are mentioned in the text include: 1) linear separable time—events proceed in an orderly sequence and different times are well defined; 2) procedural time—people ignore the clock completely; and 3) circular or cyclic time—people are governed by natural cycles (Latino cultures).*

*Marketing implications that correspond to these concepts are: 1) under linear separable time—people sell clocks, watches, timers, have lunch hour specials, happy hours, and after dinner drinks. 2) under procedural time—people do things when the "time is right" so marketers need to show causal relationships to let the consumer know that "the time is now"; and 3) under circular or cyclic time—the future doesn't make sense, so we live for now. These consumers will not wait for a better product, they will buy whatever is available now. Don't bother trying to sell them insurance.*

8.    The movement away from a "disposable consumer society" toward one that emphasizes creative recycling creates many opportunities for marketers. Can you identify some?

*Products can be disposed of by storage, temporary disposal, and permanent disposal. Recycling is an important disposal option as well. Students are likely to generate many and diverse examples of marketing opportunities in light of this new consumer emphasis. For example: A company may pick up yard waste for a fee and then turn that into compost to sell back to the homeowner! A company could pick up used oil that could be re-refined. One farmer lets companies dump old tires on his farm for a fee, and he grinds them up and resells them as a road surfacing material.*

9.    Some retailers work hard to cultivate a certain look or image, and they may even choose employees who fit this look. Abercrombie & Fitch, for example, seems to link itself to a clean-cut, all-American image. A federal lawsuit filed in 2003 claimed that Abercrombie & Fitch systematically "refuses to hire qualified minority applicants as brand representatives to work on the sales floor and discourages applications from minority applicants." Abercrombie has said the complaints are without merit, and that the company has "zero tolerance for discrimination."

The Hooters restaurant chain is known for its attractive female waitresses. Should a retailer have the right to recruit employees who are consistent with its image even if this means excluding certain types of people (e.g. non-Caucasians, men) from the sales floor?

*Traditionally, the law has allowed for hiring people with a certain look or body type if it can be proven that this is a necessary component of the product or service. For example, airlines can refuse to hire flight personnel that exceed a weight and size limitation (or terminate them if they exceed the limitations after being hired) because there is limited space to work on the airplanes. Ethnic restaurants can choose to only hire people of that ethnicity. Modeling agencies and movie/TV production companies make hiring decisions based almost exclusively on the way people look. However, for many chains such as Abercrombie & Fitch, it is difficult to justify this link. And in a case such as theirs, they would be unwise to attempt such a link for reasons of public perception. Since this lawsuit, Abercrombie & Fitch has implemented personnel policies to ensure that this problem will be eliminated.*

10.    The mall of the future will most likely be less about purchasing products than exploring them in a physical setting. This means that retail environments will have to become places to build brand images, rather than just places to sell products. What are some strategies stores can use to enhance the emotional/sensory experiences their customers receive?

*Students will likely focus on strategies being used by large retailers, including the swank environments in new malls (leather furniture, premium floor coverings, HD big-screen monitors, fountains and landscaping, high-end play areas, and family bathrooms). But they may be reminded of the many themed restaurants that have opened (including those that feature live high-divers).*

11.    The store environment is heating up as more and more companies put their promotional dollars into point-of-purchase efforts. Shoppers are now confronted by videos at the checkout counter, computer monitors attached to their shopping carts, and so on. We're increasingly exposed to ads in non-shopping environments. Recently, a health club in New York was forced to remove TV monitors that showed advertising on the Health Club Media Networks, claiming that they interfered with workouts. Do you feel that these innovations are overly intrusive? At what point might shoppers "rebel" and demand some peace and quiet while shopping? Do you see any market potential in the future for stores that "countermarket" by promising a "hands-off" shopping environment?

*Student opinion will vary based on their knowledge/experience and feelings/beliefs about place-based media. You might ask your students if they have encountered this type of promotion and explore their reaction at the time of exposure. Students might also be asked to consider a more objective opinion, in light of what they have learned from this course. They should be challenged to view the advantages and disadvantages of these practices from the perspectives of both consumers and retailers.*

12.    Court cases in recent years have attempted to prohibit special interest groups from distributing literature in shopping malls. Mall management claims that these centers are private property. On the other hand, these groups argue that the mall is the modern-day version of the town square and as such is a public forum. Find some recent court cases involving this free-speech issue and examine the arguments pro and con. What is the current status of the mall as a public forum? Do you agree with this concept?

*This exercise will challenge the student to conduct primary and secondary research. Encourage exploration of this issue with other students, faculty members, and consumer advocacy groups. A search should be conducted of published sources such as court cases and the* Law Review. *They might call the management office of a local mall for additional information.*

## Application Questions

13.    Conduct naturalistic observation at a local mall. Sit in a central location and observe the activities of mall employees and patrons. Keep a log of the nonretailing activity you observe (e.g., special performances, exhibits, socializing, etc.). Does this activity enhance or detract from business conducted at the mall? As malls become more like high-tech game rooms, how valid is the criticism raised that shopping areas are only encouraging more loitering by teenage boys, who don't spend a lot in stores and simply scare away other customers?

*Students tend to like this exercise. Now that they have been exposed to a variety of consumer behavior constructs, they are likely to see things in the retail context that they didn't notice before. They will probably notice a wide variety of nonretailing activities in the mall. Encourage your students to think about the advantages and disadvantages of these other activities from both the consumers' and retailers' points of view. Encourage students to develop a specific plan for dealing with teenage loitering that would work, be legal, and would not interfere with normal store and mall traffic. Students might interview mall officials or security officers to get their viewpoint about loitering. (Possible Field Project Idea)*

14.     Select three competing clothing stores in your area and conduct a store image study for them. Ask a group of consumers to rate each store on a set of attributes and plot these ratings on the same graph. Based on your findings, are there any areas of competitive advantage or disadvantage you could bring to the attention of store management?

*Students should review the section on store image (including Atmospherics) before beginning this exercise. You might encourage the students to select stores that are very different from each other rather than "direct competitors." Consider using this as an opportunity to discuss the strengths and weakness of this type of market research. (Possible Field Project Idea)*

15.     Using Table 10.1 as a model, construct a person/situation segmentation matrix for a brand of perfume.

*You might want to ask different groups of students to construct a matrix for other very different types of products such as convenience versus specialty goods. Tell students to look up these terms in the glossary and index for further information. Allow students to experiment with variables to construct their matrix. (Possible Field Project or In-Class Group Project Idea)*

16.     What applications of queuing theory can you find employed among local services? Interview consumers who are waiting on lines to determine how (if at all) this experience affects their satisfaction with the service.

*The students should consider the explanation of queuing theory—the mathematical study of waiting in lines—as part of the psychological time construct. As suggested, a consumer's experience of waiting can radically influence his or her perception of service quality. Although we assume that something must be pretty good if we have to wait for it, the negative feelings aroused by long waits can quickly discourage consumers. Lines at movie theaters, restaurants, ticket booths, and university class registration all provide contexts in which students might investigate the psychology of time. (Possible Field Project Idea)*

17.     New interactive tools are being introduced that allow surfers on sites such as landsend.com to view apparel product selections on virtual models in full, 360-degree, rotational view. In some cases the viewer can modify the bodies, face, skin coloring, and

hairstyles of these models. In others, the consumer can project his or her own likeness into the space by scanning a photo into a "makeover" program. Boo.com plans to offer 3-D pictures that can be rotated for close looks, even down to the stitching on a sweater, as well as online mannequins that will incorporate photos of shoppers and mimic voice patterns. Visit landsend.com or another site that offers a personalized mannequin. Surf around. Try on some clothes. How was your experience? How helpful was this mannequin? When you shop for clothes online, would you rather see how they look on a body with dimensions the same as yours or on a different body? What advice can you give Web site designers who are trying to personalize these shopping environments by creating lifelike models to guide you through the site?

*A variety of responses will emerge from this activity. Many students, particularly those who are familiar with personalized mannequins, will derive a great deal of value from this method. Others simply will not see the point.*

18. Interview people who are selling items at a flea market or garage sale. Ask them to identify some items to which they had a strong attachment. Then, see if you can prompt them to describe one or more divestment rituals they went through as they prepared to offer these items for sale.

*Student results will depend entirely on the outcomes that they receive from respondents.*

19. Identify three people who own an electric coffeemaker. Then, "go to the gemba" by observing them as they actually prepare coffee in the appliance at home. Based on these experiences, what recommendations might you make to the designer of a new coffeemaker model that would improve customers' experience with the product?

*Given the modern infatuation with coffee, responses to this will likely have something to do with upscale blends and flavors, ability to make cappuccino/espresso products, etc. Buying coffee retail is much more about the experience than the actual coffee. Home use may start to mirror this.*

# CASE STUDY TEACHING NOTES

**Chapter 10 Case Study: Giving and Receiving on Freecycle.org**

## Summary of Case

Started as the brainchild of a city employee in Tucson, Arizona, as a means of relieving strain on public landfills, **Freecycle.org** has grown to immense proportions. Freecycle.org is a virtual garage sale where the main rule is that all things given and taken must be done on a completely free basis. No money or product exchanges are to be made. Participants can register for their own geographic area, then post things that they want to get rid of or take things that they need. As of January 2005, the population of Freecycle.org had grown to over 900,000 members in over 2,200 communities in over 45 countries. And this growth was achieved through word-of-mouth and free publicity. The initial goal of land-fill relief has also been accomplished as an estimated 40 billion tons of garbage avoid such a fate every day.

## Suggestions for Presentation

The most direct link for presenting and discussing this case is in the section, "Product Disposal" with the concepts of lateral cycling and disposal options. Freecycling is briefly highlighted in the second Marketing Opportunity special feature box.

## Suggested Answers for Discussion Questions

1.  Why do you think Freecycle.org has achieved such high levels of growth in such a short period of time?

    *The most obvious answer to this question is that the market was ready, even craving some kind of product disposal option such as this. People often have things to get rid of that don't have much resale value. Often, items would cost more to have someone haul them away than they are worth. Many people also feel a bit of guilt in throwing away something that is perfectly usable. So, if they find someone who can use the item, there is great satisfaction in that. On the taking end, who doesn't want free stuff? There are all too many people waiting to snag up the free stuff. As long as this supply-demand dynamic continues, freecycling is around forever.*

2.  Freecycle.org has created an alternative disposal option that is rapidly growing. Discuss ways that freecycling might affect the purchase habits of consumers.

    *There are at least two main ways that freecycling affects the purchase habits of people. People who have become involved in freecycling are much more likely to think about whether or not they really need items that they are buying new. The second way is that people might forego buying something new or even used if they can find it for free on Freecycle.org.*

# Additional Support Material

# STUDENT PROJECTS

## Individual Projects

1.      Have students employ the method of Day Reconstruction to document their own behavior for a day and report on the findings. What trends do they notice? Are there things that they found that they did not expect?

2.      Have students go to a shopping mall. Have them analyze the behavior of shoppers based on observation only. Can they determine the nature of people's reasons for shopping? Have them keep track and present the results to the class.

3.      Ask a student to visit competing discount houses, supermarkets, department stores, or specialty shops in your area and describe the image they have of each store. What factors account for the image differences? For the poorest image store, design a strategy for upgrading its image.

4.      Ask one of your students to dress in older (perhaps shabby) clothes and visit one of the finer clothing stores in your area. Have the student express an interest in trying on some clothes and observe the reaction of the store employees. Then ask the student to return in a few days in better clothes and repeat the process. Have the student explain his or her observations to the class.

5.      Have students talk to other students at the university or college. What forms of complaint behavior do they observe? What strategies could the university or college follow to alleviate these complaints?

6.      Have someone visit a local supermarket and question the manager regarding how shelf space is allocated. What and who determines which products are placed on the shelves, how much space they are allocated, and at what level they are displayed on the shelf?

7.      Many consumers have become more interested in conserving than in "throwing away." Have students think of ideas they have for creative recycling. Then, see if they can figure out ways to profitably market these ideas to the public?

8.      Ask a student to relate to the class a purchase experience in which dissatisfaction resulted from the product or service purchased. Have the student tell the class how he/she reacted in terms of postpurchase dissonance. How could the seller avoid future similar incidents?

9.      Have students interview someone older than fifty. What do they look for in a shopping environment? Compare this with your own and/or the student's expectations. Discuss the differences.

10.     Give students the assignment of selling something through an online auction site that they think is worthless junk. Have them share their results with the class. Were the results unexpected? Was it worth the time to do this? What was the highest selling price of a person's "junk"?

11.     Freecycle something. Then, take something off of Freecycle.org. Report on the experience including the feelings of giving/receiving, the benefit or value to the giver/receiver, etc.

12.     Have each student think of a time when they had to get rid of something that had been significant to them. Analyze this situation in terms of divestment rituals.


## Group Projects

1.      Student teams should go to an activity store to interview the manager. Given that the concept of the store is built around participating in the production of a good, ask the manager what benefits they perceive in this model, both from the consumer perspective and from the company perspective.

2.      Assign each student group a competitive task. Each member of the group should attempt to get an item off of Freecycle.org. The competition is: Which member of the group can come up with a free item that is worth the most?, Which did the most good for the giver? and, Which Did the most good in terms of keeping it out of a landfill?

3.      Student groups should visit three small clothing stores and assess their layouts. What differences do they observe? What factors might account for these differences? Would the student recommend any layout changes based on observation?

4.      Have groups or pairs of students interview a complaint handler for a local department store to describe a recent experience with a dissatisfied customer. The complaint handler should explain why the customer was unhappy. Do the complainers seem to have any common traits?

5.      Ask a group of students to bring to class advertisements that demonstrate a store's effort to cultivate a particular image among consumers. Do they think the ads are effective?

6.      Ask a team of students to visit a nearby popular mall to observe the activities of customers and employees. What nonretailing activities do they observe (e.g., art exhibits, performances, fitness walking, socializing, etc.)? Are these activities beneficial or harmful to retailers?

7.      Have a group of students bring several mail-order catalogs to class and discuss with the class the differences between the in-store and non-store purchasing processes. You might have the students draw up a "profile" of a typical purchaser from each of these catalogues.

8.      Assign student groups (they can either go as a group or individually and then compare notes) to go to a Saturday morning garage sale or a flea market. Observe the behavior of the participants. Characterize the behavior based on concepts from the chapter.


# eLAB

## Individual Assignments

1.      Go to **www.mountaindew.com**. One of the primary features of this Web site is the entertainment provided for the viewer. What features do you find? Were you entertained or was this page really for another market segment (if so, who)? What would an entertaining Web site have to do with encouraging the consumer to buy the product? Because the consumer cannot buy the product online, does this Web site make much sense? Explain.

2.      Go to **www.bestbuy.com**. The Best Buy Web site promises interactivity with the customer. What evidence do you find that this has occurred (if any)? Evaluate the Best Buy Web site as to ease of use and customer involvement? What are your impressions about the Best Buy approach? What is the company doing right and what are they doing wrong with respect to customer buying?

3.      Go to **www.starbucked.com.** What is the overall purpose of this Web site? Based on the information given on this Web site, discuss how consumers can become so dissatisfied that they would create or participate in such a Web site. Give examples of the different possible courses of action for reacting to poor service.

4.      Go to **www.buy.com**. Spend some time shopping on this Web site. What are the benefits and disadvantages that you perceive to shopping online? Discuss this in terms of the main motives given in the chapter for shopping.


## Group Assignments

1.      Go to **www.bananarepublic.com** and **www.oldnavy.com**. Have your group compare these two Web sites as to online atmosphere. Next, if possible, go to a Banana Republic and Old Navy store to determine the differences between in-store atmospheres. Comment on what you find. How have the two organizations positioned themselves? Is there consistency between the approaches used on the Web versus the approaches used in the retail environment? Explain. What improvements should either or both of the organizations make with respect to consumer buying? Explain how you arrived at your suggestion(s).

2.    Go to **www.customerssuck.com** and **www.northworstair.org**. As a group, examine accounts given by both employees and customers as to the outrageous behavior observed in retail settings. Summarize the findings. What conclusions can be made from this?

# *GROUP INFLUENCE AND OPINION LEADERSHIP*

## CHAPTER OBJECTIVES

When students finish this chapter they should understand why:

- A consumer doesn't make purchase decisions in a vacuum. He often is heavily influenced by others whose opinions and product choices exert various kinds of power over the individual.

- Consumers often seek out others who share similar interests in products or services.

- We may be motivated to buy or use products in order to be consistent with what other people do.

- The things that other consumers tell us about products (both good and bad) are often more influential than the advertising we are exposed to about those products.

- Online technologies are accelerating the impact of word-of-mouth communication.

- Certain people are particularly likely to influence others' product choices.

## CHAPTER SUMMARY

Consumers belong to or admire many different groups and are often influenced in their purchase decisions by a desire to be accepted by others. One form of group that has a definite impact on consumer behavior is the reference group. A *reference group* is "an actual or imaginary individual or group conceived of having significant relevance upon an individual's evaluations, aspirations, or behavior." Reference groups have a *normative influence* (that is, the reference group helps to set and enforce fundamental standards of conduct) and/or a *comparative influence* (where decisions about specific brands or activities are affected). Groups now appear on the Internet. A *virtual community of consumption* is a collection of people whose online interactions are based on shared enthusiasm for and knowledge of a specific consumption activity.

Individuals have influence in a group to the extent that they possess *social power*. Types of power include: *information power, referent power, legitimate power, expert power, reward power,* and *coercive power.* The chapter explores each of these power formats and gives examples that apply to the contemporary study of consumer behavior.

We conform to the desires of others for one of two basic reasons. People who model their behavior after others because they take others' behavior as evidence of the correct way to act are conforming because of comparative influence. People who conform to satisfy the expectations of others and/or to be accepted by the group are affected by normative influence. Although people often like to compare their judgments and actions to those of others, they tend to be selective about precisely whom they will use as benchmarks. This choice of models is of interest to the marketer. On the other hand, there can be resistance to conformity or there can be a loss of individuality. These side effects are some of the consequences of group membership and behavior.

Groups have the effect of exerting pressures to conform on individuals. These pressures are based on the norms that groups develop. Various factors influence the likelihood of conformity, including cultural pressures, fear of deviance, and group size. As strong as the pressures are to conform, however, individuals may exert their own independence and may even defy the group through anticonformity.

Much of what we know about products comes about through *word-of-mouth communication (WOM)* rather than formal advertising. The marketer must study how this process occurs and learn how to influence it if strategies are to be successful. The chapter examines these issues. It has been observed that product-related information tends to be exchanged in casual conversations. Although word of mouth is often helpful for making consumers aware of products, it can also hurt companies when damaging product rumors or negative word of mouth occurs. Boycotts can even occur based on negative word of mouth.

*Opinion leaders* who are knowledgeable about a product and whose opinions are highly regarded tend to influence others' choices. Specific opinion leaders are somewhat hard to identify, but marketers who know their general characteristics can try to target them in their media and promotional strategies. Some opinion leaders, however, do not fit this pattern. *Market mavens* (who have a general interest in the marketplace activities) and *surrogate consumers* (who are compensated for their advice about purchases) are examples.

The chapter concludes with a discussion of *sociometric methods* that attempt to trace referral patterns. This information can be used to identify opinion leaders and other influential consumers. Marketers may use these methods to learn about those that exert an influential role in the selection of products and services.

# CHAPTER OUTLINE

### 1. Reference Groups
    a. Humans are social animals. We all belong to groups, try to please others, and take cues about how to behave by observing the actions of those around us. We will often go to great lengths to please the members of a group whose acceptance

we covet.

1) A **reference group** is "an actual or imaginary individual or group conceived of having significant relevance upon an individual's evaluations, aspirations, or behavior."

2) Reference groups influence consumers in three ways:
   a) *Informational*.
   b) *Utilitarian*.
   c) *Value-expressive*.

---

*****Use Table 11.1 Here *****

---

*Discussion Opportunity—Have students make a list of all the groups that they are a member of. Next, have them identify what type of influence each group has on their behavior. Based on the list, which groups are the most influential? How could a marketer use this information to be more effective?*

---

*Discussion Opportunity—Ask: How important are groups to you? What role do they play in formulating your purchase decisions? Illustrate.*

---

3) Reference groups are not always equally powerful. Two dimensions that influence the degree to which reference groups are important are whether the purchase is to be consumed publicly or privately and whether it is a luxury or a necessity.

4) Reference groups derive their persuasiveness through **social power**, the capacity to alter the actions of others. The following are types of social power:
   a) **Referent power**—when a person admires a person or group and tries to imitate them.
   b) **Information power**—power from merely possessing valuable information that others do not have access to.
   c) **Legitimate power**—power that is granted by social agreement.
   d) **Expert power**—power based on possessing specific knowledge about a content area.
   e) **Reward power**—when a person or group has the means to provide positive reinforcement.
   f) **Coercive power**—the power to influence a person by social or physical intimidation.

---

*****Use Figure 11.1 Here; Use Consumer Behavior Challenges #1, #2, and #3 Here *****

---

*Discussion Opportunity—Have students think of an individual who has power over them. On what basis does this person derive their power? Is more than one basis applicable?*

Types of Reference Groups

b. The term *reference group* may be used loosely to identify anyone that has an influence on your behavior. The primary types of reference group influence are:

1) **Normative influence**—that is, the reference group helps to set and enforce fundamental standards of conduct (e.g., our family's influence).

2) **Comparative influence**—where decisions about specific brands or activities are affected (e.g., a club that you belong to).

*Discussion Opportunity—Give an illustration of normative influence and comparative influence. Ask: Which form of influence do you think is the strongest? Explain.*

c. Reference groups can be large or small.

1) A **formal group** has a recognized structure, regular meeting times, and officers.

2) An **informal group** is usually small and configured like a group of friends.

*Discussion Opportunity—Ask: What are some formal and informal groups to which you belong? How do they influence your behavior?*

d. A more contemporary look at reference groups has identified **brand communities** as a set of consumers who share a set of social relationships based on usage or interest in a product.

1) Such communities often meet for brief periods at organized events known as *brandfests.*

2) A **consumer tribe** is a similar concept that refers to people who share a lifestyle based on an allegiance to an activity or product. **Tribal marketing** seeks such groups as target markets.

*Discussion Opportunity—Ask the students if any of them fell that they belong to a brand community or consumer tribe? Have them describe their associations with this group.*

e. Although some groups consist of people the consumer actually knows, others are composed of people the consumer can either identify with or admire.

1) **Membership reference groups**.

2) **Aspirational reference groups**—what you want to be, not what you are (strong relationship with our *ideal selves*).

3) Both of these group types are closely watched by marketers.

4) The likelihood that people will become part of a consumer's identification reference group is affected by several factors, including:

a) *Propinquity*—physical nearness.

b) *Mere exposure*—frequency of contact.

c) *Group cohesiveness*—the degree that members of a group are attracted to each other and value their group membership.

*Discussion Opportunity—Give an example of an aspirational group of yours. How could the marketer use this aspiration in their marketing efforts?*

f. Reference groups may exert either a positive or negative influence on consumption behaviors.
   1) *Avoidance groups*—groups the consumer wishes to distance themselves from.
   2) In most instances, consumers model their behavior to be consistent with what they think the group expects of them.

*Discussion Opportunity—Have students think of an avoidance group. How could a marketer use this information in constructing strategy?*

## 2. Consumers Do It in Groups

a. The general effect of group behavior on individual behavior is that the identity of the individual is submerged in a group. Less single attention is given. This can be characterized as **deindividualization**. Several things can occur when shopping with a group:
   1) *Social loafing*—people do not devote as much to a task when their contribution is part of a larger group effort.
   2) Group members are willing to consider riskier alternatives. This is called **risky shift**.
   3) As more people are involved in a decision, each individual is less accountable for the outcome. This is called a *diffusion of responsibility*. Another explanation can be the *value hypothesis* where riskiness is a culturally valued characteristic.
   4) A more general effect is that of **decision polarization**. This occurs where the group adopts an even riskier decision (or conservative) after discussion.
   5) Shopping behaviors change when people shop in groups. **Home shopping parties** capitalize on group pressures to boost sales.

*****Use Consumer Behavior Challenge #6 Here *****

*Discussion Opportunity—Ask: Have you ever gone shopping with a group of people your own age? Do you remember buying (or encouraging others to buy) something that you probably wouldn't have if you were alone? Did you take it back, give it away, or throw it away? Did a group ever dissuade you from buying something you wanted? Did you go back later by yourself and make the purchase?*

b. **Conformity** refers to a change in beliefs or actions as a reaction to real or imagined group pressure.
   1) For a society to function, its members develop **norms**, or informal rules that governs behavior.
   2) Norms change slowly over time.
   3) Unspoken rules govern many aspects of consumption.

*****Use Consumer Behavior Challenge #4 Here *****

*Discussion Opportunity—Cite an unspoken rule of consumer behavior. Ask: How do we learn these rules? What happens if we violate them? How do foreigners to our system learn these rules? How do we learn their rules? How can the marketer aid in this process?*

   c. Among the factors that affect the likelihood of conformity are the following:
     1) *Cultural pressures*— teenagers tend to "follow the crowd."
     2) *Fear of deviance*—the group applies penalties to "rule violators."
     3) *Commitment*—the more dedication, the stronger the follower.
     4) *Group unanimity, size,* and *expertise*—the "law of large numbers."
     5) *Susceptibility to interpersonal influence*—the individual's need to identify
       or enhance his or her image in the opinion of significant others.

**\*\*\*\*\*Use Consumer Behavior Challenge #4 (Used Previously) Here \*\*\*\*\***

*Discussion Opportunity—Think of an illustration of each of the reasons for conformity. Think of ways the marketer either can or does use this tendency to conform in their strategies and advertising messages.*

   d. Sometimes we look to the behavior of others to provide a yardstick about reality.
     1) **Social comparison theory** asserts that this process occurs as a way to increase
       the stability of one's self-evaluation, especially when physical evidence is
       unavailable.
     2) Consumers are selective about whom they use for benchmarks. Similarity
       boosts confidence.
     3) In general people tend to choose a *co-oriented peer*, or a person of
       equivalent standing, when undergoing a social comparison.

**\*\*\*\*\*Use Consumer Behavior Challenge #5 Here \*\*\*\*\***

*Discussion Opportunity—Give an illustration of social comparison theory. Ask: Can this theory be applied to the construction of an advertisement? If so, how? Provide an illustration.*

<u>Resisting Conformity</u>
   e. We take pride in our individualism and uniqueness or in our ability to resist the best
     sales efforts of salespeople and advertisers.
     1) In the study of consumer behavior it is important to distinguish between
       *independence* and *anticonformity* (where there is a defiance of the group).
     2) People have a deep-seated need to preserve freedom of choice.
      a) **Reactance** is a negative emotional state wherein people try to overcome a
        loss of freedom. For example, censorship makes us want things more.

**\*\*\*\*\*Use Consumer Behavior Challenge #7 Here \*\*\*\*\***

*Discussion Opportunity—Ask: What are some things that you own that are unique? How do you feel when people talk about this? When was the last time you reacted to censorship by buying the censored product (if at all)?*

*Discussion Opportunity—Bring in a package or a picture of Black Jack chewing gum. Have the students consider that they have been put in charge of developing a new ad campaign for Black Jack chewing gum. This black, licorice-flavored gum is not for everybody. Have them make suggestions for a campaign using a reactance and individuality theme in their ad.*

## 3. Word-of-Mouth Communication

a. Much information about the world is actually communicated by individuals on an informal basis. This is called **word-of-mouth communication (WOM)**.

   1) Word-of-mouth communication is viewed as being reliable and trustworthy by most people.

   2) WOM is often backed up by social pressure that conform to recommendations.

*Discussion Opportunity—Ask: When was the last time you gave someone advice about buying a product? Describe the situation, the information, and the outcome.*

*Discussion Opportunity—Ask: When was the last time you received WOM advice to purchase a product? Was there social conformity pressure? If so, describe the pressure and what eventually happened.*

Negative WOM

b. Word of mouth is not only rapid, it can be a double-edged sword for marketers.

   1) **Negative WOM** is weighted more heavily than positive WOM.

   2) Rumors are the chief form. Rumors can easily be spread online.

   3) Though most people would rather tell positive than negative information, rumors tend to reveal the underlying fears of society.

   4) Rumors often result in boycotts of products, companies, or services. These boycotts can be successful or unsuccessful depending on their popularity, duration, and strength.

*****Use Figure 11.2 Here *****

*Discussion Opportunity—Ask: When was the last time you distributed negative information about something? Listened to negative information? What was the reason and result of this process?*

*Discussion Opportunity—Ask: Have you ever been involved in a boycott? What was the result? If so, what would you do differently this time?*

c. Various strategies have been used by marketers to try to influence WOM among consumers. One of these is to create an environment for a **virtual community of**

**consumption** to grow and thrive.
1) Forms of these communities include:
   a) *Multi-User Dungeons (MUD)*—environments where fantasy game players meet.
   b) *Rooms, rings,* and *lists*—chat rooms, organizations of related home pages, and groups of people on a single mailing list who share information.
   c) *Boards*—online communities organized around interest-specific electronic bulletin boards.
   d) *Blogs*—**Weblogs** are online personal journals containing random thoughts of thousands of individuals. The universe of active Weblogs is known as the **Blogosphere.**
2) The intensity of identification with a virtual community depends on two factors:
   a) The more central the activity to a person's self-concept, the more likely he or she will be to pursue an active membership in a community.
   b) The intensity of the social relationships the person forms with other members of the virtual community helps to determine his or her extent of involvement.
3) Types of members include:
   a) **Tourists.**
   b) **Minglers.**
   c) **Devotees.**
   d) **Insiders.**

---

*****Use Figure 11.3 Here*****

---

d. **Guerrilla marketing** consists of promotional strategies that use unconventional locations and intensive word-of-mouth campaigns to push products.
e. **Viral Marketing** is the strategy of getting customers to sell a product on behalf of the company that creates it. This strategy is well suited to the Web.

---

*****Use Consumer Behavior Challenges #8 and #15 Here*****

---

*Discussion Opportunity—Ask: What word-of-mouth sources do you check (if any) when you (a) buy a car, (b) go to a movie, (c) buy perfume or cologne, and (d) buy a CD or tape? How important (if at all) is WOM to these situations? How could the marketer use this information to construct better strategy?*

---

*Discussion Opportunity—Give an illustration of a guerrilla marketing effort you have seen. Critique it.*

---

*Discussion Opportunity—Discuss when viral marketing is most likely to take place. From a company perspective, what would be the advantages and disadvantages to this technique?*

---

**4. Opinion Leadership**
   a. Although consumers get information from personal sources, they do not tend to

to ask just *anyone* for advice about purchases.

The Nature of Opinion Leadership

b. Everyone knows people who are knowledgeable about products and whose advice
   is taken seriously by others. These people are called **opinion leaders**. Reasons
   for opinion leaders being taken seriously as information providers include:
   1) They are technically competent.
   2) They have prescreened, evaluated, and synthesized (in an unbiased way)
      product information.
   3) They are socially active and interconnected in their community.
   4) They are similar to the consumer in value and beliefs, a characteristic described by the
      term **homophily**.
   5) They are often among the first to buy new products. They often absorb risk
      because they purchase products first.

---

*Discussion Opportunity—Ask students to consider the following: Whom do you know that you
would classify as an opinion leader? In what areas is he/she a leader? Are you an opinion
leader? Under what circumstances and to whom do you perform this role?*

---

c. When marketers and social scientists initially developed the concept of the
   opinion leader, it was assumed that certain influential people in a community
   would exert an overall impact on group members' attitudes.
   1) There is a question today as to whether there is such a thing as a *generalized
      opinion leader*.
   2) Opinion leaders tend to be concentrated in their field of interest or expertise.
   3) Some opinion leaders overlap into other fields, but not into all fields.
      a. *Monomorphic*—experts in a limited field.
      b. *Polymorphic*—experts in several fields (but usually concentrated).
d. It is thought that opinion leadership is more complex than a set static process.
   1) Opinion leaders may or may not be purchasers of products they recommend.
   2) Characteristics of opinion leaders include:
      a) *Innovators*.
      b) Early and *innovative communicators*.
      c) Socially active.
      d) Appearance conscious and narcissistic.
      e) Like music and contemporary music culture.
      f) Magazine readers.
      g) Own more clothing and have a broader range of styles.
      h) *Opinion seekers*.

---

**\*\*\*\*\*Use Figure 11.4 Here; Use Consumer Behavior Challenges #9 and #10 Here \*\*\*\*\***

---

*Discussion Opportunity—Ask students to consider an opinion leader that they know and see how
many of the characteristics of opinion leaders match to that individual. What other
characteristics apply?*

---

e. A consumer category called the **market maven** has been proposed to describe people who are actively involved in transmitting marketplace information of all types. Market mavens are closer to the conception of a general opinion leader.

*Discussion Opportunity—Ask students to describe a market maven that they know. What information do you get from them? How do you think they got the information they transmit?*

f. A **surrogate consumer** is a person who is hired to provide input into purchase decisions. The surrogate consumer is usually compensated for this involvement.
  1) Examples would include interior decorators, stockbrokers, professional shoppers, or college consultants.

Identifying Opinion Leaders

g. Marketers are interested in identifying opinion leaders. Many ads are intended to reach these consumers.
  1) Unfortunately, opinion leaders are hard to find.
  2) Methods of identifying opinion leaders include:
    a) The *self-designing method*—ask individual consumers whether they consider themselves to opinion leaders.
      1. A *bona fide* opinion leader.
      2. A *key informant*.
    b) *Sociometry*—tracing communication patterns among group members. This is called **sociometric method**.
      1. Examines *referral behavior*.
      2. Examines *networks*.
      3. Examines *cliques*.

*****Use Figure 11.5 Here;*
*Use Consumer Behavior Challenges #11, #12, #13, and #14 Here *****

*Discussion Opportunity—Ask: Is there any category of consumer products in which you think you might be considered an opinion leader?*

# End-of-Chapter Support Material

# SUMMARY OF SPECIAL FEATURE BOXES

## 1.    Marketing Opportunity

This box highlights the trend of people paying big money to go to *fantasy camps*. These are camps where people are given the opportunity to play sports with their idols.

## 2. Marketing Pitfalls I

This box addresses the social problem of binge drinking among college students. This activity represents the dark side of deindividualization. This feature supports the section "Consumers Do It in Groups."

## 3. The Tangled Web I

This box takes a look at the ever-growing trend of online hoaxes. Various examples are given of how this dynamic employs WOM communication at very powerful levels. This feature supports the section "Word-of-Mouth Communication."

## 4. The Tangled Web II

This box takes a look at the concept of **determined detractors.** These are persistent critics of a company or product that mount their own public relations offensive. Most commonly, these detractors create a Web site that publicly criticizes the company.

## 5. Net Profit I

This box highlights the efforts of major corporations to increase brand awareness through online gaming. Toyota and Sony have launched very successful games that have reached cult-status. This feature supports the section "Virtual Communities."

## 6. The Tangled Web III

This box takes a look at the ever-growing trend of online hoaxes. Various examples are given of how this dynamic employs WOM communication at very powerful levels. This feature supports the section "Word-of-Mouth Communication."

## 7. The Tangled Web IV

A fake ad was made and circulated on the Internet. The ad showed a terrorist detonating a bomb inside of a Volkswagen Polo. The car, unharmed and containing the blast, was shown with the tag line, "Small but Tough." The makers of the ad ended up apologizing to Volkswagen.

## 8. Net Profit I

WOM communication regarding consumption has increased exponentially with the Internet. **E-fluentials** are individuals who influence the purchase and consumption behaviors of others through communication on the Internet. Information is presented on different research agencies that have identified groups of e-fluentials. This feature supports the section "Opinion Leadership."

# REVIEW QUESTIONS

1. Name two dimensions that influence whether reference groups have an impact on an individual's purchase decisions. *Two dimensions that influence the degree to which reference groups are important are whether the purchase is to be consumed publicly or privately and whether it is a luxury or a necessity.*

2. List three types of social power, giving an example of each. *There are six types of social power:*
   1. *Referent power: If a person admires the qualities of a person or a group, he will try to imitate those qualities by copying the referent's behaviors (e.g., choice of clothing, cars, leisure activities) as a guide to forming consumption preferences.*
   2. *Information power: A person can have power simply because she knows something others would like to know.*
   3. *Legitimate power: Sometimes we grant power by virtue of social agreements, such as the authority we give to policemen, soldiers, and yes, sometimes even professors.*
   4. *Expert power: To attract the casual Internet user, U.S. Robotics signed up British physicist Stephen Hawking to endorse its modems.*
   5. *Reward power: When a person or group has the means to provide positive reinforcement (see Chapter 3), that entity will have reward power over a consumer to the extent that he values this reinforcement.*
   6. *Coercive power: A threat is often effective in the short term, but it does not tend to produce permanent attitudinal or behavioral change.*

3. Which tend to be more powerful influences on behavior, large formal groups or small informal groups? Why? *It is small, informal groups that exert a more powerful influence on individual consumers. Small, informal groups tend to be more a part of our day-to-day lives and more important to us, because they are high in normative influence. Larger, formal groups tend to be more product- or activity-specific and thus are high in comparative influence.*

4. What is a brand community, and why is it of interest to marketers? *A brand community is a group of consumers who share a set of social relationships based upon usage or interest in a product.*

5. Tell the difference between a membership and an aspirational reference group, giving an example of each. *Some reference groups consist of people the consumer actually knows (a membership reference group); others are composed of people he doesn't know but admires. These aspirational reference groups comprise idealized figures such as successful business people, athletes, or performers.*

6. Name one factor that makes it more likely a person will become part of a consumer's membership reference group. *Propinquity, mere exposure, and group cohesiveness.*

7.    Define deindividuation and give an example of this effect. *With more people in a group, it becomes less likely any one member will be singled out for attention. People in larger groups or those in situations in which they are likely to be unidentified tend to focus less attention on themselves, so normal restraints on behavior are reduced. You may have observed that people sometimes behave more wildly at costume parties or on Halloween than they do normally. We call this phenomenon deindividuation, a process in which individual identities become submerged within a group.*

8.    What is the risky shift, and how does it relate to going shopping with friends? *The risky shift refers to the observation that in many cases, group members show a greater willingness to consider riskier alternatives following group discussion than they would if members made their own decisions with no discussion.*

9.    What is the difference between normative and informational social influence? *Home shopping parties, as the Tupperware party epitomizes, capitalize on group pressures to boost sales. A company representative makes a sales presentation to a group of people who have gathered in the home of a friend or acquaintance. This format is effective because of informational social influence: Participants model the behavior of others who can provide them with information about how to use certain products, especially because the home party is likely to be attended by a relatively homogeneous group (e.g., neighborhood homemakers) that serves as a valuable benchmark. Normative social influence also operates because actions are publicly observed. Pressures to conform may be particularly intense and may escalate as more and more group members begin to "cave in" (this process is sometimes termed the "bandwagon effect").*

10.   Define conformity and give three examples of it. Name three reasons why people conform. *Conformity refers to a change in beliefs or actions as a reaction to real or imagined group pressure. Among the reasons why people conform are cultural pressures, fear of deviance, commitment, group unanimity/size/expertise, and susceptibility to interpersonal influence.*

11.   How does the principle of least interest relate to your success in a romantic relationship? *According to the principle of least interest, the person or group that is **least** committed to staying in a relationship has the most power, because that party won't be as affected by rejection from the other person.*

12.   What is social comparison? *What type of person do we usually choose to compare ourselves to? Sometimes we look to the behavior of others to provide a yardstick about reality. Social comparison theory asserts that this process occurs as a way to increase the stability of one's self-evaluation, especially when physical evidence is unavailable. In general people tend to choose a co-oriented peer, or a person of equivalent standing, when performing social comparison.*

13.   What is the difference between independence and anticonformity? *It is important to distinguish between independence and anticonformity; in anticonformity, defiance of the group is the actual object of behavior.*

14. Define reactance and give an example. *Reactance is the negative emotional state that results when we are deprived of our freedom to choose. This feeling can drive us to value forbidden things even if they wouldn't be that interesting to us otherwise. Many efforts to censor books, television shows, or music lyrics that some people find objectionable ironically result in an increased desire for these products.*

15. What is word or mouth, and why is it more powerful than advertising? *Word of mouth (WOM) is product information transmitted by individuals to individuals. Because we get the word from people we know, WOM tends to be more reliable and trustworthy than recommendations we get through more formal marketing channels.*

16. Which is more powerful, positive or negative word or mouth? *Consumers weigh negative word or mouth more heavily than they do positive comments.*

17. Describe some ways in which marketers are using the Internet to encourage positive WOM. *A virtual community of consumption is a collection of people whose online interactions are based upon shared enthusiasm for and knowledge of a specific consumption activity. Like the brand communities we discussed earlier, these groups form around a shared love for a product, whether it's Barbie dolls or Blackberry PDAs. However, members remain anonymous because they only interact with each other in cyberspace.*

18. What is viral marketing? Guerrilla marketing? Give an example of each. *Guerrilla marketing is the use of promotional strategies that use unconventional locations and intensive word-of-mouth campaigns to push products. The train line CSX launched a safety-awareness campaign that included hiring people to throw eggs at the company's outdoor billboards. The billboards carry the stark black-on-white words "Cars hitting trains." Eggs smashing against the billboard are intended to demonstrate the impact of a car hitting a train. The idea is to get people to be careful when crossing railroad tracks.*

    *Viral marketing refers to the strategy of getting visitors to a Web site to forward information on the site to their friends in order to make still more consumers aware of the product—usually by creating online content that is entertaining or just plain weird. Viral marketing for an oil? Pretty slick. WD-40 quadrupled visitors to its fan club Web site by offering 1,000 AM/FM radios in the shape of oil cans to individuals who signed up 10 other members.*

19. What is an opinion leader? Give three reasons why they are powerful influences on consumers' opinions. What are some characteristics of opinion leaders? *An opinion leader is a person who is frequently able to influence others' attitudes or behaviors.*

    - *They are technically competent and thus convincing because they possess expert power.*
    - *They have prescreened, evaluated, and synthesized product information in an unbiased way, so they possess knowledge power. Unlike commercial endorsers, opinion leaders do not actually represent the interests of one company. Thus, they are*

*more credible because they have no "axe to grind."*

- *They tend to be socially active and highly interconnected in their communities. They are likely to hold offices in community groups and clubs and to be active outside of the home. As a result, opinion leaders often have legitimate power by virtue of their social standing.*

- *They tend to be similar to the consumer in terms of their values and beliefs, so they possess referent power. Note that although opinion leaders are set apart by their interest or expertise in a product category, they are more convincing to the extent that they are homophilous rather than heterophilous. Homophily refers to the degree to which a pair of individuals is similar in terms of education, social status, and beliefs. Effective opinion leaders tend to be slightly higher in terms of status and educational attainment than those they influence, but not so high as to be in a different social class.*

- *Opinion leaders are often among the first to buy new products, so they absorb much of the risk. This experience reduces uncertainty for others who are not as courageous. Furthermore, whereas company-sponsored communications tend to focus exclusively on the positive aspects of a product, the hands-on experience of opinion leaders makes them more likely to impart both positive and negative information about product performance.*

20. Is there such a thing as a generalized opinion leader? Why or why not? *When marketers and social scientists initially developed the concept of the opinion leader, they assumed that certain influential people in a community would exert an overall impact on group members' attitudes. Later work, however, began to question the assumption that there is such a thing as a generalized opinion leader, somebody whose recommendations we seek for all types of purchases. Very few people are capable of being expert in a number of fields. Sociologists distinguish between those who are monomorphic, or expert in a limited field, and those who are polymorphic, or expert in several fields.*

21. What is the relationship between an opinion leader and an opinion seeker? *The fact that we transmit advice about products does not mean other people **take** that advice. For someone to be considered a bona fide opinion leader, opinion seekers must actually heed his advice. An alternative is to select certain group members (key informants) who we ask to identify opinion leaders. The success of this approach hinges on locating those who have accurate knowledge of the group and on minimizing their response biases (e.g., the tendency to inflate one's own influence on the choices of others).*

22. What is the difference between a market maven and a surrogate consumer? *In addition to everyday consumers who are instrumental in influencing others' purchase decisions, a class of marketing intermediary called the surrogate consumer is an active player in many categories. A consumer category called the market maven describes people who are actively involved in transmitting marketplace information of all types.*

23. How can marketers use opinion leaders to help them promote their products or services? *If the opinion leaders will adopt the products, then there is an automatic effect of those opinion leaders promoting the same products to the public through word or mouth.*

24. What are sociometric techniques? Under what conditions does it make sense to use them? *Sociometric methods trace communication patterns among members of a group. These techniques allow researchers to systematically map out the interactions that take place among group members.*

# CONSUMER BEHAVIOR CHALLENGE

## Discussion Questions

1. The chapter describes four types of virtual community members. Which are you? *Student responses should fall into one of the following categories:*

   - *Tourists lack strong social ties to the group, and maintain only a passing interest in the activity.*
   - *Minglers maintain strong social ties, but are not very interested in the central consumption activity.*
   - *Devotees express strong interest in the activity, but have few social attachments to the group.*
   - *Insiders exhibit both strong social ties and strong interest in the activity.*

2. The average Internet user in the United States spends three hours a day online, with much of that time devoted to work and more than half of it to communications. Researchers report that , the Internet has displaced television watching and a range of other activities. Internet users watch television for one hour and 42 minutes a day, compared with the national average of two hours. One study reported increasing physical isolation among Internet users; it created a controversy and drew angry complaints from some users who insisted that time they spent online did not detract from their social relationships. However, the researchers said they had now gathered further evidence showing that Internet use has lowered the amount of time people spend socializing with friends and even sleeping. According to the study, an hour of time spent using the Internet reduces face-to-face contact with friends, co-workers and family by 23.5 minutes, lowers the amount of time spent watching television by 10 minutes and shortens sleep by 8.5 minutes. What's your perspective on this issue—does increasing use of the Internet have positive or negative implications for interpersonal relationships in our society?

   *The answer to this question all depends on how "interpersonal" is defined. If the definition sticks to that of traditional face-to-face communication, then it will be hard to argue that increased time online does not detract from interpersonal communication. Time is a limited resource. And as is shown above in the question itself, there is research to back this up. However, if students lean toward defining interpersonal communication as any type of communication between people, then there will be strong argument for the fact that increased time online enhances such. Given that many people spend time emailing, IMing, chatting, interacting in forums, blogs, etc., then in many cases, the time spent online is providing opporunities to interact with others that would otherwise not be there.*

3.   The Word of Mouth Marketing Association recently announced a new set of rules and guidelines for word-of-mouth advertising. The trade group maintains that marketers must make sure that people talking up products or services disclose whom they are working for. They also must use real consumers, not actors, who discuss what they really believe about a product. The rules were prompted by several controversial incidents such as a campaign the U.S. arm of Sony Ericsson Mobile Communications created for a camera phone. The company hired 60 actors to hang out at tourist attractions and ask unsuspecting passersby to take their pictures with the Sony Ericsson devices. The actors were told to identify themselves only when asked directly. What do you think about "stealth" campaigns like this? Should marketers be required to disclose their true intentions when they try to initiate positive word or mouth?

*Traditionally, most students will respond that there is nothing wrong or even ethically questionable about such stealth practices as those described above. Even when they are lead toward thinking that such practices are unethical, most will say that this is just another promotional practice, and that companies are within their rights to do such; that no harm is done. With in inclusion of the information that the AMA has actually censured such practices, the responses by students might be different.*

4.   Do you agree that deindividuation encourages binge drinking on campus? What can or should a college do to discourage this behavior?

*If indeed students are more likely to binge drink when they go through the process of deindividuation, then campuses should embark on some type of awareness campaign that would make student consciously aware of the effects of binge drinking on a personal, individual level.*

5.   The adoption of a certain brand of shoe or apparel by athletes can be a powerful influence on students and other fans. Should high school and college coaches be paid to determine what brand of athletic equipment their players will wear?

*Student opinion will vary. You might want to raise the issue of consumer needs versus wants, the role of advertising in determining needs and wants, and the general ethics of marketing products to children and youth.*

6.   The strategy of viral marketing gets customers to sell a product to other customers on behalf of the company. That often means convincing your friends to climb on the bandwagon, and sometimes you get a cut if they wind up buying something. Some might argue that means you're selling out your friends (or at least selling to your friends) in exchange for a piece of the action. Others might say you're just sharing the wealth with those you care about. Have you been involved in viral marketing by passing along names of your friends or sending them to a Web site such as hotmail.com? If so, what happened? How do you feel about this practice?

*Although this strategy has a fancy new name, it has been in practice for decades (anyone recall the vacuum cleaner salesperson or knife salesperson asking for names of friends and family?). Students may not be old enough to have been exposed to some of these more traditional applications of the concept. But many will have been confronted by other more modern applications. With the advent of the Internet, there are various ways that viral marketing is being applied. Be sure to try to bring out those cases where individuals were given some type of incentive to provide names of friends or for getting them to sign up for something.*

7.  Are home shopping parties that put pressure on friends and neighbors to buy merchandise ethical?

    *Such tactics are similar to those employed by official sales people. The AMA's code of ethics stipulates that marketers should reject high pressure manipulations and misleading sales tactics. If it is unethical for sales people to do it, then it is unethical for friends and neighbors to do it as well. In fact, it may be more so because often, people go to these parties under the impression that it is to be more of a social event. Once they get there and find that their friend is really a sales rep and is putting on the pressure, then essentially, they have been deceived.*

8.  What is the best way for a company to deal with determined detractors?

    *The response to determined detractors should follow similar tactics pursued by companies for any kind of negative publicity. The response should depend on the situation. If no real damage is apparent (or if the negative publicity is actually having a net-positive effect), then nothing should be done. Measures should be taken to defray or stop the negative publicity only if the potential damage is seen as being greater than any risk taken to countering such. Because most detractors work through Web sites, if anything needs to be done, efforts might be made to arrive at a settlement with those running such Web sites.*

## Application Questions

9.  The power of unspoken social norms often becomes obvious only when these norms are violated. To witness this result first hand, try one of the following: stand facing the back wall in an elevator; serve dessert before the main course; offer to pay cash for dinner at a friend's home; wear pajamas to class; or tell someone not to have a nice day.

    *Students can be creative here. Encourage them to conduct these investigations and use a debriefing session in class to discuss some of their finding, reactions, and attitudes.*

10. Identify a set of avoidance groups for your peers. Can you identify any consumption decisions that are made with these groups in mind?

    *Students will think of many diverse examples. Two potential avoidance groups may be a local gang and students who fail this course. If you are against gangs, you will try to avoid using any products that are associated with gangs; if you don't want to fail this course, you will avoid many of the behaviors that are associated with failing students. (Possible Field Project Idea)*

11. Identify fashion opinion leaders on your campus. Do they fit the profile discussed in the chapter?

    *The class might agree to focus on a particular group of fashion opinion leaders. After deciding on the group, they could go through an opinion leader profile and determine whether or not the group members actually are fashion experts. (Possible Field Project Idea)*

12. Conduct a sociometric analysis within your dormitory or neighborhood. For a product category such as music or cars, ask each individual to identify other individuals with whom they share information. Systematically trace all of these avenues of communication and identify opinion leaders by locating individuals who are repeatedly named as providing helpful information.

    *Students should include a discussion of sociometry in their responses and recognize that sociometric methods allow researchers to systematically point out the interactions that take place among group members. Conducting a study of this type should highlight for students how difficult and expensive such activities can be. (Possible Field Project Idea)*

13. See if you can demonstrate the risky shift. Get a group of friends together and ask each to privately rate the likelihood on a scale from one to seven that they would try a controversial new product (e.g. a credit card that works with a chip implanted in a person's wrist). Then ask the group to discuss the product and then rate the idea again. If the average rating changes from the first, you've just observed a risky shift

    *Any type of controversial practice can be substituted into this exercise.*

14. Trace a referral pattern for a service provider such as a hairstylist by tracking how clients came to choose him or her. See if you can identify opinion leaders who are responsible for referring several clients to the businessperson. How might the service provider take advantage of this process to grow his or her business?

    *Students are likely to come up with all types of incentive programs that will motivate customers to refer friends. Once something like that is in place, the likely hood of a referral network emerging is greater.*

# CASE STUDY TEACHING NOTES

## Chapter 11 Case Study: Jimmy Buffett Fans Unite

## Summary of Case

This case spotlights the phenomenon of Jimmy Buffett fans and their fanatical behavior. Known as parrot-heads, such fans are willing to travel long distances to see the artist perform and will tailgate for hours before an event. But that's just the tip of the iceberg. Buffett fans take Buffett-themed vacations, have Buffett-themed rooms, homes, RVs, boats, weddings, etc. The artist is more popular now than he ever was during his "hay-day" in the late 70s. The single biggest factor driving this popularity is the degree to which fans have united as a literal and virtual brand community.

## Suggestions for Presentation

The most direct application for this is to virtual communities and brand communities. However, this material can easily be used to illustrate concepts of reference groups, word-of-mouth communication, conformity, social comparison, and even opinion leadership, guerilla marketing, and viral marketing. In short, this case has application to almost every concept in the chapter.

## Suggested Answers for Discussion Questions

1.  How can Jimmy Buffett fans be considered as members of a reference group? A brand community? A consumer tribe?

    *Reference group—these are defined as groups that have a significant impact on an individual's evaluations and behavior. Because much of the Buffett fan behavior is carried out in groups, it can be argued that many of these fans would not develop attitudes and behaviors to the extent that they do without the influence of the group.*

    *Brand community—Jimmy Buffett is a brand. Because his fans have formed relationships almost entirely around the consumption of Jimmy Buffett's product offerings, these groups definitely qualify as a brand community.*

    *Consumer tribe— these go beyond brand communities, identified as groups that share a lifestyle because of shared allegiance to a product. Although Buffett fans come from many walks of live, the more involved fans definitely adhere to a particular lifestyle.*

2.  Consider your responses to question 1. What kind of opportunities does the existence of the Buffet-community present to marketers? Develop a list of specific marketing and promotional tactics.

*Brands such as Jeep and Harley-Davidson have recognized the brand communities that have formed around their brands. While initially, such groups formed without any help from the companies, at some point, the companies began to sponsor activities such as brandfests and online forums. By doing this, the companies create and facilitate forums for more extensive networking. They also then have some control over the flow of information in such groups. Also, by engaging in dialogue with such consumers, the consumers take greater ownership in the company.*

# Additional Support Material

# STUDENT PROJECTS

## Individual Projects

1. Have students write down the various groups to which they are members. In which of these groups are conformity pressures the greatest? Why do they think this is the case?

2. Ask each student to think about individual family members, friends, and acquaintances. On paper, have them identify the people who act as opinion leaders, product innovators, and market mavens. Describe what each person does. Have a few students share their observations with the class.

3. Students should collect ads that attempt to influence or promote word-of-mouth communications. Have them comment on the credibility of the ads. Is the promoter used in the ad an effective influencer?

4. Have each student try to purchase all of their necessities for one week using nothing but online purchasing. Describe the process, its successes, and its failures. What was learned? Have them evaluate the future of online purchasing.

5. Ask a student to find one magazine advertisement for a consumer product that uses "the expert" as a reference group appeal and another that features a top corporate executive. Have the student discuss the impact of each appeal on consumers.

6. Have a student think about some goods and services that he/she has purchased recently. To what extent did word-of-mouth communication influence purchases?

7. Encourage a student to think of something he/she recently purchased in which advice was actively sought from others. For what reasons was advice sought? Why was the particular person selected to provide this advice?

8.      Ask a student to interview someone who has attended a home party where products were sold (e.g., Amway, cookware, Tupperware, Sarah Coventry jewelry, Mary Kay, lingerie). What types of group power (such as referent, expert, reward, coercive) can be identified?

9.      Comment on when misinformation can be a valid strategy. What ethical issues might be involved in transmitting misinformation?

10.     Have each student identify one case of guerrilla marketing. It should be the objective to find a case where the maximum amount of promotional benefit was achieved with the least amount of resources. They should attempt to find information that will allow for estimates of these figures. Upon sharing cases with the class, keep track to determine the most effective campaign, based on this ROI-type measure.


## Group Projects

1.      Each student group will have the task of forming or joining a brand community. Have them decide upon a brand that none of them really use. Then, have them research the brand extensively and begin their own pro-product dialogue among themselves. If they wish to establish an online chat room or message board, that would be all the better. After having done this for a set period of time, have group members discuss how they feel about the brand. Whether they have purchased or not, do they feel more "loyal"? Have they developed positive attitudes? Do they find themselves engaging in WOM outside the group?

2.      Have the students video tape interviews with three individuals regarding a product they recently purchased for the first time. Why did they purchase it? What was the role of "word of mouth" and personal influence (whether real or simulated)? The group should edit the tape to present a summary illustration of their findings.

3.      Describe how opinion leaders can be formed and found on the Internet. Describe the advantages and disadvantages of using opinion leaders on the Web. How would this form of opinion leadership be different from any other form of opinion leadership (if at all)?

4.      Have student groups do an analysis of a rumor that was started about a product or company (e.g., a human finger found in a can of Pepsi, the "Satanic" connection in Procter & Gamble's moon-and-stars logo; Pop Rocks candy will make your stomach explode; McDonald's puts worms in its hamburgers; there are spider eggs in Bubble Yum, etc.). What effect did these rumors have on sales? How did the company handle the situation?

5.      Ask a group of students to make a list of aspirational groups that are of interest to many college students. Then ask them to bring to class a few print ads that are targeted to college students with these particular aspirations.

6. Have groups of students consider and identify what special language, clothes, props, and sets are characteristic of various groups present in society. You may wish to require students to make actual observations in a public place such as a shopping mall or airport.

7. Social norms tend to become obvious only when they are broken. Send a few brave students out to violate one or more social norms. (Tell them to shake hands with their left hand, eat their desserts first, belch during class, wear shoes that don't match, walk with their books on their head, make the narrow end of their ties extend a little below the wide end, sing in the elevator, or ask them to violate a social norm of their own. *Note*: Remind them to make sure they are only violating norms—not a law—unless you or your university is willing to provide bail money!) Have one group member violate a norm and the others observe from afar. What do these students observe when the social norm is violated?

8. Have a group prepare a sociometric analysis of online grocery shoppers. How is this group different and similar to in-store shoppers?

# eLAB

## Individual Assignments

1. Go to **www.jeep.com/jeep_life/index.html.** Comment on the role that reference groups and opinion leadership plays in selecting a Jeep vehicle. What were your feelings (describe them carefully) after visiting the Web site? How were these feelings formed? Did you learn anything new?

2. Go to **www.nra.org**. The National Rifle Association is one of the most vocal of all special interest groups. How does the organization use reference groups to spread its message? What type of power did you observe on the Web site? Explain how the NRA uses opinion leadership to influence public opinion.

3. Go to **http://forums.prospero.com/foxidol/start**. This is the main forum page on the official Web site for American Idol. Register as a user (if necessary). Then, read through the message threads posted by members. Document and summarize communications that are brand-building, and those that are brand-damaging.

4. Go to **www.gogorillamedia.com/gogorillamedia.html**. This is an agency that specializes in guerilla marketing tactics. Summarize five such tactics, identifying benefits and examples of using each.

5. Go to **www.hairclub.com**. One of the great problems facing men in our day and age is the prospect of going bald. Some find it beautiful and some find it socially unacceptable. How does the Hair Club for Men play to male fears? How do they use reference groups

and opinion leaders to persuade prospective customers to give their products a try? What do you think of the organization's promotional campaigns and ethics? Explain.

## Group Assignments

1.     Go to **www.ihatestarbucks.com** and **www.homedepotsucks.com**. Have your group evaluate the tactics of these anti-sites. How did they get started? Do you think they are effective? Are they distributing information or misinformation? Were you motivated to see the organizations' other Web sites? What was of interest to you on these sites? How should the affected companies respond?

2.     Go to **www.saladmaster.com**. Examine the concept behind using Saladmaster waterless cookware. Become familiar with their products. Your group's task is to assume the role of a market maven. Design an approach that would encourage your sphere of influence to try the Saladmaster approach. Explain your thoughts and procedures. What would it take to cause a shift in tastes and preferences in your influence sphere? Explain.

# 12

# *ORGANIZATIONAL AND HOUSEHOLD DECISION MAKING*

## CHAPTER OBJECTIVES

When students finish this chapter they should understand why:

- Marketers often need to understand consumer's behavior rather than consumer behavior, since in many cases more than one person is involved in deciding what to buy.

- Companies as well as individuals make purchase decisions. The decision making process differs when people are choosing what to buy on behalf of a company versus a personal purchase.

- Many important demographic dimensions of a population relate to family and household structure.

- Our traditional notions about families often are outdated.

- Members of a family unit play different roles and have different amounts of influence when making purchase decisions.

- Children learn over time what and how to consume.

## CHAPTER SUMMARY

Many purchasing decisions are made by more than one person. *Collective decision making* occurs whenever two or more people are involved in evaluating, selecting, or using a product or service. Marketers must be aware of this phenomenon if correct strategy is to be constructed.

*Organizational buyers* are people who make purchase decisions on behalf of a company or other group. Although they are influenced by many of the same factors that affect how they make decisions in their personal lives, organizational buying decisions tend to be more rationally based. They are also likely to involve more financial risk, and as they become more complex, it is probable that a greater number of people will be involved in making them.

The amount of cognitive effort that goes into organizational decisions is influenced by internal factors, such as individuals' psychological characteristics and by external factors, such as the company's willingness to tolerate risk. One of the most important determinants is the type of purchase being considered: The extent of problem solving required depends on whether the product or service to be procured is simply to be reordered (a *straight rebuy*), is ordered with minor modifications (*modified rebuy*), or has never been purchased before or is complex and risky (*new task*).

In organizations and in families, several different roles must be played during the decision-making process. These roles include initiator, gatekeeper (who determines the flow of information within the group), influencers, buyers, and users.

The modern family is a complicated unit. The family can be *extended* (several generations) or *nuclear* (the mother, father, and children). A *household* is an occupied housing unit. The number and type of U.S. households is changing in many ways, including increasing movement by consumers to southern and western states, delays in getting married and having children, and in the composition of family households that are increasingly headed by single parents. New perspectives on the *family life cycle*, which focuses on how people's needs change as they move through different stages in their lives, are forcing marketers to more seriously consider such consumer segments as divorcees and childless couples when they develop targeting strategies.

Families must be understood in terms of their decision-making dynamics. Product involvement, responsibility, and power must all be considered in the family decision-making process. Spouses in particular have different priorities and exert varying amounts of influence in terms of effort and power. Children are also increasingly influential during a widening range of purchase decisions.

Children undergo a process of *socialization*, whereby they learn how to be consumers. Parents and friends instill some of this knowledge, but a lot of it comes from exposure to mass media and advertising. Because children are in some cases so easily persuaded, the ethical aspects of marketing to them are hotly debated among consumers, academics, and marketing practitioners.

# CHAPTER OUTLINE

## 1. Introduction
   a. Purchase decisions often involve two or more people who may not have the same level of investment in the outcome, the same tastes and preferences, or the same consumption priorities.
   b. **Collective decision making** is where more than one person is involved in the purchasing process for products or services that may be used by multiple consumers.

## 2. Organizational Decision Making
   a. **Organizational buyers** are people who purchase goods and services on behalf of

companies for use in the process of manufacturing, distribution, or resale.

   1) These individuals buy from **business-to-business marketers**, who specialize in meeting the needs of such organizations as corporations, government agencies, hospitals, and retailers.

   2) Roughly, $2 trillion worth of products and services changes hands among organizations—more than is purchased by end consumers.

b. The organizational buyer's perception of the purchase situation is influenced by a number of factors:

   1) *Expectations* of the supplier.

   2) The *organizational climate* of his/her own company.

   3) The buyer's *assessment* of his/her own performance.

### Organizational Decision Making Versus Consumer Decision Making

c. Many factors have been identified to distinguish organizational and industrial purchase decisions from consumer decisions (where a product is purchased for personal use). Some of these differences are:

   1) Purchase decisions frequently involve many people.

   2) Products are often bought according to precise, technical specifications.

   3) Impulse buying is rare.

   4) Decisions are often of high risk.

   5) Dollar volume of purchases is often substantial.

   6) There is more emphasis on personal selling than on other types of promotion (especially in B2B relationships).

---

*Discussion Opportunity—Ask: How are decisions made by organizations and decisions made by individuals the same? How are they different? How are strategies the same? Different?*

---

### How Do Organizational Buyers Operate?

d. Like end consumers, organizational buyers are influenced by both internal and external stimuli. Cultural factors should also be considered by the organizational buyer.

---

*Discussion Opportunity—Give an example of a cultural factor that may influence organizational buying. Try to be specific.*

---

   1) The nature of the item to be purchased is one of the greatest influences on the organizational buyer's decision-making process.

     a) Typically, more complex organizational decisions tend to be made by a group of people (members of a **buying center**) who play different roles in the decision.

   2) Organizational buying decisions can be divided into three types (that range from the most to the least complex). The classification scheme is called the ***buyclass theory of purchasing***. Dimensions are:

     a) The level of information that must be gathered prior to making a decision.

     b) The seriousness of all possible alternatives.

     c) The buyer's familiarity with the purchase.

---

*****Use Table 12.1 Here *****

---

*Discussion Opportunity—Ask: If you were in charge of your university, who are the people you would want involved in making a decision about a purchase of a new management information system software package that would run most of the functions of the university? Who would be most important in this group? Would you rather have joint decision making or make the decision yourself? Explain.*

e. Types of decisions include:
   1) A **straight rebuy** is like a habitual decision. This is an automatic decision (as in an inventory reorder).
   2) A **modified rebuy** situation involves limited decision making. This is a repurchase with some minor modifications.
   3) A **new task** involves extensive problem solving. This decision has not been made before and usually involves a team decision.

---

*****Use Table 12.1 (Used Previously) Here *****

---

*Discussion Opportunity—Ask students to give examples of products that would be classified as straight rebuys, modified rebuys, and new task products for a business organization. Use any example organization to illustrate your descriptions.*

f. A number of specific roles are played when a collective decision must be made, either by members of a household or by individuals in an organizational buying center. The roles include:
   1) *Initiator*—the person with the idea or need.
   2) *Gatekeeper*—the person who controls the flow of information to the group.
   3) *Influencer*—the person who tries to sway the outcome of the decision.
   4) *Buyer*—the one who makes the decision.
   5) *User*—the person who winds up using the product.

---

*Discussion Opportunity—Create a series of examples that illustrate each of the decision roles that can be played out in a consumption process. How can a marketer appeal to each of these roles? With which role does most of the power lie? Explain.*

---

B2B E-Commerce
g. The Web is radically changing the way organizational buyers learn about and select products for their companies.
   1) **Business-to-business (B2B) e-commerce** refers to Internet interactions between two or more businesses or organizations.
   2) In the simplest form of B2B e-commerce, the Internet provides an online catalog of products and services needed by businesses.

*Discussion Opportunity—Research B2B. Find one example of a B2B transaction. Detail the transaction. Why has the Internet become such an important tool in B2B? How does the Internet save a B2B relationship money?*

## 3. The Family

a. The typical American family is not necessarily one with two parents living with their children at home. Other forms of family units have emerged in the last decade.

*Discussion Opportunity—Ask: Describe your family structure. Would you say that it is traditional? What impact does your family structure have on purchasing? How could an advertiser design an ad to appeal to your family? What would be in that ad?*

Defining the Modern Family

b. Types of families include:
1) The **extended family** was once the most common family unit. It consisted of three generations living together and often included not only the grandparents, but aunts, uncles, and cousins.
2) The **nuclear family**—a mother, father, and one or more children—became the modern family. This, however, is no longer the realistic view of the family.
3) Today, a **family household** is defined as being at least two people who are related by blood or marriage.

*Discussion Opportunity—Ask students to write down their definition of "family." Compare the answers with the rest of the class. How does this definition match with alternative lifestyles?*

*Discussion Opportunity—Ask: Why is it important for marketers to know how to define a family? What difference does it make to an e-marketer?*

*****Use Consumer Behavior Challenge #11 Here *****

c. The overall demographics of the modern family:
1) More than 1 million couples divorce in a typical year.
2) Approximately 20 million children younger than 18 live with just one parent. In 84 percent of these cases, the mother is the primary parent.
3) The average family size is projected to be 2.5 people by 2010.
4) The **fertility rate** is determined by the number of births per year, per 1,000 women of child-bearing age. This rate has climbed in recent years.
d. There is a broad shift toward non-family and childless households.
1) Ironically, the traditional extended family is very much a reality. Many adults care for their parents as well as their children.
2) Middle-aged adults have been termed "***the sandwich generation***" because they must attend to those older and younger than them in age.
3) Many adults are surprised when children that have left home return to the nest. These **boomerang kids** seem to keep coming back (primarily because of economic conditions, failed marriages, or live-in failures).

*Discussion Opportunity—Ask: How can marketers appeal to "the sandwich generation"?*

**\*\*\*\*\*Use Consumer Behavior Challenges #1 and #2 Here \*\*\*\*\***

*Discussion Opportunity—Ask: Is the phenomenon of "boomerang kids" new? What brought the kids back to the nest in previous years? If you are a "boomeranger" describe your situation and why you returned. Why is this phenomenon important to marketers?*

*Discussion Opportunity—Watch TV (or read a TV Guide) for a week. List and describe the various ways families are depicted. Are these realistic depictions or not? Explain.*

**\*\*\*\*\*Use Consumer Behavior Challenges #8 and #17 Here \*\*\*\*\***

   e. A family's needs and expenditures are affected by factors such as the number of people (children and adults) in the family, their ages, and whether one, two, or more adults are employed outside the home.
     1) Two important factors that determine how a couple spends time and money are whether they have children and whether the woman works.
   f. Recognizing that family needs and expenditures change over time, the concept of the **family life cycle (FLC)** has been widely used by marketers. The FLC combines trends in income and family composition with the changes in demands placed on this income.
     1) Four variables are important to the FLC. They are:
       a) Age.
       b) Marital status.
       c) The presence or absence of children in the home.
       d) Ages of children (if any).

**\*\*\*\*\*Use Figure 12.1 Here; Use Consumer Behavior Challenge #16 Here \*\*\*\*\***

*Discussion Opportunity—After reviewing the material found in Figure 12.1, identify where your family falls in the FLC. Have students do the same. Of what value would this be to marketers? What stage is coming next for you? For your family?*

     2) It is obvious by studying the FLC that marked differences occur in the consumption patterns among the various categories.

**\*\*\*\*\*Use Consumer Behavior Challenges #6, #9, #12, and #13 Here \*\*\*\*\***

*Discussion Opportunity—After reviewing the material found in Figure 12.1, ask students if there are any other categories that they think might be added to the family life cycle that aren't included? As an experiment to help you understand the concept, try to find advertisements that fit the different categories.*

## 4. The Intimate Corporation: Family Decision Making

Household Decisions

a. There are two basic types of decisions made by families:

 1) In a **consensual purchase decision**, the group agrees on the desired purchase, differing only in terms of how it will be achieved.

 2) In an **accommodative purchase decision**, group members have different preferences or priorities and cannot agree on a purchase that will satisfy the minimum expectations of all involved.

*Discussion Opportunity—Provide an illustration from your family where consensual purchase decisions and accommodative purchase decisions occurred. Which form is the most normal? Explain.*

b. Conflict occurs when there is not complete correspondence in family members' needs and preferences. Although money is the most common source of conflict between marriage partners, television choices come in a close second. Factors include:

 1) *Interpersonal needs.*

 2) *Product involvement and utility.*

 3) *Responsibility.*

 4) *Power.*

*Discussion Opportunity—Ask: Are there other areas that you believe cause conflict in family units? What do these variables depend on (such as who is involved)? How can marketers use knowledge of conflict in their marketing strategy? Can you think of any products that are designed to enhance conflict? Reduce it? Explain.*

Sex Roles and Decision-Making Responsibilities

c. Who "wears the pants" in the family?

 1) When one family member chooses the product, this is called an **autonomic decision**.

*Discussion Opportunity—Ask: In the traditional family, who generally makes the decision to buy a car? A computer? A couch? A vacation?*

 2) Roper research services sees signs of a shift in marital decision making toward more compromise and turn taking. **Syncratic decisions** are made jointly.

*Discussion Opportunity—Ask: Would you suspect more syncratic decisions in today's society by a family unit? If not, explain why.*

d. Researchers have paid special attention to which spouse plays the role of what has been called the **family financial officer (FFO)**, who keeps track of the family's bills and decides how any surplus funds will be spent. This role changes and shifts over time.

*****Use Figure 12.2 Here *****

*Discussion Opportunity—Ask: What might a marketing firm do to discover who the FFO is in a family? What strategies might be used to reach this person? Why is the role of the FFO changing over time?*

e. Four factors appear to determine the degree to which decisions will be made jointly or by one or the other spouse. They are:
   1) *Sex-role stereotypes*—men buy masculine products and females buy feminine products.
   2) *Spousal resources*—the spouse who contributes the most has the greater influence.
   3) *Experience*—time constraints and expertise establishes one decision maker.
   4) *Socio-economic status*—middle-class families make more joint decisions.

*****Use Table 12.2 Here *****

*Discussion Opportunity—Demonstrate how marketers can use information about spousal decision making in their strategy. You might wish to bring ads to demonstrate your points.*

f. Despite recent changes in decision-making responsibilities, women still are primarily responsible for the continuation of the family's **kin-network system**. They perform the rituals intended to maintain ties among family members.
g. The **synoptic ideal** calls for the husband and wife to take a common view and act as joint decision makers. One common technique for simplifying the decision-making process is the use of *heuristics*. Some frequently observed decision-making patterns include:
   1) A couple "reaches" rather than makes a decision (i.e., focus on salient, objective dimensions rather than more subtle, hard-to-define cues).
   2) A couple agrees on a system of task specialization.
   3) Concessions based on intensity of each spouse's preferences.

*Discussion Opportunity—Ask students to consider what heuristics couples use to make decisions? Give an example of a typical situation.*

## 5. Children as Decision Makers: Consumers-in-Training
   a. Children are recognized as consumers that deserve attention. Children make up three distinct markets:
   1) Primary market—kids spend a lot on their own wants and needs.
   2) Influence market—**parental yielding** occurs when a parental decision maker is influenced by a child's request and "surrenders." This is somewhat dependent on family dynamics.
   3) Future market—the Web surfers or those who are taking increased responsibility at home because of working parents.

---

**\*\*\*\*\*Use Table 12.3 Here; Use Consumer Behavior Challenges #5 and #7 Here \*\*\*\*\***

---

*Discussion Opportunity—Prompt the class to discuss how children are taking more responsibility at home. How can knowledge of this be of value to marketers? Explain.*

---

Consumer Socialization
b. **Consumer socialization** is defined as the process by which young people acquire skills, knowledge, and attitudes relevant to their functioning in the marketplace.
  1) Parents' influence in the socialization process is both direct and indirect.
  2) The process begins with infants when they accompany their parents on shopping trips.

---

*Discussion Opportunity—Have the class brainstorm all the ways we socialize the consumer (especially children) in our society.*

---

c. Three dimensions combine to produce different segments of parental styles.
  1) Authoritarian parents—restrictive with negative view about ads.
  2) Neglecting parents—detached from kids and exercise little control.
  3) Indulgent parents—less restrictive and want children to learn about buying.
d. One of the strongest influences on children is television. It teaches children about culture's values and myths. Television is often called the "electronic babysitter."

---

**\*\*\*\*\* Use Figure 12.3 Here; Use Consumer Behavior Challenge #14 Here \*\*\*\*\***

---

*Discussion Opportunity—Ask: How do you plan to teach your children how to become well-informed buyers?*

---

*Discussion Opportunity—Ask your students how many of them grew up with television. What is right and wrong with it? How can marketers use it constructively? Because you are now older, what do you wish you had done differently with respect to television when you were younger? How do you plan to handle television watching with your children? Compare this to the way your parents handled television with you.*

---

Sex-Role Socialization
e. Children pick up on the concept of gender identity at an earlier age than was previously believed (sometimes at age 1 or 2).
  1) One function of child's play is to rehearse for adulthood.
  2) Often "traditional" sex roles are stressed in children's products; the same item might be positioned and designed differently for boys and girls.

---

*Discussion Opportunity—Think of products that are sex-role specific. Comment on how they are designed and positioned. Does this cause you any problems? Should girls be encouraged to play with trucks? Boys with dolls? Explain.*

---

Cognitive Development

f. The ability of children to make mature, "adult" consumer decisions obviously increases with age (not that grown-ups always make mature decisions).

   1) Kids can be segmented by age in terms of their **stage of cognitive development**, or ability to comprehend concepts of increasing complexity.

   2) According to Swiss psychologist Jean Piaget, children pass through different cognitive structure stages.

      a) *Limited*—younger than 6, children do not employ storage and retrieval strategies.

      b) *Cued*—between 6 and 12, children employ these strategies when prompted.

      c) *Strategic*—12 and older, people spontaneously employ these strategies.

Marketing Research and Children

g. Despite the buying power, relatively little real data on children's preferences or influences on spending patterns is available.

   1) Children are difficult subjects for research.

   2) A particularly helpful type of research with children is product testing.

   3) Because children differ in their abilities to process product-related information, many serious ethical issues are raised when advertisers try to appeal directly to children.

   4) Kids' cognitive defenses are not yet sufficiently developed to filter out commercial appeals. Today, Web sites are of concern to regulators.

   5) Children's levels of understanding are especially hard to assess, because preschoolers aren't very good at verbal responses.

---

*****Use Figure 12.4 Here;*
*Use Consumer Behavior Challenges #4, #5 (Used Previously), and #15 Here *****

---

*Discussion Opportunity—Ask: Should commercials be able to advertise to young children? Should there be any restrictions? Who should determine this? Should children's Web sites be controlled? What about free speech?*

# End-of-Chapter Support Material

# SUMMARY OF SPECIAL FEATURE BOXES

1.     **Marketing Opportunity I**

This box takes a look at a new trend in organizational decision making, the use of **prediction markets.** This concept is based on the idea that groups of people are betting at making decisions than individuals.

## 2.    Net Profit I

This box takes a look at the impact that the Internet has had on B2B transactions. Specifically, it addresses purchasing, sales, and product design. This feature supports the section "B2B E-Commerce."

## 3.    Marketing Opportunity II

This box highlights how Coca-Cola is recognizing different family structures in the United Kingdom. Discussed is the introduction of a new product that appeals to smaller household units. This feature supports the section "Nontraditional Family Structures."

## 4.    Net Profit II

First came Tamagotchi pets (electronic pets on a hand-held gadget), now the world of Neopets is thriving. A website devoted to the creation and care of virtual pets has drummed up so much traffic, that MTV bought it for $160 million.

## 5.    The Tangled Web

PC rooms are becoming more and more popular. The modern-day version of the game arcade, these are businesses that house PCs hooked up to high-speed Internet connections. One of the controversial trends that has accompanied the number of PC rooms is the number of children playing violent games online.

## 6.    Marketing Pitfalls I

Following an outcry by animal rights activists that its products encouraged children to be cruel to animals, in 2005 Kraft Foods halted production of candy shaped like roadkill. The fruity-flavored Trolli Road Kill Gummi Candy was shaped like flattened snakes, chickens, and squirrels, complete with tire treads.

## 7.    Marketing Pitfalls II

This box addresses the efforts of marketers of traditionally adult-oriented products to target children. The impact of such efforts on the socialization of children is discussed. This feature supports the section "Cognitive Development."

## 8.    Marketing Opportunity III

This box illustrates how television programs and networks are incorporating principles of consumer psychology. Specifically, the application of multiple-intelligence theory is examined. This feature supports the section "Marketing Research and Children."

# REVIEW QUESTIONS

1. What are some factors that influence how an organizational buyer evaluates a purchase decision? *A number of factors influence the organizational buyer's perception of the purchase situation. These include his expectations of the supplier (e.g., product quality, the competence and behavior of the firm's employees, and prior experiences in dealing with that supplier), the organizational climate of his own company (e.g., perceptions regarding how the company rewards performance and what it values), and the buyer's assessment of his own performance (e.g., whether he believes in taking risks).*

2. What is a prediction market? *A prediction market is one of the hottest new trends in organizational decision making techniques. This approach is based on the idea that groups of people with knowledge about an industry are jointly better predictors of the future than are any individuals.*

3. Summarize the buyclass model of purchasing. How do decisions differ within each class? *The buyclass theory of purchasing uses three decision making dimensions to describe the purchasing strategies of an organizational buyer:*

   *1. The level of information that must be gathered prior to making a decision.*
   *2. The seriousness with which all possible alternatives must be considered.*
   *3. The degree to which the buyer is familiar with the purchase.*

   *In practice, these three dimensions relate to how much cognitive effort the buyer will expend in making a purchase decision. Three types of "buyclasses," or strategies based on these dimensions encompass most organizational decision situations.*

4. What are some of the ways organizational decisions differ from individual consumer decisions? How are they similar? *Many factors distinguish organizational and industrial purchase decisions from individual consumer decisions. Some of these differences are as follows:*

   - *Purchase decisions companies make frequently involve many people, including those who do the actual buying, those who directly or indirectly influence this decision, and the employees who will actually use the product or service.*
   - *Organizational and industrial products are often bought according to precise, technical specifications that require a lot of knowledge about the product category.*
   - *Impulse buying is rare (industrial buyers do not suddenly get an "urge to splurge" on lead pipe or silicon chips). Because buyers are professionals, their decisions are based on past experience and a careful weighing of alternatives.*
   - *Decisions often are risky, especially in the sense that a buyer's career may be riding on his demonstration of good judgment.*
   - *The dollar volume of purchases is often substantial, dwarfing most individual consumers' grocery bills or mortgage payments. One hundred to 250 organizational customers often account for more than half of a supplier's sales volume that gives the buyers a lot of influence over the supplier.*

- *Business-to-business marketing often involves more of an emphasis on personal selling than on advertising or other forms of promotion. Dealing with organizational buyers typically requires more face-to-face contact than is necessary in the case of end consumers.*

*We must consider these important features when we try to understand the purchasing decisions organizations make. Still, there are actually more similarities between organizational buyers and ordinary consumers than many people realize. True, organizational purchase decisions do tend to have a higher economic or functional component compared to individual consumer choices, but emotional aspects enter the scene as well. For example, although organizational buyers may appear to the outsider to be models of rationality, their decisions are sometimes guided by brand loyalty, by long-term relationships they have established with particular suppliers or salespeople, or even by aesthetic concerns.*

5.  List at least three roles people play in the organizational decision making process.
    - *Initiator: The person who brings up the idea or identifies a need.*
    - *Gatekeeper: The person who conducts the information search and controls the flow of information available to the group. In organizational contexts the gatekeeper identifies possible vendors and products for the rest of the group to consider.*
    - *Influencer: The person who tries to sway the outcome of the decision. Some people may be more motivated than others to get involved, and participants also differ in terms of the amount of power they have to convince others of their choice. In organizations, engineers are often influencers for product information, whereas purchasing agents play a similar role when the group evaluates the vendors that supply these items.*
    - *Buyer: The person who actually makes the purchase. The buyer may or may not actually use the product. This person may pay for the item, actually procure it, or both.*
    - *User: The person who winds up using the product or service.*

6.  What is a nuclear family, and how is it different from an extended family? *The extended family was once the most common family unit. It consists of three generations living together and it often includes grandparents, aunts, uncles, and cousins. As evidenced by the Cleavers of Leave It to Beaver and other TV families of the 1950s, the nuclear family—a mother and a father and one or more children (perhaps with a sheepdog thrown in for good measure)—became the model family unit over time.*

7.  How is a nation's fertility rate calculated? What fertility rate is required to ensure that population size does not decline? *The fertility rate is determined by the number of births per year, per 1,000 women of childbearing age.*

8.  What are boomerang kids? *Adult children who move back in with mom and dad after having moved out on their own.*

9.    What is the FLC, and why is it important to marketers? *Recognizing that family needs and expenditures change over time, marketers apply the family life cycle (FLC) concept to segment households. The FLC combines trends in income and family composition with the changes in demands placed upon this income. As we age, our preferences and needs for products and activities tend to change.*

10.   List some variables we must consider when trying to understand different stages in the FLC. *Researchers have proposed a number of models to describe family life-cycle stages, but their usefulness has been limited because in many cases they have failed to take into account such important social trends as the changing role of women, the acceleration of alternative lifestyles, childless and delayed-child marriages, and single-parent households. We need to focus upon four variables to adequately describe these changes: 1) age; 2) marital status; 3) the presence or absence of children in the home; and 4) the ages of children, if present.*

11.   What is the difference between a consensual and an accommodative purchase decision? What are some factors that help to determine how much conflict the family will experience when making a decision? *In a consensual purchase decision, members agree on the desired purchase, differing only in terms of how it will be achieved. In an accommodative purchase decision, group members have different preferences or priorities and cannot agree on a purchase that will satisfy the minimum expectations of all involved.*

12.   Summarize the difference between an autonomic and a syncretic decision. *When one family member chooses a product, this is called an autonomic decision. In traditional households, for example, men often have sole responsibility for selecting a car, whereas decorating choices fall to women. Syncretic decisions, such as choosing a vacation destination, are made jointly.*

13.   What are some differences between "traditional" and "modern" couples in terms of how they allocate household responsibilities? *Among newlyweds, this role tends to be played jointly, and then over time one spouse or the other takes over these responsibilities. In traditional families (and especially those with low educational levels), women are primarily responsible for family financial management—the man makes it, and the woman spends it. Each spouse "specializes" in certain activities. The pattern is different among families in which spouses adhere to more modern sex-role norms. These couples believe that there should be shared participation in family maintenance activities. In these cases, husbands assume more responsibility for laundering, housecleaning, grocery shopping, and so on, in addition to such traditionally "male" tasks as home maintenance and garbage removal.*

14.   What factors help to determine if decisions will be made jointly or by one spouse or the other?
      - *Sex-role stereotypes: Couples who believe in traditional sex-role stereotypes tend to make individual decisions for sex-typed products (i.e., those considered to be "masculine" or "feminine" as we discussed in Chapter 5).*

- *Spousal resources: The spouse who contributes more resources to the family has the greater influence.*
- *Experience: Couples who have gained experience as a decision-making unit make individual decisions more frequently.*
- *Socioeconomic status: Middle-class families make more joint decisions than do either higher- or lower-class families.*

15. What is a kin-network system? *Despite recent changes in decision-making responsibilities, women are still primarily responsible for the continuation of the family's kin-network system: they perform the rituals intended to maintain ties among family members, both immediate and extended. This function includes activities such as coordinating visits among relatives, calling and writing family members, sending greeting cards, and arranging social engagements.*

16. Describe a heuristic a couple might use when making a decision, and provide an example of it. *Some decision-making patterns frequently observed when a couple makes decisions in buying a new house illustrate the use of heuristics:*

    - *The couple's areas of common preference are based on salient, objective dimensions rather than subtler, hard-to-define cues. For example, a couple may easily agree on the number of bedrooms they need in the new home, but will have more difficulty achieving a common view of how the home should look.*
    - *The couple agrees on a system of task specialization in which each is responsible for certain duties or decision areas and does not interfere on the other's "turf." For many couples, these assignments are likely to be influenced by their perceived sex roles. For example, the wife may scout out houses that meet their requirements in advance, and the husband determines whether the couple can obtain a mortgage.*
    - *Concessions are based on the intensity of each spouse's preferences. One spouse will yield to the influence of the other in many cases simply because his or her level of preference for a certain attribute is not particularly intense, whereas in other situations he or she would be willing to exert effort to obtain a favorable decision. In cases where intense preferences for different attributes exist, rather than attempt to influence each other, spouses will "trade off" a less-intense preference for a more strongly felt one. For example, a husband who is somewhat indifferent about kitchen design may give in to his wife, but expect that in turn he will be allowed to design his own garage workshop.*

17. What are three reasons why children are an important segment to marketers? *Because children are important parts of three distinct market segments; a primary market, an influence market, and a future market.*

18. What is consumer socialization? Who are some important players in this process? How do toys contribute? *Consumer socialization is the process "by which young people acquire skills, knowledge, and attitudes relevant to their functioning in the marketplace. Especially for young children, though, the two primary socialization sources are the family and the media.*

19.    Discuss stages of cognitive development and how these relate to the comprehension of marketing messages.
- *Limited: Below the age of 6, children do not employ storage and retrieval strategies.*
- *Cued: Children between the ages of 6 and 12 employ these strategies, but only when prompted.*
- *Strategic: Children 12 and older spontaneously employ storage and retrieval strategies.*

20.    Why is it difficult to conduct marketing research with children? *They tend to be undependable reporters of their own behavior, they have poor recall, and they often do not understand abstract questions. This problem is compounded in Europe, where some countries restrict marketers' ability to interview children. Still, market research can pay off, and many companies, as well as a number of specialized firms, have been successful in researching some aspects of this segment.*

# CONSUMER BEHAVIOR CHALLENGE

## Discussion Questions

1.    Is the family unit dead?

*Responses to this question will vary around the definition of family. Those that take the approach of defining family according to the U.S. census bureau (at least two people related by blood or marriage) might say that the family unit is dying or becoming less of the norm. However, even according to this definition, there is evidence that this traditional view of family is making a comeback. Others will define family non-traditionally as any household occupied by someone. As people consider the "family" to be something other than the traditional family, then people will perceive no threat to the family.*

2.    Discuss the pros and cons of the voluntarily childless movement. Are followers of this philosophy selfish?

*The pros and cons will emerge in this discussion. If we define selfish as those that put their own well-being above that of others, there is still more than one response to this. Those choosing not to have children are selfish because they are putting their own wants and needs above that of others (the potential future child, the grandparents, society, etc.). However, there are also those that will say that those that are choosing not to have kids are not committed to raising children, and therefore would not be good parents. Thus, they are protecting the well-being of the unwanted child.*

3.    Are marketers robbing kids of their childhood?

*Young children have become the target of grown-up designers. As a spokesperson for Donna Karan observed, "These seven-year-olds are going on 30. A lot of them have their own sense of style." Maybe so, but perhaps one of the consequences is that they are forced to adopt adult values earlier than they should. One author of a book about kids complains, "We are seeing the deliberate teening of childhood. Parents are giving their kids a lot more choices on what to wear at ever younger ages. The advertisers know this, and they are exploiting the kids' longing to seem sophisticated and grown-up. One of the great things about childhood in the U.S. used to be that kids were protected by the market and allowed to grow their own ideas. Now there is no time to be a kid separate from those pressures. You may have always had kids who are little princesses, but now there are eight-year-old boys that are extremely uptight if they don't get the right Abercrombie & Fitch sweatshirt." Maybe that explains why preteens now account for $200 million of the $3 billion mass-market sales of makeup; a survey of 8- to 12.year-old girls found that two-thirds regularly used cosmetics. So much for the Age of Innocence.*

4.    The Defense Department had to shut down a controversial research program following a public outcry. Its intent was to create a prediction market to try to forecast terrorist activities. Was the decision to terminate the program warranted? Why or why not?

*Two camps will emerge from this question: 1) national security is much more important than protecting the privacy and civil rights of a minority, and 2) if privacy and civil rights of a few are violated, that is a step toward the rights of everyone being violated. Regardless, nothing justifies violating civil rights.*

5.    Do you think market research should be performed with children? Give the reasons for your answer.

*Discussion of this issue will most likely revolve around the student's opinion and experiences with children as consumers. As the chapter made clear, children are a large part of the economy both as consumers and as influences on consumption. Therefore a firm would be careless not to gather and use information on the tastes and habits of children. Many students may object to this line of reasoning, however, by stating that children are a particularly susceptible group and so marketing efforts aimed at them should not exist or should be controlled. An important distinction that needs to be made in this matter is the difference between marketing research and marketing communication—although the former is done to assist the latter, the two concepts are separate. Discussion could best be focused on the suitability of market research using children and then proceed to the propriety of marketing to children as a market.*

6.    What do you think of the practice of companies and survey firms collecting public data (e.g., from marriage licenses, birth records, or even death announcements) to compile targeted mailing lists? State your opinion from both a consumer's and a marketer's perspective.

*Ethics questions, such as this and others in this section, are best presented and framed as an opportunity for students to analyze both sides of the issue. Many students will use their own ethical framework, and also their own experiences, to answer these types of questions. There should not be any attempt to state "the" correct answer, but listing and discussing the advantages and disadvantages of the practice is the goal. This can also be accomplished by considering the different perspectives of consumers and marketers. Students likely will view such practices as reasonable from the marketer's perspective but as potential violations of privacy from the individual consumer's perspective. Ask students: How private do they really want to be?*

7.      Marketers have been criticized for donating products and services to educational institutions in exchange for free promotion. Is this a fair exchange, in your opinion, or should corporations be prohibited from attempting to influence youngsters in school?

*Here again discussion of this question will reflect the student's attitude regarding marketing toward younger consumers but with a twist—donating products to schools has obvious positive consequences for those students. Some students will view this as a positive exchange, as the school and the students receive educational materials they otherwise might not. On the other hand, some will see this as a cynical attempt to ensnare a captive audience. There would appear to be some truth in both positions— the donation of products can contribute to a child's education and it can also promote current and future purchases of those goods.*

*For example, Apple Computer Corporation made special efforts to provide computer equipment to schools, and they developed special promotions to sell equipment to teachers and school-age children. It would be hard to deny that such efforts contributed to Apple's success, but the benefits to both parties are also obvious. Discussion of this topic should be aimed at setting some guidelines that both groups could benefit from, while safeguarding the practice from exploiting children's less-developed discriminatory abilities.*

8.      For each of the following five product categories—groceries, automobiles, vacations, furniture, and appliances—describe the way in which you believe a married couple's choices would be affected if they had children.

*The question provides an excellent opportunity to exhibit the direct and indirect influence that children have on purchases. If possible, students who have children should be encouraged to contribute to the discussion by relating their experiences. Students who do not have children should be encouraged to relate their own attempts to influence their parents' purchase decisions in these and other areas. In addition, discussing the types of product categories that children are more likely to influence would be interesting. Of the product categories listed, the presence of children in the household will produce the need for more of each product (e.g., more room in the car, more groceries to consume, more variety of foods, more capacity in the appliances, etc.). What will also be influenced is the type of product bought under each category and this aspect should form the basis for discussion.*

- *Groceries—baby food, snack foods, health foods.*
- *Automobiles—two-door, four-door, van, station wagon.*
- *Vacations—if the destination has recreation facilities (e.g., pool, tennis courts, etc.) or is appropriate for children of different ages.*
- *Furniture—baby furniture, special beds for younger children (e.g., bunk beds, canopy beds), new furniture for older children.*
- *Appliances—microwave ovens and other convenience appliances for busy children and families.*

9. In identifying and targeting newly divorced couples, do you think marketers are exploiting these couples' situations? Are there instances where you think marketers may actually be helpful to them? Support your answer with examples.

   *This question is much like questions 1–3 in that it asks the student to consider a specific target market and whether marketing to it is appropriate. In addition to examining each of these groups separately, a more general question may be: What are the limits, or the parameters, of appropriate targeting? At a broader level, the whole notion of target marketing may be reexamined as to whether it is appropriate to attempt to persuade a group to purchase a product. A discussion of this scope could quickly get so broad and unfocused that students become confused, so care must be taken to keep the discussion centered on one topic at a time. Those students who accept target marketing should be asked to describe situations where target marketing should be curbed and why. Those students who feel that target marketing is wrong should be encouraged to consider that it is a necessary tool for firms to market their products. They should be encouraged to describe their set of guidelines for properly using target marketing. The situation described here, that of divorced couples, could be used to exemplify the use and abuse of target marketing. Students should also be able to describe the advantages and disadvantages of target marketing to this particular group and how marketers should handle other sensitive situations.*

10. Industrial purchase decisions are totally rational. Aesthetic or subjective factors don't— and shouldn't—play a role in this process. Do you agree?

    *The buyer's perception in organizational marketing is affected by expectations, organization climate, and "organizational memory." In most cases: 1) purchase decisions frequently involves many people; 2) products are often bought according to precise specifications; 3) impulse buying is rare; 4) decisions are high-risk; 5) dollar volume of purchases is often substantial; and 6) there is more emphasis on personal selling than other types of promotion.*

    *Aesthetic or subjective factors do enter the picture, however, because the people who make purchase decisions are human and consequently make decisions based on both thinking (cognitive) and feeling (affect). Business knows that pleasant surroundings do affect the amount and quality of work. Many times an organizational buyer is buying more than a product or service, he/she is really buying the salesperson and the company—relationship marketing.*

11.     We can think of college students living away from home can be thought of as having a substitute "family." Whether you live with your parents, with a spouse, or with other students, how are decisions made in your college residence "family"? Do some people take on the roles of mother, father, or children? Give a specific example of a decision that had to be made and the roles that were played.

*This question should prompt responses from all students. Certainly, all students will have different residence circumstances. Likely, the definition of family will be expanded by students more toward the U.S. census definition of household—any occupied housing unit—and family roles will easily be considered flexible for this scenario.*

## Application Questions

12.     Arrange to interview two married couples, one younger and one older. Prepare a response form listing five product categories—groceries, furniture, appliances, vacations, and automobiles—and ask each spouse to indicate, without consulting the other, whether purchases in each category are made by joint or unilateral decisions and to indicate whether the unilateral decisions are made by the husband or the wife. Compare each couple's responses for agreement between husbands and wives relative to who makes the decisions and compare both couples' overall responses for differences relative to the number of joint versus unilateral decisions. Report your findings and conclusions.

*Students' discussion of this question should consider the text material on spousal influence. Married students should be encouraged to provide their insight into these issues.*

13.     Collect ads for three different product categories in which the family is targeted. Find another set of ads for different brands of the same items in which the family is not featured. Prepare a report on the effectiveness of the approaches. Which specific categories would most likely benefit from a family emphasis?

*You might encourage students to look at magazines that target different social groups to see if there is a difference.*

14.     Observe the interactions between parents and children in the cereal section of a local grocery store. Prepare a report on the number of children who expressed preferences, how they expressed their preferences, and how parents responded, including the number who purchased the child's choice.

*If a student stands near a family in the cereal aisle, he/she could note who actually picks up the cereal and puts it in the basket or otherwise chooses the brand. You might also ask that student who made the cereal choices when he/she was young.*

15.     Watch three hours of children's programming on commercial television stations and evaluate the marketing techniques used in the commercials in terms of the ethical issues raised in the final section of this chapter. Report your findings and conclusions.

*Advise students to have a pad of paper and make good notes throughout the viewing of the programming. Find out how the student reaches his conclusions concerning the ethical issues.*

16.     Select a product category and using the life-cycle stages given in the chapter, list the variables that will affect a purchase decision for the product by consumers in each stage of the cycle.

*You might encourage students to develop their own list of categories in the family life cycle, define them, and then determine the types of products people in each of those categories would probably need.*

17.     Consider three important changes in modern family structure. For each, find an example of a marketer who has attempted to be conscious of this change as reflected in product communications, retailing innovations, or other aspects of the marketing mix. If possible, also try to find examples of marketers who have failed to keep up with these developments.

*If students have trouble getting information for this project, you might ask them to contact various retailers (e.g., department stores, specialty stores, discount houses, etc.) and ask the manager if he/she is aware of any product modification, promotions, or displays that have been made.*

# CASE STUDY TEACHING NOTES

**Chapter 12 Case Study: Children—The Final Frontier . . . for Cell Phones.**

### Summary of Case

Targeting children for the marketing of goods and services is controversial. Different countries have different regulations. Some outlaw it entirely. The cell phone industry in the United States. has identified children as the next frontier to combat flattening sales growth. Although there are many who are speaking out against the tactics of companies designing and selling child-friendly phones, the industry is defending itself by saying that they are not targeting kids. They are targeting parents. The key to this campaign is positioning the purchase of a cell phone for one's child as a purchase that is not over indulgent, but as one that is caring for the safety of the child.

**Suggestions for Presentation**

This case will be best presented in conjunction with the sections of the family life cycle, cognitive development, and marketing research and children. Most students will admit that there is a line in marketing to children. However, deciding where that line should be is the question. This case shows an example of an industry that is not targeting kids, but is targeting their parents. So what is the difference? That will be one of the main points of discussion for this case.

**Suggested Answers for Discussion Questions**

1.      When it comes to cell phones for kids, who is the customer? Discuss the dynamics of this.

*The same question can be asked for many products that will ultimately be used by kids. Educational videotapes, toys, cold cereal, clothing, etc. It is the child that will most directly use the products. However, the parents also get benefits from such products. Students should be prompted to identify such benefits. What are the benefits received in this case on cell phones by the child and by the parent?*

*Another issue at hand is that children generally do not have their own funds. At least, not enough to buy something like a cell phone and cell service. Thus, the parent has to be the one to buy the product. But how much influence do kids have on what parents purchase? This will be another key point in answering this question.*

2.      How do current trends in the family life cycle affect the marketing of cell phones to children?

*There is an increasing number of single parent households, whether it is due to divorce, death, or people having children without marrying. There is also an increasing in the number of two-parent homes where both parents work. In both cases, it is becoming more likely that children spend more time outside the direct supervision of parents. There have been many products and services directed to such parents (including online Webcams monitoring child care). Parents feel some need to stay connected to their kids when they are not in their presence.*

# Additional Support Material

# STUDENT PROJECTS

## Individual Projects

1.  Conduct this as an in-class activity with each student doing their own work. Distribute a list of ten products/services and have each student indicate on the list whether the decision to purchase each product is probably made by the husband alone, the wife alone, or jointly by both parties. Does there seem to be a trend developing? If so, what evidence does the class have that they are probably correct?

2.  Have each student research the pager market. What is the current status of this market? How has it evolved since the early 1990s? Why?

3.  Have students compile a list of magazines that appeal to young women. Then, have them do the same for young men. How are appeals used in such magazines similar and/or different from each other? Have students bring in example ads to illustrate their conclusions.

4.  Have students go to the library and research advertisements in a women's magazine (i.e., *Good Housekeeping, Ladies' Home Journal, Family Circle,* and *Woman's Day*) over the past twenty years. How have advertisers adapted their copy and art work to account for the changing roles of women? Are there things that have not changed?

5.  Each student should consider the market for cell phones. In segmenting the market for cell phones and cell phone service, discuss the impact of family life cycle stage, sex, age, education, or important factors? What marketing and promotional strategies would you devise to reach the segment(s) you selected? Why?

6.  Have students conduct the following exercise: Bring in ads for two different product categories in which the family is targeted. Find another set of ads for two different brands of the same items in which the family is not targeted. Evaluate the ads as to their effectiveness. Why do you prefer one ad more than another?

7.  Ask a student to go to a toy store, a toy department, or a cereal aisle in the grocery store and watch several interactions between a parent and child. Have the student make an oral report on how the children "made their wishes known" and how parents reacted to their children's "needs and wants."

8.  Ask a student to visit a store (e.g., clothing store, shoe store, furniture store, appliance store, restaurant, etc.) and interview the store manager regarding how the family life cycle concept is employed in their inventory selection, pricing, and/or advertising and sales promotion.

9.    Have a student bring to class three advertisements that show the changing roles of men and women. Also bring in three ads that show the traditional roles of men and women. Which ads does the class like best? Which do they find more credible? Try to analyze their responses.

10.   Interview the purchasing manager of a small- to medium-sized organization about how the organization does purchasing. Does the organization have a buying center? If so, describe it. If not, who fulfills the roles as defined by the buying center?

11.   Have each student consider a purchase that they were recently a part of that involved multiple individuals (room mates, their family, a fraternity, etc.). Have them analyze this purchase by identifying specific people who played each of the roles in the buying center (initiator, gatekeeper, influencer, buyer, and user).

12.   Research "boomerang kids." How can marketers appeal to this group? Should appeals be made to this group? What are the special characteristics of this group?

13.   Have students find someone who could be classified as a member of the sandwich generation. Interview this person with the intent of determining how this role affects their purchase patterns and the use of their income. Why would identification of the sandwich generation be important to marketers?

## Group Projects

1.    Student groups should interview a corporate purchase agent at length about their purchasing practices. What are the factors that affect the purchase decision? Are there multiple individuals involved in the process? Who affects the purchase decision and in what way?

2.    Student groups should interview youth of three different age groups (early, mid, and late teens; mall intercept format may work best) as to the purchases that they typically make in a week. Find out about how much they usually spend and on what types of things they usually spend it. How do they get their spending money? About how much do they have to spending on average? Results should be reported, including the identification of developing patterns.

3.    Groups should identify three local restaurants that seem to target clientele in three different family life cycle stages (e.g., young singles; young married without children; married with young children; married with youngest child older than six; empty nesters with the breadwinner still in the work force; empty nesters out of the work force; sole survivors). Each restaurant should be visited by a team member. How does each establishment attract its target market? Sometimes it is fun to run about a 2-minute video of the clientele entering and leaving each different type of restaurant.

4. Ask a student or a group of students to describe different purchase situations in which they (or another family member) plays the role of initiator, influencer, information gatherer, decision maker, purchaser, or user.

5. You or one or more of your students should select a product category such as a car, a tie, jewelry, restaurant, shoes, or an apartment. Using the life-cycle stages given in the chapter, ask the class to explain the variables that will affect a purchase decision by consumers in each stage of the cycle.

6. Have your group discuss the differences between Generation X, Generation Y, and the Digital Generation. Next, forecast the characteristics of the generation that is currently five to ten years old. How will this generation be different from the three previous ones? What opportunities await the marketer with this group?

7. Have your group interview a group of senior citizens about what was "hot" and what was not when they were teens. How has the world changed for teens since these seniors were teens? Are there value similarities, music preferences, and relationships with peers that are worth commenting about? How can marketers use information about a senior's past to market to them today? Explain.

8. Have groups of students analyze television ads broadcast during programs targeted toward children. Have them identify the types of products, the companies and brands, the nature of the appeals, and execution techniques used in such ads. Results should be compiled in some type of summary that provides the frequency of different categories.

# eLAB

## Individual Assignments

1. Go to **www.kids.us**. What is the objective of this website? Explain how a company could use a website such as this in taking a proactive approach to responsibly marketing toward children. Outline a strategy that would include the use of this website.

2. **www.hotwheels.com/index_hwkids.aspx**. Examine all parts of this website. Discuss at least three different segments that are targeted by this brand and this website. How does this website facilitate customer interactions?

3. Go to **www.bradkent.com**. No, this isn't Clark Kent's brother—instead it's a great site for examining candy wrappers. That's right—candy wrappers! Pick a few of the displayed products and comment on how the design of the wrapper segments the market for the product. How do these wrappers aid the decision-making process (if they do)? Which one caught your attention significantly? Why? Explain.

4.	Go to **www.nabisco.com**. Spend some time becoming familiar with the many pages within this Web site. How can the concepts in the chapter relating to the children as decision makers be applied to the content of the Web site?

5.	Go to **www.givingupsmoking.co.uk**. Want to quit smoking (or never start)? This is the site for you. After visiting the Web site, comment on which portion of the decision role alternatives found in the chapter come into play here. How could this site affect decision making? Do you think this method would work to help someone quit smoking? Explain why or why not.

6.	Go to **www.barnesandnoble.com.** How can a Web site as large and as broad as this be discussed in terms of the family life cycle? Explain how each aspect of the FLC can or cannot be applied here.


## Group Assignments

1.	Go to **www.smugmug.com**. What is the service offered by this company? What family members might be the best prospects for this product? What generations? Explain and justify your answers.

2.	Go to **www.tigerbeatmag.com**, **www.teenmag.com**, **www.teenpeople.com**, **www.alloy.com**, and **www.studentcenter.org**. Visit these sites and you will enter the world of Teens. Have your group analyze the differences and similarities between the Web sites. Which are primarily for boys and which are primarily for girls? How can you tell? Which primary features are used to attract teens? Remembering that you were once a teen, what would have attracted you to these sites? Why do these sites no longer attract you (if they do not)? Is the non-attraction just a function of age or is some other variable important? Find three Web sites that are attractive to your age range. Explain this attractiveness.

# CHAPTER

# 13

# INCOME AND SOCIAL CLASS

## CHAPTER OBJECTIVES

When students finish this chapter they should understand why:

- Our decisions about whether to spend our money are influenced by both personal and social conditions.

- We can group consumers into social classes that say a lot about an individual's standing in society.

- Consumer behavior often is affected by a person's desire to make a statement about her social class, or the class to which she would like to belong.

## CHAPTER SUMMARY

The field of behavioral economics considers how consumers decide what to do with their money. In particular, discretionary expenditures are made only when people are able and willing to spend money on items above and beyond their basic needs. *Consumer confidence*—the state of mind consumers have about their own personal situation, as well as their feelings about their overall economic prospects—helps to determine whether they will purchase goods and services, take on debt, or save their money.

A consumer's *social class* refers to his or her standing in society. It is determined by a number of factors, including education, occupation, and income.

Virtually all groups make distinctions among members in terms of relative superiority, power, and access to valued resources. This *social stratification* creates a *status hierarchy*, where some goods are preferred over others and are used to categorize their owners' social class.

Although income is an important indicator of social class, the relationship is far from perfect because social class is also determined by such factors as place of residence, cultural interests, and worldview.

*Purchase decisions* are sometimes influenced by the desire to "buy up" to a higher social class or to engage in the process of conspicuous consumption, where one's status is flaunted by the deliberate and nonconstructive use of valuable resources. This spending pattern is a characteristic of the nouveau riches, whose relatively recent acquisition of income, rather than ancestry or breeding, is responsible for their increased social mobility.

Products often are used as *status symbols* to communicate real or desired social class. Parody display occurs when consumers seek status by deliberately avoiding fashionable products.

# CHAPTER OUTLINE

**1. Consumer Spending and Economic Behavior**
   a. Products are frequently bought and displayed as markers of social class; they are valued as **status symbols**.

Income Patterns
   b. Income shifts are linked to two key factors:
   1) A shift in women's roles in the workplace—women are getting more high-paying jobs.
      a) In almost two-thirds of all families earning more than $50,000 (approximately 18 million), it is the wife's paycheck that is propelling the couple up the income ladder.
   2) Increases in the attainment of an education—college graduates earn 50 percent more than high school graduates.
      a) A big portion of consumer spending power comes from college grads.

> *Discussion Opportunity—Research which jobs are most attractive to female college graduates. Where is the future heading with respect to female employment in the workforce? What psychological penalties might working mothers pay? What perks must be offered to working mothers to keep them in the labor force?*

To Spend or Not to Spend, That Is the Question
   c. Consumer demand for goods and services depends on ability to buy and willingness to buy.
   1) **Discretionary income** is the money available to a household over and above that required for a comfortable standard of living.
      a) American consumers spend about $400 billion in a year in discretionary ways.
      b) People aged 35 to 55, whose incomes are at a peak, account for about half of this amount.
   2) As the population ages and income levels rise, the typical U.S. household is changing the way it spends its money.
   3) The most noticeable change is that a much larger share of the budget is spent on shelter and transportation and less on food and apparel.

a) Households are spending more on entertainment, reading, and education than in the past.

> *Discussion Opportunity—Ask: Can you think of some item that you have the ability to buy but you don't intend to buy? Why won't you buy it? Can you think of some object you would be willing to buy but you just don't have the means to buy it? How are you planning to resolve this?*

d. Consumers tend to equate money with security and comfort. Many anxieties result.
   1) Acquiring and managing money is more a state of mind than of wallet.

> ***\*\*\*\*\*Use Table 13.1 Here; Use Consumer Behavior Challenge #1 Here \*\*\*\*\****

> *Discussion Opportunity—Ask: How do you feel about money? What does it represent to you? Would you classify yourself as a saver or a spender? Do you think other people would agree with this? On a scale of one to ten, where does money fall on your personal scale of priorities?*

> *Discussion Opportunity—Ask: What are your greatest fears with respect to money? Explain. What do you expect of a spouse with respect to money? Are you stingy or sharing with respect to money? Where do you think this feeling comes from?*

Consumer Confidence

e. The field of **behavioral economics**, or economic psychology, is concerned with the "human" side of economic decisions (including biases).
   1) A consumer's beliefs about what the future holds is an indicator of **consumer confidence**, which reflects the extent to which people are optimistic or pessimistic about the future health of the economy and how they will fare down the road.
   2) The Survey Research Center at the University of Michigan has developed the following questions to survey consumer confidence:
      a) Would you say that you and your family are better off or worse off financially than a year ago?
      b) Will you be better off or worse off a year from now?
      c) Is now a good time or a bad time for people to buy major household items such as furniture or a refrigerator?
      d) Do you plan to buy a car in the next year?

> *Discussion Opportunity—Ask: Do you think these four questions are good for measuring consumer confidence? Do you think people would truthfully answer all these questions? Would you? What other questions might be added to the list? Why?*

f. The overall savings rate is influenced by the individual consumer's pessimism or optimism about his or her personal circumstances, world events, and cultural differences in attitudes toward saving.

> *Discussion Opportunity—Ask students to evaluate how each of the following groups feels about savings and the general state of our economy (and their position in it): (a) a teenager, (b) a senior in college, (c) your parents, and (d) your grandparents (or other people in this age range).*

### 2. Social Class

    a. A consumer's standing in society, or **social class**, is determined by a complex set of variables, including income, family background, and occupation.

      1) The place one occupies in the social structure is an important determinant not only of how much money is spent, but it also influences how it is spent.

      2) Consumers' view toward money varies widely.

> *Discussion Opportunity—Ask: What other variables can you think of that might have a strong association (determinant of) with social class?*

    b. In most animal species the most assertive or aggressive animals exert control over the others.

      1) People are not much different.

      2) People tend to try and improve their lot in life by moving up the social order.

      3) Social class affects access to resources.

        a) According to Karl Marx, the "haves" control the resources and the "have nots" provide the labor.

        b) According to Max Weber, multidimensional people are ranked by social status, power, wealth, and property.

      4) Social class affects taste and lifestyles. People in each group tend to socialize with each other, share many ideas and values, and have similar education.

        a) Social class is as much a state of mind as it is of having.

        b) The tendency to marry within one's own social class in known as **homogamy**.

> *Discussion Opportunity—Have your students comment on the phrase "Social class is as much a state of being as it is of having." How important is social class to you? Explain.*

Social Stratification

    c. The phenomenon of **social stratification** refers to the creation of artificial divisions in a society. ("Those processes in a social system by which scarce and valuable resources are distributed unequally to status positions that become more or less permanently ranked in terms of the share of valuable resources each receives.")

      1) Status is either earned (***achieved status***) or inherited (***ascribed status***).

      2) Most groups exhibit a structure, or **status hierarchy**, in which some members are somehow better off than others. They may have more authority or power, or they may simply be better liked or respected.

> *Discussion Opportunity—Ask: How do advertisers use social stratification and status hierarchy in advertising? How are authority, power, money, and respect shown in advertisements?*

d. One of the most famous social class scales is the one developed by Lloyd Warner
in 1941. Warner's six divisions are:
  1) Upper Upper (old rich).
  2) Lower Upper (new rich).
  3) Upper Middle (professionals and owners).
  4) Lower Middle (lower-paid, white-collar workers and high-paid, blue-collar workers).
  5) Upper Lower (blue-collar workers).
  6) Lower Lower (underemployed and unemployed).

*****Use Figure 13.1 Here;
Use Consumer Behavior Challenges #4 and #5 Here *****

e. Every society around the world has some form of class structure. Some people are
mobile and some are not.
  1) In China, a middle class is rapidly developing. This has made a market for all kinds of
  goods and services.
  2) Japan is a very status-conscious society where upscale, designer labels are quite
  popular. This is especially true with the large working female demographic.
  3) Shopping is a major pastime for Arab women, most of whom do not work outside the
  home.
  4) The United Kingdom is very class conscious, with class structure being traditionally
  preordained. **Chavs** are a lower-class group that has been traditionally overlooked by
  marketers, but is now being targeted by various companies.
f. The concept of **mass class** recognizes that there is a huge segment of consumers worldwide
who now enjoy a level of purchasing power that is sufficient to let them afford high-
quality products.
g. **Social mobility** refers to the passage of individuals from one social class to another.
This passage can be:
  1) *Horizontal mobility*—movement from one position to another roughly
  equivalent in social status (a nurse to a school teacher).
  2) *Downward mobility*—movement from one position to one farther down the

scale (losing a job and being placed on welfare).
3) *Upward mobility*—movement from one position to one farther up the scale (the child of a blue-collar worker becomes a physician).

Components of Social Class

h. The most important components of social class are (in descending order):
1) *Occupational prestige* (the "worth" of people). These hierarchies tend to be stable over time and similar in different societies.
  a) A person's occupation tends to be strongly linked to one's use of resources and time (among other things).
  b) This variable is often considered to be the single best indicator of social class.
2) *Income.* Wealth is not distributed evenly. Income per se is not a very good indicator of social class (e.g., the blue-collar worker who earns $90,000 a year working an industrial crane), however, most equate it to social class.

*****Use Consumer Behavior Challenge #11 Here *****

i. There are relationships between income and social class. A few of these are:
1) Social class appears to be a better predictor of purchases that have symbolic aspects but low to moderate prices (e.g., cosmetics, liquor).
2) Income predicts the purchase of expensive products without status or symbolic value (e.g., a major appliance).
3) Both social class and income are needed to predict the purchase of expensive symbolic products (e.g., cars, homes).

Measurement of Social Class

j. Because social class is a complex concept that depends on a number of factors, not surprisingly, it has proven difficult to measure.

*****Use Figure 13.2 Here; Use Consumer Behavior Challenge #10 Here *****

k. Market researchers were among the first to propose that people from different social classes can be distinguished from each other in important ways. Problems include:
   1) The shift away from the traditional nuclear family structure.
   2) The inability to use the reputational method because we as a society are becoming more anonymous. Early studies relied on the **reputational method** (extensive interviewing done in a neighborhood to determine reputations and backgrounds of individuals).
   3) Status inconsistency. Examples include:
      a) A person from a low status ethnic background has a high-status job. This can be called **status crystallization** (assesses the impact of inconsistency on the self and social behavior).
      b) A person that is undereducated in a traditional sense succeeds in position, wealth, and power.
      c) *Overprivileged consumers*—lottery winners.
      d) *Underprivileged consumers*—sacrifice to look good.
      e) Women and their roles.
         1. Women have traditionally borrowed their social status from their husbands.
         2. Today, more women are marrying without regard to the social position of the man.

---

***\*\*\*\*\*Use Figure 13.3 Here; Use Consumer Behavior Challenge #2 Here \*\*\*\*\****

---

*Discussion Opportunity—Give an example of someone who suffers from status inconsistency.*

---

*Discussion Opportunity—Give examples of couples who come from different backgrounds (with respect to social class and occupation type) and have become romantically involved. Will this cause problems? Do you see any evidence in our entertainment shows (such as on television or in the movies)? In our advertising?*

---

l. Marketers have failed to use social class information as effectively as they could for the following reasons:
   1) They have ignored status inconsistency.
   2) They have ignored intergenerational mobility.
   3) They have ignored subjective social class.
   4) They have ignored consumers' aspirations to change their class standing.
   5) They have ignored the social status of working wives.

---

*Discussion Opportunity—How might Web marketers use social class in designing appealing opening Web pages for e-commerce companies? Give an illustration of a firm that you believe uses social class in designing an opening page.*

---

**3. How Social Class Affects Purchase Decisions**
  a. Different products and stores are perceived by consumers to be appropriate for certain social classes.
    1) Working classes tend to evaluate products in more utilitarian terms (such as sturdiness or comfort).
    2) More affluent consumers tend to evaluate products based on appearance and body image.

Class Differences in Worldview
  b. A major social class difference involves the ***worldview*** of consumers.
    1) Working classes are more concerned with immediate needs and are more dependent on relatives for emotional support, are family-oriented, and the appearance of home is a priority.
    2) Higher classes tend to focus on more long-term goals; quest for riches often results in depression and deviant behavior.
    3) The concept of a **taste culture**, which differentiates people in terms of their aesthetic and intellectual preferences, is helpful in understanding the important yet subtle distinctions in consumption choices among the social classes.

*****Use Figure 13.4 Here *****

*Discussion Opportunity—Illustrate taste culture with ads from magazines. How are the magazines matched to market segments (which are matched to the ads)?*

  c. Another approach to social class focuses on differences in the types of ***codes*** (the ways meanings are expressed and interpreted by consumers) used within different social strata. Examples of the codes are:
    1) **Restricted codes** are dominant among the working class. These codes focus on content of objects not on the relationship among objects.
    2) **Elaborated codes** tend to be used by the middle and upper classes. These codes focus on more complex issues and have a worldwide view.

*****Use Table 13.2 Here *****

*Discussion Opportunity—Ask: What are some physical cues that you can observe to determine whether a person is in the upper, middle, or lower socio-economic class? Do you think you can easily be misled? How are these cues used in advertising?*

*Discussion Opportunity—Bring in ads that appear (in your opinion) to be directed toward the blue-collar and white-collar classes. Point out codes that are restricted and elaborated.*

  d. Clearly not all cultures are created equal when it comes to tastes. Forms of ***capital*** for which people compete are:
    1) ***Economic capital*** (financial resources).
    2) ***Social capital*** (organizational affiliations and networks).

3) The way that people view the world is heavily influenced by economic and social background, a process known as **habitus**.

4) **Cultural capital** (a set of distinctive and socially rare tastes and practices—knowledge of "refined" behavior that admits a person into the realm of the upper class).

---

*****Use Figure 13.4 Here *****

---

*Discussion Opportunity—Give illustrations of cultural capital. Give illustrations of ads that use cultural capital symbols.*

---

Targeting the Poor

e. About 14 percent of Americans live below the poverty line, and this segment has been largely ignored by marketers.

1) Many of the poor feel alienated by society.

2) Some marketers are developing products and services for low-income consumers.

3) Some marketers are trying to educate the low-income consumer on how to stretch their dollar. Many are also trying to improve relationships in the hopes that the consumer will choose them as their lives become more prosperous.

---

*Discussion Opportunity—Think of five products that could be specifically targeted toward the poor. How would you change the existing marketing strategy to accommodate this shift toward this segment? Do you think this new approach would be successful? What would be the key variables necessary for success?*

---

Targeting the Rich

f. Social class is also about money.

1) Many marketers target affluent, upscale markets.

2) The number of millionaires is increasing at roughly 20 times the rate of the population.

3) It is a mistake to assume that everyone with a high income should be placed in the same market.

---

*****Use Consumer Behavior Challenge #7 Here *****

---

g. *Old money* is linked to inherited money.

1) The point with this segment is not how much money, but where did it come from and how is it spent.

2) People who earned their money are not usually included in this group.

3) This group has a history of service and philanthropy.

h. The *nouveau riches* are not accepted by old rich. They are considered to be "rags to riches." *Nouveau riches* is a term often used in a negative manner by the old rich.

1) Many nouveu riches are plagued by ***status anxiety*** (wearing the right clothes or seen in the right places).

> *Discussion Opportunity—Ask: How do spending patterns differ between the "old rich" and the "new rich"?*

> *Discussion Opportunity—Have the students classify some of America's richest men as either "old rich" or "new rich" (e.g., Ted Turner, Bill Gates, or Michael Eisner).*

> *Discussion Opportunity—When Ted Turner tried to shame America's rich into being more philanthropic by giving a billion dollars to the United Nations (over ten years), what did they think of him? What do you think of his effort? Does it make you like him? Does it make you want to use him as a role model?*

## 4. Status Symbols

a. People have a tendency to evaluate themselves, their professional accomplishments, their material well-being, and so on, relative to others.

1) Status symbols can be thought of as "badges of achievement."
2) "He who dies with the most toys, wins" is a trite but (to many) a true phrase. Status-seeking is a significant source of motivation.

> *Discussion Opportunity—Have the class create a list of ten status symbols that are important to them. Then have them share their lists with the class. How are these symbols linked to success? If a marketer knew your list, how would it affect their strategy for marketing to you?*

> *Discussion Opportunity—Ask: What are the "new status" symbols for Generation X, Generation Y, and the digital generation? How are these different from the status symbols for the baby boomers?*

Conspicuous Consumption

b. Thorstein Veblen felt that a major role of products was for **invidious distinction**. They were used to inspire envy in others through a display of wealth or power.

1) Veblen coined the phrase **conspicuous consumption** to refer to people's desire to provide prominent visible evidence of their ability to afford luxury goods.

> *****Use Consumer Behavior Challenges #7 (Used Previously) and #12 Here *****

> *Discussion Opportunity—Have students give examples of conspicuous consumption or invidious distinction that have either affected you or been done by you. Can you think of your real reasons for participating in this behavior?*

2) Forms of conspicuous behavior might include:
   a) ***The billboard wife***.
   b) ***The modern potlatch***—a feast where the host gives elaborate gifts to

guests and guests are expected to reciprocate, forcing poor guests into bankruptcy. (The best modern example is the large and expensive wedding.)

c) ***The leisure class***—people for whom productive work is taboo and who engage in conspicuous waste.

d) **Parody display**—avoiding status symbols and going in the reverse direction.

---

*****Use Consumer Behavior Challenges #6 and #12 (Used Previously) Here *****

---

*Discussion Opportunity—Give an example of the billboard wife, the modern potlatch, the leisure class, and parody display as status symbol display. Please be specific in your examples. Use ads to display your thoughts if possible.*

---

# End-of-Chapter Support Material

## SUMMARY OF SPECIAL FEATURE BOXES

### 1.  Marketing Pitfalls

This box highlights the problems faced by lottery winners. These problems are due to the fact that they not only receive a windfall of money overnight, but they change social classes.

### 2.  Marketing Opportunity I

A chain of stores in California called La Curacao has had tremendous success by targeting low-income Hispanics with items from their country and culture. They also offer them something really unique—credit. They have taken on the risk of offering credit cards to low income individuals. This feature supports the section "Targeting the Poor."

### 3.  Marketing Opportunity II

This box examines the status symbol that cuts across age groups—the cell phone. Results of research are given that identify how the cell phone has reached status symbol position with youth as well as adults. This feature supports the section "Status Symbols."

## REVIEW QUESTIONS

1.  How have women contributed to the overall rise in income in our society? *One reason for this increase in income is that there also has been a larger proportion of people of working age participating in the labor force. Mothers with preschool children are the fastest-growing segment of working people. Furthermore, many of these jobs are in high-*

*paying occupations such as medicine and architecture that used to be dominated by men. Although women are still a minority in most professional occupations, their ranks continue to swell. The steady increase in the numbers of working women is a primary cause of the rapid growth of middle- and upper-income families. There are now more than 18 million married couples making over $50,000 a year—but in almost two-thirds of these families, it is the wife's paycheck that is propelling the couple up the income ladder.*

2.   Define discretionary income. *Discretionary income is the money available to a household over and above that required for a comfortable standard of living.*

3.   How does consumer confidence influence consumer behavior? *Consumers' beliefs about what the future holds is an indicator of consumer confidence that reflects the extent to which people are optimistic or pessimistic about the future health of the economy and how they will fare down the road. These beliefs influence how much money they will pump into the economy when making discretionary purchases.*

4.   What is a pecking order? *In many animal species, a social organization develops whereby the most assertive or aggressive animals exert control over the others and have the first pick of food, living space, and even mating partners. Chickens, for example, develop a clearly defined dominance–submission hierarchy. Within this hierarchy, each hen has a position in which she is submissive to all of the hens above her and dominates all of the ones below her (hence, the origin of the term pecking order). People are not much different. They also develop a pecking order that ranks them in terms of their relative standing in society. This standing determines their access to such resources as education, housing, and consumer goods. People try to improve their ranking by moving up in the social order whenever possible. This desire to improve one's lot in life, and often to let others know that one has done so, is at the core of many marketing strategies.*

5.   What is social class? Is it different from income and if so how? *We use the term social class more generally to describe the overall rank of people in a society. People who are grouped within the same social class are approximately equal in terms of their social standing in the community. They work in roughly similar occupations, and they tend to have similar lifestyles by virtue of their income levels and common tastes. These people tend to socialize with one another and share many ideas and values regarding the way life should be lived. Indeed, "birds of a feather do flock together."*

6.   What is the difference between achieved and ascribed status? *Think back to groups to which you've belonged. You'll probably agree that in many instances some members seem to get more than their fair share of goodies, whereas other individuals are not so lucky. Some of these resources may have gone to people who earned them through hard work or diligent study. This allocation is due to achieved status. The person may have obtained other rewards because she was lucky enough to be born with "a silver spoon in her mouth." Such good fortune reflects ascribed status.*

7.      What is a chav? *The British use this term widely; it refers to young, lower-class men and women who mix flashy brands and accessories from big names like Burberry with track suits. Their style icons include soccer star David Beckham and his wife, Victoria, who was known as Posh Spice as a member of the Spice Girls pop group. Despite their (alleged) tackiness, chavs are attractive to marketers because they have a lot of disposable income to spend on fashion, food, and gadgets.*

8.      Describe what is meant by the term "mass class" and tell what is causing this phenomenon. *Mass class refers to the hundreds of millions of global consumers who now enjoy a level of purchasing power that's sufficient to let them afford high-quality products—except for big-ticket items like college educations, housing, or luxury cars.*

9.      Define social mobility and what different forms can it take? *In some societies, such as India, one's social class is very difficult to change, but America is reputed to be a country in which "any man (or woman?) can grow up to be president." Social mobility refers to the "passage of individuals from one social class to another."*

10.     What one variable is the best indicator of social class? What are some other important indicators? *When we think about a person's social class, there are a number of pieces of information we may consider. Two major ones are occupation and income. A third important factor is educational attainment that is strongly related to income and occupation.*

11.     Why does earning more money often not result in a corresponding change in social class? *One problem is that even if a family increases household income by adding wage earners, each additional job is likely to be of lower status. A homemaker who gets a part-time job is not as likely to get one that is of equal or greater status than the primary wage earner's full-time job. In addition, the extra money earned is often not pooled toward the common good of the family. Instead, the individual uses it for his own personal spending. More money does not then result in increased status or changes in consumption patterns because it tends to be devoted to buying more of the usual rather than upgrading to higher-status products.*

12.     What are some of the problems associated with efforts to measure social class? *One reason is that most measures of social class were designed to accommodate the traditional nuclear family, with a male wage earner in the middle of his career and a female full-time homemaker. Such measures have trouble accounting for two-income families, young singles living alone, or households headed by women, who are so prevalent in today's society. Another problem with measuring social class is the increasing anonymity of our society. Earlier studies relied on the reputational method, in which extensive interviewing was done within a community to determine the reputations and backgrounds of individuals. This information, coupled with the tracing of interaction patterns among people, provided a very comprehensive view of social standing within a community. However, this approach is virtually impossible to implement in most communities today. One compromise is to interview individuals to obtain demographic*

*data and to combine these data with the subjective impressions of the interviewer regarding the person's possessions and standard of living.*

13. Define status crystallization and give an example. *Social scientists developed the concept of status crystallization to assess the impact of inconsistency on the self and social behavior. The logic behind this idea is that because the rewards from each part of such an "unbalanced" person's life would be variable and unpredictable, stress would result. People who exhibit such inconsistencies tend to be more receptive to social change than are those whose identities are more firmly rooted.*

14. How does the worldview of blue-collar and white-collar consumers tend to differ? *Although they would like to have more in the way of material goods, working-class people do not necessarily envy those who rank above them in social standing. They may not view the maintenance of a high-status lifestyle as worth the effort. As one blue-collar consumer commented, "Life is very hectic for those people. There are more breakdowns and alcoholism. It must be very hard to sustain the status, the clothes, and the parties that are expected. I don't think I'd want to take their place."*

15. What is a taste culture? *A taste culture differentiates people in terms of their aesthetic and intellectual preferences. This concept helps to illuminate the important yet sometimes subtle distinctions in consumption choices among the social classes.*

16. Describe the difference between a restricted and an elaborated code, giving an example of each. *Restricted codes are dominant among the working class, whereas the middle and upper classes. tend to use elaborated codes. Restricted codes focus on the content of objects, not on relationships among objects. Elaborated codes, in contrast, are more complex and depend on a more sophisticated worldview. These code differences extend to the way consumers approach basic concepts such as time, social relationships, and objects.*

17. What is cultural capital, and why is an etiquette class a way to accumulate it? *This refers to a set of distinctive and socially rare tastes and practices—knowledge of "refined" behavior that admits a person into the realm of the upper class. The elite in a society collect a set of skills that enable them to hold positions of power and authority, and they pass these on to their children (such as etiquette lessons and debutante balls). These resources gain in value because access to them is restricted. That's part of the reason why people compete so fiercely for admission to elite colleges. Much as we hate to admit it, the rich are different.*

18. How would you differentiate between consumers who are "old money" versus "nouveau riche?" *We call consumers who have achieved extreme wealth and have relatively recently become members of upper social classes the nouveau riches, a term that many people use in a derogatory manner to describe newcomers to the world of wealth.*

19. What is conspicuous consumption? Give a current example. *Conspicuous consumption refers to people's desire to provide prominent visible evidence of their ability to afford luxury goods.*

20. What is a current example of parody display? *As the competition to accumulate status symbols escalates, sometimes the best tactic is to switch gears and go in reverse. One way to do this is to deliberately avoid status symbols—that is, to seek status by mocking it. Social scientists call this sophisticated form of conspicuous consumption parody display. Hence, the popularity of old, ripped blue jeans, and "utility" vehicles such as Jeeps among the upper classes.*

# CONSUMER BEHAVIOR CHALLENGE

## Discussion Questions

1. Sears, J.C. Penney, and, to a lesser degree, KMart, have made concerted efforts in recent years to upgrade their images and appeal to higher-class consumers. How successful have these efforts been? Do you believe this strategy is wise?

   *J.C. Penney has not been very successful in changing its image. Because consumers have always thought of stores like J.C. Penney, Sears, and KMart as discount or low-price stores, it is likely that these stores will have difficulty changing their images among the general public. Attempting to change a store's image when consumers have a strong perception of the store's image—and one that is largely inconsistent with the proposed image—can be a very risky strategy. As in the case of J.C. Penney, retailers run the risk of alienating a significant group of loyal consumers with these attempts.*

2. What are some of the obstacles to measuring social class in today's society? Discuss some ways to get around these obstacles.

   *Some of the obstacles in measuring social class in today's society are changes in family structure, anonymity, and status inconsistency. Students should refer to the text discussion for suggestions on how to get around some of these obstacles.*

3. Do you believe "affluenza" is a problem among Americans your age? Why or why not?

   *Well-off consumers seem to be stressed or unhappy despite or even because of their wealth, a condition sometimes termed affluenza. Given the supporting information for this concept in the text, there should be some that feel that this is an issue.*

4.    What consumption differences might you expect to observe between a family characterized as underprivileged versus one whose income is average for its social class?

*An example of the consumption differences one might expect to observe between a family characterized as underprivileged versus one whose income is average for its social class include the brands of clothing worn, the types of cars driven, types of vacations (flying versus driving, hotels versus camping), and vacation destinations (local state park versus Hawaii). Students likely will identify a number of factors in their own lives that distinguish them as members of the "middle" class. Ask students if they have a tendency to overestimate the class they are in. Why would they do this?*

5.    How do you assign people to social classes, or do you at all? What consumption cues do you use (e.g., clothing, speech, cars, etc.) to determine social standing?

*As discussed in the text, people are assigned to social classes by virtue of their social standing in the community. People are grouped according to their occupation, lifestyle, ideas and values, and income. Consumption cues that may be used to determine people's social standing include their cars, homes, clothing, speech, and types of people with whom they socialize.*

6.    Thorstein Veblen argued that women were often used as a vehicle to display their husbands' wealth. Is this argument still valid today?

*The instructor should expect students to differ in their level of agreement with Thorstein Veblen's notion that women often are used as a vehicle to display their husbands' wealth. They should be encouraged to defend and support their views with examples from today's society. Does advertising perpetuate this process? If so, how?*

7.    Given present environmental conditions and dwindling resources, what is the future of "conspicuous waste"? Can the desire to impress others with affluence ever be eliminated? If not, can it take on a less dangerous form?

*The goal of this question is to make the student think about current environmental conditions, depleting resources, and how "conspicuous waste" plays a major role in this decay process. The view of conspicuous waste from both consumer and marketer perspectives should be included.*

8.    The chapter observes that some marketers are finding "greener pastures" by targeting low-income people. How ethical is it to single out consumers who cannot afford to waste their precious resources on discretionary items? Under what circumstances should this segmentation strategy be encouraged or discouraged?

*Student opinions will vary. Possible ethical issues include: Do people with low incomes need special protection? Does low income equate with low intelligence? Do you take away freedom of choice from people with low incomes? Who should decide how people use their money? Will society have to provide essential items if those with low incomes*

331

*spend their money on discretionary items? The argument of which discretionary items should not be promoted to low-income people seems to be centering on "sin products" (e.g., tobacco, alcohol, etc.). When a special cigarette, a special wine, and a special ale were targeted toward people who live in the inner city, many groups spoke out saying that it was immoral to use billboards in these neighborhoods to encourage sales. The companies involved have either dropped the product or changed their promotional strategies, but these same products with different brand names are still appearing on billboards in the inner city. Some argue that because low-income people have the right to use tobacco products and alcoholic beverages, manufacturers should have the right to communicate about their products to every potential consumer.*

9.  Status symbols are products that are valued because they show others how much money or prestige a person has, such as Rolex watches or expensive sports cars. Do you believe that your peer group values status symbols? Why or why not? If yes, what are the products that you think are regarded as status symbols now for consumers your age?

    *Obviously, there will be two groups of students here; those who think their peer group values status symbols and those who think their peer group does not. For the latter, you might probe individuals in this group by dropping some brands or objects that you think might be valued by them. For those that do feel they and their peers value status symbols, the symbols given may vary quite a bit from the traditional. Although they may give the obvious such as BMW or Rolex, they will likely provide more items that their college-student peers are actually using and wearing.*

## Application Questions

10. Using the Status Index presented in Figure 13.3, compute a social class score for people you know, including their parents if possible. Ask several friends (preferably from different places) to compile similar information for people they know. How closely do your answers compare? If you find differences, how can you explain them?

    *Students should enjoy using this exercise to analyze their parents' social class standing, as well as that of their peers' parents. They might be encouraged to compute a hypothetical score for themselves, based on expectations for the future. (Possible Field Project Idea)*

11. Compile a list of occupations, and ask a sample of students in a variety of majors (both business and nonbusiness) to rank the prestige of these jobs. Can you detect any differences in these rankings as a function of students' majors?

    *The students should be encouraged to try this exercise with a variety of individuals, not just students in different majors. It would be interesting to see differences in perceptions of prestige due to gender, age, current occupation, level of education, etc. (Possible Field Project Idea)*

12.   Compile a collection of ads that depict consumers of different social classes. What generalizations can you make about the reality of these ads and about the media in which they appear?

*The instructor might review this exercise after students have completed it and attempt to identify the aspects of the advertisements that students used to classify consumers as members of different social classes. A discussion of how our attitudes and perceptions are influenced by stereotypical beliefs could then be used with the students' own examples as evidence of stereotypical beliefs and their potentially negative consequences. (Possible Field Project Idea)*

# CASE STUDY TEACHING NOTES

## Chapter 13 Case Study: Predatory Lending—All Loans Are Not Created Equal

### Summary of Case

Low income consumers generally have poor credit ratings. Thus, it has been a practice for some time for lenders to offer credit to individuals at higher interest rates, a practice known as sub-prime lending. However, there is a practice which goes way beyond the ethical parameters of sub-prime lending. Predatory lending is the practice of extending loans with extremely high rates (up to 100 percent annual rate), hidden fees, and substantial prepayment penalties. This practice is growing rapidly. And it is targeted at the poor, those who can least afford it. Most companies that engage in this practice are small chains. However, it is evident that some of the biggest names in financial services have been involved in the practice. Legislative attempts are being made to regulate this practice.

### Suggestions for Presentation

This is a good case to address ethical issues of specific marketing practices. In this case, it is the practice of not only targeting the poor, but doing so by taking advantage of their weaknesses. As the discussion questions should bring out, this case can be tied to the reasons that the poor are susceptible to this practice.

### Suggested Answers for Discussion Questions

1.   Discuss all of the reasons that low income consumers are "falling for" predatory loans.

*There are at least a couple of issues here. First, low income individuals tend to be of lower education levels. Second, they are also likely to have less experience with business contracts and having used credit. Third, they do not have many (if any) options for credit.*

*All of these things tend to lead low income customers to take the predatory options because they do not recognize the disadvantages of doing so.*

2.     What are all of the ways that predatory lending hurts individuals as well as communities?

*The effects on individuals are that people end up not being able to pay the loan back and have their merchandise repossessed. These situations also likely hurt the already bad credit ratings of such individuals. These problems may set of a chain of events that cause the consumer to draw even more debt to cover for that which they are already in.*

*Communities are damaged because low income individuals often live close to each other in neighborhoods. If multiple individuals on the same street or in the same area are affected negatively by this practice, then that has a negative effect on the economy of the geographic area.*

## Additional Support Material

# STUDENT PROJECTS

### Individual Projects

1.     Have a student visit a high-end specialty store for a luxury good (i.e., Louis Vuitton, Coach, Burburry, etc.). Have them interview a sales associate or manager in regard to the existence of the mass class segment. Can they identify the difference between upper-class people and middle- to lower-class people who buy the products? What are the noted differences? How prevalent are the mass culture members?

2.     Students should conduct an assessment of consumer confidence in their home country according to the accepted measures of such. Do this for each year in the last 5 years. What is the trend? What are the economic implications of this?

3.     Conduct a brief secondary research project on what happens to people after they win a large lottery. Summarize the results and share them with the class.

4.     Conduct this as an in-class activity. Prepare a list of 15 occupations and distribute copies to the class. Ask each student to rank the occupations according to prestige. Compile the results (either during class, or after for the next class period). Discuss the results with the class. Are there consistencies? Why do these form? What implications do these perceptions have on consumer behavior?

5. Ask students to find at least two manufacturer's ads for the same type of product (e.g., clothing, food product, personal care product, etc.) that they think are aimed at different social classes. How do these ads differ?

6. Ask a student to compile a collection of ads that depict consumers of different social classes. What medium and vehicle is each ad found in? Have students generalize about the reality of the stories told in these ads.

7. Ask a student to bring in an ad in which the brand being marketed was at one time a status symbol, but fell out of fashion for a time (e.g., Cadillac, Parker Pen, Izod-Lacoste, etc.). Have the student discuss whether the ad still attempts to create that perception. What new product, if any, has replaced the featured product as a status symbol?

8. Have a student interview one or more salespeople from one of the following product categories: new or used cars, stereo equipment, clothing, insurance, or real estate. Ask the student to determine the social classes or status of their customers. Does the student recommend that the sales approach will vary depending on the customer's social class?

9. Ask a student to bring in a collection of magazines aimed at different social classes. Have the student comment on the products advertised, the physical appearance and layout, and the editorial content of the magazines.

10. Chart your own discretionary spending for one week. What patterns do you notice? How could this information be of value to marketers?

11. What status symbols motivate you to purchase? Pick an example product and give an illustration.

12. How can online marketers use social class in marketing efforts? Give examples of good and bad usage. Go online to do this if possible.

## Group Projects

1. Have a group of students compile a list of ten colleges and universities. Then, have them go out and have other students rank them. Have the students comment on the results. Are there any marketing implications to the results?

2. Have a student interview small business owners, large business owners, or a couple of both for their opinions of the state of the economy. How do they think an increase in Social Security Taxes—or Americans with Disabilities Act, Flat Tax Proposal, NAFTA, or some other currently proposed federal regulation or mandate—would affect them? Have the student find out what major signals the owners study and watch before making their business forecasts.

3.  Have students prepare a survey designed to measure the attitude toward various global U.S. companies (i.e., Nike, Coca-Cola, McDonald's, etc.). For each company, they should have questions designed to assess general attitudes as well as perceptions of the global expansion and business practices of such companies. Then, have the groups distribute the survey to international students. They should be certain to have the respondents note their home country.

4.  Have student groups visit two sections of a community—one where residents are professionals and business people and one where residents are mostly working class. Ask them to note how the homes vary in terms of color, architecture, and the general appearance of the lawn and landscape. Have them check the paper or call a realtor to find the general value of homes in the area. What types of stores are in the neighborhood and how are they promoted?

5.  Bring to class copies of the types of magazines described in the chapter that appeal to various social classes. Pass the magazines around and have students look through them. Ask the class to discuss the differences and similarities that they noted.

6.  Students usually enjoy this project. Ask a group to classify the major retail stores (department and specialty stores) in your community according to their estimation of the social class of their target market. Have them explain how the marketing strategy is different for each of the stores profiled.

7.  Ask students to make a list of slang terms that are used to disparage social classes. Why are these terms used? How do marketers disparage or make fun of social classes (which they do not target)? What is the best way to treat all classes with ethics and dignity?

8.  Have your group designate which social class would most accurately describe each member's current position. Where do the members expect to be in 5 years with respect to social class? What differences will occur if the anticipated movement in social class occurs? Discuss the changes in class.

9.  Assign groups of students to go to an airport (or other location where they will find lots of foot traffic) to people watch. Have them classify as many people as possible according to social class based on the appearance and behaviors of individuals. Have the class as a whole discuss their results. What lessons can be learned from this?

# eLAB

## Individual Assignments

1.  Go to **www.burberry.com**. How does this prestige fashion label use social class and status to sell its products? Critique their approach. Does this approach make you want to buy such products? Explain.

2.       Go to **www.maxlang.com**. How much would you pay for a belt for casual or business wear? How much does Max Lang charge? Is Max Lang selling belts or status? How can the Max Lang Web site overcome problems such as sizing and the desire to personally see prestige products? What do you think of the organization's strategy?

3.       Go to **www.cadillac.com**. Once the ultimate status symbol, Cadillac's image began a slow decline around 1980. The brand is now on a major quest to reclaim its title. Although they are seeing some success, they may be hitting certain target markets with some of their products that actually detract from the image they are trying to achieve. Specifically regarding the Escalade line of SUVs, how do you perceive the conflict between Cadillac's traditional target market, and that of new market segments that are embracing the brand (i.e., hip hop culture)? How should Cadillac address this issue? Design a promotional strategy outline.

4.       Go to **www.hammacher.com**. How does Hammacher Schlemmer use prestige and the desire to be different in its marketing effort? Give illustrations from the company's Web site to support your conclusions. Is this a good strategy for the company to follow? Explain.

5.       Go to **www.deutsche-wurlitzerusa.com**. Ever want your own jukebox. If so, Wurlitzer is the place to go. How does the company use prestige, memories, the desire to be different, status, and affluence to sell their products? Explain.

## Group Assignments

1.       Go to **www.miserlymoms.com**. Have your group analyze the advantages of this Web site. What benefits are offered? How would this site get upscale, affluent consumers to use the Web site? How would the site get poorer, less affluent consumers to use the Web site? What evidence do you see that the organization is trying for both markets? Explain. How does the site appeal to upscale consumers who have greater amounts of discretionary income? Downscale consumers who have less?

2.       Visit **www.fashion-era.com**. Take some time as a group and browse the fashion trends from different time periods. Find trends that are in fashion at one time period, then out of fashion, then back in fashion at some other time period. What governs these trends? Discuss this and draw some conclusions based on the concepts in the chapter.

3.       Visit both **www.macaronigrill.com** and **www.dennys.com.** Have your group analyze the approaches that both of these Web sites have taken to appeal to their target markets. What elements and cues in these Web sites reflect the principles contained in this chapter on social status and cultural capital?

# CHAPTER 14

# *ETHNIC, RACIAL, AND RELIGIOUS SUBCULTURES*

## CHAPTER OBJECTIVES

When students finish this chapter they should understand why:

- Consumers' memberships in ethnic, racial, and religious subcultures often play a big role in guiding their consumption behaviors.

- Additional influences come from our identification with microcultures that reflect a shared interest in some organization or activity.

- Many marketing efforts appeal to ethnic and racial identity.

- African Americans, Hispanic Americans, and Asian Americans are the three most important ethnic/racial subcultures in the United States.

- Religion and spirituality are increasingly being used to market products.

## CHAPTER SUMMARY

Consumers identify with many groups that share common characteristics and identities. These large groups that exist within a society are *subcultures*, and membership in them often gives marketers a clue about individuals' consumption decisions. A large component of a person's identity is often determined by his or her ethnic origins, racial identity, and religious background. The three largest ethnic/racial subcultures are African Americans, Hispanic Americans, and Asian Americans, but consumers with many diverse backgrounds are beginning to be considered by marketers as well.

Recently, several minority groups have caught the attention of marketers as their economic power has grown. Segmenting consumers by their ethnicity can be effective, but care must be taken not to rely on inaccurate (and sometimes offensive) *ethnic stereotypes*.

African Americans are a very important market segment. Although in some respects the market expenditures of these consumers do not differ that much from whites, blacks are above average consumers in such categories as personal-care products. In the past, blacks were either ignored or portrayed negatively in mainstream advertising, but such depictions are changing as more blacks actually work on the development of campaigns and as specialized black media increases in importance.

Hispanic Americans and Asian Americans are other ethnic subcultures that are beginning to be actively courted by marketers. The size of both groups is increasing rapidly and in the coming years will dominate some major markets. Asian Americans on the whole are extremely well educated, and the socioeconomic status of Hispanics is increasing as well. Key issues for reaching the Hispanic market are consumers' degree of acculturation into mainstream American society and the recognition of important cultural differences among Hispanic subgroups (e.g., Puerto Ricans, Cubans, Mexicans). Both Asian Americans and Hispanic Americans tend to be extremely family oriented and are receptive to advertising that understands their heritage and reinforces their traditional family values.

Although the impact of religious identification on consumer behavior is not clear, some differences among religious subcultures do emerge. Some of these factors are closely related to social class. The market power of religious groups is uncertain, however, researchers closely monitor trends.

# CHAPTER OUTLINE

## 1. Subcultures and Consumer Identity

a. Consumers' lifestyles are affected by group memberships *within* the society-at-large. These groups are known as **subcultures**, whose members share beliefs and common experiences that set them apart from others.

b. **Microcultures** form around a strong shared identification with an activity or art form.

> *Discussion Opportunity—Have the class identify as many subcultures as possible. Which of these match up with those in the text? Which go beyond the text?*

## 2. Ethnic and Racial Subcultures

a. Ethnic and religious identity often are significant components of a consumer's self-concept. An **ethnic subculture** consists of a self-perpetuating group of consumers who are held together by common cultural and/or genetic ties and are identified both by its members and by others as being a distinguishable category.

> *Discussion Opportunity—Ask: What are some of the ways that members of ethnic and racial minorities identify with and support each other? What implications does this have for marketers?*

> *Discussion Opportunity—Ask: What are the good and bad points of adherence to ethnicity? Give illustrations if possible. How should marketers deal with ethnicity?*

Ethnicity and Marketing Strategies

b. People's racial and ethnic differences should be explicitly taken into account when formulating marketing strategies.

1) These subcultural memberships are frequently paramount in shaping people's needs and wants.

2) Membership in ethnic subcultures is often predictive of certain consumer variables such as level and type of media exposure, food and apparel preferences, political behavior, and leisure activities.

*Discussion Opportunity—Give an illustration of how membership in an ethnic subculture predicts level and type of media exposure, food and apparel preferences, political behavior, and leisure activities. Be specific in the illustrations.*

c. The way marketing messages should be structured depends on subcultural differences in how meanings are communicated.

1) **High-context cultures**—group members are tight-knit, symbols and gestures carry much weight, and they are sensitive to nuances in ads. Most minorities fall in this category.

2) **Low-context culture**—group members are less sensitive to ethnicity. Most Anglos are in this group.

3) Ethnicity is a moving target. There is a trend toward blurring of ethnic and racial backgrounds. This is expected to increase over time.

   a) There is an increase in mixed marriages and mixed dating.

   b) Many from diverse ethnic backgrounds are now blending. A multicultural household is an attractive target for marketers.

   c) The Census Bureau is having difficulty putting "blends" in the right categories.

4) Products that are marketed with an ethnic appeal are not necessarily intended for consumption only by the ethnic subculture from which they originate. **De-ethnicization** refers to the process whereby a product formerly associated with a specific ethnic group is detached from its roots and marketed to other subcultures (e.g., bagels—from the Jewish culture—which now can be bought in a jalapeño version—Hispanic culture).

*Discussion Opportunity—Ask: Why would a multicultural household be an attractive target for marketers? Explain your thoughts.*

*Discussion Opportunity—Think of three de-ethnicization products that you may have bought recently. How did you first hear about them? Do you think of them as being ethnic in their nature?*

5) The Census Bureau identifies the "Big Three" subcultures in the United States. These are projected to be (in 2013):

   a) Hispanic Americans—42.1 million.

   b) African American—42 million.

   c) Asian Americans—smallest in number, but the most rapidly growing.

6) The bulk of American immigrants historically came from Europe.

7) The new immigrant is more likely to be Asian or Hispanic.

8) Some new immigrants target particular professions—30 percent of Indian Americans are employed in professional specialty occupations.

> **\*\*\*\*\*Use Figure 14.1 Here \*\*\*\*\***

*Discussion Opportunity—Have students consider whether or not immigrants should be advertised to in their own language or in English? Have different students defend their point of view.*

Ethnic and Racial Stereotypes

d. Many subcultures have powerful stereotypes associated with them. These stereotypes can be viewed positively or negatively.

1) Ethnic symbolism has been used in the past by marketers as a shorthand to connote certain product attributes. The images employed were often crude and unflattering.

2) The use of subtle (and sometimes not so subtle) ethnic stereotypes in movies illustrates how the media can perpetuate assumptions about ethnic or racial groups.

> **\*\*\*\*\*Use Consumer Behavior Challenges #1, #8, and #9 Here \*\*\*\*\***

*Discussion Opportunity—Identify a specific ethnic or racial minority. Have the students make a list of some of the negative stereotype descriptions that are associated with the group. In a column next to the negative word, write a positive word that describes the same behavior or characteristic. How might this analysis be useful to marketers? Note: This is a sensitive discussion topic and should be approached with caution and professionalism.*

*Discussion Opportunity—Even though this project may take some time, look through contemporary magazines and find illustrations of what you perceive to be ethnic stereotyping or insensitivity. Explain why you think your examples qualify.*

*Discussion Opportunity—Ask: What are some of the ethnic products (e.g., foods, clothes, accessories, etc.) that have become part of the mainstream U.S. culture?*

**3. African Americans**

a. African Americans comprise a significant racial subculture and account for 12 percent of the U.S. population. Though alike in some ways, this market also has differences within it.

1) Some commentators have argued that black/white differences are largely illusory.

2) The primary differences seem to occur because of income levels and place of residence.

a) Both blacks and whites spend about two-thirds of their incomes on housing, transportation, and food.

Black/White Consumption Differences
b. The differences might be summarized as being that:
1) If African Americans comprised a separate nation, their buying power would rank twelfth in Western countries.
2) Blacks tend to drink their coffee with sugar and cream much more than their white counterparts do.
3) Of black cigarette smokers, 69 percent prefer menthol.

> *****Use Consumer Behavior Challenges #2 and #4 Here *****

> *Discussion Opportunity—Ask: What other purchase differences have you noticed between African American consumers and those of other groups in the United States? Examine traditional African American magazines and their respective ads. What products seem to be emphasized?*

**4. Hispanic Americans**
a. The Hispanic subculture is a sleeping giant, a segment that was until recently largely ignored by many marketers.

> *Discussion Opportunity—Ask: Why might marketers have ignored the Hispanic American market?*

b. Demographically, two important characteristics of the Hispanic market are worth noting:
1) It is a young market—the median age is 23.6 (the U.S. average is 32).
2) The Hispanic family is much larger than the rest of the population's—the average is 3.5 (compared to the 2.7 U.S. average).
c. Other characteristics include:
1) Movie attendance tends to be a family outing experience.
2) Children's clothing purchases are a matter of pride.
3) Convenience products and those that save time tend to not be very important to this market.
4) Brand loyalty means that generic products do not do well in this market.

> *Discussion Opportunity—What are some further research characteristics of the Hispanic subculture that you have noticed? How might these be used by the marketer?*

d. Marketers are starting to take notice of the Hispanic subculture, specifically the following:
1) It's the fastest-growing sub-segment.
2) Cuban Americans are the wealthiest of the Hispanic group.
3) Blunders must be avoided—this is especially noticeable in print magazine translations.

> *Discussion Opportunity—What should marketers emphasize when trying to appeal to the Hispanic market? What should they avoid?*

Understanding Hispanic Identity

e. Native language and culture are important concerns of Hispanic identity and self-esteem, and these consumers are very sympathetic to marketing efforts that acknowledge and emphasize the Hispanic cultural heritage.

  1) Many Hispanics prefer products that show an interest in the Hispanic consumer.

  2) Many Hispanics are also working hard to maintain their ethnicity.

  3) A profile would include:

    a) A need for status.

    b) A strong sense of pride.

    c) A high value on self-expression.

    d) A high value on family.

f. One important way to distinguish among members of a subculture is to consider the extent to which they retain a sense of identification with their country of origin versus the host country. **Acculturation** refers to the process of movement and adaptation to one country's cultural environment by a person from another country. This factor is very important when considering the Hispanic market.

---

**\*\*\*\*\*Use Table 14.1 Here \*\*\*\*\***

---

g. The acculturation of Hispanic consumers may be understood in terms of the **progressive learning model**. This perspective assumes that people gradually learn a new culture as they increasingly come in contact with it. The new culture becomes a blend of the original culture and the **host culture**. The Hispanic market differs from this in some ways (such as):

  1) They have negative attitudes toward business in general.

  2) They make high use of the Spanish language media.

  3) They are brand loyal and store loyal (prefer prestige labels).

  4) They buy brands specifically advertised to Hispanics.

---

**\*\*\*\*\*Consumer Behavior Challenge #5 Here \*\*\*\*\***

---

*Discussion Opportunity—Find magazine illustrations where the advertisement is specifically directed toward the Hispanic consumer. Share your findings with the class.*

---

h. For many Hispanics, crossing borders is a way of life. The "crossing to a new life" is a popular theme. Examples would be:

i. **Acculturation agents**—people and institutions that teach the ways of a culture are crucial to success in the new environment. Factors include:

  1) *Culture of origin*.

  2) *Culture of immigration*.

  3) *Movement*—physically uprooting one's self or family.

  4) *Translation*—mastering new rules for operating in a foreign environment.

  5) *Adaptation*—forming new consumption patterns.

  6) *Assimilation*—adopting new products, habits, and values.

  7) *Maintenance*—keeping old practices from the old culture.

8) *Resistance*.

9) *Segregation*—shopping in ethnic places only.

```
*****Use Figure 14.2 Here; Use Consumer Behavior Challenge #10 Here *****
```

*Discussion Opportunity—What are some ways that marketers are trying to help Hispanic consumers more easily assimilate into the mainstream U.S. culture? What are some ways marketers are trying to keep the Hispanic subculture separate?*

## 5. Asian Americans

a. Although their numbers are relatively small, Asian Americans are the fastest-growing minority group in the United States. Interesting statistics include:

1) The average household income is $2,000 greater than whites; $7,000–$9,000 greater than African Americans and Hispanics.

2) College graduation rate is twice that of whites and quadruple that of African Americans and Hispanics.

*Discussion Opportunity—Ask: Why do you think Asian Americans put such an emphasis on education? How can marketers capitalize on the high education level of Asian Americans?*

Segmenting Asian Americans

b. Despite the potential, this group is hard to market to because it is actually comprised of many subgroups that may have different languages and cultures. Characteristics of this diverse group include:

1) Chinese is the largest, followed by Filipino and Japanese.

2) Mass marketing techniques are often not viable to this group.

3) They generally save more of their wages and borrow less.

4) They are status conscious and buy premium brands.

*Discussion Opportunity—Ask: How are the various Asian American groups different from each other? What can marketers do to avoid embarrassment and costly cultural blunders in their promotions?*

*Discussion Opportunity—The text indicates that the term* Asian *refers to 20 ethnic groups. Do research to determine what these groups are. Comment on the diversity.*

c. Some rules for reaching this market would include:

1) Use English in the broadcast media and use the native language in print.

2) The most frequently spoken languages are Mandarin Chinese, Korean, Japanese, and Vietnamese. Filipinos predominately speak English.

3) Consider adding Asian versions of American products for this market.

*Discussion Opportunity—What should marketers emphasize when trying to appeal to the Asian market? What should they avoid?*

> *Discussion Opportunity—Research the Chinese belief of feng shui. What ramifications could this have for marketers? Explain.*

## 6. Religious Subcultures

a. Recent years have witnessed a resurgence of interest in religion and spirituality. Spiritually oriented books are a growing segment in adult publishing.

b. More churches are adopting aggressive marketing orientations, including the more than 400 **megachurches** (churches serving more than 2,000 congregants per week).

The Impact of Religion on Consumption

c. Religion influences attitudes toward sexuality, birthrates, household formulation, income, and political attitudes.

  1) There are 2 billion Christians, 1.2 billion Muslims, 900 million Hindus, 315 million Buddhists, 15 million Jews, and 190 million in a category called Primal Indigenous.

  2) The primary American religion is Protestant (57 percent) followed by Catholic (25 percent).

  3) Because of religious freedom, America has long been a place where new religions could develop.

  4) Various new religious movements are flourishing throughout the world. Such groups include the Raelians, the Ahmadis, Brahma Kumaris World Spiritual University, Cao Dai, Soka Gakkai International, the Toronto Blessing, and Umbanda.

---

**\*\*\*\*\*Use Consumer Behavior Challenges #3, #6, and #7 Here \*\*\*\*\***

---

  5) Most religious-oriented marketing activity in the United States can be traced to **Born-Again Christians**. These are those who follow literal interpretations of the Bible and who acknowledge being born again through belief in Jesus.

    a) Some 72 million of the 235 million Christians in the United States claim to be born-again.

    b) Christian bookstore revenues are more than $2 billion per year.

> *Discussion Opportunity—Bring examples of how religion seems to affect consumption or promotion.*

> *Discussion Opportunity—Ask: Can you think of some products that appeal primarily to Catholics? How should these be marketed?*

> *Discussion Opportunity—Ask: Can you think of products that would appeal more to Protestants than to any other religious subculture? How do you feel about adding religion into a marketing effort?*

> *Discussion Opportunity—Ask: How do the values and attitudes of a born-again Christian affect consumer behavior and consumption?*

> *Discussion Opportunity—Ask: What products appeal more to Jews than to members of other religious subcultures?*

# End-of-Chapter Support Material

# SUMMARY OF SPECIAL FEATURE BOXES

**1.     Net Profit I**

This box illustrates how the Internet has been used to form "countries." Various individuals have started their own micronations and have promoted and developed them through the Internet. This feature supports the section "Subcultures and Consumer Identity."

**2.     Marketing Pitfalls I**

This box illustrates the problems that arise when commercial products feature sacred religious and cultural symbols. This feature supports the section "Ethnicity and Marketing Strategies."

**3.     The Tangled Web**

This box summarizes various popular video games that are centered around racial stereotypes and have come under fire by consumer groups. This feature supports the section "Ethnic and Racial Stereotypes."

**4.     Marketing Opportunity I**

Hispanic Americans use the Internet almost twice as frequently as the overall population to listen to music and watch video clips. Big advertisers are responding through this medium. This feature supports the section "Hispanic Americans."

**5.     Net Profit II**

This box focuses on how the growing level of affluence among the Asian immigrant population is creating a new market for Asian products. Examples for Chinese products are given. This feature supports the section "Asian Americans."

**6.     Marketing Opportunity II**

This box examines how multilevel marketing companies have been able to penetrate closed religious subcultures by recruiting members. Various examples are given. This feature supports the section "Religious Subcultures."

### 7.     The Global Looking Glass

This box provides an illustration of how "Americanization" is not the only global cultural trend.

### 8.     Net Profit III

This box features the expanding applications of the Internet for religious purposes. Not only are religious-oriented Web sites using the Net to disseminate information and recruit, but the Internet is increasingly being used by worshippers as a substitute for more traditional activities. This feature supports the section "Religious Subcultures."

### 9.     Marketing Pitfalls II

This box features various examples of how marketing efforts that reference religious themes can result in negative reactions. This feature supports the section "Religious Subcultures."

# REVIEW QUESTIONS

1.     What is a subculture? How does it differ from a microculture? *Consumers' lifestyles are affected by group memberships within the society-at-large. We call these groups subcultures, whose members share beliefs and common experiences that set them apart from others. Every consumer belongs to many subcultures. These memberships can be based on similarities in age, race or ethnic background, or place of residence. Other groups form around a strong shared identification with an activity or art form; these are called microcultures. A good example is the microculture that automobile hobbyists call "Tuners."*

2.     What is the difference between a high-context and a low-context culture? What is an example of this difference? *In a high-context culture, group members tend to be tightly knit, and they are likely to infer meanings that go beyond the spoken word. Symbols and gestures, rather than words, carry much of the weight of the message. In contrast, people in a low-context culture are more literal.*

3.     Why is it difficult to identify consumers in terms of their ethnic subculture membership? *In the 2000 U.S. Census, some 7 million people identified with two or more races, refusing to describe themselves as only white, black, Asian, Korean, Samoan or one of the other categories listed*

4.     What is de-ethnicization? Give an example. *De-ethnicization refers to the process whereby a product formerly associated with a specific ethnic group is detached from its roots and marketed to other subcultures.*

5.     Why are Hispanic American consumers attractive to marketers? *The Hispanic subculture is a sleeping giant that until recently many U.S. marketers largely ignored. The growth*

*and increasing affluence of this group has now made it impossible to overlook, and major corporations avidly court Hispanic consumers. Marketers especially like the fact that Hispanics tend to be brand loyal. In one study, about 45 percent reported that they always buy their usual brand, whereas only one in five said they frequently switch brands. Another study found that Hispanics who strongly identify with their ethnic origin are more likely to seek Hispanic vendors, to be loyal to brands used by family and friends, and to be influenced by Hispanic media. This segment is also highly concentrated geographically by country of origin, which makes them relatively easy to reach. More than 50 percent of all Hispanic Americans live in the Los Angeles, New York, Miami, San Antonio, San Francisco, and Chicago metropolitan areas.*

6. What is acculturation? How does it differ from enculturation? *Acculturation refers to the process of movement and adaptation to one country's cultural environment by a person from another country.*

7. Who are acculturation agents? Give two examples. *The person's contact with acculturation agents—people and institutions that teach the ways of a culture—are also crucial. Some of these agents are aligned with the culture of origin (in this case, Mexico), including family, friends, the church, local businesses, and Spanish-language media that keep the consumer in touch with her country of origin. Other agents are associated with the culture of immigration (in this case, America) and help the consumer to learn how to navigate in the new environment. These include public schools, English-language media, and government agencies.*

8. Describe the processes involved when a person assimilates into a new host culture. *Several processes come into play as immigrants adapt to their new surroundings. Movement refers to the factors motivating people to physically uproot themselves from one location and go to another. In this case, people leave Mexico because of the scarcity of jobs and the desire to provide a good education for their children. On arrival, immigrants encounter a need for translation. This means attempting to master a set of rules for operating in the new environment, whether learning how to decipher a different currency or figuring out the social meanings of unfamiliar clothing styles. This cultural learning leads to a process of adaptation, by which people form new consumption patterns. For example, some of the Mexican women interviewed started to wear shorts and pants since settling in the United States, although this practice is frowned upon in Mexico.*

*During the acculturation process, many immigrants undergo assimilation, where they adopt products, habits, and values that are identified with the mainstream culture. At the same time, there is an attempt at maintenance of practices associated with the culture of origin. Immigrants stay in touch with people in their country and, like Maria, many continue to eat Spanish foods and read Spanish newspapers. Their continued identification with Mexican culture may cause resistance, as they resent the pressure to submerge their Mexican identities and take on new roles. Finally, immigrants (voluntarily or not) tend to exhibit segregation; they are likely to live and shop in places that are physically separated from mainstream Anglo consumers. These processes illustrate that ethnicity is a fluid concept, and the boundaries of a subculture are constantly being re-created.*

9.    Why are Asian Americans an attractive market segment? Why can they be difficult for marketers to reach? Why all the interest? *Asians not only make up the fastest-growing population group, but they are generally the most affluent, best educated, and most likely to hold technology jobs of any ethnic subculture. Indeed, Asian Americans are much more likely than average Americans to buy high-tech gadgets. They are almost three times as likely to own a digital camcorder and twice as likely to have an MP3 player. About 32 percent of Asian households have incomes of more than $50,000 compared to 29 percent in the entire U.S. population. Estimates put this segment's buying power at $253 billion annually. That explains why the brokerage firm Charles Schwab now employs more than 300 people who speak Chinese, Korean, and Vietnamese at its call centers.*

*Despite its potential, this group is hard to market to because it actually is composed of subgroups that are culturally diverse and speak many different languages and dialects. The term* Asian *refers to 20 ethnic groups, with Chinese being the largest and Filipino and Japanese second and third, respectively. Filipinos are the only Asians who predominantly speak English among themselves; most Asians prefer media in their own languages. The most frequently spoken languages among Asian Americans are Mandarin Chinese, Korean, Japanese, and Vietnamese.*

10.   How can we compare consumers' allegiance to some products as a form of religious observance? *You don't have to be active in an organized religion to "worship" products. A recent study of a brand community centered on the Apple Newton illustrates how religious themes can spill over into everyday consumption, particularly in the case of "cult products." Apple abandoned the Newton PDA years ago, but many avid users still keep the faith.*

11.   How do religious subcultures affect consumption decisions? *In some cases dietary or dress requirements create demand for certain products, and these items then may gain in popularity among other groups. For example, less than one-third of the 6 million consumers who buy kosher products are Jewish. Seventh-Day Adventists and Muslims have very similar dietary requirements, and other people simply believe that kosher food is of higher quality. That's why some of the nation's largest manufacturers get involved. About two-thirds of Pepperidge Farm's products, for example, are kosher.*

*In addition to food products, religious subcultures in particular may exert a significant impact on consumer variables such as personality, attitudes toward sexuality, birthrates and household formation, income, and political attitudes. Church leaders can encourage consumption, but more importantly, they can* discourage *it—sometimes with powerful effects.*

# CONSUMER BEHAVIOR CHALLENGE

## Discussion Questions

1.  Some industry experts feel that it's acceptable to appropriate symbols from another culture even if the buyer does not know their original meaning. They argue that even in the host society there is often disagreement about these meanings. What do you think?

    *This is delicate territory. Most all companies are going to offend someone or some group at some point. But when taking on cultural symbols, companies should have the responsibility to at least know the meaning and the potential impact of using such symbols in a commercial sense. Then, if they wish to use them anyway, at least they will have done so in an informed manner.*

2.  The prominence of black characters in videogames containing violent story lines is all the more striking because of the narrow range of video games in which blacks have been present over the years. One study found that of 1,500 videogame characters surveyed, 288 were African American males—and 83 percent of those were athletes. Do you think this is a problem, and if so how would you address it?

    *Students will have various takes on this. The prevalence of black athletes in video games is reflective of the prevalence of African American athletes in real life. These individuals have achieved great success in professional sports at a ratio much higher than that of the general population or any other ethnic group. So, why should anyone be offended? The flip side will be that the games are propagating stereotypes and that that is not responsible.*

3.  Should members of a religious group adapt marketing techniques that manufacturers customarily use to increase market share for their products? Why or why not?

    *Most students will probably say that some level of marketing used by churches and religious groups is fine. After all, without any kind of promotion, how are the members of an organization supposed to be informed about the services that a church offers? Worshippers and potential worshippers have needs and desires, just like any consumers in any consumer context. So, it seems fitting that churches attempt to meet the needs of the members of their congregation. However, some students will probably raise the issue that there is a line in marketing something like religion. A Starbucks outlet in a church? It has happened.*

4.  Several years ago R. J. Reynolds announced plans to testmarket a menthol cigarette called Uptown specifically to black consumers. According to the company, about 70 percent of black smokers prefer menthol, more than twice the average rate. After market research showed that blacks tend to open cigarette packs from the bottom, the company decided to pack Uptowns with the filters facing down. Reynolds cancelled its plans after private health groups and government officials protested. Does a company have the right to exploit a subculture's special characteristics, especially to increase sales of a harmful

product such as cigarettes? What about the argument that virtually every business that follows the marketing concept designs a product to meet the needs and tastes of a preselected segment?

*The instructor should anticipate a high level of interest and involvement with the issues represented in the RJR case. As in the case of targeting gays and the handicapped, there is likely to be a difference of opinion. It would be particularly interesting to hear the perspectives of both white and black students on this specific case. Generally, students should be able to think about and critically examine the issues regarding segmentation (on any basis) in order to meet the unique needs and wants of consumers and to increase overall sales of the product.*

5.  Describe the progressive learning model and discuss why this phenomenon is important when marketing to subcultures.

*The progressive learning model states that people gradually learn a new culture as they increasingly come in contact with it. As stated in the text, this model leads us to expect the consumer behavior of Hispanic Americans, for example, to be a mixture of practices taken from their original culture (e.g., Spanish, Mexican, etc.) and those of the new host culture (United States). Students should focus their discussions on the implications of this model for marketing strategy.*

6.  Born-again Christian groups have been instrumental in organizing boycotts of products advertised on shows they find objectionable, especially those that they feel undermine family values. Do consumer groups have a right or a responsibility to dictate the advertising a network should carry?

*As with many of the previous exercises, the answer to this question is a matter of individual opinion. As always, the instructor should encourage students to consider both sides of the argument and develop examples or cases to defend both positions, regardless of their personal opinions.*

7.  Religious symbolism increasingly is being used in advertising, even though some people object to this practice. For example, a French Volkswagen ad for the relaunch of the Golf model showed a modern version of the Last Supper with the tag line, "Let us rejoice, my friends, for a new Golf has been born." A group of clergy in France sued the company and the ad had to be removed from 10,000 billboards. One of the bishops involved in the suit said, "Advertising experts have told us that ads aim for the sacred in order to shock, because using sex does not work anymore." Do you agree? Should religion be used to market products? Do you find this strategy effective or offensive? When and where is this appropriate, if at all?

*In answering this question, students may come up with numerous related incidents to illustrate the impact of highlighting religion in popular culture and advertising. One interesting approach to this issue (and related issues of offenses based on any other group or subculture) might be to suggest that there should be no censure of such material at all; that in a society where free speech is a core value, such material should not need to be censured or regulated. If indeed companies cross the line, then the market should take care of itself by a decrease in demand for products produced by such companies.*

## Application Questions

8.    Locate current examples of marketing stimuli that depend on an ethnic stereotype to communicate a message. How effective are these appeals?

*Students are likely to identify beer companies for their practice of ethnic segmentation in advertising. To target Hispanic Americans or African Americans, for example, advertisers are employing well-known Hispanic American and African American personalities (e.g., movie stars, professional athletes, etc.) to promote their products. It is likely that these appeals are effective when the consumer feels a sense of identity or affinity with the spokesperson.*

9.    To understand the power of ethnic stereotypes, conduct your own poll. For a set of ethnic groups, ask people to anonymously provide attributes (including personality traits and products) most likely to characterize each group using the technique of free association. How much agreement do you obtain across respondents? To what extent do the characteristics derive from or reflect negative stereotypes? Compare the associations for an ethnic group between actual members of that group and nonmembers.

*Students should be encouraged to conduct their own research for this exercise and many others. This may be a good time for the instructor to emphasize the importance and value of market and consumer research efforts.*

10.   Locate one or more consumers (perhaps family members) who have emigrated from another country. Interview them about how they adapted to their host culture. In particular, what changes did they make in their consumption practices over time?

*You might want to ask the class if anyone personally knows someone who has emigrated to the United States or if they personally know a foreign student at your university before making this assignment. The class will be able to discuss this question in more depth if someone who personally knows an immigrant conducts this interview.*

# CASE STUDY TEACHING NOTES

## Chapter 14 Case Study: Rollin' in My Es-Co-Lade

## Summary of Case

It is no secret that the Cadillac Escalade has become a status symbol within the hip-hop culture. May rappers have sung about the vehicle and have featured customized versions in their videos. It is one of the vehicles of choice for NBA players. But what students may not know prior to reading this case is that Cadillac is on board with this. They have taken a proactive approach to recognizing and targeting this segment. This is a challenge for a company led by aging white males who are, for the most part, targeting aging white consumers. But the revenues brought in by young African Americans has brought such profits that the group cannot be ignored. This case features efforts by the company to make the next generation Escalade a big hit with its fans.

## Suggestions for Presentation

This case has an obvious direct link to the section on African Americans. However, the principles of this application will stretch to any of the ethnic or even religious groups discussed in the chapter. The basic concept is that subcultures are verifiable groups with values, characteristics, desires, and so on. If they are wanting or needing something, then in many respects, it is the responsibility of the marketer to recognize that. Have students read this case and prepare responses to the discussion questions as a means of illustrating the core principles of this chapter.

This case also has application to Chapter 13 and the section on status symbols.

## Suggested Answers for Discussion Questions

1.    Describe Cadillac's "new customer" as a subculture.

     *The case gives plenty of information about this. This new customer is predominantly young, African American, and has some money. Although many of the figures in the media who choose these vehicles are larger-than-normal males (professional athletes) that is not necessarily the characteristic of the subculture that is following the trend set by these individuals. The new customer is defined by the hip-hop subculture. This means that other products are included as part of the customer description, including music, fashion, food, and beverages.*

2.    Discuss the features and attributes (tangible and intangible) of the Escalade that have made it a hip-hop hit. Do you think that Cadillac can extend this appeal to its other models? Why or why not?

*The vehicle is large and has a looming presence. It has an edgy design. It can handle the biggest customer wheels available as aftermarket add-ons. It has a powerful motor. Fashion trends are tricky. What is cool today may be old school tomorrow. However, given the efforts that Cadillac is making, the new model should be successful as long as it does not deviate too much from the basic formula that has made it a hit with this subculture.*

# Additional Support Material

# STUDENT PROJECTS

## Individual Projects

1.  Using the Model of Consumer Acculturation in Figure 14.2 as a guide, have students find examples of how marketing campaigns have played a significant role in this process for some ethnic subculture.

2.  Have each student list four or five major religions, then have them list products that each religion would or would not buy because of their faith. Can they find any examples of how companies have catered to such patterns?

3.  Bring some magazines to class that are primarily targeted toward either African American or Caucasian audiences. Ask the students to look through each type of magazine and select advertisements that are similar, except for the models. Are there any other differences between the ads (e.g., language, models, social situation, etc.)? Explain.

4.  Have individual students bring to class print ads aimed at a particular subculture and show how the ads attempt to address the group. Do the students think they are effective?

5.  Conduct this as an in-class activity. Discuss the differences between Middle Eastern consumers, Indian consumers, and Chinese consumers. Are all of these cultural and racial groups labeled Asian? If not, how are they labeled? Are the labels important from a consumer behavior standpoint?

6.  Assign students to interview a member of a subculture other than his or her own (e.g., African American, Hispanic American, Asian American, white, Catholic, Mormon, Jewish, etc.) to discover what types of products or services are purchased because of membership in this particular group. What are some marketing implications?

7.  Have students interview a member of an ethnic or religious subculture (e.g., African American, Hispanic American, Asian American, Lutheran, Jewish, Baptist, etc.) to see if the person can identify additional subcultures within the subculture. What are the subtle differences and are any of these significant to marketers?

8.      Have a student visit a toy store to observe the various types of toys that are for sale to ethnic subcultures. Have them give a report on the range of toys available and specify the intended racial or ethnic markets.

9.      Send students to a retail store of their choice and have them comment on ethnic symbols that may or may not be used in marketing the store's products. For example, are mannequins racially diverse? Should retail stores follow a policy of appealing to ethnic groups with symbols? Explain.

10.     Have students watch television programs based on ethnicity or subcultures. Watch one and describe how the show might appeal to an ethnic or subculture group. Notice the ads. Were there any differences between the products or services advertised in the show? Were there any differences between the ways the ads appeared? Comment.

11.     Assign students to talk to a religious professional (e.g., minister or priest) about his views toward marketing to consumers based on religious preferences. What is his opinion? Does he market his religion? If so, how? Comment on whether you agree with this policy or not.

## Group Projects

1.      Have student groups research a church. This should be done through secondary methods as well as visiting the church and making observations. An interview with the pastor might also be appropriate. How are these churches focusing on recruiting new members as well as retaining existing members? Does it appear that there is any compromising of doctrines in engaging in such activities?

2.      Assign student groups to visit two local supermarkets to find out if either has segmented their market on the basis of the subculture or ethnic background of their customers. How many subcultures are recognized by each supermarket? Have the students talk to the store manager if possible.

3.      Assign a student group to interview an account executive from an advertising agency and ask this person about marketing to ethnic subcultures, particularly the African American and Hispanic American markets. Among other things, have them question the person on whether they see a line between marketing responsibly to such groups and carrying out racial stereotypes.

4.      Have student groups assume that they are a product management team in charge of developing a promotional strategy for a product of their choice. Have students use the knowledge gained while reading this chapter to design an effective campaign for an ethnic or religious subculture, also of their choice.

5.      So that students can better understand the power of ethnic stereotypes, have them conduct a poll. Assign each group of students an ethnic group (e.g., white, black, Hispanic,

Asian). Have them then ask people to anonymously provide attributes (including personality traits and product purchases) most likely to characterize that group (for any group that is highlighted, have students poll individuals who are not from that group). Have each group share their results. Initiate a discussion as to what these stereotypes imply. Are any of them true? What does this imply for marketers?

6. Have groups prepare a list of holidays that are oriented toward a particular subculture (e.g., Cinco de Mayo, Martin Luther King's Birthday, Passover, Easter, St. Patrick's Day, etc.). Now have them ask a few people if they celebrate or commemorate these holidays. What are the marketing implications? (Make sure that some of the people interviewed belong to the subcultures chosen.)

7. Have the class discuss the concept of interracial marriage. Remember that this discussion should be sensitive to the feelings of all class members. How do marketers treat interracial marriage in campaigns? How do marketers treat adoption of children who are outside the adoptive parents' race? What might be the ethical considerations of either of these questions?

8. Have students discuss where they believe the greatest influx of immigrants will come from in the next 10 years. What marketing ramifications will this cause?

9. Assign student groups to attend a function (e.g., a movie, dance, church, or social gathering) where they are in the minority. This may be difficult if the group is ethnically diverse. They may need to go to more than one function. Have them describe their . experience and feelings to the members of the group. Have the group reach a consensus on racial harmony and bigotry based on the group's experiences. Relate these feelings to marketing efforts to market to racial groups. Do marketers help or hurt integration of racial groups and positive diversity? Explain.

# eLAB

## Individual Assignments

1. Go to the following: **www.bet.com**, **www.jetmag.com**, **www.ebony.com**, and **www.vibe.com**. What do these African American interest Web sites have in common? How do they use desire for ethnicity to their advantage? Would members of other races be attracted to these sites? If so, why? State your general impressions of these sites. Do you think they will succeed in the long run? Explain.

2. Go to **www.tigerwoods.com**. Tiger Woods has been lauded as a person who has broken the barrier of race in professional golf. His heritage is that of many different races. Find evidence on this Web site to support the concept of de-ethnicization.

3.      Go to **www.catholic.org**, **www.lds.org**, **www.scientology.com**, and **www.baptist.org**. Each of these sites expresses thoughts about religion and religious freedom. What techniques do the sites use to stimulate their audiences to follow their messages and commit to participation? How can marketers use religious Web sites to their advantage? Is there a potential conflict of interest or ethical dilemma in using religious Web sites for commercial purposes? Explain.

4.      Go to **www.indiaprofile.com** and **www.goindiago.com**. These interesting Web sites give the viewer information on the Indian culture and fashion. How could these sites increase their appeal to a more diverse audience? What aspect of Indian culture would you like to learn more about? How could you do this? What Indian products might be of interest to you? Where could you purchase these items?

5.      Go to **www.margaritaville.com**, **www.fubu.com**, **www.p-diddy.com**, and **www.anime.com**. What techniques learned in the chapter are used by these Web sites to attract their audiences? What evidence of ethnicity do you observe? Is there anything "cultish" about the Web sites? If so, is that bad? Explain. How could these sites attract larger audiences?


## Group Assignments

1.      Have your group explore **www.starwars.com** and **www.lucasfilm.com**. How do these sites make appeals to their selected audiences? What are the strongest features of the Web sites? Write a brief marketing plan for each of the Web sites to attract more African American, Hispanic American, and Asian American visitors. What do your plans have in common? Predict the success of your marketing planning effort.

2.      Go to **www.bratzpack.com**. Have your group analyze how this popular toy site attempts to broaden its base to various ethnic groups. After analyzing the Web site, write a brief summary plan that demonstrates your group's ideas for broadening the ethnic appeal of the Web site. Could the site appeal to religious groups? If so, how could this be done without offending existing and future customers? Explain.

# CHAPTER 15

# *AGE SUBCULTURES*

## CHAPTER OBJECTIVES

When students finish this chapter they should understand why:

- People have many things in common with others merely because they are about the same age.

- Teens are an important age segment for marketers, but they are undergoing many changes that influence their behavior as consumers.

- Baby boomers continue to be the most powerful age segment economically.

- Seniors will increase in importance as a market segment.

## CHAPTER SUMMARY

People have many things in common with others merely because they are about the same age or live in the same part of the country. Consumers who grew up at the same time share many cultural memories and belong to the same *age cohort*. Consumers often feel positively about products they used when they were younger, so they may be receptive to marketers' *nostalgia* appeals that remind them of these experiences.

Four important age cohorts are teens, college students, baby boomers, and senior consumers. Teenagers are making a transition from childhood to adulthood, and their self-concepts tend to be unstable. They are receptive to products that help them to be accepted and enable them to assert their independence. Because many teens earn money but have few financial obligations, they are a particularly important segment for many nonessential or expressive products, ranging from chewing gum to clothing fashions and music. Due to changes in family structure, many teens also are taking more responsibility for their families' day-to-day shopping and routine purchase decisions.

College students are an important market, but they are hard to reach via conventional media. In many cases, they are living alone for the first time, so they are making important decisions about setting up a household. Many marketers appeal to this group by staging events or other elaborate promotions.

*Baby boomers* are the most powerful age segment because of their size and economic clout. As this group ages, its interests have changed and marketing priorities have changed as well. The needs and desires of baby boomers affect demands for housing, childcare, automobiles, and clothing. Only a small proportion of boomers are as affluent and materialistic as all are assumed to be.

As the population ages, the needs of mature consumers will also become increasingly influential. Many marketers traditionally ignored seniors because of the stereotype that they are too inactive and spend too little. This stereotype is no longer accurate. Most of the seniors are healthy, vigorous, and interested in new products and experiences—and they have the income to purchase them. Marketing appeals to this age subculture should focus on consumers' self-concepts and perceived ages, which tend to be more youthful than their chronological ages. Marketers also should emphasize concrete benefits of products, because this group tends to be skeptical of vague, image-related promotions. Personalized service is of particular importance to this segment.

# CHAPTER OUTLINE

## 1. Age and Consumer Identity

  a. The era in which a consumer is born creates for that person a cultural bond with the millions of others born during that same time period. As we grow older, our needs and preferences change, often in unison with others who are close to our own age.

    1) Marketers must recognize age changes and figure out how to effectively communicate with each age group.

      a) Age exerts a significant influence on one's identity.

      b) Communication must be in an age group's own particular language.

---

*Discussion Opportunity—Give an example of how a person's age group affects his or her identity.*

---

  Age Cohorts: "My Generation"

  b. An **age cohort** consists of people of similar ages who have undergone similar experiences. They often share similar memories (i.e., cultural heroes and important historical events).

    1) Marketers often target products and services to one or more specific age cohorts.

    2) Campaigns can be developed to attract consumers of different ages.

---

*****Use Figure 15.1 Here; Use Table 15.1 Here *****

---

*Discussion Opportunity—Have students make a list of products (services, people, ideas) that have special appeal or memories to their age group. Have them make a similar list including the same categories for their parents or grandparents and for consumers younger than 12. How are the lists similar? How are they different? Ask: Do you find that you are beginning to have more in common with your parents than with someone younger than 12? Why do you think this is occurring?*

*Discussion Opportunity—Ask: After examining the age cohorts found in Figure 15.1, what do you think would be a better way to subdivide the chart? Explain.*

   c. Values and symbolism used to appeal to age cohorts can evoke powerful feelings of nostalgia.
     1) Adults older than 30 are the most susceptible to nostalgia. Many advertising campaigns appeal to nostalgia for groups by using music from the nostalgic time period.

***\*\*\*\*\*Use Table 15.1 Here (Used Previously);***
***Use Consumer Behavior Challenge #1 Here \*\*\*\*\****

*Discussion Opportunity—Ask: What is nostalgic to you? Think back to earlier school years. What products were popular? Do you still use these products (if you can find them)? What is your all-time favorite musical group? How do marketers revive markets for nostalgic products? Would the technique work with you?*

## 2. The Youth Market
   a. The concept of a teenager is a relatively new idea (originating in the 1950s).
     1) The teenager is often described as being rebellious.
     2) Teens today are called **Generation Y** kids (among other things). This generation was born between 1979 and 1994.

***\*\*\*\*\*Use Figure 15.2 Here \*\*\*\*\****

Teen Values, Conflicts, and Desires
   b. This can be the best of times and the worst of times. It is a time of uncertainty and development of choices in activities, friends, and looks. There are serious social consequences to almost everything.
     1) Teens search for cues from their peers and from advertising for the "right" way to look and behave.
     2) Teens use products to express their identities, to explore the world and their newfound freedoms in it, and also to rebel against the authority of their parents and other socializing agents. Marketers often do their best to assist in this process.

360

   c. According to research done by Saatchi & Saatchi, there are four themes common
     to all teens:
     1) ***Autonomy versus belonging***—want independence but need support.
     2) ***Rebellion versus conformity***—rebellion against social norms but want acceptance.
     3) ***Idealism versus pragmatism***—must reconcile how the world should be with reality.
     4) ***Narcissism versus intimacy***—obsessed with appearance but want sincere relationships.
   d. The nature of teens in different countries and cultures is similar in many ways but has
     some differences.

   e. Some teenagers fall into special categories (ages 8 to 14) where they are
     neither children nor real teenagers. This group is called **tweens**.
   f. Generation Y kids go by various names, including Echo Boomers and Millennials.
     1) They spend $170 billion a year.
     2) They are very tech-savvy, being the first to always have had PCs in their lives.
     3) They tend to "fit in" more than their older siblings or even their parents.
     4) Gen Y-ers are jugglers who place high value on being both footloose and connected
       through technology, a condition known as **connexity**.
   g. This group has been raised on television, however, many believe that the advertising
     found on television is based on "lies and hype." They may be more "savvy" than
     older generations went it comes to electronic media. Because of this skepticism, there
     are rules of engagement for marketers to engage with young consumers:
     1) Rule 1: Don't Talk Down.
     2) Rule 2: Don't Try to Be What You're Not.
     3) Rule 3: Entertain Them. Make It Interactive and Keep the Sell Short.
     4) Rule 4: Show That You Know What They're Going Through, but Keep It Light.
   h. Consumer tribes are most common among youth and teenagers.

Teen Values, Conflicts, and Desires
i. Because of the unique characteristics of the Generation Y segment, research firms are
   coming up with innovative ways of tapping into them.
j. Some firms employ **coolhunters**, youth who are employed to roam the streets and report
   back on the cutting-edge trends.
   1) Being "cool" is extremely important to teens.
   2) Marketers view teens as "consumers-in-training."
   3) Teens exert a big influence on the purchase decisions of their parents. Many
     become the shoppers for the home because of working parents.
   4) Today's teens are more difficult for marketers to reach because they do not like being

marketed to. Marketers must then tread lightly and target this group without them knowing it.

***

*****Use Consumer Behavior Challenges #6, #9, and #10 Here *****

***

*Discussion Opportunity—Ask: What do you think are three of the greatest problems facing a typical teenager (high school student) today? Can you suggest anything that marketers can do to help a teenager during this growing-up period? What would you do differently during your teenage years if you had a "do over"?*

*Discussion Opportunity—Ask: Can you think of ways you influenced your parents' buying decisions when you were a teenager? What was your "track record"?*

  k. Advertisers spend more than $100 million a year to influence the purchases of college students, who in turn purchase $20 billion worth of products a year. Most students have about $200 in discretionary money per month after expenses.
    1) College students pose a special challenge because they are difficult to reach with traditional media.
    2) Sampler boxes have proven to be successful (often distributed through dorms).
      a) Posters in dorms (called **wall media**) are also useful in reaching this market.
      b) Spring Break is also a time (and place) where many marketers are investing money to reach college students.

***

***** Use Figure 15.3 Here; Use Consumer Behavior Challenges #2 and #3 Here *****

***

*Discussion Opportunity—Ask: If you were hired to sell a new type of product directly to college students, what do you think would be the best way to reach them? What would your plan include?*

*Discussion Opportunity—Provide the following scenario to the class: Let's say that you were going to design a set that would show a typical dorm room for a college student attending a college or university today. This dorm room would provide the setting in which you would shoot a commercial to sell some product to the student. What would the room look like? What would be in it? What would be on the walls? How would this room be different from 10 or 20 years ago?*

*Discussion Opportunity—Ask: Remember the last time you went on Spring Break? How did marketers attempt to reach you and your fellow students? Evaluate the effectiveness of these techniques.*

Baby Busters: "Generation X"
  l. The cohort of consumers born between 1960 and 1976 consists of 46 million Americans who will be a powerful force through the end of this decade and beyond.
    1) This generation has been labeled "Generation X," "slackers," or "baby busters."

2) Their sense of alienation is echoed by their choices in music, media, and in fashion.

---

*Discussion Opportunity—Regardless of whether you are in "Generation X" or not, what are your impressions of this cohort? Do you think it is misunderstood? What problems and opportunities will this generation face? If you were given the task of appealing to this generation, what approach or theme would you use? Why?*

---

m. Perhaps one reason why marketers' efforts to appeal to X-ers with messages of alienation, cynicism, and despair have not succeeded is that many people in their 20s aren't so depressed after all. This group is actually quite diverse.

## 3. Baby Boomers

a. The **baby boomers** age segment is the source of many fundamental cultural and economic changes. The reason: power in numbers. This group was born between 1946 and 1964.

Economic Power: He Who Pays the Piper Calls the Tune

b. Because of the size and buying power of the boomer group during the last 20 years, marketers pay a lot of attention to this age cohort.

c. The "Woodstock Generation" created a revolution in style, politics, and consumer attitudes.

1) This generation is much more active and physically fit than its predecessors.

---

*****Use Consumer Behavior Challenge #4 Here *****

---

*Discussion Opportunity—Ask: If you were to characterize the baby boomers, how would you describe them? What do you think would "turn them on"? What do you admire about them? What do you dislike about them?*

---

*Discussion Opportunity—Why did Woodstock have such an impact on this generation? How does this impact affect purchasing habits?*

---

d. Consumers aged 35 to 44 spend the most on housing, cars, and entertainment. These consumers also spend the most on food, apparel, and retirement programs.

---

*****Use Consumer Behavior Challenge #4 Here *****

---

*Discussion Opportunity—Propose a plan for marketing to this age group. What factors would you consider? What would be the prime opportunities? What difficulties might you have to face?*

---

## 4. The Gray Market

a. The old image of the elderly person as being one who is infirm, stays at home, and leads a thoroughly depressing life is rapidly changing as an image in the twenty-first century.

Gray Power: Seniors' Economic Chart

b. By 2010, one in every seven Americans will be older than 65. The **gray market** is those consumers aged 55 and older.

   1) Senior citizens have economic clout and will continue to gain in that area.

   2) They currently have 50 percent of all discretionary income and spend $60 billion annually.

   3) Most elderly people lead more active, multidimensional lives than we assume.

   4) Their economic health is good and getting better.

      a) Seniors spend increasing amounts on exercise facilities, cruises and tourism, cosmetic surgery and skin treatments, and "how-to" books and university courses.

      b) Most seniors no longer have the economic burden of their children.

---

*****Use Consumer Behavior Challenge #7 Here *****

---

*Discussion Opportunity—List three university courses that you think might be interesting to seniors. Have the class suggest their own choices. Discuss these choices.*

Understanding Seniors

c. The key values of the elderly are:

   1) *Autonomy*—they want to lead active lives and to be self-sufficient.

   2) *Connectedness*—they want to keep bonds with friends and family.

   3) *Altruism*—they want to give something back to the world.

*Discussion Opportunity—Ask: What do you think are the key values of the elderly? How could these be incorporated into advertising to stimulate their interest in products?*

d. Most elderly perceive of themselves as being 10 to 15 years younger than they actually are.

   1) Age is a state of mind.

   2) A better yardstick to categorize the elderly is **perceived age**—how old a person feels.

   3) There is a "feel age" and a "look age."

   4) Many marketers emphasize product benefits rather than age appropriateness in marketing campaigns, because many consumers will not relate to products targeted to their chronological age.

*Discussion Opportunity—Give illustrations of "feel age" versus "look age." Can you find these differences in advertisements?*

e. Four subsegments appear:

   1) Older—aged 55–64

   2) Elderly—aged 65–74

   3) Aged—aged 75–84

   4) Very old—85+

f. **Social aging theories** try to understand how society assigns people to different

roles across the life span.
1) **Gerontographics** divides the mature market into groups based on both level of physical well-being and social conditions such as becoming a grandparent or losing a spouse.

*****Use Table 15.2 Here *****

*Discussion Opportunity—Taking the information found in Table 15.2, present five good selling ideas for marketing to seniors. Confirm your ideas with the next section—Selling to Seniors. What were the similarities and differences between the text's and your approaches?*

Selling to Seniors
g. Seniors lead more active, multidimensional lives than we assume.
1) Of those older than 65, 80 percent own their own homes (80 percent outright).
2) Businesses are starting to use seniors more and more in their businesses.
3) Products and packages are adapting to seniors.
4) Carmakers are adapting to the special needs of seniors.

*Discussion Opportunity—Find five examples of products or packages that have adapted to the special needs of seniors. Show why you think these adaptations have occurred.*

h. Some suggestions have been offered for advertising to the elderly. They include:
1) Keep language simple.
2) Use clear, bright pictures.
3) Use action to attract attention.
4) Speak clearly and keep the word count low.
5) Use a single sales message and emphasize brand extensions to tap consumers' familiarity.
6) Avoid extraneous stimuli (i.e., excessive pictures and graphics, which can detract from the message).

*****Use Consumer Behavior Challenge #8 Here *****

*Discussion Opportunity—Collect some senior citizen ads. Critique them as per the suggested list given in the text. Point out effective and ineffective characteristics.*

*Discussion Opportunity—Ask: What do you think about old age? How old do you think you will live to be? What do you look forward to? What do you fear? What products do you think you will always use? If you could give three pieces of advice to a 5 year old (based on your life experience so far), what would they be? What pieces of advice have your parents given to you that have proved to be wise statements for living life?*

# End-of-Chapter Support Material

# SUMMARY OF SPECIAL FEATURE BOXES

### 1. Marketing Opportunity I

This box demonstrates how marketers are profiting from high school reunion attendees. The reason for this is that those who tend to go are self-selected successes (failures tend not to show up). This feature supports the section "Age and Consumer Identity."

### 2. Net Profit

This box illustrates how teens are using the Internet to experiment with identity. The anonymity provided by the Net has prompted many teens to go online and communicate with others by either pretending to be someone they are not or by not revealing their identity to friends. This feature supports the section "Teens, Values, Conflicts, and Desires."

### 3. The Global Looking Glass

This box examines how advertising parallels the attitudes of society by showing how European ad campaigns have reflected differing views on Americans over the years.

### 4. Marketing Opportunity II

In order to appeal to the uniqueness of today's youth market, many corporations are engaging in very unlikely partnerships. This special feature supports the section "Marketing to Gen Y."

### 5. Marketing Opportunity III

Teens spend an average of $386 per year to decorate their rooms, more than double the figure a decade ago. Marketers are recognizing this and focusing on it. This special feature supports the section "Marketing to Gen Y."

### 6. Marketing Pitfalls

This box highlights Calvin Klein's strategy of using adolescent sexuality as a basis for ad campaigns since the 1980s. This feature supports the section "Researching the Youth Market."

### 7. Marketing Opportunity IV

This box highlights the current trend in dorm room décor. Marketers have cashed in by targeting designer products to college students. This feature supports the section "Big (Wo)Man on Campus: We're Talking to You!"

## 8. Marketing Opportunity V

Women are now joining men for the midlife crisis. This is especially true with the purchase of an automobile. Women older than 45 are purchasing "mid-sized sporty" cars.

## 9. Net Profit II

This box presents a write-up on how the Internet can be the perfect distribution channel for seniors who can't leave the house. Various Web sites have arisen that target this age group. This feature supports the section "Segmenting Seniors."

## 10. Marketing Opportunity VI

Seniors are fueling a leisure travel boom, seeking out exotic locations. This is due to the fact that once the children leave the nest, people seek experiences rather than possessions.

# REVIEW QUESTIONS

1. What is an age cohort, and why is it of interest to marketers? *An age cohort consists of people of similar ages who have undergone similar experiences. They share many common memories about cultural heroes (e.g., John Wayne versus Brad Pit, important historical events (e.g., World War II versus the 2001 terrorist attacks), and so on. Although there is no universally accepted way to divide up people into age cohorts, each of us seems to have a pretty good idea of what we mean when we refer to "my generation."*

2. List three basic conflicts teens face and give an example of each.

   - *Autonomy versus belonging: Teens need to acquire independence, so they try to break away from their families. On the other hand, they need to attach themselves to a support structure, such as peers, to avoid being alone. One survey of teens found that only 11 percent view themselves as "popular."*
   - *Rebellion versus conformity: Teens need to rebel against social standards of appearance and behavior, yet they still need to fit in and be accepted by others. They prize "in-your-face" products that cultivate a rebellious image like those the retail chain Hot Topic sells for this reason.*
   - *Idealism versus pragmatism: Teens tend to view adults as hypocrites, whereas they see themselves as being sincere. They have to struggle to reconcile their view of how the world should be with the realities they perceive around them.*
   - *Narcissism versus intimacy: Teens are often obsessed with their own appearance and needs. On the other hand, they also feel the desire to connect with others on a meaningful level.*

3.  How are Gen Y kids different from their older brothers and sisters? *Unlike their parents or older siblings, Gen Y-ers tend to hold relatively traditional values and they believe in the value of fitting in rather than rebelling. Their acculturation agents (as we discussed in the previous chapter) stress teamwork—team teaching, team grading, collaborative sports, community service, service learning, and student juries. Violent crime among teenagers is down 60 to 70 percent. The use of tobacco and alcohol are at all-time lows. So is teen pregnancy. Five out of ten echo boomers say they trust the government, and virtually all of them trust mom and dad.*

4.  What are tweens, and why are so many marketers interested in them? *Marketers use the term* tweens *to describe the 27 million children aged 8 to 14 who spend $14 billion a year on clothes, CDs, movies, and other "feel good" products. Tweens are "between" childhood and adolescence and they exhibit characteristics of both age groups. As one tween commented, "When we're alone we get weird and crazy and still act like kids. But in public we act cool, like teenagers.*

5.  How do tribal gatherings represent a marketing opportunity? *Tribal gatherings provide manufacturers with an opportunity to strengthen the group bond by offering accessories such as shoes, key chains, belts and hats, backpacks, sunglasses, T-shirts, and other goodies that reinforce membership. Although many brands of skates are available including K2, Razors, Oxygen, Tecnica, and Nike, the original Rollerblade product retains cult status within the tribe.*

6.  What are some of the most efficient ways for marketers to connect with college students? *Online advertising is very effective: Fully 99 percent of college students go online at least a few times per week and 90 percent do so daily. In addition, enterprises like mtvU.com are blossoming because they reach students where they live and play. These specialized networks are providing college students with irreverent programming designed to appeal to their sense of humor. Other strategies to reach students include the widespread distribution of sampler boxes containing a variety of personal care products in student centers and dormitories and the use of posters (termed* wall media*). In addition, a growing number of marketers are capitalizing on the ritual of Spring Break to reach college students; they estimate that about 40 percent of students now make the annual trek to points south.*

7.  What is a "reward car" and who buys this type of vehicle? *A "reward car" is a sporty car that a woman buys after her kids have grown. Sales of "reward cars" among women older than 45 are skyrocketing.*

8.  What are some industries that stand to benefit most from the increasing affluence and vitality of the senior market? *Travel and hospitality, car sales and rentals, apparel, banking, and others.*

9.  What are some effective ways to segment the senior market? *In addition to chronological age, marketers segment the elderly along such dimensions as the particular years a person came of age (age cohort), current marital status (e.g., widowed versus married),*

*and a person's health and outlook on life. Several segmentation approaches begin with the premise that a major determinant of elderly marketplace behavior is the way a person deals with being old. Social aging theories try to understand how society assigns people to different roles across the life span. For example, when people retire they may reflect society's expectations for someone at this life stage—this is a major transition point when people exit from many relationships. Some people become depressed, withdrawn, and apathetic as they age; some are angry and resist the thought of aging; and others accept the new challenges and opportunities this period of life has to offer. Table 15.2 summarizes some selected findings from one segmentation approach called gerontographics, which divides the mature market into groups based on both level of physical well-being and social conditions such as becoming a grandparent or losing a spouse.*

# CONSUMER BEHAVIOR CHALLENGE

## Discussion Questions

1.  What are some possible marketing opportunities present at reunions? What effects might attending such an event have on consumers' self-esteem, body image, and so on?

    *The marketing opportunities present at reunions are abundant and varied. Many are based on the appeal of nostalgia. Because consumers within an age group confront crucial life changes at roughly the same time, the values and symbolism used to appeal to them can evoke powerful feelings of nostalgia. Marketers have realized that the people who attend reunions often represent a valuable customer base that can be used for new products tests and special promotional activities.*

    *Students are likely to recognize the type of social pressure that is experienced by individuals attending high school, college, or family reunions. Many will be able to relate to individuals' desires to be thin, younger looking, and successful or to be associated with others (e.g., husbands or wives) who are such, when they have an opportunity to see friends, acquaintances, or extended family members on an infrequent basis. In preparation for such an event, many people will spend a lot of time and money to present the perfect image—who they want to be or how they want to be seen in others' eyes—by, among other things, dieting and buying special clothing.*

2.  The chapter describes members of Gen Y as much more traditional and team-oriented than their older brothers and sisters. Do you agree?

    *Given that the traditional college students of today fall into the Gen Y category, this should be an interesting discussion. Do students want to see themselves as "traditional"? If this is a good thing, then they are likely to agree. However, even if this is true, it will be interesting to see if students will want to "fess up."*

3.  What are some of the positives and negatives of targeting college students? Identify some specific marketing strategies that you feel have either been successful or unsuccessful at appealing to this segment. What characteristics distinguish the successes from the failures?

    *According to material found in the chapter, advertisers spend approximately $100 million per year to try and influence this $20 billion market. As noted, the average college student has approximately $200 in discretionary funds each month beyond their basic needs. The marketers would certainly like to capture those dollars. Advantages of pursuing this market include the facts that they have money to spend and they are willing to try new products. Many, however, are inexperienced buyers, are hard to reach through traditional media, and tend to be specialized in the way they receive their information.*

    *As noted in the chapter, one unique way of reaching the college student is the use of sampler boxes and wall media. Students should be challenged to think of other media forms and strategies that might prove to be successful with their market. This question usually results in a lively discussion.*

4.  Why have baby boomers had such an important impact on consumer culture?

    *As stated in the text, the baby boomer segment is the source of many fundamental cultural and economic changes in our society, largely due to its significant size, but also due to the current position of many boomers in lucrative jobs with high levels of responsibility. Because of the size and buying power of the boomer group during the past two decades, marketers have focused their attention on this market and popularized many of its values and lifestyle characteristics, increasing their impact on society at large.*

5.  How has the baby boomlet changed attitudes toward child-rearing practices and created demand for different products and services?

    *As described in the chapter, the baby boomer decided to have children later in life and not have as many. The new emphasis on career by boomer women also has impacted the birth rate. Because many of the boomer women have started hearing the ticking of their "biological clock," there has been a surge in birth rates. It is generally thought that these children (because of pampering) will have more attention and products directed toward them than previous generations. New trends are toward vans (for the family), services (day care facilities for working parents), and new magazines (Working Mother).*

6.  "Kids these days seem content to just hang out, surf the Net, and watch mindless TV shows all day." How accurate is this statement?

    *Students should be encouraged to approach this answer seriously. Once they formulate an answer, they should devise a strategy for reaching this generation of consumers. What impact will this generation of consumers have on marketing in the next century? What about the generation following behind them?*

7.   Is it practical to assume that people age 55 and older constitute one large consumer market? What are some approaches to further segmenting this age subculture?

*Marketers have become convinced that the 55 and older age segment is diverse, with a minimum of four subsegments represented by the 55–64, 65–74, 75–84, and 85 and older categories. Clearly, with people living longer lives, there are going to be considerable differences in the health and general welfare of these individuals. Many will have more income relative to expenditures than at any other time in their lives, affording opportunities for full and rich lifestyles. Ultimately, the most influential characteristic of older adult consumers is their perceived age, or how old they feel.*

## Application Questions

8.   Find good and bad examples of advertising targeted to older consumers. To what degree does advertising stereotype the elderly? What elements of ads or other promotions appear to determine their effectiveness in reaching and persuading this group?

*First, the instructor can use information provided in the preceding question. Second, consider that this question will be an interesting exercise for students and is likely to draw their attention to issues they have not carefully considered to date. Encourage them to find examples of what they view as both positive and negative treatment of the elderly in the media. They can also interview senior citizens to get their view.*

9.   If you were a marketing researcher assigned to study which products are "cool," how would you do this? Do you agree with the definitions of "cool" provided by the young people in the chapter?

*One of the best ways to aid students in answering this question is to pick one of the eLab projects and have them do it for homework. These practical projects will help the students synthesize the material found in the chapter and will aid them in seeing "cool" from someone else's view. It is recommended that time be saved for an in-class discussion—it will be "cool."*

10.  Marketers of entrenched brands like Nike, Pepsi, and Levi Strauss are tearing their hair out over Gen Y consumers. Image-building campaigns (e.g., Michael Jordan endorsing Nike) are not as effective as they once were. Compared to their predecessors, these young consumers seem to be more interested in individuality than in fitting in. For example, Kodak is successfully marketing its "Sticky Film" to young people who use the product to express themselves in original ways. Perhaps this change is partly due to the amount of time young people spend surfing alone on the Web. As a Nike executive put it, "Television drives homogeneity. The Internet drives diversity." What advice would you give to a marketer who wants to appeal to Gen Y? What are major do's and don'ts? Can you provide some examples of specific marketing attempts targeted to Gen Y that work or don't work?

*Considering that the typical college junior and senior at the time of this edition will be in use are Gen Y-ers, the responses to this should be interesting. This question basically asks, "How can marketers get to you?" Considering that most of these students will be marketing majors, they may have different attitudes about marketing than the status quo Gen Y-er. Thus, they may be more willing to reveal their "secrets." Some of the responses that come out may mirror suggestions given in the chapter itself. But because this generation seems to be defined by more diversity, responses may include ideas that reflect more customization in products and services.*

# CASE STUDY TEACHING NOTES

### Chapter 15 Case Study: Scion's Quest to Crack Generation Y

### Summary of Case

This case features Toyota's new division, Scion (pronounce *sigh-on*). The division was created because Toyota was not having much success reaching Generation Y. Highlighted here are not only the characteristics of Generation Y as Toyota has discovered them, but specific tactics that Scion has employed for such characteristics. While this brand is still unknown to many, it is on the charts for the target market. First year sales are exceeding projections by 30 percent, with 85 percent of customers new to Toyota. And Scion has achieved an average age that is among the lowest in the industry.

### Suggestions for Presentation

One of the Marketing Opportunity boxes in the chapter mentions an effort by Toyota to reach Gen Y by creating a Roxy version of the Echo. That project occurred prior to the launch of Scion in 2004. The case of Scion is the perfect illustration of what an aging corporation needs to do to reach Generation Y. The most direct presentation of this case should take place as part of the coverage of Generation Y. However, the concepts of how a company reaches an age cohort are applicable to any of the other segments covered in the chapter.

As a side note to this case, Scion has found unexpected success with people in older age brackets, even though Gen Y has been their target. Gen X and even boomers have looked right past the body-pierced, tattooed image of Scion to recognize true value: small, economical vehicles that are surprisingly roomy, packed with standard features, and have the price of a Hyundai.

## Suggested Answers for Discussion Questions:

1.  Is Toyota wasting its time by paying so much attention to age as a segmentation variable? Explain.

    *Absolutely not. One of the biggest challenges in the automotive industry is that of continuing to appeal to the core customer of a given brand while at the same time trying to appeal to new customers in a younger age bracket. Companies that fail to do this suffer the fate of Oldsmobile and the struggles faced by Cadillac, Buick, Lincoln, Mercury, and other automotive divisions. Toyota is hardly in the same boat as Buick . . . yet. But they took the proactive approach to ensure that they would never be there. Age cohorts have enough similarities within themselves that they are very sound market segments. Generation Y is so unique from the other age segments that going after this segment as a means of garnering new customers was a very smart move by Toyota.*

2.  Considering the characteristics of Generation Y, what do you see as some of the challenges that Scion faces in the future as their brand grows?

    *One of the challenges will be the same as that faced by other car companies: How do you continue to appeal to the target group (especially given their uniqueness and diversity) while trying to appeal to the next generation coming in?*

    *One of the standard trends in the automobile industry is for cars to be introduced as small, low-end vehicles only to grow larger, heavier, and more expensive (Honda Accord and Toyota Camry are cases in point). So, another challenge for Scion will be to adhere to the original value formula that is providing them with success, while also giving the customers the "next big thing."*

    *One last challenge is simply keeping up with nontraditional promotional methods that work on Gen Y. How do you remain incognito and appear as though you are not promoting to someone when, invariably, they will discover that you are? Thus, promotional tactics will need to be very dynamic and flexible.*

# Additional Support Material

# STUDENT PROJECTS

## Individual Projects

1.  Choose a basic product that is used by people of all age groups (soft drink, toothpaste, automobile, etc.). Identify different brands of this product that target different age groups

(Gen Y-ers, Gen X-ers, boomers, seniors). Identify key differences in the product itself as well as in how these brands are promoted, priced, and distributed.

2. Have students bring to class print ads that are aimed at a particular age group and show how these ads attempt to address that group.

3. Ask a student to think of a product that she believes was specifically designed for and marketed to her age group. Why does she believe this? What is her reaction when she sees either younger or older consumers using the product?

4. Have students contact their parents or grandparents. What is nostalgic to them? How have you seen this used in advertising? What products have a nostalgic appeal for them? Do they say that nostalgic appeals work on them? Have them give examples.

5. Have students collect a series of ads for beauty products from magazines published in the 1950s and 1960s and magazines published today. (Check the library and photocopy the old ads.) Have them then estimate the age of the models in the ads. Do they feel these idealized depictions are different today? Is more or less of an age mixture found in magazines today?

6. Ask students to use a product example (i.e., food products, automobiles) to illustrate how the marketer might promote to youths to take advantage of the influence they exert on family-purchase decisions.

7. Ask students to visit two mall stores that are not department stores (i.e., Abercrombie & Fitch, American Eagle, Aeropostale, the Buckle, etc.). How do these stores appeal to the teen market? How does the design of the store differ from that of other stores targeted at other age groups? Do salespeople differ? Does promotion seem to differ?

8. Large shopping malls draw in people of all ages. Have students visit a large mall and note the tactics used to target Gen Y-ers, Gen X-ers, boomers, and seniors. Are there any other single products that seem to be able to simultaneously target multiple age segments?

9. What do you think are the best ways to reach the: (a) teen market, (b) baby boomer market, and (c) senior market with advertising messages? Demonstrate and explain.

10. Have students interview a 6 year old. How are his or her values, product needs, and feelings for what is "cool" different from yours when you were 6? What do you feel you have in common with the 6 year old? How do you feel alienated from him or her?

11. Have students interview someone in his early to mid teens. Ask him about his values, interests, and perceptions of what is "cool." What kinds of products (clothing, electronics, etc.) does he like? After doing this, each student should compare the results to a description of him- or herself at the same age.

12.     Have students give a one-page description of themselves, their time period, and their thoughts in their teenage years. How could a marketer use this information to make appeals to them? What were their favorite expressions? Do they still use these? Do they now seem very out of place except to someone of their generation?


## Group Projects

1.     Find magazine ads from the 1970s targeted at boomers. Locate ads from current publications targeted at the same people. What are the similarities and differences? To what extent are these similarities and differences due to the phase of life, and to what extent are they due to the actual characteristics of the age cohort?

2.     Have student groups go to a senior citizen gathering (this can be any kind of gathering) and interview three men and three women about nostalgia. What were they most nostalgic about? How could this be used in marketing to capture their attention? What did you learn from this experience?

3.     Have student groups visit a local retirement village and observe how the complex is designed to meet the needs of the market segment it is serving. Have the students review the literature provided by the complex to see what techniques are used to market the facility to "seasoned citizens." Is it "cool" to live in a senior's complex? Why or why not?

4.     Have student groups interview men from different age groups (older than 60, 40-60, and 30–39, and 18–29). Ask them about how they watch sporting events. Do they have a preferred ritual (place to watch, with someone or alone, certain food items, etc.)? What are the similarities and differences? What are the implications of these results for the sports teams, networks, and other products mentioned by the respondents?

5.     Have student groups interview a working and a nonworking woman who have children in grade school. Have them write down the menu that they served for the previous evening meal. Ask them about the specific brands that they used to prepare the meal (e.g., bread, beverage, entree, vegetables, fruits, dessert, etc.). Have them then collate this information to discover any similarities and differences.

6.     Have groups look through magazines targeted to a specific age group (e.g., *Seventeen, YM, Boys Life, Modern Maturity,* etc.) and describe the types of articles and advertisements contained in each magazine. How effective are these publications at reaching their target markets?

7.     Have groups find good and bad examples of advertising targeted toward "seasoned citizens." To what extent do these ads stereotype the elderly? Do you think that the elderly would like or resent the implications? Are there any elements in these ads that make them effective in reaching and persuading the elderly? Explain.

8. Ask groups to select two product categories that appear to have good potential for sales to older people but are presently not marketed very well. Design a plan for more effective marketing to take advantage of this opportunity.

9. Have groups interview teens and tweens to determine their feelings toward advertisements and marketers. You may design the experiment any way you choose. After the survey is completed, make a judgment about the teens' and tweens' values and discuss any differences you may see. Were these differences random; due to the respondents' sex; the respondents' age; the respondents' socio-economic status or factors; or something else? Did the group treat advertisements and marketers fairly? Explain. What did you learn from this interview experience?

# eLAB

## Individual Assignments

1. Go to **www.peapod.com** and **www.iping.com**. Each student should identify how the services offered by these Web sites would benefit senior citizens. How can these Web sites better target this age group?

2. Go to **www.snowball.com** and **www.bolt.com**. These are portals geared toward teens. How do these sites differ from Yahoo or Google for information search, ecommerce, and the presentation of other information?

3. Go to **www.teenpeople.com**. Examine what is in style or "cool" for teens. How has style and "coolness" changed since you were a teen? What marketing efforts to persuade teens were used on the Web site? Did you find the style changes attractive and appealing? Explain your feelings.

4. Go to **www.mtv.com**. MTV has been around for a long time. Did you watch it when you were a teen? How has it changed? What new strategies is the organization using to reach its target market of today? Where will the organization be heading in the future? How could it keep its customers and viewers from "growing up" and leaving it as a source of entertainment and information? Plot a strategy that might help with this.

5. Go to **www.cosmogirl.com** and **www.cosmomag.com**. How are these two sites different? What are their two target markets? What messages and values are being transmitted by the two Web sites? How can age and gender be combined by marketers to ensure success? Find two illustrations on the two Web sites to illustrate your thoughts or feelings.

## Group Assignments

1.      Go to **www.selectquote.com**. Run a quote for at least two different types of life insurance for both a male and a female at 20, 40, and 60 years of age. Summarize the results. What are the differences and why do these differences exist? Discuss how companies could effectively target each age group.

2.      Go to **www.groups.yahoo.com**. Have your group join an online community. Over the next week, try to find out information about values from at least three different age cohorts. Prepare a paper that illustrates your findings and the methodology used. Would online communities be a good way to do research on consumers and their values? Explain. What would be the advantages and disadvantages of doing research in this way? What did your group learn from this online experience?

# CHAPTER

# *CULTURAL INFLUENCES ON CONSUMER BEHAVIOR*

## CHAPTER OBJECTIVES

When students finish this chapter they should understand why:

- A culture is a society's personality and our membership in a culture plays a big role in shaping our identities as individuals.

- Myths are stories that express the shared ideals of a culture, and in modern times marketing messages are used to hand these stories down to members.

- Many of our consumption activities including holiday observances, grooming, and gift-giving are based upon deeply ingrained rituals.

- We can describe products as either sacred or profane, and it's not unusual for some products to move back and forth between the two categories.

## CHAPTER SUMMARY

A society's *culture* includes its values, ethics, and the material objects and services produced by its people. It is the accumulation of shared meanings and traditions among members of a society. A culture can be described in terms of ecology (the way people adapt to their habitat), its social structure, and its ideology (including people's moral and aesthetic principles). This chapter describes the primary aspects of culture and focuses on how cultural meanings are created and transmitted across society by its members.

*Myths* are stories containing symbolic elements that express the shared ideals of a culture. Many myths involve some *binary opposition*, where values are defined in terms of what they are and what they are not (e.g., nature versus technology). Modern myths are transmitted through advertising, movies, and other media.

A *ritual* is a set of multiple, symbolic behaviors that occur in a fixed sequence and that tend to be repeated periodically. Rituals are related to many consumption activities that occur in popular culture. These include holiday observances, gift giving, and grooming.

A *rite of passage* is a special kind of ritual that involves the transition from one role to another. These passages typically entail the need to acquire products and services, called ritual artifacts, to facilitate the transition. Modern rites of passage include graduations, fraternity initiations, weddings, debutante balls, and funerals.

Consumer activities can be divided into *sacred* and *profane consumption* domains. Sacred phenomena are "set apart" from everyday activities or products. People, events, or objects can become sacralized. *Objectification* occurs when sacred qualities are ascribed to products or items owned by sacred people. *Sacralization* occurs when ordinary objects, events, and even people take on sacred meaning to a culture or to specific groups within a culture. *Desacralization* occurs when objects that previously were considered sacred become commercialized and integrated into popular culture.

# CHAPTER OUTLINE

**1. Understanding Culture**
   a. Culture—a concept crucial to the understanding of consumer behavior—may be thought of as a society's personality. Put another way, **culture** is the accumulation of shared meanings, rituals, norms, and traditions among the members of an organization or society.
   1) Culture is the "lens" through which people view products.
   2) The importance of cultural expectations often is discovered only when they are violated.
   3) Sensitivity to cultural issues can come only by understanding underlying issues.

---

*Discussion Opportunity—Explain why culture is the "lens" through which people view products.*

---

   b. A consumer's culture determines the overall priorities he or she attaches to different activities and products.
   1) It also mandates the success or failure of specific products and services.
   2) Products and services resonate with the priorities of a culture at any given time.
   3) Products and services can also provide a window onto the dominant cultural ideals of that period.

---

*****Use Consumer Behavior Challenge #1 Here *****

---

*Discussion Opportunity—Ask students how each of the following has affected the American culture: automobiles, microwaves, snowboards, computers, pocket pagers, the pill, leisure time, personal data assistants, Napster, and the Internet? What do you think came first—the attitude or the product?*

c. Culture is not static. It is continually evolving, synthesizing old ideas with new ones. A cultural system consists of three functional ideas:

1) *Ecology*—the way a system adapts to its habitat.

2) *Social structure*—the way in which orderly social life is maintained.

3) *Ideology*—the way in which people relate to their environment and social groups.

    a) This revolves around the belief that members of a society possess a common *worldview* (they share certain ideas about principles of order and fairness).

    b) They also share an ethos (a set of moral and aesthetic principles).

*Discussion Opportunity—State what you think the U.S. culture would have to say about the culture's role in a worldview. State five ethos (principles) that we share.*

d. Although every culture is different, four dimensions appear to account for much of this variability.

1) *Power distance*—how interpersonal relationships form when power differences exist (e.g., employee/boss, student/teacher).

2) *Uncertainty avoidance*—threat created by ambiguous situations.

3) *Masculinity/femininity*—degree to which sex roles are clearly delineated.

4) *Individualism*—do they emphasize individuality or common good of the group.

    a) Cultures differ in their emphasis on individualism versus collectivism.

    b) In **collectivist cultures**, people subordinate their personal goals to those of a stable in-group.

    c) In **individualist cultures**, there is more attachment and importance associated with personal goals, and people are more likely to change memberships when the demands of the group become too costly.

*Discussion Opportunity—Ask: How does a man prove he is masculine in our culture? How does a female prove she is feminine in our culture? How do alternative lifestyles such as homosexuality fit into our culture?*

*Discussion Opportunity—Ask: Do you think the United States puts greater emphasis on individuality or the common good? Bring in ads that demonstrate both positions, however, defend yours.*

e. Values are very general ideas about good and bad goals.

1) From these flow **norms**, or rules dictating what is right or wrong, acceptable or unacceptable. Norms can be:

    a) **Enacted norms**—explicitly decided on (e.g., go on the green light).

    b) **Crescive norms**—embedded in culture and discovered only through interaction with other members of that culture. These include:

        1. A **custom** is a norm handed down from the past that controls basic behaviors.

        2. A **more** is a custom with a strong moral overtone.

        3. **Conventions** are norms regarding the conduct of everyday life.

c) Many norms are learned *vicariously* as we watch others perform life's little rituals.

---

*****Use Consumer Behavior Challenge #11 Here *****

---

*Discussion Opportunity—Give an example of an enacted norm, a crescive norm, a custom, a more, and a convention. Can you find any advertisements that illustrate these?*

---

*Discussion Opportunity—Ask students to give an illustration of how we learn culture vicariously. Think of how you have learned something in this way in the past.*

---

## 2. Myths and Rituals
   a. Stories and practice help us make sense of the world.
   b. Every society has its "good" and "evil" and its "good luck" and "bad luck."

Myths
   c. Every society possesses a set of myths that define that culture. A **myth** is a story containing symbolic elements that express the shared emotions and ideals of a culture.
      1) It often features a conflict between two opposing forces.
      2) It often sets good against evil.
      3) It reduces anxiety because it provides consumers with guidelines about their world.
      4) Strategies can be patterned after these myths.

---

*Discussion Opportunity—Ask students to share their favorite myth. Have them explain how it is used.*

---

   d. Myths serve four interrelated functions in culture:
      1) *Metaphysical*—they help explain the origins of existence.
      2) *Cosmological*—all components are part of a single picture.
      3) *Sociological*—establish a social code to maintain order.
      4) *Psychological*—establish models for personal conduct.

---

*****Use Consumer Behavior Challenges #12 and #13 Here *****

---

*Discussion Opportunity—Think of myths that seem to fall into the categories (functions) mentioned in the chapter (i.e., metaphysical, cosmological, sociological, and psychological). How can these be tied (if they can) to purchasing?*

---

   e. Myths can be analyzed by examining their underlying structures. It has been noted that many stories involve **binary opposition**, where two opposing ends of some dimension are represented. Characters or products are often characterized as to what they "are not" rather than what they "are."

1) Conflict is often resolved by a *mediating figure* (animals are often given human characteristics).
2) A myth common to many cultures is a **monomyth**—a hero emerges from the everyday world and often has super powers (e.g., comic book heroes).
3) Examples of mythic movies include:
   a) *Gone With the Wind*
   b) *E.T.: The Extraterrestrial*
   c) *Star Trek*

*Discussion Opportunity—Have the class explain common myths from their cultures. How do these myths affect their purchase decisions or life?*

*Discussion Opportunity—Bring in an advertisement that you believe uses a myth to sell its products or services.*

*Discussion Opportunity—Ask: What movies do you think are mythical in nature and have changed our culture? What is the most recent mythical movie in your opinion? Why has it achieved this status?*

Rituals
f. A **ritual** is a set of multiple, symbolic behaviors that occur in a fixed sequence and that tend to be repeated periodically. Rituals can occur at a variety of levels.
   1) Many businesses owe their livelihoods to their ability to supply **ritual artifacts**, or items used in the performance of rituals, to consumers.

*****Use Table 16-1 Here *****

*Discussion Opportunity—Ask: What is your morning ritual? What products do you need to support it? What are your primary rituals while at school? Isn't it interesting to think how all of these rituals will change in a few years when you enter the work place full -time (and learn new rituals)?*

*Discussion Opportunity—Ask: What ritual from college, your work place, or your family do you find to be the most fulfilling? Irritating? Explain and describe.*

2) There are many grooming rituals that are dominant themes in commercials.
3) Two sets of binary oppositions expressed in personal rituals are:
   a) *Private/public*.
   b) *Work/leisure*.

*Discussion Opportunity—Ask: What "beauty ritual" do you go through each day?*

g. In the **gift-giving ritual**, consumers procure the perfect object (artifact), meticulously remove the price tag (symbolically changing the item from a commodity to a unique good), carefully wrap it, and deliver it to the recipient.
   1) Westerners see this ritual as a form of *economic exchange*.
   2) Gift giving can be a *symbolic exchange*.
   3) Every culture prescribes certain occasions and ceremonies for giving gifts.

---

*****Use Table 16-2 Here *****

---

*Discussion Opportunity—Ask: What differences are there when you purchase something for someone else versus when you purchase something for yourself?*

---

*Discussion Opportunity—Ask: How do marketers use gift giving to stimulate purchasing? What new occasions have recently been invented for doing this?*

---

h. The gift-giving ritual can be broken down into three distinct stages:
   1) *Gestation*—the giver is motivated by an event to buy a gift.
      a) *Structural*—prescribed by culture (e.g., Christmas present).
      b) *Emergent*—decision is more personal (e.g., husband brings a love gift for his wife).
   2) *Presentation*—recipient responds to gift and donor evaluates the response.
   3) *Reformation*—bonds between parties are adjusted (looser or tighter).
      a) When given a gift, one may feel pressure to respond. The **reciprocity norm** must then be considered.

---

*Discussion Opportunity—Ask: Did you ever receive a present that you did not think was good enough or was too good? How did you respond? Have you ever given a gift where the recipient's response made you wish you had not bought the gift? How did this affect your purchases in the future?*

---

i. One can also give a gift to themselves.
   1) One can reward one's self with a self-gift.

---

*****Use Figure 16-1 Here; Use Consumer Behavior Challenges #2, #5, and #9 Here *****

---

*Discussion Opportunity—Ask: What was the last self-gift you gave yourself? What was different or memorable about the purchase process? Did you feel guilty? How can the marketer deal with this potential guilt as being a reason not to purchase?*

---

j. Holidays are filled with rituals. Common holidays (for gifts) are:
   1) Thanksgiving.
   2) Valentine's Day.
   3) Secretaries' Day.
   4) Grandparents' Day.
   5) Christmas.

6) New Year's.
7) Halloween.

---

*****Use Consumer Behavior Challenge #8 Here *****

---

*Discussion Opportunity—Share examples of gifts that could be associated with these days.*

---

*Discussion Opportunity—Ask: How do you think Halloween should be celebrated (if at all)? What does this say about your culture and your view toward contemporary culture and values?*

---

k. **Rites of passage** can be construed as being special times marked by a change in social status. Every society sets aside times when these passages occur.
   1) Marketers attempt to reach consumers during these passage times.
   2) Stages include:
      a) *Separation*—detaching from the original group.
      b) *Liminality*—person is literally in between statuses.
      c) *Aggregation*—person reenters society after rite-of-passage.

---

*Discussion Opportunity—Ask: How did your family react when you went off to college for your freshman year? When did you first go back home? When did you get back together with your high school friends? What happened when you came back to college this year? If you did not leave home to go to college, how was this process different?*

---

l. The final rite of passage is death. This ritual is tightly scripted in most societies.

---

*****Use Consumer Behavior Challenges #4 and #6 Here *****

---

*Discussion Opportunity—Ask students to think about marketing death. Not very pleasant, is it? It is, however, a huge industry. List the rituals associated with death. How can these be marketed tastefully (to those who do not want to think about the subject)?*

---

**3. Sacred and Profane Consumption**
   a. **Sacred consumption** involves objects and events that are "set apart" from normal activities and are treated with some degree of respect or awe.
   b. **Profane consumption** involves consumer objects and events that are ordinary, everyday objects and events that do not share the "specialness" of sacred ones.

Domains of Sacred Consumption
c. This is ordinary consumption that is not "ordinary."
   1) *Sacred places* are set apart by a society because they have religious or mystical significance or because they commemorate some aspect of a country's heritage. The sacredness of these places is due to the property of **contamination** (something special happened there).
   2) Other places are created from the profane world and given special sacred qualities.

3) In many cultures, home is a particularly sacred place. This is the consumer's "inner space."

**\*\*\*\*\*Use Consumer Behavior Challenge #3 Here \*\*\*\*\***

*Discussion Opportunity—Ask: How do you attempt to make your home special, homey, and even sacred? How can marketers use this desire to market to you?*

*Discussion Opportunity—Describe a special scared place that you have been to.*

d. People themselves can also be sacred.
   1) Memorabilia can take on special meaning—from baseball cards to clothing a special person has touched or worn.

*Discussion Opportunity—Ask students to think of celebrities who have become sacred. Can you think of any of these people who were actually created by marketing people? For a fascinating treatment of the subject refer students to Irvin J. Rein, Philip Kotler, and Martin R. Stoller's* High Visibility: *Dodd, Mead & Company, 1987.*

e. Many consumers' activities (events) have also taken on a special status.
   1) Examples would include the Super Bowl, the Olympics, the World Series, Woodstock, and sometimes even a family vacation.
   2) Personal momentos from sacred events can include:
      a) Local products.
      b) Pictorial images.
      c) "A piece of the event" such as a rock or seashell.
      d) Symbolic shorthand such as a small symbol that depicts the event.
      e) A collector marker like a lapel pen.

**\*\*\*\*\*Use Consumer Behavior Challenge #7 Here \*\*\*\*\***

*Discussion Opportunity—Have students tell about an event that has become sacred to them. Ask: Have you ever seen this event used in a marketing effort? What will you tell your children about this event? Will it become part of their memory as well?*

*Discussion Opportunity—What have you collected that might be construed as being tied to a scared place, person, or event? Bring it to class.*

From Sacred to Profane and Back Again
f. Sacred things become profane and profane things become sacred.
   1) **Desacralization** occurs when a sacred item or symbol is removed from its special place or is duplicated in mass quantities, becoming profane as a result. Religion to some extent has become desacralized.

2) **Sacralization** occurs when ordinary objects, events, or even people take on sacred meaning to a culture or to specific groups within a culture.
   a) *Objectification* occurs when sacred qualities are attributed to mundane items.
   b) This process can occur through contamination.
   c) Objects can be set apart in *collections*. **Collecting** refers to the systematic acquisition of a particular object or set of objects, and this widespread activity can be distinguished from hoarding, which is merely unsystematic collecting.

> *****Use Consumer Behavior Challenge #14 Here *****

> *Discussion Opportunity—Give an example of a person, event, or object that you have sacralized. Give an example of a person, event, or object that you have desacralized. Explain why this occurred. Has it had any impact on your purchasing patterns?*

# End-of-Chapter Support Material

## SUMMARY OF SPECIAL FEATURE BOXES

### 1. Marketing Opportunity I

This special feature box highlights the group ritual of tailgating at football games. The practice has existed for more than 100 years. Tailgaters have traditionally had to improvise for supplies and accessories. However, now there are many corporations that recognize and target this market segment. This special feature supports the section "Rituals."

### 2. Net Profit

This box illustrates how the Internet has transformed the ritual of buying wedding gifts. Various online wedding sites and registries are engaged in fierce competition and as a result are offering new services and incentives to lure in customers. This feature supports the section "Gift-Giving Ritual."

### 3. Marketing Opportunity II

The Jewish ritual of the bar mitzvah and bat mitzvah has long been practiced. The ritual is often accompanied by a lavish party. Now, in some affluent communities, there are non-Jewish youth who are requesting similar coming-of-age parties.

# REVIEW QUESTIONS

1.  What do we mean by *culture*? How is it related to an individual's personality? *We can think of culture as a society's personality. It includes both abstract ideas, such as values and ethics, and material objects and services, such as the automobile, clothing, food, art, and sports, that are produced or valued by a society. Put another way,* culture *is the accumulation of shared meanings, rituals, norms, and traditions among the members of an organization or society.*

2.  How do ideology, social structure, and ecology shape a culture? Give examples of different forms these may take.

    -   *Ecology—The way a system adapts to its habitat. Ecology is shaped by the technology a culture uses to obtain and distribute resources (e.g., industrialized societies versus Third World countries). The Japanese, for example, greatly value products designed for efficient use of space because of the cramped conditions in that island nation.*
    -   *Social structure—The way in which orderly social life is maintained. This includes the domestic and political groups that are dominant within the culture (e.g., the nuclear family versus the extended family; representative government versus dictatorship).*
    -   *Ideology—The mental characteristics of a people and the way in which they relate to their environment and social groups. This revolves around the notion that members of a society possess a common worldview (an idea we introduced in Chapter 13). They share certain ideas about principles of order and fairness. They also share an ethos, or a set of moral and aesthetic principles. A theme park in Bombay that caters to India's emerging middle class, called Water Kingdom, illustrates how a culture's worldview can be distinctive. Many consumers there are unfamiliar with mixed-sex public activities of this nature, so the park rents swimsuits to women who have never worn one before. No thongs here, though: The suits cover the women from wrists to ankles.*

3.  What is the difference between an enacted norm and a crescive norm? Give three examples of crescive norms. *Some norms, called enacted norms, are explicitly decided on, such as the rule that a green traffic light means "go" and a red one means "stop." Many norms, however, are much more subtle. These crescive norms are embedded in a culture and we discover them only when we interact with other members of that culture.*

4.  What is binary opposition and how does a mediating character fit into this structure? *Binary opposition occurs when there are two opposing ends of some dimension (e.g., good versus evil, nature versus technology). Characters, and in some cases products, are often defined by what they are* not *rather than what they* are *(e.g., "This is not your father's Oldsmobile," "I can't believe it's not butter.").*

    *Recall from the discussion of Freudian theory in Chapter 6 that the ego functions as a kind of "referee" between the opposing needs of the id and the superego. In a similar fashion, the conflict between mythical opposing forces is sometimes resolved by a mediating figure that can link the opposites by sharing characteristics of each. For example, many myths contain animals that have human abilities (e.g., a talking snake) to bridge the gap between humanity and nature, just as marketers often give cars (technology) animal names (nature) such as Cougar, Cobra, or Mustang.*

5. What is a monomyth? Give an example. *A monomyth is a myth that is common to many cultures. The most prevalent monomyth involves a hero such as Superman who emerges from the everyday world with supernatural powers and wins a decisive victory over evil forces. He then returns with the power to bestow good things on his fellow men.*

6. Give examples of public versus private rituals. Name some ritual artifacts we use to perform these rituals. *Public rituals like the Super Bowl, presidential inaugurations, and graduation ceremonies are communal activities that affirm our membership in the larger group and reassure us that we are reading from the same script as everyone else. Other rituals occur in small groups or even in isolation. Market researchers discovered that for many people (like Katie) the act of late-night ice cream eating has ritualistic elements, often involving a favorite spoon and bowl!*

7. What ritualistic functions does a bath perform? *Two sets of binary oppositions personal rituals express are private/public and work/leisure. Many beauty rituals, for instance, reflect a transformation from a natural state to the social world (as when a woman "puts on her face") or vice versa. She may view the bath as a sacred, cleansing time, a way to wash away the "sins" of the profane world.*

8. Describe the three stages of the gift-giving ritual. *The gift-giving ritual has three distinct stages: During gestation, the giver is motivated by an event to procure a gift. This event may be either structural (i.e., prescribed by the culture, as when people buy Christmas presents) or emergent (i.e., the decision is more personal and idiosyncratic). The second stage is presentation, or the process of gift exchange. The recipient responds to the gift (either appropriately or not), and the donor evaluates this response. In the third stage of reformulation, the giver and receiver adjust the bond between them (either looser or tighter) to reflect the new relationship that emerges after the exchange is complete. Negativity can arise if the recipient feels the gift is inappropriate or of inferior quality.*

9. What is an antifestival? *Because of these oppositions, we can think of Halloween as an antifestival, an event that distorts the symbols associated with other holidays. For example, we can regard the Halloween witch as an inverted mother figure. The holiday also parodies the meaning of Easter by stressing the resurrection of ghosts and of Thanksgiving by transforming the wholesome symbolism of the pumpkin pie into the evil jack-o-lantern.*

10. Define a *rite of passage*. Specify the stages involved and give two examples. *What does a dance for recently divorced people have in common with a fraternity Hell Week? Both are examples of modern rites of passage, or special times marked by a change in social status. Every society, both primitive and modern, sets aside times at which such changes*

*occur. Much like the metamorphosis of a caterpillar into a butterfly, consumers' rites of passage consist of three phases:*

- *The first stage, separation, occurs when the individual is detached from his original group or status (e.g., the college freshman leaves home).*
- *Liminality is the middle stage, in which the person is literally between statuses (e.g., the new arrival on campus tries to figure out what is happening during orientation week).*
- *The last stage, aggregation, takes place when the person reenters society after the rite of passage is complete (e.g., the student returns home for Christmas vacation as a college "veteran").*

11. What is the difference between sacred and profane consumption? *Sacred consumption involves objects and events that are "set apart" from normal activities and are treated with some degree of respect or awe. They may or may not be associated with religion, but people tend to regard most religious items and events as sacred. Profane consumption involves consumer objects and events that are ordinary, everyday objects and events that do not share the "specialness" of sacred ones.*

12. Are sports events sacred? Why or why not? *For many people, the world of sports is sacred and almost assumes the status of a religion. We can find the roots of modern sports events in ancient religious rites, such as fertility festivals (e.g., the original Olympics). Indeed, it is not uncommon for teams to join in prayer prior to a game. The sports pages are like the scriptures (and we describe ardent fans as reading them "religiously"), the stadium is a house of worship, and the fans are members of the congregation. Devotees engage in group activities, such as tailgate parties and the "Wave" where sections of the stadium take turns standing up. The athletes who fans come to see are godlike; they are reputed to have almost superhuman powers. Athletes are central figures in a common cultural myth, the hero tale. In these stories, the player must prove himself under strenuous circumstances, and victory is achieved only through sheer force of will.*

13. Describe the two processes of sacralization and desacralization, providing an example of each. *Sacralization occurs when ordinary objects, events, and even people take on sacred meaning to a culture or to specific groups within a culture. As we've seen, events such as the Super Bowl and people such as Elvis Presley now are sacred. Indeed, virtually anything can become sacred. Skeptical? Consider that a Web site is thriving by selling unlaundered athletic wear worn by members of the Dallas Cowboys football team. Shoes worn by quarterback Troy Aikman sell for $1,999, and an unwashed practice jersey that retains the sweat of an unknown player goes for $99. Used socks are flying out the door at $19.99 a pair. Says the owner, "Fans who have never been able to touch the Cowboys before now have an opportunity."*

*Desacralization occurs when a sacred item or symbol is removed from its special place or is duplicated in mass quantities, becoming profane as a result. For example, souvenir reproductions of sacred monuments such as the Washington Monument or the Eiffel*

*Tower, artworks such as the Mona Lisa or Michelangelo's David, or adaptations of important symbols such as the American flag by clothing designers, eliminate their special aspects by turning them into unauthentic commodities produced mechanically with relatively little value.*

14. What is collecting, and how does it differ from hoarding? *Collecting refers to the systematic acquisition of a particular object or set of objects. We can distinguish this activity from hoarding, which is merely unsystematic collecting. Hoarding is becoming a problem in some areas where consumers' refusal to throw things away in some extreme cases has resulted in fires, eviction, and even the removal of children from the home.*

# CONSUMER BEHAVIOR CHALLENGE

## Discussion Questions

1. We can think of culture as a society's personality. If your culture were a person, could you describe its personality traits?

   *Students likely will describe the U.S. culture as young, aggressive, independent, healthy, and fit. Some of the following American core values will probably be discussed: freedom, youthfulness, achievement, materialism, activity, conformity, individuality, mastery over the environment, efficiency, equality, humanitarianism, and religious orientation.*

   *In contrast, other cultures may be described in ways that are equally as distinctive and reflective of their unique (or stereotypical) characteristics. Instructors may be alerted to students' tendencies to describe the U.S. culture as positive and other cultures as negative, in which case a discussion of ethnocentrism may be beneficial.*

2. The chapter argues that not all gift giving is positive. In what ways can this ritual be unpleasant or negative?

   *The text clearly states that negativity can arise if the recipient feels the fit is inappropriate or of inferior quality. The giver/donor may feel the response to the gift was inadequate, insincere, or a violation of the reciprocity norm, which obliges people to return the gesture of a gift with one of equal value. Both participants may feel resentful for being forced to participate in the gift-giving ritual.*

3. For many Disneyland is a sacred place. Do you agree? Why or why not?

   *This question should be used to make sure that students understand the definition of "sacred" as it applies in consumer behavior (objects and events that are "set apart" from normal activities and are treated with some degree of respect or awe). Once they understand this, most all should agree that Disneyland is a sacred place to some . . . to many.*

4.    Describe the three stages of the rite of passage associated with graduating from college.

*Rites of passage includes three phases:*

1.   *Separation—detached from original group (e.g., college freshman leaves home).*
2.   *Liminality—person is literally in between statuses (e.g., freshman during orientation).*
3.   *Aggregation—person reenters society after rite of passage (e.g., goes home for Christmas as a "college veteran").*

*For the college graduation example:*
1.   *Students should recognize the college graduate's separation involves detachment from his or her college friends, roommates, fraternity brothers/sorority sisters, and professors.*
2.   *During the liminality phase, the college graduate is in between stages—college and career—and experiences a period of adjustment to the new environment.*
3.   *Aggregation occurs when the graduate becomes part of the professional society, identifying with his or her career rather than college.*

5.    Have you ever given yourself a gift? If so, why did you do it and how did you decide what to get?

*Research has shown that the most common reasons that people buy themselves gifts are to reward themselves for good deeds, to console themselves after negative events, or to motivate themselves to accomplish some goal. As students respond, relate their responses to these reasons for buying self-gifts.*

6.    "Fraternity hazing is just a natural rite of passage that should not be prohibited by universities." Do you agree?

*Whether or not something is a rite of passage does not correlate with whether or not it is morally correct. If a rite of passage causes harm to people, then it can easily be argued that it is an unethical practice. In such cases, it can be argued that such practices should not be allowed. Making the link between this concept and whether or not fraternity hazing is harmful will be a bit "hazy."*

7.    Identify the ritualized aspects of football that are employed in advertising.

*Students should be able to generate a long list of ritualized behaviors associated with high school, college, and professional football. These include wearing school/team colors, pre-game tailgating activities, singing school/team songs, cheers, the "wave," and half-time entertainment (including performance by the marching band). Any and all of the rituals can be employed in advertising.*

8.    "Christmas has become just another opportunity to exchange gifts and stimulate the economy." Do you agree? Why or why not?

*To some extent the answer to this question will reflect each students' upbringing, their appreciation of this religious event and season, their sense of tradition, and their cynicism. Marketers and consumers are both to blame for the over-commercialization of the season. Many, however, still regard this season as one of the most religious on the calendar. Have students talk about Christmas traditions. Most can remember more traditions than details of presents they have received or given. Ask them to describe how their family feels about Christmas (from their mother and father's standpoint). Is the Christmas season a time for family renewing and gathering (most will say yes)? This question should provide for a lively debate. Be sure to include the marketing aspects of the season and whether this is right or wrong.*

9.    Bridal registries lay out very clearly the gifts that the couple wants. How do you feel about this practice—should people actually specify what you should buy for them, or should a gift be a more personal expression from you?

*There should be representatives that emerge to support both sides of this debate. Although, because this practice has become so culturally accepted, younger people will probably see nothing wrong with it. However, traditionally, the nature of gift giving was more symbolic in nature. As the Net Profit special feature box points out: "Because the wedding couple specifies exactly what they want in advance, the giver doesn't really have to know very much about the recipients. As we'll see later in this chapter, part of gift giving is developing or reinforcing a symbolic relationship, but now the process is much more automated. As one etiquette expert disdainfully points out, in the old days (pre-Internet) people were supposed to be "zealous with creativity" when selecting a gift. Now, it's just gimme, gimme, gimme with a dollar amount attached.*

10.    Rituals can provide us with a sense of order and security. In a study of the drinking rituals of college students, the researchers found that drinking imposed order in students' daily lives—from the completion of assignments to what and when to eat. In addition, ritualizing an activity such as drinking provided security and fellowship at a time fraught with confusion and turbulent change. Obviously, though, there's a dark side to drinking rituals. Consider the highly publicized death of a Massachusetts Institute of Technology student who died three days after falling into an alcohol-induced coma as the result of a fraternity pledge. Indeed, binge drinking is probably the most widely practiced ritual among college students; it has been described as the most significant health hazard on college campuses today. What role does drinking play in the social life on your campus? Based on your experience, how does it fit into rituals of college life? Should these practices be changed? If so, how?

*Student responses will likely mirror the research on this topic; the majority of students at some point in their college experience are involved in ritualistic drinking. Thus, most everyone will have something to share—some (obviously) more than others. Their responses to whether or not such practices should be changed will likely be based on whether or not they have had or have witnessed any negative experiences associated with drinking.*

## Application Questions

11.  When you go out on a first date, identify the set of crescive norms that are operating. Write a report (preferably when the date is over) describing specific behaviors each person performed that made it clear you were on a first date. What products and services are affected by these norms?

     *Social norms that are subtle and embedded in a culture, those that are discovered only when people interact with other members of that culture, are known as crescive norms. First dates are about getting to know one another. So, specific behaviors as to the nature of discussion should emerge. Additionally, there may be such norms as one party holding doors or pulling out chairs for the other. Being polite, on one's best behavior, is a crescive norm that often changes as people get to know each other. Even the act of going to dinner might be counted as a first date norm, because it facilitates the "getting to know" factor. Students might include norms of ommission, such as going home to meet the family on the first date.*

12.  Interview people you know about any "magic" items they own (e.g., How many of your friends have a lucky charm or keep a St. Christopher's medal or some other object hanging from their rear-view mirrors?). Get them to describe their feelings about these objects and tell how they acquired their magical properties. How would they feel if they lost these special items?

     *The nature of "magic" as described in the text simply refers to the fact that marketers of many different types of goods will imply that their product will result in extraordinary effects. Most people will probably refer to items in their possession around which they themselves have somehow developed a sense of the supernatural. Be sure to make special note of any student who responds with an example that demonstrates that a company has actually played a role in the development of such perceptions.*

13.  Identify modern day myths that corporations have created. How do they communicate these stories to consumers?

     *Be sure to note that this question specifies how corporations create the myths about themselves. If information is communicated through mainstream channels (i.e., mass advertising or direct mail), then people will associate it very directly with the company and it likely will not be perceived as a myth. But in today's world of marketing, companies have strategies such as stealth marketing and viral marketing, where information can be seeded without the consumer knowing the source.*

14.     Interview people you know who collect some kind of object. How do they organize and describe their collections? Do you see any evidence of sacred versus profane distinctions (for example, a person who collects matchbooks might have one set that you can actually use to light a candle, whereas other matchbooks can't ever be touched).

*The very nature of collecting should result in people applying some element of sacredness to the items being collected. However, there will likely be a range, with items that are more sacred and items that are less sacred.*

15.     Ask friends to describe incidents where they received a gift they thought was inappropriate. Why did they feel this way, and how did this event influence the relationship between them and the gift-giver?

*According to the text, research has shown that gift giving is more exchange-oriented (instrumental) in the early stages of a relationship, but becomes more altruistic as the relationship develops. In addition, third parties can exert strong influences on gift giving as people are influenced by others in their social network when selecting gifts for recipients. So student responses to this question should depend upon which stage of a relationship the gift giving took place in. But given that this perspective on gift giving identifies a social and relationship component, a gift perceived as inappropriate will certainly affect the relationship between the receiver and the giver.*

# Additional Support Material

# CASE STUDY TEACHING NOTES

**Chapter 16 Case Study: Camera Phones Invade the Middle East**

**Summary of Case**

Camera phones have become very popular in many countries. But these cameras have also brought on controversy as social practices have unfolded that involve the cameras. Nowhere is this controversy greater than in Arab countries. Cultural values in these countries are very sensitive to privacy issues, especially where unveiled women are concerned. Very strict legal regulation has been put into place in many countries. In Saudi Arabia, camera phones were completely outlawed for some time, until public outcry led to a reversal of that action. Very stiff penalties for violating cultural norms with a camera phone continue to be imposed in Arab countries.

## Suggestions for Presentation

The material in this case is to be presented in conjunction with the section "Sacred and Profane Consumption." While taking camera phone pictures of people in an unsuspecting manner has been an issue in many parts of the world, it is a much greater issue in Arab countries. In most parts of the world, taking a picture of a woman without a veil on her face would not be considered inappropriate. However, in the Arab world, women are not to be seen in public without veils on. In that manner, the unveiled image of a woman has been sacralized. It is apparent as people in these countries have fought for the right to have such cameras that such images may be leaning toward desacralization. The very harsh fines and penalties that exist in such countries for the use of phones to circulate pornographic images of any kind is another example of that which the core culture considers to be sacred.

## Suggested Answers for Discussion Questions

1.  Why do you think that Saudi Arabia and other Middle Eastern countries have taken a stronger stance to regulating the use of camera phones? Discuss this question in the context of sacred and profane consumption.

    *The culture in Arab countries is rooted in the Muslim religion. Cultural values have established a very conservative line between that which is moral and that which is immoral regarding images of women and sexuality. Thus, although in most countries viewing a woman without a veiled face is totally normal, in the Arab world, it would be highly inappropriate and immoral. In the same manner, nude and pornographic images of any kind are widely considered to be immoral. The image of a woman and issues of sexuality are sacred. The connection has been made by religious leaders between the use of the cameras and acts that are immoral by the Muslim faith. Thus, the phones have been the center of a religious controversy.*

2.  Consumer acceptance of camera cell phones in Saudi Arabia has obviously been strong. What do you think this says about the culture in this country?

    *At the very least, this says that there are many people who recognize that camera phones can be used without violating the cultural norms that exist in such countries. The denouncing of these phones by religious leaders and political conservatives has been based on the assumption that such phones lead to immoral behavior. Certainly, there are many people who want the phones and do not engage in the defined immoral behavior.*

    *The popularity of the phones also may indicate that some people may not agree with the definition of immoral behavior by the mainstream culture.*

# STUDENT PROJECTS

## Individual Projects

1.     Invite a person from a foreign culture to come to your class to discuss products commonly used in the guest's country that are seldom used in this country. In preparation, have the students develop a list of products commonly used in the United States. Ask the guest how available these products are in their country, where they can be purchased, and the frequency of use.

2.     Invite someone from the funeral industry to come to talk to the class on marketing practices in the industry. Collect literature from various funeral homes to study prior to the guest speaker's visit. Have students formulate questions prior to the class.

3.     Invite someone from the wedding industry to come to talk to the class on marketing practices in the industry. Collect literature from various wedding related businesses to study prior to the guest speaker. Have students formulate questions prior to the class.

4.     Have a student briefly summarize an episode of a weekly television series that he or she watched recently. Have the class describe how the program transmitted cultural beliefs, values, and customs.

5.     Ask students to identify what they perceive to be a sacred place on campus. How is this place honored? Marketed? How is information about this place passed on to future students? How does the university or college use this sacred place to market the university or college? Is this proper?

6.     Ask students to interview a person from a different or foreign culture. During the interview have the student observe any nonverbal communication that is taking place, then ask what similarities and differences he or she has noticed between the nonverbal language of his culture and the American culture. Have the student report on these similarities and differences.

7.     Have students interview two people from two different foreign cultures. Have the students ask what major differences they see between the cultural values in their country and those in the American culture. Ask the students to explain these to the class.

8.     Ask students to describe rituals they follow when visiting a shopping mall, movie theater, or restaurant. How could marketers capitalize on these rituals?

9.     Have students comment on the practice of drinking while attending college. What are their opinions and perceptions of the role of drinking in the college experience? Is it ritualistic? If so, how do marketers capitalize on this ritual? If a college really wanted to discourage drinking, what would be the best way to do this culturally?

10. If you were a marketing manager for a local charity, how could you use gift-giving rituals to encourage contributions to your charitable cause?

11. Why has Halloween become such a popular holiday? Is the popularity just with children or has it spread to adults? What gifts have become fashionable to give on Halloween? Explain your feelings about Halloween.

12. Each student should identify and describe a possession that most people would consider to be ordinary, but to them is sacred. Have them describe how this sacredness developed.

## Group Projects

1. Have student groups identify an American custom, more, and convention. Then, have them design a new product or service (or multiple if necessary) that would take advantage of the existence of these crescive norms.

2. More and more, email messages are forwarded that represent incorrect or even mythical information (i.e., that Bill Gates will pay people money to forward an email). Have student groups locate an email that would qualify as a myth and research the origin of the message as well as its truthfulness.

3. Have student groups interview three people from different cultures. Ask about differences between their culture and the country in which they are now living. How did each person state that his or her culture was different? Students should note whether they had ever noticed these differences/ How could advertisers use these differences to promote their products (use an example)?

4. Have student groups observe a group of fraternity or sorority members watching a favorite program. If necessary, they should ask questions before or after to help determine the nature of the group's behavior during the viewing of the program. What are the rituals of this group for watching this program?

5. Have student groups identify what they feel is the most sacred symbol on campus and establish the reasons for this. Then, have the class come together and compare their results.

6. Ask groups to prepare a list of products that people tend to buy more for what the products mean than for what the products do. Are there other products that could satisfy the same need and even perhaps sell for less? What makes these products have lesser status?

7. Ask groups to compare a list of rituals that will probably be performed (or that were performed) at their wedding ceremony and reception. What are the marketing implications of these rituals? (It is interesting to point out the different rituals based on a religious, ethnic, or racial subculture and rituals that seem to be solely American.) An

added question might be: How are wedding plans affected when people from different subcultures get married?

8. Have group members interview a ball player, an actress or actor, a student preparing for exams, a trial lawyer, or others you might choose to see if each has a certain ritual or superstition that he tends to follow in preparing for and performing his activity. Does he remember when he first started performing this ritual?

9. Have group members interview a middle school or high school student (and, if possible, that person's closest friend). Find out what new words their group is using this year. What do they mean? What new products are they using to prove that they are "in"? How can they spot persons who obviously do not belong to their groups? What words or products are now "out"?

10. Ask each group to design a new holiday to be implemented in the nation. This holiday should have a theme, a date for celebration, and a unique idea that could be marketed. Have the class vote on the best idea.

# eLAB

## Individual Assignments

1. Go to **www.menscience.com**. Everyone has grooming rituals. Who grooms the most, men or women? Examine this Web site and the implications that it has for male grooming. Describe how the design of the Web site seeks to enhance male grooming rituals that would then require the use of products that they sell.

2. Go to **www.1800flowers.com**. Flowers have become one of America's favorite gifts. After reading the material in the chapter, write a short one- to two-page paper on the art of flower giving. What useful data does this site supply for this form of gift giving? Critique the ease and convenience of using the Web site. How do you think flower giving has changed since the advent of the Internet?

3. Go to **www.elvis.com**. After exploring this Web site, comment on the myth and legend of Elvis Presley. What marketing techniques are used? How has "the King" been able to retain a loyal following after all these years? Using data found on the Web sites, construct a brief strategy for introducing the Presley music to today's teen generation. Don't treat this as an impossible task. How would "the King" do it if he were alive today? Remember, teens from the '50s made him a superstar.

4. Go to **www.hardrock.com**. How does the Hard Rock Cafe make it easy for you to become a "collector" of their memorabilia? What secrets about our contemporary culture has the organization learned? Do you have any Hard Rock gear? If not, why not? With which generation would Hard Rock gear be most popular? Why?

5. Go to **www.brighton.com** and **www.longaberger.com**. How do these two different sites seek to make you into purchasers and collectors of their products? What strategies do you see?

6. Go to **www.itunes.com**. Digital music and music players are all the rage. At least, they are with younger generations. Your task is to design a strategy to get your father and mother to use the Web site for their music needs. Anticipate the problems you might encounter with your task and build in separate strategies for overcoming these difficulties. Do the difficulties arise from the service or from cultural differences? Try out your strategy on your parents to see if it will work. Report your results.

## Group Assignments

1. Go to **www.marvel.com** and **www.dccomics.com**. After visiting these two Web sites, have your group discuss and comment on the use of heroes and antiheroes in these two organizations' products and Web sites. What magical qualities have been bestowed on the characters you have found? How are these characters used to deliver messages? How have marketers used these characters for merchandising purposes? Why do these characters remain popular? Which is your group's favorite? Why?

2. Go to **www.snopes.com**. As a group, spend some time on this Web site. Then, choose an urban myth that you find most interesting (regardless of whether it is true or not). Apply the four interrelated functions of myths to the one that you chose. How can the concepts of binary opposition, mediating figure, or monomyth be applied to the myth that you chose? In your opinion, has the Internet made urban myths and legends more commonplace? Why?

# CHAPTER  17

# *THE CREATION AND DIFFUSION OF GLOBAL CONSUMER CULTURE*

## CHAPTER OBJECTIVES

When students finish this chapter they should understand why:

- Styles are a mirror that reflects underlying cultural conditions.

- We can distinguish between high and low culture.

- Many modern marketers are reality engineers.

- New products, services, and ideas spread through a population. Different types of people are more or less likely to adopt them.

- Many people and organizations play a role in the fashion system that creates and communicates symbolic meanings to consumers.

- Fashions follow cycles.

- Products that succeed in one culture may fail in another if marketers fail to understand the differences among consumers in each place.

- Western (and particularly American) culture has a huge impact around the world, though people in other countries don't necessarily ascribe the same meanings to products as we do.

## CHAPTER SUMMARY

The styles prevalent in a culture at any point in time often reflect underlying political and social conditions. The set of agents responsible for creating stylistic alternatives is termed a *culture production system*. Factors such as the types of people involved in this system and the amount of competition by alternative product forms influence the choices that eventually make their way to the marketplace for consideration by end consumers.

*Culture* is often described in terms of high (or elite) forms and low (or popular) forms. Products of popular culture tend to follow a *cultural formula* and contain predictable components. On the other hand, these distinctions are blurring in modern society as imagery from "high art" is increasingly being incorporated into marketing efforts.

*Reality engineering* occurs as elements of popular culture are appropriated by marketers and converted to vehicles for promotional strategies. These elements include sensory and spatial aspects of everyday existence, whether in the form of products appearing in movies, odors pumped in to offices and stores, billboards, theme parks, and video monitors attached to shopping carts.

*Diffusion of innovation* refers to the process whereby a new product, service, or idea spreads through a population. *Innovators* and *early adopters* are quick to adopt new products, and *laggards* are slow. A consumer's decision to adopt a new product depends on his or her personal characteristics as well as on characteristics of the innovation itself. Products stand a better chance of being adopted if they demand relatively little change in behavior from users, are easy to understand, and provide a relative advantage compared to existing products.

The *fashion system* includes everyone involved in the creation and transference of symbolic meanings. Meanings that express cultural categories (e.g., gender distinctions) are conveyed by many different products. New styles tend to be adopted by many people simultaneously in a process known as *collective selection*. Perspectives on motivations for adopting new styles include psychological, economic, and sociological models of fashion. Fashions tend to follow cycles that resemble the product life cycle. The two extremes of fashion adoption, *classics* and *fads*, can be distinguished in terms of the length of this cycle.

Because a consumer's culture exerts such a big influence on his or her lifestyle choices, marketers must learn as much as possible about differences in cultural norms and preferences when marketing in more than one country. One important issue is the extent to which marketing strategies must be tailored to each culture versus standardized across cultures. Followers of an *etic perspective* believe that the same universal messages will be appreciated by people in many cultures. Believers in an *emic perspective* argue that individual cultures are too unique to permit such standardization—marketers must instead adapt their approaches to be consistent with local values and practices. Attempts at global marketing have met with mixed success; in many cases this approach is more likely to work if the messages appeal to basic values and/or if the target market consists of consumers who are more internationally rather than locally oriented.

The United States is a net exporter of popular culture. Consumers around the world have eagerly adopted American products, especially entertainment vehicles and items that are linked symbolically to a uniquely American lifestyle (e.g., Marlboro cigarettes, Levi's jeans). Despite the continuing "Americanization" of world culture, some consumers are alarmed by this influence and are instead emphasizing a return to local products and customs. In other cases, they are integrating these products with existing cultural practices in a process known as *creolization*.

401

# CHAPTER OUTLINE

## 1. Introduction

<u>The Creation of Culture</u>

a. Big corporations are currently working hard to capture market share in the rapidly growing black urban culture. They are looking for the next hot fashion.

b. It is quite common for mainstream culture to modify symbols identified with "cutting edge" subcultures and present these to a larger audience.

   1) As this occurs, these cultural products undergo a process of **co-optation**, where their original meanings are transformed by outsiders.

   2) In many instances, cultural changes are brought to the average person via advertising and the fashion industry.

> ***\*\*\*\*\*Use Figure 17.1 Here \*\*\*\*\****

> *Discussion Opportunity—Ask: Can you think of an example where co-optation has occurred? What evidence of this was in advertising or on the mass media?* Hint: *Think of slang language used by African-American rappers that has become common to our daily expressions.*

> *Discussion Opportunity—Ask: What evidence is there that the Vietnam War and the "Flower Power" generation still influences the culture of today's youth (if it does)? Give examples.*

<u>Cultural Selection</u>

c. We inhabit a world brimming with different styles and possibilities. Consumers may at times feel overwhelmed by the sheer number of choices in the market-place.

   1) The selection of certain alternatives over others (such as an automobile) is the culmination of a complex filtration process resembling a funnel.

   2) Many possibilities initially compete for adoption, and these are steadily winnowed down as they make their way down the path from conception to consumption in a process of **cultural selection**.

> ***\*\*\*\*\*Use Figure 17.2 Here \*\*\*\*\****

> *Discussion Opportunity—What new styles have you seen appear in the last six months? How many of these have begun to appear on television (either in the ads or on the shows)? How long do you think the styles will last?*

   3) Styles are not formed in a vacuum.

d. Some of the characteristics of fashion and popular culture are:

   1) Styles often are a reflection of deeper social trends (e.g., politics and social conditions).

   2) Styles usually originate as an interplay between the deliberate inventions of designers and business people and spontaneous actions by ordinary consumers.

3) These cultural products can travel widely.

4) A style begins as a risky or unique statement by a relatively small group of people.

5) Most styles eventually wear out.

<u>Culture Production Systems</u>

e. The set of individuals and organizations responsible for creating and marketing a cultural product is a **culture production system (CPS)**.

1) The nature of these systems helps to determine the types of products that eventually emerge from them.

2) Factors such as the number and diversity of competing systems and the amount of innovation versus conformity that is encouraged are important.

3) The different members of a culture production system may not necessarily be aware of or appreciate the roles played by the other members, yet many diverse agents work together to create popular culture.

f. A culture production system has three major subsystems:

1) *Creative subsystem*—responsible for generating new symbols and/or products.

2) *Managerial subsystem*—responsible for selecting, making tangible, mass producing, and managing the distribution of new symbols and/or products.

3) *Communications subsystem*—responsible for giving meaning to the new product and providing it with a symbolic set of attributes that are communicated to consumers.

---

*****Use Table 17.1 Here; Use Consumer Behavior Challenge #9 Here *****

---

*Discussion Opportunity—Think of an example of a culture production system and identify the members of the system for a popular custom or trend that impacts college students.*

---

g. Many judges or "tastemakers" influence the products that are eventually offered to consumers. These **cultural gatekeepers** are responsible for filtering the overflow of information and materials intended for consumers (collectively, this is known as the *throughput sector*).

---

*Discussion Opportunity—Ask: Who do you know that might be classified as a cultural gatekeeper? Explain.*

---

<u>High Culture and Popular Culture</u>

h. Culture production systems create many diverse products, but some basic distinctions can be offered regarding their characteristics.

1) Arts versus crafts.

a) An **art product** is viewed primarily as an object of aesthetic contemplation without any functional value.

b) A **craft product** is admired because of the beauty with which it performs some function (such as a ceramic ashtray).

*****Use Consumer Behavior Challenge #2 Here *****

2) High art versus low art.
3) Mass culture churns out products specifically for a mass market. Many of these products follow a **cultural formula** (where certain roles and props often occur consistently—as in a pulp detective story or a romance novel).

*****Use Table 17.2 Here; Use Consumer Behavior Challenge #10 Here *****

*Discussion Opportunity—Think of an illustration where a cultural formula might be used in marketing a product.*

*Discussion Opportunity—Ask: Can any cultural formulas be applied to college life? Explain.*

4) Aesthetic marketing research.
   a) Creators of aesthetic products are increasingly adapting conventional marketing methods to fine tune their mass-market offerings.
   b) Marketing research is used to test audience reactions to concepts.
   c) Content of movies is often influenced by consumer research.

*****Use Consumer Behavior Challenge #3 Here *****

Reality Engineering
i. **Reality engineering** occurs as elements of popular culture are appropriated by marketers and converted to vehicles for promotional strategies.
   1) These elements include sensory and spatial aspects of everyday existence.
   2) Reality engineering is accelerating due to the current popularity of product placements by marketers.
   3) Media images appear to significantly influence consumers' perceptions of reality, affecting viewers' notions about such issues as dating behavior, racial stereotypes, and occupational status.
   4) Studies of the **cultivation hypothesis**, which refers to media's ability to distort consumers' perceptions of reality, have shown that heavy television viewers tend to overestimate the degree of affluence in the country, and these effects also extend to such areas as perceptions of the amount of violence in one's culture.
   5) **Product placement** refers to the insertion of specific products and/or use of brand names in movie and television scripts.
   6) Some researchers claim product placement helps in consumer decision making.

*****Use Consumer Behavior Challenges #1, #5, and #12 Here *****

*Discussion Opportunity—Do a little research on the practical applications of product placement. Rent a movie or watch TV for an evening prior to this class discussion. Count the number of products that have been placed in the movie. How many were there? What effect (if any) did these product placements have on you? What do you think of product placement in children's movies?*

    7) A concept related to product placement is **advergaming**, the practice of merging interactive advertisements with online games.

## 2. The Diffusion of Innovations
    a. An **innovation** is any product or service that is perceived to be new by consumers (even if it has been used by others in other places).
    b. **Diffusion of innovations** refers to the process whereby a new product, service, or idea spreads through a population.

*Discussion Opportunity—Ask: What product have you recently purchased that you would classify as an innovation? Where did you hear about it? What thought process did you go through before you made the purchase?*

*Discussion Opportunity—Ask: Is the diffusion of innovation process different via the Internet as opposed to more normal channels? Explain your answer and give an example.*

Adopting Innovations
    c. A consumer's adoption of an innovation resembles the decision-making sequence discussed in Chapter 9.
    1) Not all people adopt a product at the same time.
      a) Categories of adopters can be related to phases of the product-life-cycle concept used widely by marketing strategists.

*****Use Figure 17.3 Here *****

    2) Adopter categories include:
      a) **Innovators**—the first to buy; will buy novel products.
        1) A **lead user** is an involved, experienced customer who is very knowledgeable about the field.

*****Use Consumer Behavior Challenge #6 Here *****

      b) **Early adopters**—share many of the characteristics with the innovators, however, they have a higher degree or concern for social acceptance.
      c) Early majority—sometimes called late adopters.
      d) Late majority—**late adopters** are the mainstream public.
      e) **Laggards**—the last to adopt a product.

> *****Use Figure 17.3 (Used Previously) Here *****

> *Discussion Opportunity—Bring in magazine ads that you think would be directed at the various adopter categories. Explain your reasoning.*

> *Discussion Opportunity—Create an illustration of the types of adopters using a high-tech product or the e-commerce on the Internet.*

<u>Behavioral Demands of Innovations</u>
  d. Innovations can be categorized in terms of the degree to which they demand changes in behavior from adopters. Three major forms are:
    1) A **continuous innovation** refers to a modification of an existing product.
    2) A **dynamically continuous innovation** is a more pronounced change in the existing product.
    3) A **discontinuous innovation** creates major changes in the way we live.

> *Discussion Opportunity—With input from students, make a list of products that fit the three forms of innovations. Discuss the significance of these innovations. How does the promotion for these products differ?*

<u>Prerequisites for Successful Adoption</u>
  e. Regardless of how much behavioral change is demanded by an innovation, several factors are desirable for a new product to succeed. These may be classified and summarized as being:
    1) **Compatibility**—must fit the consumer's lifestyle.
    2) **Trialability**—reduce risk by letting the consumer try it.
    3) **Complexity**—the lower the better.
    4) **Observability**—innovations that are observable spread faster.
    5) **Relative advantage**—must give advantages other products don't.

> *Discussion Opportunity—Ask: What do you think were the three most important innovations in your lifetime (so far)? In your parents' lifetime? In your grandparents' lifetime? How did the innovations you just listed match with the prerequisites for successful adoption list?*

> *Discussion Opportunity—Using an example of your own choosing, illustrate how the prerequisites for successful adoption influenced your purchase of a product or service.*

**3. The Fashion System**
  a. The **fashion system** consists of all those people and organizations involved in creating symbolic meanings and transferring those meanings to cultural goods.
    1) Fashion can be thought of as a **code** or language.
      a) It is **context-dependent**.
      b) Fashion products are often **undercoded**.
    2) **Fashion** is the process of social diffusion by which a new style is adopted by some group(s) of consumers.

a) *A fashion*, in contrast, refers to a particular combination of attributes.

b) *In fashion* means that this combination is currently positively evaluated by some reference group.

> ***\*\*\*\*\*Use Consumer Behavior Challenge #8 Here \*\*\*\*\****

Cultural Categories

b. The meaning that does get imparted to products reflects underlying **cultural categories**, which correspond to the basic ways we characterize the world.

1) These cultural categories affect many different products and styles.

2) Costumes worn by celebrities can affect the world of fashion.

> *Discussion Opportunity—Ask: What are some fashions (fads) that have been started by popular movies?*

c. The process by which certain symbolic alternatives are chosen over others has been termed **collective selection**. As with the creative subsystem, members of the managerial and communications subsystems also seem to develop a common frame of mind.

> ***\*\*\*\*\*Use Consumer Behavior Challenge #7 Here \*\*\*\*\****

> *Discussion Opportunity—Ask: What would you say is the current fashion theme or motif? How has this affected advertising, movies, and marketing? How long do you think it will last?*

Behavioral Science Perspective on Fashion

d. Fashion is a very complex process and operates on many levels.

1) Many psychological factors help to explain why people are motivated to be in fashion. These include:

a) Conformity.

b) Variety-seeking.

c) Personal creativity.

d) Sexual attraction.

2) An early theory of fashion proposed that "shifting *erogenous zones*" (sexually arousing areas of the body) accounted for fashion changes, and that different zones become the object of interest because they reflect societal trends.

3) Economists approach fashion in terms of the model of supply and demand.

4) Veblen's notion of conspicuous consumption applied.

e. The collective selection model is an example of a sociological approach to fashion.

1) **Trickle-down theory** has been one of the most influential approaches to understanding fashion. Two conflicting forces drive fashion:

a) Subordinate groups try to adopt the status symbols of the groups above them as they attempt to climb up the ladder of social mobility.

b) Those people in the superordinate groups are constantly looking below them on the ladder to ensure that they are not imitated.

2) Other theories include the *trickle-across* and *trickle-up* theories.
3) **Meme theory** has been proposed to explain the fashion process using a medical metaphor.
   a) A *meme* is an idea or product that enters the consciousness of people over time.
   b) Memes "leap" from brain to brain via a process of imitation.

---

*Discussion Opportunity—Ask: Can you think of items people buy that seem to display their wealth? How do you know that these people have these items? Can you provide illustrations of the trickle-across and trickle-up theories?*

---

*Discussion Opportunity—Ask: Can you think of a current meme? Explain it and its effect.*

---

Cycles of Fashion Adoption
f. Although the longevity of a particular style can range from a month to a century, fashions tend to flow in a predictable sequence. The **fashion acceptance cycle** is quite similar to the more familiar product life cycle.

---

*****Use Figure 17.4 Here *****

---

g. Consider how the fashion acceptance cycle works:
1) There is an *introduction stage*.
2) An *acceptance stage*.
3) A *regression stage*.
4) Events that might happen during these stages include:
   a) The item becomes a **classic** where it has an extremely long acceptance cycle.
   b) The item is a **fad** where it is very short lived.
     1. The fad is non-utilitarian.
     2. The fad is adopted on impulse.
     3. The fad diffuses rapidly.
5) There is a difference between a fad and a trend (the trend lasts for some time).
6) Questions to ask to determine if a trend is occurring include:
   a) Does it fit with basic lifestyle changes?
   b) What are the benefits?
   c) Can it be personalized?
   d) Is it a trend or a side effect?
   e) What other changes have occurred in the market (consider *carryover effects*)?
   f) Who adopted the change?

---

*****Use Figure 17.5 Here*****

---

*Discussion Opportunity—What do you think are "classics" and "fads"? What are your reactions to these products? What are "classics" from your parents' generation? How do you know they are classics?*

## 4. Transferring Product Meanings to Other Cultures

   a. Innovations know no geographic boundaries. Learning other cultures is essential to a successful marketing effort.

Think Globally, Act Locally

   b. As corporations increasingly find themselves competing in many markets around the world, the debate has intensified regarding the necessity of developing separate marketing plans for each culture. Two views exist:
   1) **Adopting a standardized strategy**—this viewpoint represents an **etic perspective**, which focuses on commonalties across cultures (it is objective and analytical).
   2) On the other hand, many marketers endorse a *localized strategy* (**emic perspective**), which focuses on variations within a culture (it is subjective and experiential).

*Discussion Opportunity—Ask: If you were in charge of international markets for Kraft Foods, would you focus primarily on the etic or emic perspectives? Would your answer change if you worked for Chrysler? Explain.*

   c. Marketers must appreciate that consumers in some cultures do not like some tastes and styles.
   d. Which perspective is best? The answer depends on a series of factors:
   1) Tastes and styles.
   2) Advertising preferences and regulations.
   3) Cultural norms toward taboos and sexuality.

*Discussion Opportunity—What are some taboos that you are aware of in other countries? In the United States? What effect might these taboos have on marketers and advertising?*

Does Global Marketing Work?

   e. Often times global marketing seems better in theory than in practice. Employing local entities to help with the marketing and advertising effort often pays off.
   f. A recent study of consumers in 41 countries identified characteristics people associate with global brands. These characteristics fell into three dimensions:
   1) *Quality Signal*—Many assume that if a company has global reach it must excel on quality.
   2) *Global Myth*—Consumers look to global brands as symbols of cultural ideals and they buy these brands to help them "bond" with like-minded people around the world.
   *Social Responsibility*—People recognize that global companies wield extraordinary influence, both positive and negative, on society's well-being.

g. The researchers grouped consumers who evaluate global brands in the same way, and they identifieid four major segments: global citizens, global dreamers, antiglobals, and global agnostics.

---

*Discussion Opportunity—What are some translation problems that you have heard of (where a simple meaning in one culture presents a problem in another culture)?*

---

The Diffusion of Consumer Culture

h. There is a constant search for the "elusive global consumer."

   1) Affluent people who are global citizens share common tastes. Many of these come from the Western world.

   2) Young people are strongly influenced by Western culture (such as through MTV).

   3) Formerly isolated cultures are now reachable through mass media and modern technology.

   4) The West is a net exporter of popular culture.

   5) The newest market to open to Western goods and services is the Asian market.

   6) Converting to a Western form of business and consumption is not without its problems. These problems include a loss of confidence and pride in the local culture, as well as alienation, frustration, and an increase in stress as leisure time is sacrificed to work ever harder to buy consumer goods.

   a) A **globalized consumption ethic** realizes that consumers worldwide have consumption desires and this desire is growing.

   b) Attaining goods, however, is not easy for consumers in **transitional economies** (those countries making the transition from controlled, centralized economies to a free-market system).

   c) As the global consumption ethic spreads, the products wished for in different cultures becomes homogenized.

   7) In some cases, the meanings of desired products are adapted to local customs and needs. The process of **creolization** occurs when foreign influences are absorbed and integrated with local meanings.

---

*****Use Consumer Behavior Challenge #4 Here *****

---

*Discussion Opportunity—Ask: Do you believe that "Creeping Americanism" is an ethical issue? Why? Do you think that it is a political problem? Why? Do you think it is a marketing problem? Why?*

---

*Discussion Opportunity—Give an example of creolization in the United States (with foreign products) and in a foreign country (with United States products).*

# End-of-Chapter Support Material

## SUMMARY OF SPECIAL FEATURE BOXES

**1.     Marketing Pitfalls I**

This box explores the controversial practice of marketing within schools. Numerous corporations have donated large sums of money and goods to schools in exchange for promotional and distribution rights to students. This feature supports the section "Reality Engineering."

**2.     Marketing Opportunity I**

This box highlights how companies in the high-tech industry have strategically employed innovators to test their products. This feature supports the section "Adopting Innovations."

**3.     Marketing Pitfalls II**

This box looks at the changing dynamics of product development. Product developments are speeding up in industries from apparel to computers. The cell phone industry is moving especially fast. Motorola and Nokia are featured. This feature supports the section "Cycles of Fashion Adoption."

**4.     Marketing Pitfalls III**

Cultural differences often cause problems in international promotions. This box takes a look at some faux pas by companies in China. This feature supports the section "Adopting a Localized Strategy."

**5.     The Global Looking Glass**

This box highlights a cultural backlash stemming from the James Bond movie *Die Another Day*. The North Koreans did not like the backward manner in which they were portrayed. The South Koreans were upset that 007 had sex with a woman in a Buddhist temple. This feature supports the section "Cultural Differences Relevant to Marketers."

**6.     Marketing Opportunity II**

The diffusion of global consumer culture has some unpredictable dynamics. A recent trend has fashion all over the world wearing a style of flip-flops worn by Brazilian peasants. Supermodels, movie starts, politicians, and other celebrities are now wearing these. This special feature supports the section "Emerging Consumer Cultures in Transitional Economies."

# REVIEW QUESTIONS

1.  What is collective selection? Give an example. *We term the process by which certain symbolic alternatives are chosen over others collective selection. As with the creative subsystem, members of the managerial and communications subsystems also seem to develop a common frame of mind. Although products within each category must compete for acceptance in the marketplace, they can usually be characterized by their adherence to a dominant theme or motif—be it "The Western Look," "New Wave," "Danish Modern," or "Nouvelle Cuisine."*

2.  Describe a culture production system (CPS) and list its three components. What is an example of a CPS with these three components? *A culture production system (CPS) is the set of individuals and organizations responsible for creating and marketing a cultural product. A culture production system has three major subsystems:*

    *   *A creative subsystem responsible for generating new symbols and products.*
    *   *A managerial subsystem responsible for selecting, making tangible, mass producing, and managing the distribution of new symbols and products.*
    *   *A communications subsystem responsible for giving meaning to the new product and providing it with a symbolic set of attributes that it then communicates to consumers.*

    *An example of the three components of a culture production system for a music release would be: 1) a singer (e.g., rapper Eminem, a creative subsystem); 2) a company (e.g., Interscope Records, which manufactures and distributes Eminem's CDs, a managerial subsystem); and 3) the advertising and publicity agencies hired to promote the CDs (a communications subsystem).*

3.  Define a *cultural gatekeeper*, giving three examples. *Many judges or "tastemakers" influence which products we as consumers get to consider. These cultural gatekeepers are responsible for filtering the overflow of information and materials intended for customers. Gatekeepers include movie, restaurant, and car reviewers; interior designers; disc jockeys; retail buyers; and magazine editors. Collectively, social scientists call this set of agents the throughput sector.*

4.  Describe the difference between arts and crafts. *We view an art product primarily as an object of aesthetic contemplation without any functional value. In contrast, we admire a craft product, because of the beauty with which it performs some function (e.g., a ceramic ashtray or hand-carved fishing lures).*

5.  What is a cultural formula? Give an example. *Mass culture churns out products specifically for a mass market. These products aim to please the average taste of an undifferentiated audience. Rather than being unique, they are predictable because they follow certain patterns. As Table 17.2 illustrates, many popular art forms, such as detective stories or science fiction, generally follow a cultural formula, in which certain roles and props often occur consistently. Romance novels are an extreme case of a*

*cultural formula. Computer programs even allow users to "write" their own romances by systematically varying certain set elements of the story.*

6.    What is new vintage? How is this an example of reality engineering? *Reality engineering occurs as marketers appropriate elements of popular culture and convert them for use as promotional vehicles. It's hard to know what's real anymore; even "used jeans" get created by specialists who apply chemical washes, sandpaper, and other techniques to make a new pair of jeans look like they're ready for retirement. The industry even has a term for this practice that sums up the contradiction:* new vintage!

7.    Define *product placement* and list three examples of it. How is this practice the same or different from branded entertainment? *Product placement refers to the insertion of specific products and the use of brand names in movie and TV scripts. This strategy actually is a long-standing tradition in movies, though the placements are more blatant and financially lucrative today. In the heyday of the major Hollywood studios, brands such as Bell telephones, Buick cars, Chesterfield cigarettes, Coca-Cola, De Beers diamonds, and White Owl cigars regularly appeared in films. For example, in a scene in the classic "Double Indemnity" that takes place in a grocery store, the director Billy Wilder had some products like Green Giant vegetables facing the camera while others "mysteriously" were turned around to hide their labels. And a scene set in a kitchen in "All About Eve" starring Bette Davis clearly shows boxes of Sunshine Hi-Hos crackers. Indeed, the practice dates at least as far back as 1896, when an early movie shows a cart bearing the brand name Sunlight (a soap made by Lever Brothers, now known as Unilever) parked on a street. Perhaps the greatest product placement success story was Reese's Pieces; sales jumped by 65 percent after the candy appeared in the film* E.T.

*The practice of product placement is becoming so commonplace (and profitable) that it's evolving into a new form of promotion called branded entertainment, where advertisers showcase their products in longer-form narrative films instead of commercials.*

8.    What is advergaming? Give an example. *As gaming goes mass market, many marketers are turning on to a new strategy called advergaming, where online games merge with interactive advertisements that let companies target specific types of consumers.*

9.    What is the diffusion of innovations? *Diffusion of innovations refers to the process whereby a new product, service, or idea spreads through a population. The rate at which a product diffuses varies. For example, within 10 years after its introduction, 40 percent of U.S. households watched cable TV, 35 percent listened to compact discs, 25 percent used answering machines, and 20 percent bought color TVs. It took radio 30 years to reach 60 million users and TV 15 years to reach this number. In contrast, within 3 years 90 million of us were surfing the Web.*

10.    What are innovators? Early adopters? Laggards? *Roughly one-sixth of the population (innovators and early adopters) are very quick to adopt new products, and one-sixth of the people (laggards) are very slow. Even though innovators represent only about 2.5 percent of the population, marketers are always interested in identifying them. These are*

*the brave souls who are always on the lookout for novel products or services and who will be the first to try a new offering. Just as generalized opinion leaders do not appear to exist (see Chapter 11), innovators tend to be category-specific as well. Early adopters share many of the same characteristics as innovators, but an important difference is their degree of concern for social acceptance, especially with regard to expressive products, such as clothing, cosmetics, and so on.*

11. Describe the differences among continuous innovations, dynamically continuous innovations, and discontinuous innovations, providing an example of each. Which type are consumers least likely to adapt? *A **continuous innovation** refers to a modification of an existing product, such as when General Mills introduces a Honey Nut version of Cheerios or Levi's promotes shrink-to-fit jeans. A marketer may do this to set a brand apart from its competitors. Most product innovations are of this type; that is, they are evolutionary rather than revolutionary. The company makes small changes to position the product, add line extensions, or merely alleviate consumer boredom.*

   *A **dynamically continuous** innovation is a more pronounced change in an existing product, as represented by self-focusing 35-mm cameras or touch-tone telephones. These innovations have a modest impact on the way people do things, requiring some behavioral changes. When IBM introduced its Selectric typewriter, which uses a typing ball rather than individual keys, the new design permitted secretaries to instantly change the typeface of manuscripts by replacing one Selectric ball with another.*

   *A **discontinuous** innovation creates major changes in the way we live. Major inventions, such as the airplane, the car, the computer, and the television have radically changed modern lifestyles. The personal computer has replaced the typewriter, and it has created the phenomenon of "telecommuters" by allowing many consumers to work from their homes. Of course, the cycle continues, as new continuous innovations (e.g., new versions of software) are constantly being made for computers. Dynamically continuous innovations such as the "mouse" and trackballs compete for adoption, and discontinuous innovations such as streaming video transmitted on cell phones start to appear in stores.*

12. What is the difference among the terms *fashion, a fashion,* and *in fashion? Fashion is the process of social diffusion by which a new style is adopted by some group(s) of consumers. In contrast, a fashion (or style) refers to a particular combination of attributes. And, to be in fashion means that some reference group positively evaluates this combination. Thus, the term* Danish Modern *refers to particular characteristics of furniture design (i.e., a fashion in interior design); it does not necessarily imply that Danish Modern is a fashion that consumers currently desire.*

13. What are cultural categories and how do they influence product designs? *The meaning that does get imparted to products reflects underlying cultural categories that correspond to the basic ways we characterize the world. Our culture makes distinctions between different times, between leisure and work, and between genders. The fashion system provides us with products that signify these categories. For example, the apparel industry*

*gives us clothing to denote certain times (e.g., evening wear, resort wear), differentiates between leisure clothes and work clothes, and promotes masculine and feminine styles.*

14. Summarize some of the major approaches to understanding fashion from the perspectives of psychologists, economists, and sociologists. *Many psychological factors help to explain why people are motivated to be in fashion. These include conformity, variety seeking, personal creativity, and sexual attraction. For example, many consumers seem to have a "need for uniqueness": They want to be different (though not necessarily too different!).*

    *Economists approach fashion in terms of the model of supply and demand. Items that are in limited supply have high value, whereas those readily available are less desirable. Rare items command respect and prestige.*

    *The collective selection model we discussed previously is an example of a sociological approach to fashion. This perspective focuses on the initial adoption of a fashion (idea, style, etc.) by a subculture and its subsequent diffusion into society as a whole. Such diffusion often begins with youth subcultures like the hip-hop segment.*

15. What is an example of a meme? *A meme is an idea or product that enters the consciousness of people over time—examples include tunes, catch-phrases ("You're fired!"), or styles such as the Hush Puppy.*

16. What is the trickle-down effect? List some reasons why it is no longer as valid as it used to be. *Trickle-down theory, first proposed in 1904 by Georg Simmel, has been one of the most influential approaches to understanding fashion. It states that there are two conflicting forces that drive fashion change. First, subordinate groups try to adopt the status symbols of the groups above them as they attempt to climb up the ladder of social mobility. Dominant styles thus originate with the upper classes and trickle down to those below.*

    *However, this is where the second force kicks in: Those people in the superordinate groups are constantly looking below them on the ladder to ensure that they are not imitated. They respond to the attempts of lower classes to "impersonate" them by adopting even newer fashions. These two processes create a self-perpetuating cycle of change—the machine that drives fashion.*

17. What is the difference between a fad, a fashion, and a classic fashion life cycle? *Fashions are characterized by slow acceptance at the beginning, which (if the fashion is to "make it") rapidly accelerates, peaks, and then tapers off. We can identify different classes of fashion by considering the relative length of the fashion acceptance cycle. Many fashions exhibit a moderate cycle, taking several years to work their way through the stages of acceptance and decline; others are extremely long-lived or short-lived. A classic is a fashion with an extremely long acceptance cycle. It is in a sense "antifashion" because it guarantees stability and low risk to the purchaser for a long period of time. A fad is a very short-lived fashion. Relatively few people usually adopt a fad product. Adopters may*

*all belong to a common subculture, and the fad "trickles across" members but rarely breaks out of that specific group.*

18. What is the difference between an emic and an etic perspective on globalization? *Marketers who endorse an emic perspective stress variations across cultures. They feel that each culture is unique, with its own value system, conventions, and regulations. This perspective argues that each country has a national character, a distinctive set of behavior and personality characteristics. An etic perspective focuses on commonalities across cultures. An etic approach to a culture is objective and analytical; it reflects impressions of a culture, as viewed by outsiders.*

19. Why is the United States a net exporter of popular culture? *This simply means that the United States exports more pop culture than it imports. The United States exerts a greater influence on the pop culture of other countries than it is influenced by those countries.*

20. What country provides an example of a transitional economy? *After the downfall of communism, Eastern Europeans emerged from a long winter of deprivation into a springtime of abundance. The picture is not all rosy, however, because attaining consumer goods is not easy for many in transitional economies. This description refers to a country (examples include China, Portugal, and Romania) that is struggling with the difficult adaptation from a controlled, centralized economy to a free-market system.*

21. Define *creolization* and provide an example. *A process called creolization occurs when foreign influences are absorbed and integrated with local meanings. Modern Christianity adapted the pagan Christmas tree into its own rituals. In India handicapped beggars sell bottles of Coke from tricycles, and a popular music hybrid called Indipop mixes traditional styles with rock, rap, and reggae.*

# CONSUMER BEHAVIOR CHALLENGE

**Discussion Questions**

1. Watchdog groups have long decried product placements for blurring the line between content and advertising without adequately informing viewers. And the networks themselves appear to be divided on how far they want to open the gate. "You've got to wonder when it starts to destroy the entertainment value," asks one former television executive. In some instances, placements are extremely subtle. For example, Polaroid handed out cameras to the band Outkast, whose hit song "Hey Ya" includes the lyric, "Take it like a Polaroid picture." How do you see the future of product placement—will it get out of hand and create a consumer backlash, or is it a valuable alternative to traditional advertising?

*Not only is the popularity of product placement as a promotional technique increasing, but product placement blatancy is also increasing. In a 2005 episode of* CSI New York, *an agent's phone rings. His partner says, "Hey, what is that song?" He replies, "Oh, that's the new Cold Play song." He then goes on very nonchalantly, but the obvious nature of the plug is surpassed only by the fact that on the next commercial break, the first ad is for Cold Play's latest release.*

2.	Is advertising an art or a craft? Which should it be?

*Remember that an art product is primarily as an object of aesthetic contemplation without any functional value. In contrast, we admire a craft product, because of the beauty with which it performs some function (e.g., a ceramic ashtray or hand-carved fishing lures). Although the people involved in the creation of advertisements are very creative, even artistic, if an advertisement has no functional value, then it is of no value to the company. In contrast, advertisements go about the function of trying to achieve some objective, often in an artistic manner.*

3.	The chapter mentions some instances where market research findings influenced artistic decisions, as when a movie ending was reshot to accommodate consumers' preferences. Many people would most likely oppose this practice, claiming that books, movies, records, or other artistic endeavors should not be designed to merely conform to what people want to read, see, or hear. What do you think?

*The instructor should encourage students to review the relevant discussion in the text concerning aesthetic marketing research and then express their thoughts and feelings regarding the use of consumer research for these purposes. Considering these practices in light of the marketing concept should generate an interesting discussion.*

4.	Due to higher competition and market saturation, marketers in industrialized countries are increasingly trying to develop Third World markets by encouraging people in underdeveloped countries to desire Western products. Asian consumers alone spend $90 billion a year on cigarettes, and U.S. tobacco manufacturers continue to push relentlessly into these markets. Cigarette advertising, often depicting glamorous Western models and settings, is found just about everywhere—on billboards, buses, storefronts, and clothing, and many major sports and cultural events are sponsored by tobacco companies. Some companies even hand out cigarettes and gifts in amusement areas—often to preteens. Should this practice be encouraged, even if the products being marketed may be harmful to consumers' health (e.g., cigarettes) or divert needed money away from the purchase essentials? If you were a trade or a health official in a Third World country, what guidelines, if any, might you suggest to regulate the import of luxury goods from advanced economies?

*This question represents a controversial aspect of marketing activities that has received considerable attention from many and diverse parties. Students should be encouraged to review popular press commentaries and raise this question with others, both inside and outside the business arena. An interesting discussion is likely to ensue.*

5.   Comment on the growing practices described as reality engineering. Do marketers "own" our culture and should they?

*As mentioned in the text, reality engineering occurs as elements of the popular culture are appropriated by marketers and converted to vehicles for promotional strategies. In an advertisement, a company took a famous picture of World War II leaders Roosevelt, Stalin, and Churchill meeting at Yalta and superimposed women in bathing suits standing next to them and whispering in their ears. Because of modern photographic techniques, the picture looked real. Students should debate who owns history or the icons that it has produced. The picture described here might be okay in their minds, however, what if the picture had been a drawing of the Last Supper or some other religious event of significance? Ask the students to debate the issue.*

6.   If you worked in marketing research for a cosmetics firm, how might you apply the lead user concept to help you identify new product opportunities?

*A lead user is an involved, experienced customer who is very knowledgeable about the field. One approach to using this concept would be to conduct focus groups of identified lead users. These are the ones who would know what is happening in the industry from the consumer's perspective.*

7.   Boots with six-inch heels are the latest fashion rage among young Japanese women. Several teens have died after tripping over their shoes and fracturing their skulls. Followers of the style, however, claim they are willing to risk twisted ankles, broken bones, bruised faces, and other dangers associated with the platform shoes. One teenager said, "I've fallen and twisted my ankle many times, but they are so cute that I won't give them up until they go out of fashion." Many consumers around the world seem to be willing to suffer for the sake of fashion. Others argue that we are merely pawns in the hands of designers who conspire to force unwieldy fashions down our throats. What do you think? What is and what should be the role of fashion in our society? How important is it for people to be in style? What are the pros and cons of keeping up with the latest fashions? Do you believe that we are at the mercy of designers?

*This is another question that is very opinion oriented. Responses will largely be based on how consumers view fashion and how willing they are to sacrifice to incorporate fashion into their lives. The "should" element of this question may bring forward some idealistic responses. Most students will likely take the approach that consumers are free to do as they choose and that fashion "should" be what consumers want it to be.*

## Application Questions

8.   If you were a consultant to a toy company, what would you forecast as the next big trend in this market? Survey toy stores and watch what kids are playing with now to help you with your prediction.

*Such trends are very difficult to predict. But as students provide their comments on this question, highlight the concepts of fashions, fads, and classics. Which type is likely to be responsible for the next hit?*

9.	How might the rise of peer-to-peer music sharing influence the structure of the music CPS? One hypothesis is that this method erodes the dominance of the big labels because listeners are more likely to access music from lesser-known groups. Survey your friends to determine if this in fact happening—are they listening to a wider variety of artists or just downloading more of the big-time groups?

*We term the set of agents responsible for creating stylistic alternatives a culture production system (CPS). Factors such as the types of people involved in this system and the amount of competition by alternative product forms influence the choices that eventually make their way to the marketplace for consideration by end consumers. There is strong evidence that with the advent of digital music file formats, peer-to-peer file sharing, and digital music players, people are listening to a greater variety of music and being exposed to groups and genres that they otherwise might not be. The case study for Chapter 6 highlights the practice of pod swapping or poaching, where people exchange their iPods with others for a period of time.*

10.	Read several romance or action novels to see if you can identify a cultural formula at work. Do you see parallels among the roles different characters play (e.g., the hero, the evildoer, the temptress, etc.)?

*Be sure to refer people to Table 17.2 that illustrates how popular art forms follow a cultural formula in which certain roles and props often occur consistently. Romance novels are an extreme case of a cultural formula. Computer programs even allow users to "write" their own romances by systematically varying certain set elements of the story. Given that, it should be fairly easy for students to define a cultural formula by simply scanning various romance novels.*

11.	Watch 12 hours of TV shows and keep a log of all product placements you see. What are the dominant products being inserted in the shows?

*As students report their results, be sure to discuss the implications of these placements for the product categories as well as the brands involved.*

# CASE STUDY TEACHING NOTES

## Chapter 17 Case Study: "Beh-Ding Ding-Ding," The Crazy Frog Sings

### Summary of Case

The ringtone industry is pulling in more than $4 billion annually. This case focuses on the evolutionary popularity of the Crazy Frog ringtone series. The audio track that serves as the basis for Crazy Frog was created by a Swedish teen as high-tech mimicry of a motorcycle. Another Swede created the graphic and combined the two. The combination took off like wildfire on the Internet. So popular that Jamba/Jamster, the largest ringtone company, acquired the rights to Crazy Frog and began selling it. The case goes on to illustrate how the ringtone industry is not only influenced by traditional music channels, but how the ringtone industry is actually influencing pop music.

### Suggestions for Presentation

The discussion questions for this case present two main concepts from the chapter that should be applied to this case. These are how art and pop culture influence each other, and the diffusion of innovations. This case also illustrates other concepts. This is a case not only of how something can break pop culture barriers, but how companies can capitalize on this popularity by commercializing pop culture. Additionally, the difference between an art product and a craft product could be illustrated. Crazy Frog began life as an art product, an object of aesthetic contemplation without any real functional value. Once it evolved to the level of commercially distributed ringtone, then it was definitely a craft product, one that accomplishes the utilitarian function in an artistic manner.

### Suggested Answers for Discussion Questions

1.    In the case of Crazy Frog, how have art and media influenced popular culture? Is the reverse also true?

*Which came first, the art, or the pop culture icon? Sometimes, it is difficult to tell. In this case, Crazy Frog was created as an "artistic" venture by a teenager. From there, the popularity of Crazy Frog took on a life of its own. Crazy Frog's creators have even commented on how control quickly left their hands. So, in the first place, art influenced pop culture. But various media played a role in this rise to popularity (Internet, cellphones, media players). So, it is difficult to untangle this influence. Ultimately, it is easy to define the influence that a specific medium had on pop culture as Jamster made a commercial purchase and began officially marketing the Crazy Frog product line through media channels.*

2.  Discuss the spread of Crazy Frog in the context of the concept of "diffusion of innovations."

    *Diffusion of innovations refers to the process whereby a new product, service, or idea spreads through a population. The rate at which a product diffuses varies. This question can certainly be discussed in terms of diffusion rates. At each level of development (audio only, audio/video, ring tone), Crazy Frog began to diffuse at a faster rate. Crazy Frog can also be applied to a diffusion life cycle. Innovators may have been the only ones with access to the Crazy Frog audio due to the limited nature of distribution. Early adopters were likely to pick it up when the graphic was added and it started being distributed more widely. Then, once Crazy Frog achieved a level of mass distribution through Jamster, the remaining early adopters and late adopters accepted it. You may want to ask students whether they think the Crazy Frog itself is a continuous innovation, dynamically continuous innovation, or a discontinuous innovation.*

# Additional Support Material

# STUDENT PROJECTS

## Individual Projects

1.  Go through magazines to find ads that display fashion used in association with some other product. Discuss the ramification of this and present your findings to the class.

2.  Rent a movie of your choice. Find ten different consumer products that would be natural fits for product placement in the movie you have just watched (these should be products for which a branded placement does not already exist in the film). Position the products (through description of the scene) where they should most appropriately be used. Explain why companies (the ten products) should be willing to pay for the exposure your group has suggested.

3.  Visit an upscale-fashion department store or boutique. Interview the manager about fashion. How does the manager decide on which fashion merchandise to purchase? What does he or she do with fashion merchandise once it has run its course? How does he or she know when a fashion is becoming unfashionable? Relate your results to the class.

4.  Discuss issues of ethics as they apply to reality engineering. Support your ideas with examples.

5.  Go to a contemporary magazine and find illustrations of high and low culture. Indicate what type of consumers might be attracted to these different messages.

6.   Find a product and describe how it was first introduced and how it has become diffused into our economy. Does it seem to fit the stages described in the text?

7.   What role do MTV and other teen media programs have in establishing fashion? How do older adults get information on fashion? How do older adults get information on fashion in business attire?

8.   It should be apparent from the chapter that art and culture are in a constant state of influencing each other. It is the dynamics of how these two elements of society influence each other that they also influence themselves. Discuss how fashion, music, and entertainment influence each other through pop culture.

9.   Find a product placement agency. Interview someone at this agency as to the general nature of product placement and how these "deals" come about. How is the practice of product placement changing? What is different about this practice today as opposed to 10 or 20 years ago?

10.  Describe three illustrations of trickle-down theory, trickle-up theory, and trickle-across theory.

11.  Is it appropriate for large corporations to market small boutique brands and hide the true origins of these products? Write a one-page paper that examines this issue.

12.  Some consumers complain that they are "at the mercy" of designers: They are forced to buy whatever styles are in fashion, because nothing else is available. Do you agree that there is such a thing as a "designer conspiracy"? Give ample evidence to support your position.

## Group Projects

1.   This is one for groups to give some thought to and even do some research on. How have styles in fashion and in our economy impacted political and social conditions? Which came first, the style or the conditions?

2.   Have groups select a product category of interest to them. Have them develop a formal strategy to reality engineer the product. Include specific tactics relating to different components of the marketing mix.

3.   Seinfeld, the program, advanced the use of product placement perhaps more than any other program in modern times. As a group, rent a series of episodes from one of the latter seasons. Make note of all brand placements. What is the nature of each (foreground/background, visual/audio, degree of exposure)? What impact do you think each of the placements had for the brand?

4. As groups, research the current fashion trends that are influencing the purchasing patterns of teenagers, college students, middle-aged business people, and senior citizens?

5. Based on research from the previous question, have groups develop predictions as to what they think upcoming fashion trends will be. How will they come about and how long will they last?

6. Meet together and discuss how fashion, trends, and fads impact the computer and computer software industry. What trends do you see for the future?

7. Divide the class into teams. Have one group take the perspective that the correct way to market is to take the etic perspective. Have one group take the perspective that the correct way to market is to take the emic perspective. Debate the issue.

8. Divide the class into teams. Have one group take the perspective that the "Americanization" of foreign cultures and media is a proper path to take. Have one group take the perspective that the "Americanization" of foreign cultures and media is wrong and will eventually cause conflict. Debate the issue.

9. Have your group design a fashion assessment instrument (questionnaire). Test it. Critique your effort.

10. Have your group design a fashion trend. Explain what it is and how you might get it adopted.

# eLAB

## Individual Assignments

1. Go to **www.dkny.com** and **www.esteelauder.com**. What's new in fashion, style, and cosmetics? Either of these sites might give you some clue. After visiting the Web sites, list what you perceive to be the top five trends in female fashion for this year. Remember, fashion may be more than just clothing. Report your opinions to the class.

2. Go to **www.oxygen.com** and **www.oprah.com**. Oprah Winfrey's multi-media empire is summarized on these two Web sites. She has dedicated herself to expanding women's influence in the world. What issues seem to be most important on these Web sites? How is female self-esteem treated on both of the Web sites? What cultural issues are described? Do you feel the opinions presented on the Web sites are fair or are they political and biased? Support your feelings.

3. Go to **www.cadillac.com**. Find all the information that you can on the newest model of the Cadillac Escalade. What changes have been made to this vehicle? To what extent do

you think these changes have been made in response to the desires of the target market? Discuss the nature of pop culture in the development of this model.

4.　　Go to **www.myreplicawatch.com** and **www.fashionknockoffs.com**. Why do you think that the knockoff industry has become so big? Discuss this in terms of the fashion concepts discussed in the chapter. Also, include a discussion of the economics of buying such brands (how much does the real thing cost?).

5.　　Go to **www.brandchannel.com/brandcameo_films.asp**. Select five different films that have a high number of brands placed in them. Then, look up reviews for each film as well as how the film did at the box office and in home video. What impact do you think each of the placements had for the brand?

## Group Assignments

1.　　Go to **www.disney.com**, **www.universalstudios.com**, **www.seaworld.com**, and **www.sixflags.com**. How do these organizations use reality engineering? What evidence does your group find that the technique is being used? Which site did your group find to be the most attractive? Why? Which site seemed to cross cultural lines in its appeal to the consumer? How did you know this? What evidence do you see of trends in entertainment? Do any of the sites advertise "virtual" experiences? If so, which ones and how do they do it? Report your group's findings to the class.

2.　　Go to **www.originalsoupman.com**. Do some research to find out the relationship between this company and the Soup Nazi of Seinfeld fame. How do you think the program influenced the success of this company?

# Video Guide

# VIDEO GUIDE
## Solomon, *Consumer Behavior* 7<sup>th</sup> edition

## Segment 1: Procter & Gamble

Summary

The cornerstone of P&G's success is building brands. Over the 100 plus years the company has been in existence, P&G has built 250 brands. It has sales of $40 billion and is in 130 countries. Ivory soap was the first consumer product developed and became the model for other product development. In the process of making Ivory soap, air bubbles mistakenly ended up in the bar. The result was floating soap – a product that met a consumer need. This is how P&G builds other products and brands – by understanding the customer.

Discussion Questions

1.     P&G believes that if accompanied by the right marketing efforts a brand can virtually live forever. Yet, in Principles of Marketing you learned that products have a life-cycle – they mature and eventually become obsolete. Which viewpoint is correct?

Most products are indeed destined to die – but there are notable exceptions including Dove soap which has been a market leader for over a century. The key to longevity is steady innovation that keeps the brand relevant to consumers while at the same retaining its brand identity. Chapter 2 discussed some of the issues related to subtle yet constant changes in packaging that help to accomplish this goal. This is a good opportunity to discuss the concept of brand equity and to emphasize the strategic importance of maintaining a brand promise that doesn't change even though some of its surface characteristics might evolve to keep up with the times.

2.  P&G repositioned Pampers so that consumers view it as delivering emotional benefits instead of functional benefits. How did the company do this? How might P&G do the same thing for its other personal care products such as toothpaste?

The company moved away from emphasizing the absorptive capacity of the diapers and began to focus upon the role of diapers in good parenting and infant development. As a result it became more of an educational service provider than just a diaper manufacturer. As the video briefly notes, the new Crest White Strips product also offers an emotional benefit by enhancing appearance (rather than dental health) and perhaps increasing social confidence in the process. This is a good opportunity to discuss different kinds of motivations that can underlie purchases within even the same product category.

Teaching Suggestions

1.  The video mentions that P&G conducts a variety of marketing research studies to understand the deeper needs of its customers. Encourage your students to think about how they would design research that would enable them to go beyond simple surveys as they explore how various personal care products play significant roles in people's everyday lives. You might consider assigning a research project that would enable students to talk to "real people" (or at least roommates) in order to appreciate how seriously take these products.

2.  P&G invented the soap opera genre, and now the company is trying to target young people on the Web. Invite students to share product websites they find to be particularly good or bad in class. You might hold a competition to see who (individuals or groups) can generate the best concept to create buzz for a mundane household product.

# Segment 2: iWon.com

Summary

iWon.com is an online portal with a difference. The difference is users of this site have the opportunity to win $10,000 a day and $10 million on tax day. The business model was built on the idea that people habitually respond to giveaways, as demonstrated with the many book and magazine sweepstakes. The company started during the height of the dot.com explosion with major initial funding from CBS. It launched in 1999 with a big media blitz by giving away $10 million. The buzz was continued as the company worked with major TV shows and magazines to profile and announce sweepstakes winners. Profitability was reached in 2001, or three years after inception. iWon.com uses big money to attract potential customers and it has proven to be a successful business model so far.

But nothing is totally free, as one of the founders emphasizes. Users have the chance to win money in exchange for demographic and psychographic information. Once users give iWon.com the permission to use their information for portal site customization, iWon tailors content such as news, movies, weather, and horoscopes to the user. Additionally, iWon allows marketers to direct market to this same group of people based on customers-stated preferences. Several Fortune 500 companies are clients and buy this data from iWon, which allows them to permission market. The site has roughly 250 different ads per month. Because the site can be customized on both the content and the advertising side, people stay longer at iWon than any other site on the web. This "Play and Stay" strategy has proved to be successful since the company's inception. Further, the company purchased Excite last year, and these two sites combined are the 7th most trafficked portal sites. iWon is competing fiercely against AOL, MSN, and Yahoo! This forces iWon to reach customers more effectively and understand its customers' needs better (both users and advertisers). The success formula is simple—give customers great content and prizes.

Discussion Questions

1. Permission marketing walks the fine line between privacy and advertising. What are the ethical decisions that surround permission marketing? What issues do marketers need to be aware of?

Permission marketing is the difference between marketers using information that they have permission to use versus using information that they do not. Spam is the use of 5 or more email addresses to send unsolicited email. Students will understand spam and the irritation of receiving unsolicited email. It is important to move the discussion into a business arena and how it is unethical for a business to participate in these activities. Build this question on the Permission Marketing teaching suggestion.

2. What are the different types of Internet advertising used by iWon.com and other Internet portals?

The specific forms are:
- Banner ads: Located at the top and bottom of pages
- Buttons: Small banners
- Sponsorships: Used for brand awareness
- Pop-up ads: Open up in a separate window
- Email: Digital direct mail

3. List the reasons that iWon.com's business model has been successful in reaching target consumers?

Students will have varying answers. However, some acceptable answers would be:
- The owner's had previous business experience.
- Initial funding allowed the company to develop.
- The company caught consumer interest with a unique promotional offer and model.
- The company is in the information business—a product that is always in demand.
- The company is partnered with Fortune 500 companies.
- The company had good timing.
- The company offers something of value to the consumer in exchange for information about the consumer.
- The company acquired Excite and expanded its business.

4. After examining the Web site, list the personal consumer information that iWon.com collects on its visitors? Is this information valuable? Comment.

If students enter the Web site, they will find that demographic, preference, lifestyle, and even attitudinal information is collected. Often, this collection does not occur at one time. Consumers can be constantly queried about a variety of subjects. What kind of information is collected when the consumer customizes his or her own personal portal opening page? This area should make for a good discussion. It is a good idea for the instructor to explore this area personally so direction and comments can be given to the students.

Teaching Suggestions

1. Online Advertising

The iWon.com website is a great example of online advertising. Have students go to the site and surf the various departments and sections. How many different types of advertising appear? How many different companies? Register for the sweepstakes. Is this a good promotional tool? Why or why not?

2. Market Research
Collecting data about consumers is becoming increasingly difficult, as people are savvier to marketers' need for information. iWon.com is selling information about customer habits to

companies that need to know purchasing decisions, trends, and demographic and psychographic information. The instructor can ask students for different ways companies can collect information about their customers. The discussion can start with information available internally and then move to primary and secondary data externally.

## 3. Direct Marketing

Students should be directed to collect all physical and digital direct mail that comes to them for one week. For each physical and digital direct mail piece, assess the purpose, target audience, message, and overall communication of the piece. Select the piece that is the best and the one that is the worst.

## 4. Permission Marketing

Have students focus on the privacy issue involved in any permission marketing effort. What do the consumers get and what do they give up in any such effort? What information must be disclosed to Iwon.com to customize the portal for personal needs? Is there any other information that the company wants from its visitors? Is privacy invaded or is just good marketing occurring?

# Segment 3: Harley-Davidson

Summary
Its motorcycles are a slice of Americana. So just how did the Harley Davidson Motor Company grow to become the number one selling heavyweight motorcycle in Japan? It might be attributed to what's called "The Harley-Davidson Mystique." What is it about a Harley that has worldwide appeal? How does the company manage to preserve its image worldwide? Are advertisements altered for overseas markets? Hop on your hog and get ready for an attitude adjustment as we explore Harley-Davidson's global marketing strategies.

Discussion Questions

1. How would you describe the Harley-Davidson brand personality? What makes this personality different from other motorcycle brands?

Students will throw out words like freedom, individuality, rebelliousness, or perhaps American. They might also be prompted to think about cultural icons that they associate with the brand such as James Dean. Other brands also try to cultivate this image, but for now Harley seems to have a lock on this position (especially vis a vis its American image).

2. The Harley brand is communicated consistently around the world. This is usually a positive attribute, but in light of today's politics do you foresee any possible red flags?

Harley's strong association with the U.S.A. might cause problems in some countries where consumers' anti-American attitudes are escalating. Harley can continue to emphasize the benefit of freedom while (perhaps) downplaying its American origins – but should it take this step?

Teaching Suggestions

1. Harley-Davidson faces a classic problem it shares with other brands such as Levi-Strauss: How to retain its "outsider" image while attracting new mainstream customers? Many hardcore Harley riders, for example, resent newcomers whom they regard as wannabes. This presents a good opportunity for discussion about the tension between a need to innovate and a need to stay in step with one's target market. How can Harley maintain its' "mystique" and yet continue to grow its market?

2. Much of Harley's appeal is fostered by its riders – as the video notes, the riders are the Harley-Davidson brand. Students can be encouraged to apply the brand community concept here, and to think about other brands that might do a better job of going down the same path.

3. Harley is aggressively expanding its merchandising efforts as the company continues to license merchandise in many categories. Encourage students to come up with new ideas for Harley merchandise and also to suggest categories where the Harley brand would be a mistake.

# Segment 4: Skechers

## Summary

How do you sell style? Trends that drive a dynamic shoe market are competitive. Skechers' philosophy is to maintain a flexible image in an ever-changing market. Staying on top of the fashion trend cycle is a very difficult and challenging problem.

Kelly O'Connor explains by answering seven questions how Sketchers reaches its target market, markets its products, and continues to be a "cool" alternative for consumers. The questions are:

1.  What is Skechers and who is your target market?
It is a marketing company that happens to be in the footwear industry. 8-10% of sales revenue is the budget for advertising and marketing, substantially more than most in the footwear industry. The target market is the 12- to 24-year old. However, as the youth market widens, older consumers that consider themselves to be young are also targets of the company.

2.  How do you instill brand loyalty into your chosen market?
Skechers is in fact street slang. The company selected a street slang word of their target market for their brand name (Skechers is a "kid who is always into something new"). All of their market research is done in-house – primarily focus groups. Their international distributors represent about 100 countries, and they also participate in research efforts. The marketing team travels globally, looking for trends or ideas that are emerging at the street level. They then take the idea, put the Skechers twist on it, and enter the market in a bold way.

3.  What's the key factor in maintaining your market?
It is maintained by having street credibility with the target market – the most important factor in continuing the brand.

4.  What is your message and how do you deliver it?
Message is: "Skechers makes cool shoes for cool people." This is delivered with consistency. Whatever the market, they position their product for cool people by being seen in all the cool places, cool magazines, and cool television shows.

5.  How do you fit into the highly competitive footwear landscape?
By being on top of the trends, Sketchers has become known as a lifestyle brand – what is in and what is cool. The owner of Skechers hires people who are in reality living the youth lifestyle. Most of the design team actually lives that lifestyle, too. Whatever they see, they bring it back to the company.

6. How do you appeal to your audience in various media?
Skechers does not dictate to their target market what to wear. Many companies have failed with this practice. They simply represent what is happening based on the market research. For this reason, the company has shifted their designs over the years. In addition, they use real people as models in the advertising so the target market can relate to the people.

7. Why doesn't your advertising focus on the product itself?
Footwear has limited exposure. Skechers is more into creating a brand about lifestyle than presenting footwear. Skechers primarily uses magazines for print and MTV in television. The company may eventually move into clothing lines.

Discussion Questions

1. List and describe what Skechers perceives to be its target market.

As described in the video clip, Skechers perceives the 12- to 24-year old youth market as its primary target market. However, it also appreciates those that are older but still "young at heart." In addition, Skechers also goes after the "cool" market.

2. How does Skechers attempt to stay in touch with its identified target market?

The company uses internal focus groups, visits to malls, a Web presence, and a constant attention to the feelings of the youth market as primary research devices. Additionally, it hires younger people who are living the lifestyle that is important to the company. The company also does international research.

3. Should the company branch into clothing as an extension of its successful footwear products?

This is an opinion question. Some students will see this as a natural extension. Others will see dangers. The company could build on existing popularity but must be mindful that competitors would change.

4. How can Skechers use the Web to become more effective in reaching its target market?

As can be seen at www.skechers.com, the company already has an effective Web presence. The next step might be to use the Web site to extend its global presence. Another avenue would be to use a "design your own shoe" feature to get more ideas on what is "cool." Students will have additional suggestions that can be discussed in class.

<u>Teaching Suggestions</u>

1.  Trends and Market Segments

This company seems to have done well in predicting youth trends and focusing on the youth target market.  It also understands that "youth" may be more a state of mind than a physical age.  Therefore, Skechers also markets to the "young in mind."

Suggestion One:
Have students list current youth trends.  Examine the ads shown in the video clip.  How do these ads match the listed trends?  Comment on how well Skechers is following these trends.  Finish the discussion with comments on whether these companies create trends or follow them.

Suggestion Two:
Collect ads from the four or five leading sneaker manufacturers.  Have students characterize the images, themes, or lifestyles being portrayed by these shoes.  Where does Skechers fit in these positioning characterizations?

2.  Lifestyles in the Youth Subculture

"Skechers makes cool shoes for cool people."  Examine how cool defines youth lifestyle.

Suggestion One:
Have students define what they perceive to be "cool."  Have them list "cool" products.  How does "cool" define their lifestyle?

Suggestion Two:
Examine "cool" over time.  What was "cool" five, ten, fifteen, twenty, or thirty years ago?  How could a company like Skechers continue to appeal to a consumer's appreciation of "cool"?

# Segment 5: Subaru

Summary
The Subaru example focuses primarily on how the company moved from "customer satisfaction" to "customer loyalty" and what effects this change had on operations. The automobile industry has a significant challenge in creating loyal customers, as time between purchases can be several years. Joe Barstys is the main speaker in the video and is head of customer relationships. He realized that a satisfied customer, measured by after-purchase surveys, does not equal a loyal customer, measured by repeat purchases.

Discussion Questions

1. Joe Barstys significantly changed the focus of Subaru and, consequently, its focus toward its customers. Define Subaru's new focus. How is this focus supported throughout Subaru?

The human experience is the focus of every employee at Subaru and is the defining statement of Subaru's corporate culture. It's not just a car, a dealer, a person – it is an experience. This is supported in every area of the company, from its image to its dealer incentive program. The company rewards its employees, providing a positive experience to its customers. The company has a people-centered culture.

2. What type of market research does Subaru do, based on the information provided in the video? What are the collection methods?

Subaru does secondary research using internal sources. The internal sources are the customer satisfaction surveys and the deal services experiences report. These surveys could be considered primary research if the questions pertained to a specific problem the company is trying to solve.

3. What are the internal, social, and external influences affecting a potential customer buying a Subaru?
Students may come up with many answers to this question. Refer students to the various ads shown in the video clip for guidance. Here are sample answers:

*Internal Influences (social or psychological field):*
Perception – The Subaru brand
Motivation – Want to be associated with the Subaru image
Attitudes – Serious about purchasing decision, intelligent demeanor
Personality – Quirky
Age Group – Probably over 30
Lifestyle – Outdoors, adventurous

*External Influences:*
Culture – Independent
Social Class – Middle to upper

4. Considering what you have learned about brand loyalty from the Subaru example, describe a product or service that you believe you are strongly brand loyal toward. Explain the reasons for your loyalty.

Students may generate their own examples. However, students should see the difference between satisfaction and loyalty. A follow-up question might be for students to indicate a product or service that they are satisfied with but not brand loyal toward. How could the producer of the product or service earn their brand loyalty?

<u>Teaching Suggestions</u>

1. Measuring Customer Loyalty
In practice, measuring customer loyalty can be difficult. These two teaching suggestions are based on helping students think through how to apply this concept.

    a. Have the students compose 5 to 10 questions that Subaru might ask its customers in a "Dealer Services Survey."
    b. Students can choose any company whose operations they understand. List all points of this company that customers come in contact with and how customer loyalty can be measured for each point. Additionally, are there any overall customer loyalty measures?

2. Consumer Behavior
Car purchases are usually very involved and customers normally go through the elaborated decision process described in Figure 9.1.

    a. Suggestion One:
Based on the video, students put themselves in the place of Joe Barstys who is trying to appeal to the female consumer. Have students detail each stage of the decision process (Figure 9.1) a female consumer would go through and how the company should respond.

    b. Suggestion Two:
Ask students to think about a big purchase they recently made. Analyze this experience based on the process Figure 9.1 describes. What did they learn about their own decision making?

# Segment 6: AFLAC

Summary
That wacky quacky duck brought AFLAC to a high spot among most recognizable ads and brand names.  The insurance company is growing quickly as a result of this greater name recognition.

Discussion Question

How did the AFLAC duck build brand recognition?  Does high brand recognition translate directly into greater sales for the brand?

The duck was a unique way to expose consumers to an obscure brand and to motivate them to repeat the name amongst themselves.  However, as the video points out this awareness alone does not sell the product or service – it simply opens the door to allow the company's salespeople to elaborate about what the brand means and why it's superior to competitors.

Teaching Suggestion

The AFLAC duck succeeded partially because the advertising strategy went against accepted wisdom that financial services are high-risk products that have to be promoted seriously and conservatively.  This is a good opportunity to get students to think of other examples of campaigns that went against the grain (e.g. Intel's ingredient marketing approach) and to discuss the need for "rationality" when dealing with B2B products and services.  Should a company make fun of itself in order to sell itself?

# Segment 7: Wild Planet

Summary
Wild Planet is more than a toy company; the company thinks of itself as selling a positive play experience. Its products are more than just toys; they are created to make kids think, take them outdoors, and explore the world around them. To keep innovating and creating more toys that are attractive to kids, the company continually does market research. In fact, it interviews and works with more than 5,000 children per year, executing ethnographic and exploratory research.

Discussion Questions

1. For Wild Planet, market research is a key activity for all product development. What are the different ways the company collects data on what kids like?

Wild Planet has a kids' advisory panel, a database of families who will test toys in their homes or at play groups, the kids inventory challenge, and the kids shopper, where children are given $30 to spend and their decision making is observed.

2. Analyze the likely buying behavior of these buyers. Who are they? Why are they interested in Wild Planet? What prompts them to buy?

Wild Planet knows that children are the influencers in the buying process, but ultimately the parents make the decisions. Therefore, the products need to be cool enough for kids, but also appeal to parents. According to the video, kids buy Wild Planet toys because they are so different than other toys on the market. They appeal to a different side of kids and push their imagination. In addition to being cool, toys have to be appealing to the child's peer group because they have a big influence on buyer behavior.

Teaching Suggestions

1. Finding good online resources for secondary research can be difficult, and primary research can be expensive. Ask students to find three broad online kids' consumer resources. What types of questions can these resources help answer? What types of questions can they not answer? Instructors can combine all students' resources to provide a set of data sources for future research students will be able to refer to later.

2. Ask students to talk about gender differences in preferences for toys. Are these differences innate or learned? How did their own experiences with toys teach them about "correct" sex role behavior?

# Segment 8: Reebok

Summary

Reebok has reinvented itself from one fitness craze to the next, from aerobics, to Step, to hip-hop. Today, the company is focused on creating a pop culture around its product. It even went as far as creating a new brand (RBK) targeted at the teen market. The strategy is to start the customer relationship earlier and develop that loyalty over the years. To re-brand Reebok, the company signed big-name rappers to represent the brand. Instead of taking the athletic approach, Reebok is taking the lifestyle approach because rappers are as influential as big-name athletes.

Discussion Questions

1.  What is brand loyalty and how does Reebok hope to gain it from teen customers?

Brand loyalty is a pattern of repeat product purchases, accompanied by an underlying positive attitude toward the brand that is based on the belief that the brand makes products superior to its competition. Reebok is hoping to start this process early with its customers so they grow with the brand as they get older.

2.  What did Reebok do to rebrand itself? Why?

The original brand had lost its marketplace relevance. While it kept up with the trends from the 80s, it did not transition well in to the 90s. The company took an innovate approach to leverage the existing brand, but give it a new look. Tactics included changing the name to RBK, signing celebrity rappers, redesigning the product, and approaching the product from a lifestyle perspective instead of an athletic perspective.

Teaching Suggestion

Have students list ten sporting goods brands, then discuss why each brand is significant. What are the elements that make the brand strong? What are the marketing activities that are associated with reinforcing the brand? Have students list the names of five bad or poor brands. Why is the brand conceived negatively? More broadly, how do consumers use these brands to enact a desired lifestyle? Are there any ethical implications involved in holding out these brands as necessary for certain lifestyles?

# Segment 9: Motorola

Summary
Motorola's new Moto phone is used to illustrate how advertising helps to build a brand.

Discussion Questions

1.  In order for a global advertising campaign to succeed, the advertising agency must identify a brand's core meaning and find a way to communicate this across cultures. What is Moto's core meaning?

Motorola has positioned its Moto phone as a lifestyle concept; in a sense a versatile fashion accessory. This is a good opportunity to underscore that the purchase decision process even for high-tech products like cell phones often are dramatically influenced by "nonrational" criteria such as fashionability.

2.  Advertisers often rely upon mnemonics to increase brand awareness and encourage habitual decision making. How does Motorola do this?

Motorola has "taken ownership" of the Chinese slang term *moto*. Its global advertising consistently includes the term in various advertising executions so that the connection between the cell phone and the name Motorola is constantly being reinforced.

3.  How does an integrated marketing strategy involving advertising and direct marketing outlets influence consumer decision making?

When done properly, the same simple message (e.g. "moto") is communicated in many different outlets so that the consumer more easily associates the concept with the brand. This should simplify decision making as a consistent message is delivered both over time and in different places.

Teaching Suggestions

1.  Get students to talk in class about their attachments to their cell phones and the social functions they play. They will easily understand how fundamental this product is to their lifestyles – especially when you get them to imagine how they would behave differently if they lived in "the old days" when cell phones were not available!

2.  One of the advertising executives notes that the Motorola campaign eschews "mirror marketing" and instead is essentially aspirational (the contrast between appealing to real versus ideal selves was discussed in Chapter 5). Use this comment to develop a class discussion around the role of high-tech products in aspirational marketing and how this strategy relates to global branding (i.e. creating a common bond among consumers around the world who aspire to the same products in order to live a "modern" lifestyle).

# Segment 10: Global Business and Ethics

Summary
This video suggests that there is no absolute or definitive statement on what constitutes ethical behavior and that an individual's sense of ethics is determined by a number of social, cultural, and religious factors and influences. This video also discusses how the role of ethics in management practices, global marketing, and corporate ethics and social responsibility differs from culture to culture. In addition, the degree of enforcement with regards to ethical guidelines and standards, the practice of using connections, and the extent of gift giving may differ across borders as detailed in the video.

Discussion Questions

1.  Is there an objective standard of ethical behavior we can use to judge companies around the world? Why or why not?

Ethical standards vary widely around the world along with religious beliefs and cultural expectations regarding appropriate behavior. We need to assess ethical behavior in terms of how it conforms to local standards, not necessarily to what we personally believe is right or wrong.

2.  What is the difference (if any) between gift-giving and bribery in corporate contexts?

Gift-giving is usually engrained in local standards, and it is done as part of a general effort on a company's part to forge connections and to reward customers for their business. In contrast, bribery refers to the giving of favors, gifts, or money by an individual to win a specific deal – typically one that will directly benefit that individual and not necessarily the company as a whole.

Teaching Suggestions

1.  As the video notes, many ethical issues arise when scientific advances create opportunities that may conflict with ethical standards. This can generate a lot of good discussion in the class about such issues as the ethics of cloning, companies' possibly self-serving motives for donating drugs to developing countries, or tobacco companies' efforts to penetrate foreign markets as the number of U.S. smokers declines.

2.  Students will have strong opinions about child labor – yet not all of them are willing to boycott products they know are made by children or under sweatshop conditions. This double standard can generate heated discussion, especially when you highlight the marketing opportunities available to companies like No Sweat that position themselves in terms of their ethical labor standards. And, if child labor is considered appropriate or desirable in a host country (because of the revenue it brings to poor families) according to the video's definition of local ethical behavior should we object to this practice?

# Segment 11: The Cult of Mac

Summary
Consumer attitude toward Macintosh computers comes close to being religious. Consumer opinions transcend the product into assumed personality and lifestyle of the Mac user. Mac occupies only 4% of the computer market, but these consumers are distinguished by their fierce loyalty to the product. Apple has nourished the myth of the Mac, which has led to its sustained market share in the face of Microsoft. A large part of the following of these computers is attributed to the image of the two founders, Steve Jobs and Steve Wozniack. They embody the hero myth, saving the world from Bill Gates. The video explains the elements of the hero myth as it applies to the development of Apple computers. Explained in this myth is the history of Apple, its challenges, near bankruptcy, and current successes. Just before Apple went under, Jobs realigned the company around its original vision and released a series of highly profitable products.

Apple is trying to be different and leverage the image of creativity and innovation. Such examples are evident in the logo, product design, and advertising. This positioning explains why a large part of Mac users are creative developers. Mac users also characterize themselves as SUV drivers, consumers of whole foods, democrats, and are in general "outdoorsier" than PC users. The Mac customer loyalty is built on myth, rebellion against Microsoft, belief in a "cause," and love of the product.

Discussion Questions

1.  According to the book, there are three components to attitude – affect, beliefs, and behavior. What are Mac users' attitudes toward this product, based on these three areas, and which hierarchy best describes a Mac user?

    Affect – Mac users have very strong feelings toward this product. The feelings surpass the product and move toward the emotional connection with the company in a mythic manner.
    Behavior – Mac users are loyal and therefore are repeat customers.
    Belief – This group believes a Mac is a far superior product to the PC. Further, they believe that PC users are acting as cattle and not thinking individually.
    The experiential hierarchy best describes a Mac user, as this hierarchy is concerned with emotional response as part of attitude.

2.  Using the VALS segmentation system on page 221, which of the eight VALS types would you think Mac users most likely fall into?

    Actualizers:  successful with many resources, open to change.
    Fulfilleds:  satisfied, reflective, comfortable, practical.
    Experiencers:  impulsive, young, offbeat, love risk.
    Believers:  strong principles, favor proven brands.
    Makers:  action-oriented, self-sufficient, do-it-yourselfers.

3.  What would a psychographic analysis of Mac users contain for characteristics in the areas of activities, interests, and opinions?

> Following is a list of possible answers. Student input will vary:
> Activities: Outdoor sports, frequent stores like Trader Joes and Wild Oats, involved with other Mac users.
> Interests: Possibly a designer, likes SUVs and VWs, reads broadly, listens to NPR
> Opinions: Strongly anti-Microsoft, democrat, like to support the underdog

Teaching Suggestion

The Mac is a cult product on par with Harley Davidson and Krispy Kreme donuts. Consumers have strong relationships with their Macs and demonstrate a high level of product involvement. Conceptualizing Involvement, Figure 4.3 on page 128, shows that cause-and-effect relationships result in differing levels of involvement. Ask students to use this figure as a model to diagram the Mac user's involvement with the product.

# Segment 12: Money to Burn: Consumption by the Dead in China

Summary

The video segment provides an interesting glimpse into Chinese customs and practices relating to consumption by the dead. In China, it is common to burn paper objects, such as fake money, checkbooks, money trees, and coins, for the dead to use. Other objects, such as paper clothing, eyeglasses, brand-name luxury goods, and houses are also common. In order to ensure the goods find their way to the deceased, their name is written on each object burned. This practice is so common that the industry is estimated to be $2 billion and is focused primarily in the southern part of China, Taiwan, and Vietnam.

The primary motivation for relatives of the dead to burn paper objects is to memorialize the deceased and show respect, love, care, and honor for their life on earth. There are specific practices and customs associated with when to burn and how often. Regional, urban vs. suburban, rich vs. poor influences play a large part in the practices and types of objects burned. The video not only looks at the consumption of paper objects for the dead, but the type of paper objects are indicators of what goods Chinese people consume while alive.

Discussion Questions

1. Describe the three stages of the rite of passage associated with dying in Chinese culture.

   Rites of passage include three phases:
   - separation: detached from original group – detachment from the family, friends, and earth
   - liminality: person is literally in-between statuses – the time between death and the time paper objects are burned
   - aggregation: person reenters society after rite-of-passage – in this case the reentry is not into life on earth, but the Chinese afterlife

2. What are the crescive norms operating in funeral practices and in China? What products and services are affected by these norms?

   Crescive norms cover the gambit of customs, mores, and conventions regarding burning paper objects. The set of norms include timing and frequency of burning, which signifies respect and honor of the loved one. The type of objects burned is based on conventions, depending on whether the family is urban or suburban. The quantity and quality of the objects is also a crescive norm. All of the products and retail stores surrounding this practice are due to the norms associated with death in China.

3. Based on the video, are Chinese marketers influencing the industry of gift-giving by stimulating increased burning of paper objects? Into which of the three gift-giving stages does this fall?

Answers to the first question will vary. Burning of paper object falls into the gestation stage, where the giver is motivated by an event to buy a gift, and it is structural instead of emergent, as it is prescribed by culture.

Teaching Suggestions

1. Ask the class to compare a list of Chinese funeral rituals to American funeral rituals. What are the major differences between the cultural values in the United States and China? What are the marketing implications of these rituals? How are funerals affected when people are from different religions?

2. Ask a group of students to analyze the American and Mexican funeral industries, specifically looking at the marketing practices in both countries. Students should collect literature from various funeral homes, look for any traditional advertising, and interview a few people about the marketing messages they notice about funeral homes.

# VIDEO CORRELATION GRID

*Consumer Behavior , 7/e - Michael R. Solomon*

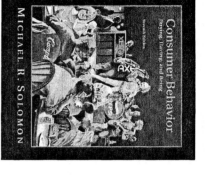

Prentice Hall - 2007©

| Segment | Title | Duration | 1 | 2 | 3 | 4 | 5 | 6 | 7 | 8 | 9 | 10 | 11 | 12 | 13 | 14 | 15 | 16 | 17 |
|---|---|---|---|---|---|---|---|---|---|---|---|---|---|---|---|---|---|---|---|
| | | | | | | | | | | | Chapter | | | | | | | | |
| 1 | Procter & Gamble | 14:53 | X | | X | | | | | X | | | | | | | | | |
| 2 | iWon.com | 11:01 | | | X | | | | X | | | | | | | | | | |
| 3 | Harley Davidson | 9:30 | | | | X | | | X | | X | | | | | | | | X |
| 4 | Skechers | 12:19 | | | | | | X | | | | | | | | | | | |
| 5 | Subaru | 9:54 | | | | | | | | | | X | | | | | | | |
| 6 | AFLAC | 8:14 | | | X | | | | | | | X | | | | | | | |
| 7 | Wild Planet | 9:00 | | | | | | X | | | | | | X | | | | | |
| 8 | Reebok | 8:50 | | | | | | X | | | | | | | | X | | | |
| 9 | Motorola | 14:28 | | | | | | | X | | | | | | | | | X | |
| 10 | Global Business and Ethics | 12:07 | X | | | | | | | | | | | | | X | X | X | |
| 11 | The Cult of Mac | 22:30 | | | | | | X | X | | | | | | X | | X | X | |
| 12 | Money to Burn: Consumption by the Dead in China | 26:41 | | | | | | | | | | | X | | | | X | | X |